Deep Reinforcement Learning in Unity

With Unity ML Toolkit

Abhilash Majumder

Apress®

Deep Reinforcement Learning in Unity: With Unity ML Toolkit

Abhilash Majumder
Pune, Maharashtra, India

ISBN-13 (pbk): 978-1-4842-6502-4   ISBN-13 (electronic): 978-1-4842-6503-1
https://doi.org/10.1007/978-1-4842-6503-1

Managing Director, Apress Media LLC: Welmoed Spahr
Acquisitions Editor: Spandana Chatterjee
Development Editor: Laura Berendson
Coordinating Editor: Shrikant Vishwakarma

Cover designed by eStudioCalamar

Cover image designed by Pexels

Distributed to the book trade worldwide by Springer Science+Business Media LLC, 1 New York Plaza, Suite 4600, New York, NY 10004. Phone 1-800-SPRINGER, fax (201) 348-4505, e-mail orders-ny@springer-sbm. com, or visit www.springeronline.com. Apress Media, LLC is a California LLC and the sole member (owner) is Springer Science + Business Media Finance Inc (SSBM Finance Inc). SSBM Finance Inc is a **Delaware** corporation.

For information on translations, please e-mail booktranslations@springernature.com; for reprint, paperback, or audio rights, please e-mail bookpermissions@springernature.com.

Apress titles may be purchased in bulk for academic, corporate, or promotional use. eBook versions and licenses are also available for most titles. For more information, reference our Print and eBook Bulk Sales web page at http://www.apress.com/bulk-sales.

Any source code or other supplementary material referenced by the author in this book is available to readers on GitHub via the book's product page, located at www.apress.com/978-1-4842-6502-4. For more detailed information, please visit http://www.apress.com/source-code.

Printed on acid-free paper

This book is dedicated to my parents, Abhijit and Sharbari Majumder,
and my late grandfather, Shri Paresh Chandra Majumder.

Table of Contents

About the Author

Abhilash Majumder is a natural language processing research engineer for HSBC (UK/India) and technical mentor for Udacity (ML). He also has been associated with Unity Technologies and was a speaker at Unite India-19, and has educated close to 1,000 students from EMEA and SEPAC (India) on Unity. He is an ML contributor and curator for Open Source Google Research, Tensorflow, and Unity ML Agents and a creator of ML libraries under Python Package Index (PyPI). He is a speaker for NLP and deep learning for Pydata-Los Angeles. He is an online educationalist for Udemy, and a deep learning mentor for Upgrad. He is an erstwhile graduate from the National Institute of Technology, Durgapur (NIT-D) majoring in NLP, Machine Learning, and Applied Mathematics. He can be reached via email at debabhi1396@gmail.com

Abhilash was a former apprentice/student ambassador for Unity Technologies, where he educated corporate employees and students on using general Unity for game development. He was a technical mentor (AI programming) for the Unity Ambassadors Community and Content Production. He has been associated with Unity Technologies for general education, with an emphasis on graphics and machine learning. He is a community moderator for machine learning (ML Agents) sessions organized by Unity Technologies (Unity Learn). He is one of the first content creators for Unity Technologies India (since 2017) and is responsible for the growth of the community in India under the guidance of Unity Technologies.

About the Technical Reviewer

Ansh Shah is pursuing an MSc Physics and BE Mechanical from Bits Pilani University, India. By day, he is a student. By night, he is a robotics and machine learning enthusiast. He is a core member of BITS ROBOCON, a technical team at college, and is currently working on quadcopter and quadruped.

Acknowledgments

The amount of dedication and support that I have received in the making of this book has left me amazed. First, I would like to thank my family, Mr. Abhijit Majumder and Mrs. Sharbari Majumder, who have been instrumental in supporting me all the way. I would also like to extend my heartfelt thanks to the entire Apress Team, without whom this would not have been possible. Special thanks to Mrs. Spandana Chatterjee, the Acquisition Editor, Mr. Shrikant Vishwakarma, the Coordinating Editor, and Laura Berendson, the Development Editor, for their constant support and thorough reviews. Ansh Shah, the Technical Reviewer of this book, has also played an important role and I extend my thanks to him.

I would also like to share this space in thanking my mentor, Carl Domingo from Unity Technologies, who has been so instrumental in guiding me from the beginning of my journey with Unity. The Unity Machine Learning team deserves mention, as this book would not have been possible without their constant efforts to make the ML Agents platform amazing. I especially thank Dr. Danny Lange, whose sessions on machine learning have been instrumental in understanding the framework and the concepts.

I am grateful to everyone who helped in the entire process to make this book, which would help readers understand the beauty of deep reinforcement learning.

Introduction

Machine learning has been instrumental in shaping the scope of technology since its inception. ML has played an important role in the development of things such as autonomous vehicles and robotics. Deep reinforcement learning is that field of learning where agents learn with help of rewards—a thought which has been derived from nature. Through this book, the author tries to present the diversity of reinforcement learning algorithms in game development as well as in scientific research. Unity, the cross-platform engine that is used in a plethora of tasks, from visual effects and cinematography to machine learning and high performance graphics, is the primary tool that is used in this book. With the power of the Unity ML Agents Toolkit, the deep reinforcement learning framework built by Unity, the author tries to show the vast possibilities of this learning paradigm.

The book starts with an introduction to state-based reinforcement learning, from Markov processes to Bellman equations and Q-learning, which sets the ground for the successive sections. A plethora of diverse pathfinding algorithms, from Dijkstra to sophisticated variants of A* star, have been provided along with simulations in Unity. The book also covers how navigation meshes work for automated pathfinding in Unity. An introduction to the ML Agents Toolkit, from standard process for installation to training an AI agent with deep reinforcement learning algorithm (proximal policy operation [PPO]) is provided as a starter. Along the course of this book, there is an extensive usage of the Tensorflow framework along with OpenAI Gym environments for proper visualizations of complex deep reinforcement learning algorithms in terms of simulations, robotics, and autonomous agents. Successive sections of the book involve an in-depth study of the variety of on- and off-policy algorithms, ranging from discrete SARSA/Q-learning to actor critic variants, deep Q-network variants, PPO, and their implementations using the Keras Tensorflow framework on Gym. These sections are instrumental in understanding how different simulations such as the famous Puppo (Unity Berlin), Tiny agents, and other ML Agents samples from Unity are created and built. Sections with detailed descriptions about how to build simulations in Unity using the C# software development kit for ML Agents and training them using soft actor critic (SAC), PPO, or behavioral cloning algorithms such as GAIL are provided.

The latter part of this book provides an insight into curriculum learning and adversarial networks with an analysis of how AI agents are trained in games such as FIFA. In all these sections, a detailed description of the variants of neural networks—MLP, convolution networks, recurrent networks along with long short-term memory and GRU and their implementations and performance are provided. This is especially helpful as they are used extensively during building the deep learning algorithms. The importance of convolution networks for image sampling in Atari-based 2D games such as Pong has been provided. The knowledge of computer vision and deep reinforcement learning is combined to produce autonomous vehicles and driverless cars, which is also provided as an example template (game) for the readers to build upon.

Finally, this book also contains an in-depth review of the Obstacle Tower Challenge, which was organized by Unity Technologies to challenge state-of-the-art deep reinforcement learning algorithms. Sections on certain evolutionary algorithms along with the Google Dopamine framework has been provided for understanding the vast field of reinforcement learning. Through this book, the author hopes to infuse enthusiasm and foster research among the readers in the field of deep reinforcement learning.

CHAPTER 1

Introduction to Reinforcement Learning

Reinforcement learning (RL) is a paradigm of learning algorithms that are based on rewards and actions. The state-based learning paradigm is different from generic supervised and unsupervised learning, as it does not typically try to find structural inferences in collections of unlabeled or labeled data. Generic RL relies on finite state automation and decision processes that assist in finding an optimized reward-based learning trajectory. The field of RL relies heavily on goal-seeking, stochastic processes and decision theoretic algorithms, which is a field of active research. With developments in higher order deep learning algorithms, there has been huge advancement in this field to create self-learning agents that can achieve a goal by using gradient convergence techniques and sophisticated memory-based neural networks. This chapter will focus on the fundamentals of the Markov Decision Process (MDP), hidden Markov Models (HMMs) and dynamic programming for state enumeration, Bellman's iterative algorithms, and a detailed walkthrough of value and policy algorithms. In all these sections, there will be associated python notebooks for better understanding of the concepts as well as simulated games made with Unity (version 2018.x).

The fundamental aspects in an academy of RL are agent(s) and environment(s). Agent refers to an object that uses learning algorithms to try and explore rewards in steps. The agent tries to optimize a suitable path toward a goal that results in maximization of the rewards and, in this process, tries to avoid punishing states. Environment is everything around an agent; this includes the states, obstacles, and rewards. The environment can be static as well as dynamic. Path convergence in a static environment is faster if the agent has sufficient buffer memory to retain the correct trajectory toward the goal as it explores different states. Dynamic environment pose a stronger challenge for agents, as there is no definite trajectory. The second use-case

© Abhilash Majumder 2021
A. Majumder, *Deep Reinforcement Learning in Unity*, https://doi.org/10.1007/978-1-4842-6503-1_1

requires sufficient deep memory network models like bidirectional long short-term memory (LSTM) to retain certain key observations that remain static in the dynamic environment. Figuratively generic reinforcement learning can be presented as shown in Figure 1-1.

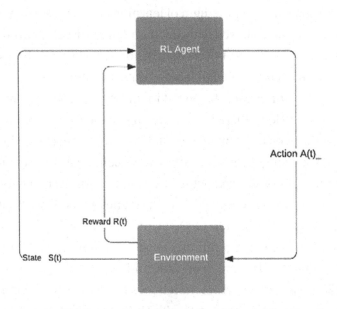

Figure 1-1. *Interaction between agent and environment in reinforcement learning*

The set of variables that control and govern the interaction between the agent and the environment includes {state(S), reward(R), action(A)}.

- State is a set of possible enumerated states provided in the environment: $\{s_0, s_1, s_2, \dots s_n\}$.

- Reward is the set of possible rewards present in particular states in the environment: $\{r_0, r_1, r_2, \dots, r_n\}$.

- Action is the set of possible actions that the agent can take to maximize its rewards: $\{A_0, A_1, A_2, \dots A_n\}$.

OpenAI Gym Environment: CartPole

To understand the roles of each of these in an RL environment, let us try to study the CartPole environment from OpenAI gym. OpenAI gym includes many environments for research and study of classic RL algorithms, robotics, and deep RL algorithms, and this is used as a wrapper in Unity machine learning (ML) agents Toolkit.

The CartPole environment can be described as a classical physics simulation system where a pole is attached to an "un-actuated" joint to a cart. The cart is free to move along a frictionless track. The constraints on the system involve applying a force of +1and -1 to the cart. The pendulum starts upright, and the goal is to prevent it from falling over. A reward of +1 is provided for every timestamp the pole remains upright. When the angle of inclination is greater than 15 degrees from the normal, the episode terminates (punishment). If the cart moves more than 2.4 units either way from the central line, the episode terminates. Figure 1-2 depicts the environment.

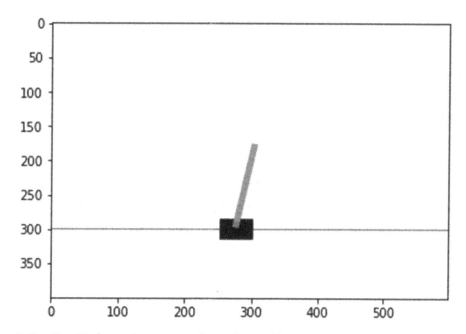

Figure 1-2. *CartPole environment from OpenAI gym*

The possible states, rewards, and actions sets in this environment include:

- States: An array of length 4.:[cart position, cart velocity, pole angle, pole tip velocity] such as [4.8000002e+00,3.4028235e+38 ,4.1887903e-01,3.4028235e+38]

- Rewards: +1 for every timestamp the pole remains upright

- Actions: integer array of size 2 : [left direction, right direction], which controls the direction of motion of the cart such as [-1,+1]

- Termination: if the cart shifts more than 2.4 units from the center or the pendulum inclines more than 15 degrees

- Objective: to keep the pendulum or pole upright for 250 time-steps and collect rewards more than 100 points

Installation and Setup of Python for ML Agents and Deep Learning

To visualize this environment, installation of Jupyter notebook is required, which can be installed from the Anaconda environment. Download Anaconda (recommended latest version for Python), and Jupyter notebooks will be installed as well.

Downloading Anaconda also installs libraries like numpy, matplotlib, and sklearn, which are used for generic machine learning. Consoles and editors like IPython Console, Spyder, Anaconda Prompt are also installed with Anaconda. Anaconda Prompt should be set as an environment PATH variable. Preview of the terminal is shown in Figure 1-3.

Note   Anaconda Navigator is installed with Anaconda. This is an interactive dashboard application where options for downloading Jupyter notebook, Spyder, IPython, and JupyterLab are available. The applications can also be started by clicking on them.

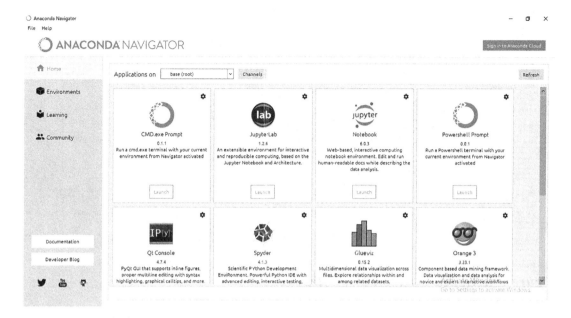

Figure 1-3. *Anaconda navigator terminal*

Jupyter notebook can be installed by using pip command as:

```
pip3 install -upgrade pip
pip3 install jupyter notebook
```

For running the Jupyter notebook, open Anaconda Prompt or Command Prompt and run the following command:

```
jupyter notebook
```

Alternatively, Google Colaboratory (Google Colab) runs Jupyter notebooks on the cloud and is saved to local Google drive. This can be used as well for notebook sharing and collaboration. The Google Colaboratory is shown in Figure 1-4.

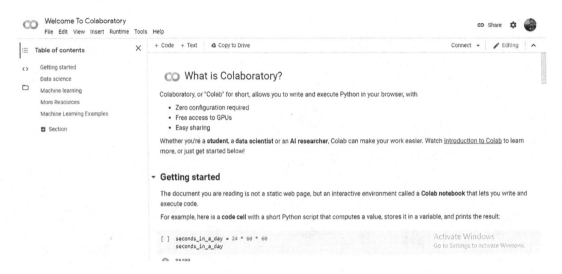

Figure 1-4. *Google Colaboratory notebook*

To start, create a new Python3 kernel notebook, and name it as CartPole environment. In order to simulate and run the environment, there are certain libraries and frameworks required to be installed.

- Install Gym : Gym is the collection of environments created by OpenAI, which contains different environments for developing RL algorithms.

  Run the command in Anaconda Prompt, Command Prompt :

  ```
  pip install gym
  ```

  Or run this command from Jupyter notebook or Google Colab notebook

  ```
  !pip install gym
  ```

- Install Tensorflow and Keras: Tensorflow is an open-source deep learning framework developed by Google that will be used for creating neural network layers in deep RL. Keras is an abstraction (API) over Tensorflow and contains all the built-in functionalities of Tensorflow with ease of use. The commands are as follows :

  ```
  pip install tensorflow>=1.7
  pip install keras
  ```

These commands are for installation through Anaconda Prompt or Command Prompt. The version of Tensorflow used later in this book for Unity ML agents is 1.7. However, for integration with Unity ML agents, Tensorflow version 2.0 can be used as well. If issues arise due to mismatch of versions, then that can be resolved by going through the documentation of Unity ML agents versioning and compatibility with Tensorflow, and the latter can be reinstalled just by using the pip command.

For Jupyter notebook or Colab installation of Tensorflow and Keras, the following commands are required:

```
!pip install tensorflow>=1.7
!pip install keras
```

Note   Tensorflow has nightly builds that are released every day with a version number, and this can be viewed in the Python Package Index (Pypi) page of Tensorflow. These builds are generally referred to as tf-nightly and may have an unstable compatibility with Unity ML agents. However, official releases are recommended for integration with ML agents, while nightly builds can be used for deep learning as well.

- Install gym pyvirtualdisplay and python opengl: These libraries and frameworks (built for OpenGL API) will be used for rendering the Gym environment in Colab notebook. There are issues with xvfb installation locally in Windows, and hence Colab notebooks can be used for displaying the Gym environment training. The commands for installation in Colab notebook are as follows:

```
!apt-get install -y xvfb python-opengl > /dev/null 2>&1
!pip install gym pyvirtualdisplay > /dev/null 2>&1
```

Once the installation is complete, we can dive into the CartPole environment and try to gain more information on the environment, rewards, states, and actions.

Playing with the CartPole Environment for Deep Reinforcement Learning

Open the "Cartpole-Rendering.ipynb" notebook. It contains the starter code for setting up the environment. The first section contains import statements to import libraries in the notebook.

```
import gym
import numpy as np
import matplotlib.pyplot as plt
from IPython import display as ipythondisplay
```

The next step involves setting up the dimensions of the display window to visualize the environment in the Colab notebook. This uses the pyvirtualdisplay library.

```
from pyvirtualdisplay import Display
display = Display(visible=0, size=(400, 300))
display.start()
```

Now, let us load the environment from Gym using the gym.make command and look into the states and the actions. Observation states refer to the environment variables that contain the key factors like cart velocity and pole velocity and is an array of size 4. The action space is an array of size 2, which refers to the binary actions (moving left or right). The observation space also contains high and low values as boundary values for the problem.

```
env = gym.make("CartPole-v0")
#Action space->Agent
print(env.action_space)
#Observation Space->State and Rewards
print(env.observation_space)
print(env.observation_space.high)
print(env.observation_space.low)
```

This is shown in Figure 1-5.

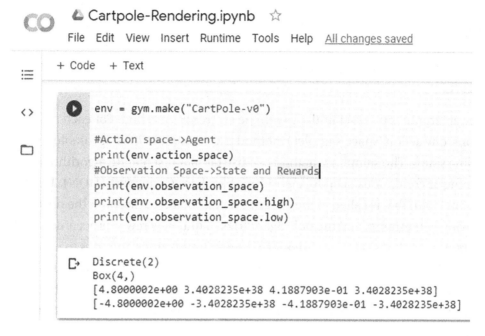

Figure 1-5. *Observation and action space in CartPole environment*

After running, the details appear in the console. The details include the different action spaces as well as the observation steps.

Let us try to run the environment for 50 iterations and check the values of rewards accumulated. This will simulate the environment for 50 iterations and provide insight into how the agent balances itself with the baseline OpenAI model.

```
env = gym.make("CartPole-v0")
env.reset()
prev_screen = env.render(mode='rgb_array')
plt.imshow(prev_screen)

for i in range(50):
  action = env.action_space.sample()
  #Get Rewards and Next States
  obs, reward, done, info = env.step(action)
  screen = env.render(mode='rgb_array')
  print(reward)
  plt.imshow(screen)
  ipythondisplay.clear_output(wait=True)
  ipythondisplay.display(plt.gcf())
```

```
  if done:
    break
```

```
ipythondisplay.clear_output(wait=True)
env.close()
```

The environment is reset initially with the env.reset() method. For each of the 50 iterations, env.action_space.sample() method tries to sample most favorable states or rewarding states. The sampling method can use tabular discrete RL algorithms like Q-learning or continuous deep RL algorithms like deep-Q–network (DQN). There is a discount factor that is called at the start of every iteration to discount the rewards of the previous timestamp, and the pole agent tries to find new rewards accordingly. The env.step(action) chooses from a "memory" or previous actions and tries to maximize its rewards by staying upright as long as possible. At the end of each action step, the display changes to render a new state of the pole. The loop finally breaks if the iterations have been completed. The env.close() method closes the connection to the Gym environment.

This has helped us to understand how states and rewards affect an agent. We will get into the details of an in-depth study of modeling a deep Q-learning algorithm to provide a faster and optimal reward-based solution to the CartPole problem. The environment has observation states that are discrete and can be solved by using tabular RL algorithms like Markov-based Q-learning or SARSA.

Deep learning provides more optimization by converting the discrete states into continuous distributions and then tries to apply high-dimensional neural networks to converge the loss function to a global minima. This is favored by using algorithms like DQN, double deep-Q-network (DDQN), dueling DQN, actor critic (AC), proximal policy operation (PPO), deep deterministic policy gradients (DDPG), trust region policy optimization (TRPO), soft actor critic (SAC). The latter section of the notebook contains a deep Q-learning implementation of the CartPole problem, which will be explained in later chapters. To highlight certain important aspects of this code, there is a deep learning layer made with Keras and also for each iteration the collection of state, action, and rewards are stored in a replay memory buffer. Based on the previous states of the buffer memory and the rewards for the previous steps, the pole agent tries to optimize the Q-learning function over the Keras deep learning layers.

Visualization with TensorBoard

The visualization of loss at each iteration of the training process signifies the extent to which deep Q-learning tries to optimize the position of the pole in an upright manner and balances the action array for greater rewards. This visualization has been made in TensorBoard, which can be installed by typing the line in Anaconda Prompt.

```
pip install tensorboard
```

To start the TensorBoard visualization in Colab or Jupyter Notebook, the following lines of code will help. While it is prompted by the Console to use the latest version of Tensorflow (tf>=2.2), there is not a hard requirement for this, as it is compatible with all the Tensorflow versions. Tensorboard setup using Keras can also be implemented using older versions (Tensorboard) such as 1.12 or as low as 1.2. The code segment is the same across versions for starting TensorBoard. It is recommended to import these libraries in Colab, as in that case, we have the flexibility to upgrade/downgrade different versions of our libraries (Tensorflow, Keras, or others) during runtime. This also helps to resolve the compatibility issues with different versions when installed locally. We can install Keras 2.1.6 for the Tensorflow 1.7 version locally as well.

```
from keras.callbacks import TensorBoard
% load_ext tensorboard
% tensorboard --logdir log
```

TensorBoard starts on port 6006. To include the episodes of training data inside the logs, a separate logs file is created at runtime as follows:

```
tensorboard_callback = TensorBoard(
log_dir='./log', histogram_freq=1,
write_graph=True,
write_grads=True,
batch_size=agent.batch_size,
write_images=True)
```

To reference the tensorboard_callbacks for storing the data, callbacks=[tensorboard_callback] is added as an argument in model.fit() method as follows:

```
self.model.fit(np.array(x_batch),np.array(y_batch),batch_size=len(x_batch),
verbose=1,callbacks=[tensorboard_callback])
```

11

The end result shows a Tensorboard graph, as shown in Figure 1-6.:

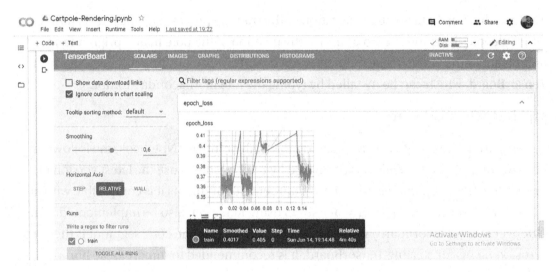

Figure 1-6. *TensorBoard visualization of CartPole problem using deep Q-learning*

To summarize, we have got some idea about what RL is and how it is governed by states, actions, and rewards. We have seen the role of an agent in an environment and the different paths it takes to maximize the rewards. We have learned to set up Jupyter Notebooks and an Anaconda environment and also installed some key libraries and frameworks that will be used extensively along the way. There was a systematic approach in understanding the CartPole environment of OpenAI Gym as a classical RL problem, along with understanding the states and rewards in the environment. Lastly we developed a miniature simulation of a CartPole environment that would make the pole upright for 50 iterations, and also had a visualization using a deep Q-learning model. The details and implementations will be discussed in-depth in later chapters along with Unity ML agents. The next section involves understanding MDP and Decision Theory using Unity Engine and will be creating simulations for the same.

Unity Game Engine

Unity Engine is a cross-platform engine that is not only used for creating games but also simulations, visual effects, cinematography, architectural design, extended reality applications, and especially research in machine learning. We will be concentrating our efforts on understanding the open-source machine learning framework developed by Unity Technologies— namely, the Unity ML Toolkit. The latest release of version 1.0 at the time of writing this book has several new features and extensions, code modifications, and simulations that will be discussed in-depth in the subsequent sections. The toolkit is built on the OpenAI Gym environment as a wrapper and communicates between Python API and Unity C# Engine to build deep learning models. Although there have been fundamental changes in the way the toolkit works in the latest release, the core functionality of the ML toolkit remains the same. We will be extensively using the Tensorflow library with Unity ML agents for deep inference and training of the models, through custom C# code, and will also try to understand the learning in the Gym environments by using baseline models for best performance measures. A preview of the environments in ML Agents Toolkit is shown in Figure 1-7.

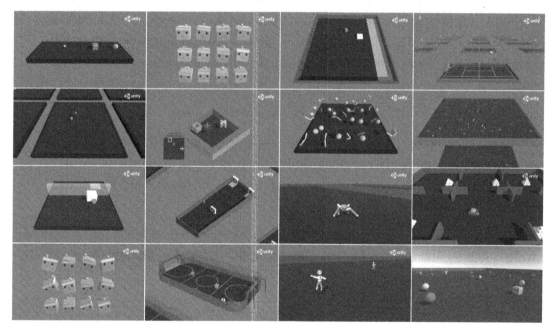

Figure 1-7. *Unity machine learning toolkit*

Note   We will be using Unity version 2018.4x and 2019 with Tensorflow version 1.7 and ML agents Python API version 0.16.0 and Unity ML agents C# version(1.0.0). However, the functionality remains the same for any Unity version above 2018.4.x. The detailed steps of installing Unity Engine and ML agents will be presented in the subsequent sections.

Markov Models and State-Based Learning

Before starting with Unity ML Toolkit, let us understand the fundamentals of state-based RL. The Markov Decision Process (MDP) is a stochastic process that tries to enumerate future states based on the probability of the current state. A finite Markov model relies on information of a current state denoted by $q^*(s, a)$, which includes state, action pair. In this section, we will be focusing on how to generate transition states between different decisions and also creating simulations based on these transitions in Unity Engine. There will be a walk-through of how state enumeration and Hidden Markov Models (HMM)s can assist an agent in finding a proper trajectory in an environment to attain its rewards in Unity.

Finite MDP can be considered as a collection of sets: {S, A, R}, where the rewards R resemble any probabilistic distribution of the rewards in state space S. For particular values of state $s_i \in S$ and $r_i \in R$, there is a probability of those values occurring at time t, given particular values of preceding state and action, where | refers to conditional probability:

$$p\,(s_i, r_i \mid s, a) = P_r\,\{S_t = s_i, R_t = r_i \mid S_{t-1} = s, A_{t-1} = a\}$$

The decision process generally involves a transition probability matrix that provides the probability of a particular state moving forward to another state or returning to its previous state. A diagrammatic view of the Markov Model can be depicted as in Figure 1-8.:

Note   Andrey Andreyevich Markov introduced the concept of Markov Chains in stochastic processes in 1906.

Markov State Models

Abhilash Majumder | June 14, 2020

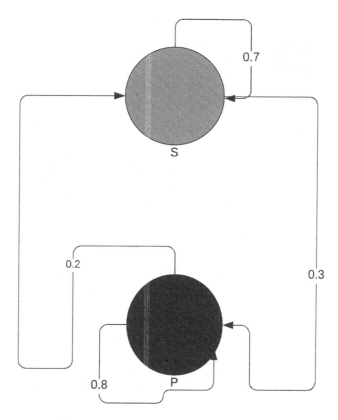

Figure 1-8. *State transition diagram of Markov Models*

Concepts of States in Markov Models

The state transition diagram provides a binary chain model having states S and P. The probability of state S to remain in its own state is 0.7, whereas that to go to state P is 0.3. Likewise, the transition probability of state P to S is 0.2, whereas the self-transition state probability of P is 0.8. According to the law of probabilities, the sum of mutual and self-transition probabilities will be 1. This allows us to generate a transition matrix of order 2 X 2, as shown in Figure 1-9.

State Transition Matrix

Abhilash Majumder | June 15, 2020

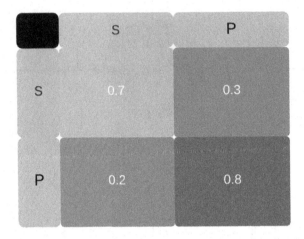

Figure 1-9. *State transition matrix*

The transition matrix at the end of each operation produces different values for self- and cross-transition of the different states. This can be mathematically visualized as computing the power of the transition matrix, where the power is the number of iterations we require for the simulation to occur as mentioned below:

$$T(t+k) = T(t)^k \; k \in R$$

The formulation shows the states of the transition matrix after k iterations are given by the power of the transition matrix at initial state times, k, under the assumption that k belongs to Real.

Let us try to extend this idea by initializing the individual states S and P with initial probabilities. If we consider V to be an array containing the initial probabilities of the two states, then after k iterations of the simulation, the final array of states F can be attained as follows:

$$F(t+k) = V(t) * T(t)^k$$

Markov Models in Python

This is an iterative Markov Process where the states get enumerated based on the transition and initial probabilities. Open the "MarkovModels.ipynb" Jupyter Notebook and let us try to understand the implementation of the transition model.

```python
import numpy as np
import pandas as pd

transition_mat=np.array([[0.7,0.3],
                         [0.2,0.8]])

intial_values= np.array([1.0,0.5])


#Transitioning for 3 turns
transition_mat_3= np.linalg.matrix_power(transition_mat,3)
#Transitioning for 10 turns
transition_mat_10= np.linalg.matrix_power(transition_mat,10)
#Transitioning for 35 turns
transition_mat_35= np.linalg.matrix_power(transition_mat,35)
#output estimation of the values
output_values= np.dot(intial_values,transition_mat)
print(output_values)
#output values after 3 iterations
output_values_3= np.dot(intial_values,transition_mat_3)
print(output_values_3)
#output values after 10 iterations
output_values_10= np.dot(intial_values,transition_mat_10)
print(output_values_10)
#output values after 35 iterations
output_values_35= np.dot(intial_values,transition_mat_35)
print(output_values_35)
```

We import numpy and pandas libraries, which would help us in computing matrix multiplications. The initial state of the sets is set to 1.0 and 0.5 for S and P, respectively. The transition matrix is initialized as mentioned previously. We then compute the value of the transition matrix for 3, 10, and 35 iterations, respectively, and with the output of each stage, we multiply the initial probability array. This provides us the final values for each state. You can change the values of the probabilities to get more results as to what extent a particular state stays in itself or transitions to another state.

In the second example, we provide a visualization of how a ternary system of transitions migrate to different states based on initial and transition probabilities. The visualization is shown in Figure 1-10.

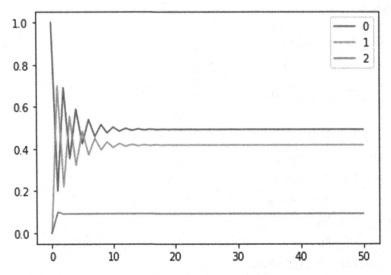

Figure 1-10. *Transition visualization of Markov states*

Downloading and Installing Unity

Now let us try and simulate a game based on this principle of Markov states in Unity. We will be using Unity version 2018.4, and it will also be compatible with versions of 2019 and 2020. The initial step is to install Unity. Download Unity Hub from the official Unity website. The Unity Hub is a dashboard that contains all the versions of Unity, including beta releases as well as tutorials and starter packs. After downloading and installing Unity Hub, we can choose a version of our choice above 2018.4. Next we proceed to get the version downloaded and installed, which would take some time. There should be sufficient space available in C: drive on Windows to make the download complete, even if we are downloading in a separate drive. Once the installation is complete, we can open up Unity and start creating our simulation and scene. Unity Hub appears as shown in Figure 1-11.

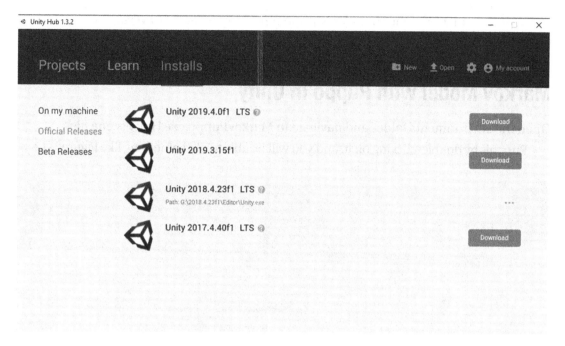

Figure 1-11. *Unity Hub and installing Unity*

Download the samples project file named DeepLearning, which contains all the codes for the lessons on this book. There is a requirement of downloading and installing preview packages for Unity ML Toolkit, since the other projects in the folder depend on them. After downloading, if error messages are received in the Console related to Barracuda engine or ML agents (mostly related to invalid methods), then go to:

Windows > Package Manager

In the search bar, type in ML agents, and the option of ML agents preview package (1.0) will appear. Click on Install to locally download the preview packages related to ML agents in Unity. To cross-verify, open the Packages folder and navigate to the "manifest. Json" source file. Open this up in Visual Studio Code or any editor and check for the following line:

```
"com.unity.ml-agents":"1.0.2-preview"
```

If errors still persist, then we can get that resolved by manually downloading Unity ML agents either from the Anaconda Prompt using the command:

```
pip install mlagents
```

or download it from the Unity ML Github repository as well. However, the installation guidelines will be presented in Chapter 3.

Markov Model with Puppo in Unity

Open the environments folder and navigate to MarkovPuppo.exe Unity scene file.

Run this by double-clicking on it, and you will be able to see something like Figure 1-12.

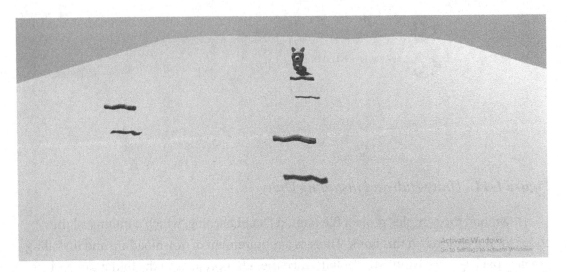

Figure 1-12. *MarkovPuppo Unity scene application*

The game is a simulation where Puppo (Puppo The Corgi from Unity Berlin) tries to find the sticks as soon as they are simulated in a Markov process. The sticks are initialized with predefined probability states, and a transition matrix is provided. For each iteration of the simulation, the stick that has the highest self-transition probability gets selected while the rest are destroyed. The task of the Puppo is to locate those sticks at each iteration, providing him a little rest of 6 seconds when he is able to reach one correctly. Since the transition probabilities are computed really fast, the steps taken by Puppo are instantaneous. This is a purely randomized distribution of Markov states where the state transition probability is computed on the go. Let us try to dig deep into the C# code to understand it better.

Open the DeepLearning project in Unity and navigate to the Assets folder. Inside the folder, try to locate the MarkovAgent folder. This contains folders called Scripts, Prefabs, and Scenes. Open the MarkovPuppo Scene in Unity and press play. We will be able to see Puppo trying to locate the randomly sampled Markov sticks. Let us try to understand the scene first.

The scene consists of Scene Hierarchy on the left and Inspector details on the right, followed by the Project, Console Tabs at the bottom with Scene, Game Views at the center. In the hierarchy, locate "Platform" GameObject and click on the drop-down. Inside the GameObject, there is a "CORGI" GameObject. Click on it to locate in the Scene View and open the details in the Inspector Window to the right. This is the Puppo Prefab, and it has an attached Script called "Markov Agent." The Prefab can be explored further by clicking on the drop-down, and there will be several joints and Rigidbody components attached that would enable physics simulation for Puppo. The Scene View is shown in Figure 1-13.

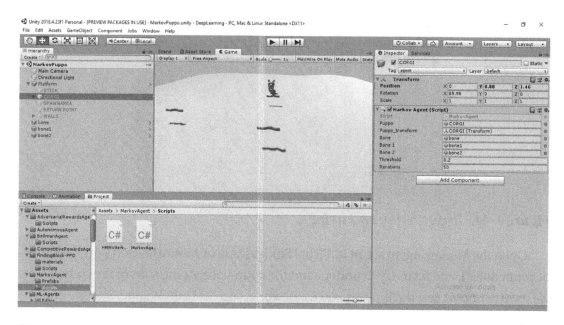

Figure 1-13. *Scene View for Markov Puppo Scene including Hierarchy and Inspector*

The Inspector Window is shown in Figure 1-14.

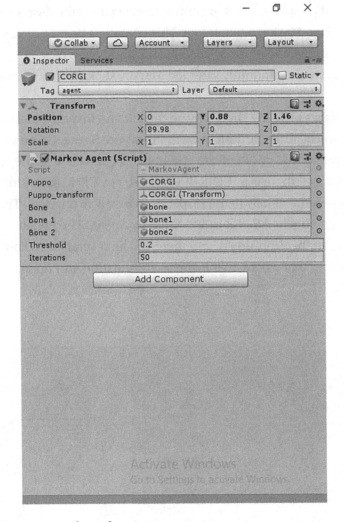

Figure 1-14. *Inspector tab and script*

Open the Markov Agent script in Visual Studio Code or MonoDevelop (any C# Editor of your choice), and let us try to understand the code-base. At the start of the code, we have to import certain libraries and frameworks such as UnityEngine, System, and others.

```
using System.Collections;
using System.Collections.Generic;
using UnityEngine;
using System;
using Random=UnityEngine.Random;
```

```
public class MarkovAgent : MonoBehaviour
 {
    public GameObject Puppo;
    public Transform puppo_transform;
    public GameObject bone;
    public GameObject bone1;
    public GameObject bone2;
    Transform bone_trans;
    Transform bone1_trans;
    Transform bone2_trans;
    float[][] transition_mat;
    float[] initial_val=new float[3];
    float[] result_values=new float[3];
    public float threshold;
    public int iterations;
    GameObject active_obj;
    Vector3 pos= new Vector3(-0.53f,1.11f,6.229f);
```

The script derives from MonoBehaviour base class. Inside we declare the GameObjects, Transforms, and other variables we want to use in the code. The GameObject "Puppo" references the Puppo Corgi agent, and it is referenced as such in Figure 1-14 in the Inspector window. GameObjects "Bone," "Bone1," and "Bone2" are the three stick targets in the scene that are randomized by Markov states. Next we have a transition matrix (named "transition_mat," a matrix of float values), an initial probability array for the three sticks (named "initial_val," a float array of size 3), and a result probability array to contain the probability after each iteration (named "result_val," a float array of size 3). The variable "iterations" signifies the number of iterations for the simulation. The GameObject "active_obj" is another variable to contain the most probable self-transitioning stick at each iteration that remains active. The last variable is a Vector3 named "pos," which contains the spawn position of Puppo after each iteration. Next we move to the details of creating the transition matrix, initial value array and try to understand how the iterations are formulated.

```
void Start()
    {
        puppo_transform=GameObject.FindWithTag("agent").
        GetComponent<Transform>();
```

```
bone=GameObject.FindWithTag("bone");
bone1=GameObject.FindWithTag("bone1");
bone2=GameObject.FindWithTag("bone2");
bone_trans=bone.GetComponent<Transform>();
bone1_trans=bone1.GetComponent<Transform>();
bone2_trans=bone2.GetComponent<Transform>();
transition_mat=create_mat(3);

initial_val[0]=1.0f;
initial_val[1]=0.2f;
initial_val[2]=0.5f;

transition_mat[0][0]=Random.Range(0f,1f);
transition_mat[0][1]=Random.Range(0f,1f);
transition_mat[0][2]=Random.Range(0f,1f);
transition_mat[1][0]=Random.Range(0f,1f);
transition_mat[1][1]=Random.Range(0f,1f);
transition_mat[1][2]=Random.Range(0f,1f);
transition_mat[2][0]=Random.Range(0f,1f);
transition_mat[2][1]=Random.Range(0f,1f);
transition_mat[2][2]=Random.Range(0f,1f);
Agentreset();
StartCoroutine(execute_markov(iterations));

}
```

In Unity C# scripting, under MonoBehaviour, there are two methods that are present by default. These are void methods named Start and Update. The Start method is generally used for initialization of variables of scene and assignment of tags to different objects; it is a preprocessing step to create the scene at the start of the game. The Update method runs per frame, and all the decision function and control logic is executed here. Since this is updated per frame, it is very computationally intensive if we are performing large complex operations. Other methods include Awake and Fixed Update. The Awake method is called before the Start thread executes, and Fixed Update has regular uniform-sized frame rates as compared to the Update method. In the first section of Start method, we assign the GameObjects to the respective tags. The tags can be created in the Inspector Window, under each selected GameObject, as shown in Figure 1-15.

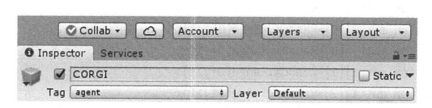

Figure 1-15. *Assigning and creating tags for GameObjects*

The tags are assigned via "GameObject.FindWithTag()" method. The next step is creation of transition matrix, which is a C# implementation of creating a generic float matrix of order 3 X 3. This is shown in the "create_mat" function.

```
public float[][] create_mat(int size)
    {

        float[][] result= new float[size][];
        for(int i=0;i<size;i++)
        {
            result[i]=new float[size];
        }
        return result;

    }
```

After creating the empty matrix, we assign values to it. The values are derived from the Random library of Unity Engine, which assigns randomized float values for the matrix.

The initial value array is also initialized in this section.

The "StartCoroutine" method calls the "IEnumerator" interface in C# Unity. Instead of updating the game each frame (using the Update method), we pass the game logic inside the Coroutine. The Coroutine runs for the number of iterations provided in the initialization and also controls the simulation. This can be explained by the code as follows.

```
private IEnumerator execute_markov(int iter)
{
    yield return new WaitForSeconds(0.1f);
    for(int i=0;i<iter;i++)
    {
```

```
transition_mat[0][0]=Random.Range(0f,1f);
transition_mat[0][1]=Random.Range(0f,1f);
transition_mat[0][2]=Random.Range(0f,1f);
transition_mat[1][0]=Random.Range(0f,1f);
transition_mat[1][1]=Random.Range(0f,1f);
transition_mat[1][2]=Random.Range(0f,1f);
transition_mat[2][0]=Random.Range(0f,1f);
transition_mat[2][1]=Random.Range(0f,1f);
transition_mat[2][2]=Random.Range(0f,1f);
mult(transition_mat,initial_val,result_values);
tanh(result_values);
initial_val=result_values;
Debug.Log("Values");
```

This part of the code has a yield return statement that releases the control of the Coroutine thread to the Start thread for 0.1 seconds (momentary pause). Then for each iteration of the simulation, the transition matrix is randomized, and the product of the initial value and transition matrix is computed by the "mult()" function. Tanh function is a nonlinear activation function for making the distributions nonlinear in the result value array.

Next we have a series of if-else statements that select the maximum probabilistic state from the result value array.

```
int bone_number=maximum(result_values,threshold);
if(bone_number==0)
{
bone.SetActive(true);
      bone1.SetActive(false);
      bone2.SetActive(false);
    active_obj=bone;
}
if(bone_number==1)
{
      bone.SetActive(false);
      bone1.SetActive(true);
      bone2.SetActive(false);
      active_obj=bone1;
}
```

```
    if(bone_number==2)
    {
          bone.SetActive(false);
          bone1.SetActive(false);
          bone2.SetActive(true);
          active_obj=bone2;
}
Debug.Log(bone_number);
```

The next step is for Puppo to determine which stick has been activated based on the previous transitions. This can be done by using RayCast in the Unity Engine Physics System. RayCast casts a ray in the direction specified by the user and also has arguments that control the depth and time limit for the ray to stay active. The requirement for the RayCast to act is that there should be a Collider object attached to the three sticks. Colliders help in understanding when collisions of physics-based GameObjects take place. In this case, we use a simple BoxCollider for the detection with RayCast upon hitting it. Based on which sticks RayCast from Puppo hits, we see that Puppo automatically transports itself to that target position by assigning the transform value of the target stick.

```
RaycastHit hit;
var up = puppo_transform.TransformDirection(Vector3.up);
Debug.DrawRay(puppo_transform.position,up*5,Color.red);
if(Physics.Raycast(puppo_transform.position,up,out hit))
 {
      if(hit.collider.gameObject.name=="bone")
      {
            Debug.Log("hit");
puppo_transform.position= bone_trans.position;
      }
                              if(hit.collider.gameObject.name=="bone1")
      {
puppo_transform.position= bone1_trans.position;
      }
                              if(hit.collider.gameObject.name=="bone2")
      {
```

```
puppo_transform.position= bone2_trans.position;
      }
  }

Debug.Log(puppo_transform.position);
Debug.Log("Rest");
Debug.Log(active_obj.GetComponent<Transform>().position);
puppo_transform.position=active_obj.GetComponent<Transform>().position;
Debug.Log(puppo_transform.position);
yield return new WaitForSeconds(6f);

Agentreset();
```

After Puppo reaches the stick for an iteration, we allow him to rest a little by calling the "yield" method for 6 seconds. Once we have understood the full functionality of the code base we can click play in the editor. We can change the values of the iterations and also the values of the initial value array in the script according to our choice to see how the distribution changes. The Debug. Log statements that are present in the Console Tab provide information regarding the values of the result array at each iteration and also which stick is getting activated. A preview of the game is shown in Figure 1-16.

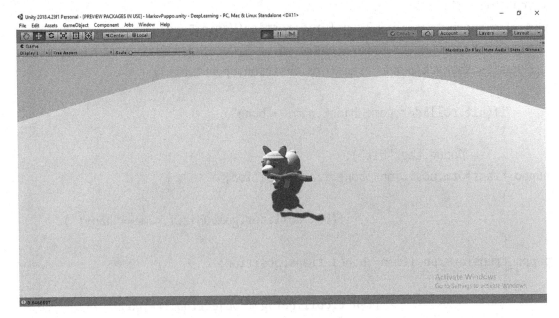

Figure 1-16. *Final game simulation of Markov Puppo*

This is a simple simulation that we created with the Unity Engine to simulate Markov states in a randomized manner. In the next section we will try to understand HMMs and Decision Process for path creation using both Python and Unity.

Hidden Markov Models

HMMs are an extension of Markov states in which some of the states are unobservable or "hidden." HMM assumes that if the state P depends on state S, then the HMM model should learn about S by observing state P. The HMM is a time-discrete stochastic process that can be mathematically explained simply between two states $\{S_n, P_n\}$ such that:

- S_n is Markov Process State and is "hidden" or not directly observable.

- $p\ (P_n \in P \mid S_1 = s_1,...,S_n = s_n) = p\ (P_n \in P \mid S_n = s_n)$

- for all n>0, $s_1,....,s_n$, where P and S are supersets of states and p() is conditional probability.

Concepts of Hidden Markov Models

Let us understand this with an example situation. We take an environment where there are friends Alice and Bob. Bob can perform only three activities : walk, shop, and clean. The choice of Bob's activities is dependent on the weather in the Environment. Alice knows the activities that Bob will perform on a particular day but does not know anything of the weather that affects Bob's activities. This can be formulated as a discrete Markov Chain model where the weather conditions resemble the states. The set of weather conditions include rainy and sunny conditions. Thus the weather conditions are hidden states that affect Bob's activities. The diagram further explains the situation. The diagram also shows the state transition probability values as well as the self-transition values. The Python simulation of the HMM has the following details:

```
states = ('Rainy', 'Sunny')

observations = ('walk', 'shop', 'clean')

start_probability = {'Rainy': 0.7, 'Sunny': 0.3}
```

```
transition_probability = {
    'Rainy' : {'Rainy': 0.8, 'Sunny': 0.2},
    'Sunny' : {'Rainy': 0.1, 'Sunny': 0.9},
    }

emission_probability = {
    'Rainy' : {'walk': 0.1, 'shop': 0.4, 'clean': 0.5},
    'Sunny' : {'walk': 0.6, 'shop': 0.3, 'clean': 0.1},
    }
```

Figure 1-17 depicts the HMM.

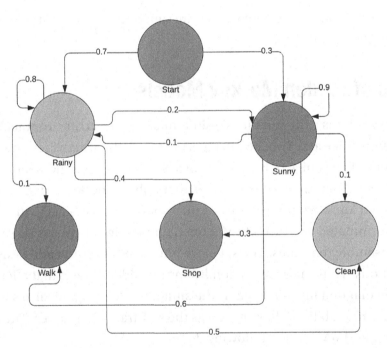

Figure 1-17. *Hidden Markov Model environment*

Hidden Markov Model with Tensorflow

Open the MarkovModel.ipynb notebook, and in the third section there is a Tensorflow implementation of HMM based on initial probability and transition matrix.

```
import tensorflow as tf
import tensorflow_probability as tfp
tf_distributions=tfp.distributions

#Generate Hidden Markov Model With Tensorflow
#Transition Probability of states
transition_mat=tf_distributions.Categorical(probs=[[0.7,0.3],
                                                   [0.2,0.8]])
#Initial Probability of states
intial_values= tf_distributions.Categorical(probs=[1.0,0.5])

#Creating a Distribution Pattern for State Observation: Mean and STD of
1st state is 2.5 and 10, respectively, and that of 2nd state is 6.5 and 7,
respectively.
observation_mat= tf_distributions.Normal(loc=[2.5,10],scale=[6.5,7])

#HMM
model=tf_distributions.HiddenMarkovModel(initial_
distribution=          intial_values,
transition_distribution=transition_mat,
observation_distribution=observation_mat,
num_steps=10,
allow_nan_stats=True,
name="HiddenMarkovModel")

#Mean of the Distribution of States
print(model.mean())
#Log probability of 0 enumerated states i.e 1st State
print(model.log_prob(tf.zeros(shape=[10])))
#Log probability of 1 enumerated states i.e 2nd State
print(model.log_prob(tf.zeros(shape=[10])))
```

The HMM is under the Tensorflow Probability library (named "tensorflow_probability") and is a method of the tf_distributions class. We initiate the values and also assign a normal distribution to each of the two initial states (having mean and standard deviation). The HMM under tf_distributions takes as arguments the initial probabilities, transition matrix, observation array that contains the normal distribution, the number of iterations to simulate, and optional arguments like name of the model and allow_nan_stats. Run this code in a notebook to get to know how the simulation values change after 10 iterations. We can also modify the values of the parameters and probabilities to produce new simulations.

Hidden Markov Model Agent in Unity

Let us try to use this principle and generate a stochastic path algorithm that uses HMM in Unity. The objective is to train an agent to detect the path where the rewards or objects are generated. At the start of each epoch, the agent tries to determine a productive path that is based on the highest probabilistic value a particular object/reward has at a particular state of time. Open the "HMMAgent" scene in Unity and click Play. The Console shows us what is the order of traversal followed by the cube agent to attain the highest valued reward or object at each point of time. For each episode or epoch of learning, the cube agent picks up any of the rewards that are present in the scene. The rewards are based in the form of highest probability an object has in a particular timestamp. Let us say, in timestamp t_0, object o_1 has the highest probability and in t_1 object o_2 has the highest probability, then the agent picks up o_1, o_2, and so on. Inside each episode, there are three timestamps, and for each episode different sequences can be observed. Certain sequences can be o_2, o_1, o_3, or even repeated states such as o_2, o_1, o_1, and so on. These sequences or paths are generated by a dynamic programming implementation of HMM known as Viterbi Algorithm. A preview of the simulation is shown in Figure 1-18.

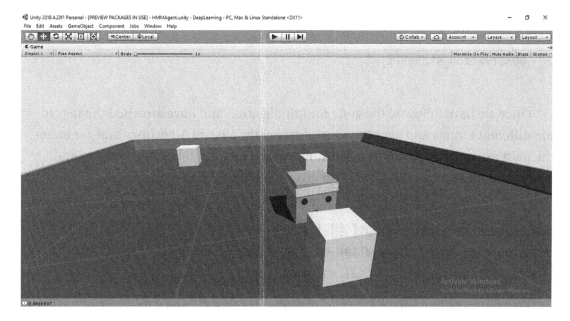

Figure 1-18. *HMMAgent Unity scene*

Let us open the associated script inside the Assets folder called "HMMViterbiAgent. cs" C# script. Most of the script is similar to the previous Markov Model script with common initialization of the transition matrix and initial and result value arrays. We have an additional inclusion of emission matrix (named "emission_mat") and observation states (named "observation_states") that have the emission probability values and the observation states, respectively.

```
float[][] emission_mat;
int[] observation_states=new int[3];
```

The initialization of both of them are as follows.

```
emission_mat[0][0]=Random.Range(0f,1f);
emission_mat[0][1]=Random.Range(0f,1f);
emission_mat[0][2]=Random.Range(0f,1f);
emission_mat[1][0]=Random.Range(0f,1f);
emission_mat[1][1]=Random.Range(0f,1f);
emission_mat[1][2]=Random.Range(0f,1f);
emission_mat[2][0]=Random.Range(0f,1f);
emission_mat[2][1]=Random.Range(0f,1f);
emission_mat[2][2]=Random.Range(0f,1f);
```

```
for(int i=0;i<3;i++)
{
    observation_states[i]=i;
}
```

Once we have followed the code for initialization and have attached the tags to the different targets and agents, we can inspect the Viterbi Algorithm that generates the path using the probabilities. The function declaration takes the matrices and arrays as arguments and fills the path array with the indices of the target objects being generated.

```
public void HMMViterbi(float[][] transition_mat,float[][]
emission_mat, int[] observation_states, float[]
hidden_states, float[] initial_val,int[] path)
```

We create a minimum weight algorithm where we try to reduce the probability of the states or objects and then try to find the highest probable object or target (among the objects) in a particular time.

```
{
    int  mini_state=0;
    float mini_weight=0f;
    float weight=0f;
    float[][]  a= create_mat(3);
    int[][] s= create_mat_int(3);
``

int i,j;
for(i=0;i<3;i++)
{
    a[i][0]=(float)(-1*Math.Log(initial_val[i])
        *(Math.Log(emission_mat[i][observation_states[0]])));
}
```

For the next steps, with the initial values of "a" matrix, we run a loop operation for each observation state and compute the minimum weight value accordingly.

```
for(i=1;i<3;i++)
{
      for(j=0;j<3;j++)
      {
          mini_state=0;
          mini_weight=a[0][i-1]-(float)
                  (Math.Log(transition_mat[0][j]));

           for(int k=1;k<3;k++)
           {
               weight=a[k][i-1] - (float)
  (Math.Log(transition_mat[k][j]));

                 if(weight<mini_weight)
                 {
                     mini_weight=weight;
                     mini_state=i;

                 }
           }

      }
```

After this, we update the "a" matrix to hold the minimum weights temporarily. We also store the state having the minimum value in state matrix "s."

```
      a[j][i]= mini_weight-(float)
      (Math.Log(emission_mat[j][observation_states[i]]));
      s[j][i]=mini_state;

   }


}
```

Once we have filled the values of "a" and "s" matrices, we get the index of the target object with highest probability and least weight. Then we do backtracking to generate the possible minimum weighted path involving the other two target objects.

```
mini_state=0;
mini_weight=a[0][i-1];
for(int k=1;k<3;k++)
{
        if(a[k][i-1]<mini_weight)
        {
                    mini_state=i;
                    mini_weight=a[k][i-1];
        }
}

        //dp backtracking
        //int[] path= new int[3];
        path[i-1]=mini_state;
        for(int k=i-2;k>=0;k--)
        {
            path[k]=s[path[k]][k+1];
        }

        float distribution_prob=(float)Math.Exp(-mini_weight);


}
```

The Viterbi algorithm is a dynamic programming algorithm that exploits Markov states and transition emission probabilities to choose a minimum weighted path that the agent can follow to collect the targets having the highest probabilities at each timestamp.

To run the function, we start a Coroutine, like before, and compute the result value array by multiplication of initial value array and transition matrix, like before, and call the HMMViterbi function.

```
mult(transition_mat,initial_val,result_values);
tanh(result_values);
initial_val=result_values;
Debug.Log("Start Path");
HMMViterbi(transition_mat,emission_mat,observation_states,
hidden_states,initial_val,path);
```

The rest of the code is similar to the previous Markov Model template where RayCast is used by the cube agent to detect the colliders of the target objects, and the transform of the cube is updated to follow the path. An interesting observation is the updates on the path after the Viterbi function is called:

```
for(int l=0;l<path.Length;l++)
{

    target_number=path[l];
    /../
}
```

After we have understood the code, we can proceed further to test the code in Play mode by assigning the script to the cube agent (named "AgentCube_Purple"). The Unity Scene View of the environment is shown in Figure 1-19.

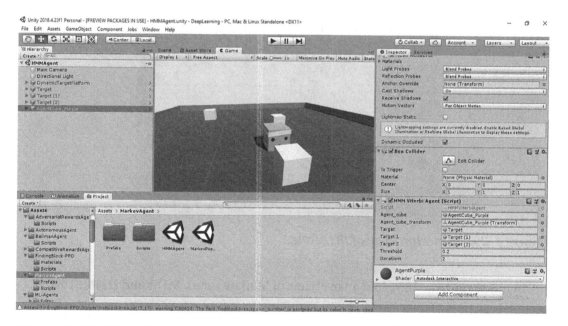

Figure 1-19. *Unity Scene with script assigned to AgentCube_Purple*

If we follow closely, in the Inspector Window, we can change the number of iterations or the epoch/episodes according to our choice. The Console shows the details of the steps that are followed in the form of indices of the target cubes. A preview of the Inspector Window is shown in Figure 1-20.

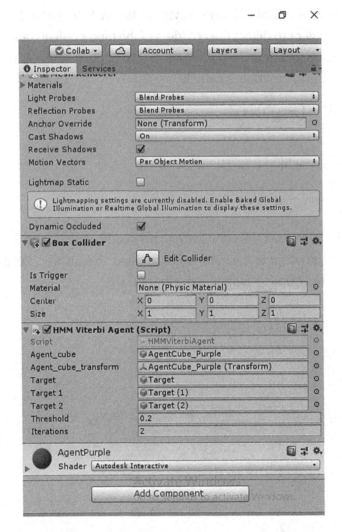

Figure 1-20. *Inspector View of the scene*

In this section, we have had an overview of Markov states, MDP, and HMM. This section is an important aspect in understanding the fundamentals of RL, as all learning algorithms in discrete RL are based on states. In this section, we have understood and implemented Markov models in Python and simulated games and understood the brief overview of dynamic programming-based HMM and also its simulation in Unity. The next section will focus on incorporating rewards to these states and make the agent learn how to attain those rewards. We will understand the core fundamentals of the Bellman equation and explore multi-armed bandits along with some variations in the iterative Bellman equation.

Bellman Equation

Now that we have an understanding of MDP, let us extend along this idea to introduce the concepts of iterated reward-based learning. The MDP and HMM provides us with an insight into how to retain past information of the states as we saw in the path tracking model. When we involve rewards in the context of Markov models, a generic learning algorithmic equation evolves. Mathematically we assume the rewards to be inside a set R and try to calculate the expectation of rewards, denoted by E[R] at the end of the episode. This can be shown as:

$$G_t = R_{t+1} + R_{t+2} + \ldots + R_t,$$

where G_t is the expectation of the rewards of time step t based on sequence of rewards received. This can be thought of as an addition on dynamic programming-based Markov models, where each state has an expectation of reward. In general, the Bellman equation has an associated discount factor y (gamma), which discounts the rewards received in the previous states. Thus a formal iterative Bellman reward discount equation can be framed as :

$$G_t = R_{t+1} + yR_{t+2} + \ldots + \sum y^k R_{t+k}$$

This is the Bellman expected reward function on Markov states with discount factor gamma on previous rewards. This enables the agent to choose the most recent value of expectation of the rewards and accordingly the most recent states that lead to more rewards. This can be visualized as a top-down tree, since this is an iterative dynamic programming approach.

The iterative Bellman equation is formulated using two fundamental algorithmic approaches :

- **Policy function**: The policy iterative function denoted by $\pi(a|s)$ is a mapping between the states and the action sets to produce an optimal policy denoted by $\pi^*(a|s)$, which attains the highest expected reward. The policy function is validated in the form of maximization of values of the policy at each step.

- **Value function**: The value function denoted by $v\pi(s)$ denotes the value or the expected return received when starting in state s and following the policy π.

Now that we have a brief idea of Bellman equations and what are value and policy functions let us try to visualize them as a top-down tree in Figure 1-21.

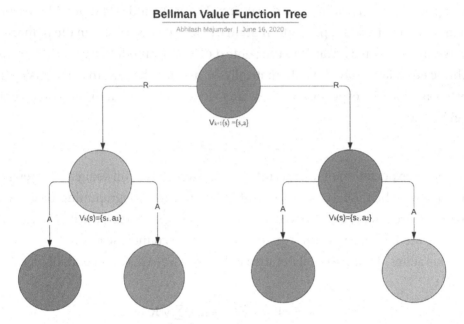

Bellman Value Function Tree
Abhilash Majumder | June 16, 2020

Figure 1-21. *Bellman value iteration tree*

The Bellman tree provided shows how in action of a policy π can control the value $v\pi(s)$ from k+1 state to k state and enumerate expected rewards from k+1, k+2 states, and so on.

Note   Richard.E. Bellman, an applied American mathematician, founded the Bellman equation as a dynamic programming method that is used in optimal control theory and later in RL.

Bellman Agent Implementation in Unity

We will discuss more on the aspects of value and policy iteration in later sections of this chapter, for now let us create another simulation based on rewards and the Bellman Iterative algorithm. Open up the Assets folder and navigate to the "BellmanAgent" folder. This contains a simulation game where the agent is on a racing kart, and there are rewards (green big cubes) that the agent has to reach and collect and after that reach the opposite end pole. The scene, when opened, would appear as shown in Figure 1-22.:

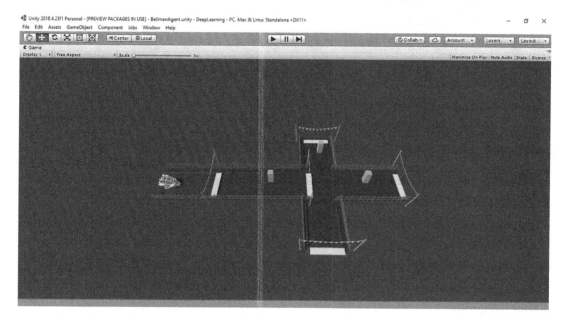

Figure 1-22. *Bellman agent Unity scene*

Let us understand the code of how the simulation works. The Kart Agent has an objective function to maximize its rewards for each episode or epoch of learning using the iterative value function of the Bellman equation. Once the agent reaches the second green target (green cube) or the end pole (finish line), the episode terminates. For the time being, the simulation is in one direction that is forward-backward along the z axis of the Kart Agent, and this can be extended to multidirectional traversal as well.

Open the "BellmanAgent.cs" C# Script. While the initialization and the variables are set according to previous templates of Markov models and HMM, there are distinct new features and variables that are required to be made.

```
float max_reward=30.0f;
public float gamma;
public float epsilon;
public GameObject TinyAgent;
public Transform tiny_transform;
```

```
public GameObject target;
public GameObject target1;
public int iter;
public GameObject target2;
public Transform target_transform;
public Transform target1_transform;
public Transform target2_transform;
float[][] states;
float[] reward=new float[9];
float[] values=new float[9];
Dictionary<float,float> state_reward= new Dictionary<float,float>();
```

The variable "max_reward" is the total value of rewards that need to be accumulated in an episode by the agent. Variable "gamma" is the discount factor. Next we have initialization of GameObject variables for Kart Agent and the targets. We create a matrix of float values called states, which is the transitional matrix in this case. There is also a float array of rewards for each state, a dictionary for mapping states with the rewards. The values array of float is required for the value function update by using the iterative Bellman equation.

The fundamental concept in creating the states in a tabular discrete manner for Bellman updates is to use the transform.z position values of the track (i.e., the road) The track may contain the green target or finish line or not. Depending on whether a particular section of the track has a target or is at the terminal position, we allocate rewards to each track section. This transforms the track into a virtual Gym-like environment containing different states and rewards, particularly similar to GridWorld (an environment in Gym).

We initialize the rewards using the Random.Range() function as follows:

```
reward[0]=Random.Range(-0.05f,0.05f);
reward[1]=Random.Range(-0.05f,0.05f);
reward[2]=Random.Range(-0.05f,0.05f);
reward[3]=Random.Range(0.05f,0.20f);
reward[4]=Random.Range(-0.05f,0.05f);
reward[5]=Random.Range(-0.05f,0.05f);
reward[6]=Random.Range(-0.05f,0.05f);
reward[7]=Random.Range(0.05f,0.2f);
reward[8]=Random.Range(-0.05f,0.05f);
```

The horizontal Track is divided into nine sections, each with an associated reward. We can manually set the rewards as well. We also populate the dictionary with the key value pair as :position value (Transform.position.z) and reward (float).

```
public void populate_state_rewards(Dictionary<float,float> state_
reward,float[] reward)
{

        state_reward.Add(-32.5f,reward[0]);
        state_reward.Add(-13.8f,reward[1]);
        state_reward.Add(-4.2f,reward[2]);
        state_reward.Add(4.9f,reward[3]);
        state_reward.Add(14.57f,reward[4]);
        state_reward.Add(23.93f,reward[5]);
        state_reward.Add(33.7f,reward[6]);
        state_reward.Add(41.7f,reward[7]);
        state_reward.Add(50.8f,reward[8]);

}
```

We then create the value array and set it using the Random.Range function. The transition matrix is also created where the diagonal elements have the same probability of 0.04 and all the others are created with the "Random.Range" function. The start method is similar like before and contains all the states, initialization of GameObjects, and linking of the tags.

Once the initialization is done, let us form a deep understanding of the code for the Bellman equation.

```
public int calculate_Bellman(float gamma,float[][] states,float[]
reward,Dictionary<float,float> state_reward,float[] values)
{
    float[] new_values=new float[9];
        new_values=values;
    values=mult(states,values,new_values);
    for(int i=0;i<9;i++)
    {
        values[i]= reward[i]+ values[i]*gamma;
    }
```

43

```
    float max_values= maxi(values);
    int max_index=maxi_index(values,max_values);
    return max_index;

}
```

The function takes arguments as the transition matrix, rewards, dictionary, and also the value array. It computes the multiplication of a transitional matrix or state with the values array. Then it applies the gamma discount factor. Finally the rewards for the current state are added to generate the new values. After the operation is done, we take the most valuable element or state with the highest value and retrieve its index from the value array. This index will help us in mapping which reward value is getting triggered. From that reward value, we can navigate to that particular track section (position) by looking up the dictionary.

```
public  float take_action(Dictionary<float,float> state_reward,int max_
index)
{    float action=0f;
    float max_reward=collect_rewards(max_index);
    foreach(KeyValuePair<float,float> i in state_reward)
        {
                if(i.Value==max_reward)
                {
                        action=i.Key;
                        break;
                }
        }
    Debug.Log(action);
    return action;
}
```

This function helps to look up the particular reward that is attained during an iteration of the game and automatically returns the position of the triggered track section.

Let us put all of these together in a Coroutine function that is the control logic for the agent. Inside the IEnumerator function, we set a for loop that runs for the number of epochs we would want.

```
Debug.Log("Start Epoch");
        float reward_now=0f;
        while(reward_now<max_reward)
         {
            Debug.Log("Start Episode");
            int max_index=calculate_Bellman(gamma,
states,reward,state_reward,values);
            Debug.Log(max_index);
            reward_now+=collect_rewards(max_index);
            Debug.Log("Rewards");
            Debug.Log(reward_now);
            float action_step=take_action(state_reward,
max_index);
            Debug.Log(action_step);
```

This segment of code runs as long as the collected rewards are less than the total expected rewards specified in the initialization step. In this segment of code, we performed the Bellman iterative value operation, attained the particular reward value that is getting triggered for that instance, and also retrieved the transform position value of the corresponding track section. The rewards are added accordingly.

```
if(action_step==target_transform.position.z )
            {
                Debug.Log("Reached first target");
                tiny_transform.position=new Vector3(0f,0f,
target_transform.position.z);
                target.SetActive(false);
                yield return new WaitForSeconds(1f);

            }
if(action_step==target1_transform.position.z )
            {
                Debug.Log("Reached Second target");
                tiny_transform.position=new Vector3(0f,0f,
```

```
target1_transform.position.z);
                target1.SetActive(false);
                yield return new WaitForSeconds(1f);

        }
tiny_transform.position=new Vector3(0f,0f,action_step);
yield return new WaitForSeconds(1f);
```

The if-else statements specify and check whether the action taken by the Kart Agent has led him to the green target or finish line. If the agent reaches the finish line or the target then we provide him a momentary rest of 1 second before the start of the next iteration. This iteration continues as long as the rewards are less than the total expected rewards.

```
if(reward_now==max_reward)
            {
                break;
            }
reset();
yield return new WaitForSeconds(2f);
  }
  Debug.Log("End Episode");

reset();
 }
Debug.Log("End Epoch")
}
```

If the conditions are met and the rewards accumulated equal the total rewards, we terminate the instance and provide the agent a rest for 2 seconds before moving to the next episode of training.

When we are comfortable with the code-base, we can play around and modify with the reward function and add more discrete rewards for different situations. Also the environment can be extended along the vertical track as well, which would also add more states on the transitional matrix as well as the value array. The motion of the agent would be then governed on both the x and the z axes. We can modify the script to accommodate more states by taking the x values of the vertically placed track section in the dictionary. Once the environment is set up as shown in Figure 1-23, we can click the Play button in the editor. Notice how the agent rapidly navigates to the highest rewarding state for each iteration and continues to do so because of the updates in the value array. The value array retains the information of the states or track sections that contain the highest rewards and also helps the agent in successive timestamps to follow that path. This can be realized as a buffer memory that retains the state having the highest values.

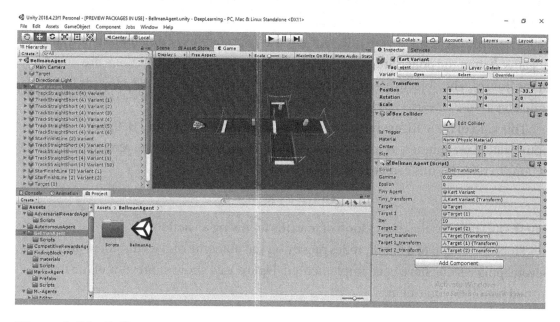

Figure 1-23. *Bellman agent Unity Scene with Inspector Window*

In this section, we have learned about the Bellman equation, which is an iterative dynamic programming equation. We have visited some important concepts of relating rewards to Markov states and the Decision Process with the help of the Bellman equation. The section also touched briefly on the value and policy iteration techniques for reward maximization or value maximization by following a particular policy. We created and simulated a Unity Game where a Kart Agent has to apply the Bellman Value Function to navigate to the highest rewarding track sections. By now, we have learned how discrete tabular environments and value/policy optimization algorithms such as the Bellman equation are useful in RL. In the next section we will discuss creating another simulation game based on Multi Armed Bandits.

Creating a Multi-Armed Bandit Reinforcement Learning Agent in Unity

Multi-armed bandits (MAB) are the simplest form of RL algorithmic simulations. This technique does not involve learning to choose maximum rewarding states but relies on a feedback mechanism. The k armed bandit problem can be described as follows: a bandit agent is in an environment where there are k different houses that can be robbed (action space). Based on the decision chosen at each step on the choice of the house, the bandit gets a reward. The reward, generally, is a stationary probabilistic distribution and can be negative (when the police are present in the house) or positive (when there are no police in the house). The objective of the bandit agent is to maximize positive rewards for n time-steps.

This kind of basic RL environment is devoid of Markov states and Bellman optimization techniques, as mathematically it is a function of only the rewards and the action. To reframe, this can be interpreted as:

$$Q(a) = E\,[\,R_t\,|\,A_t = a\,],$$

where $Q(a)$ denotes the expectation of rewards following an action a.

Since the action of a bandit relies mostly on the outcome of rewards, there are several policies that have been implemented. Figure 1-24 shows a preview of the multi-armed bandit environment.

Multi Armed Bandit Learning

Abhilash Majumder | June 16, 2020

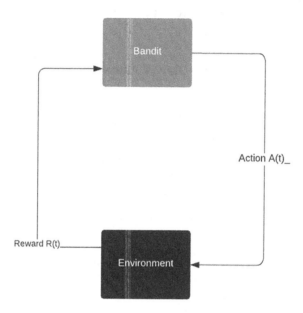

Figure 1-24. *Multi-armed bandit and environment*

Strategies Involved in Multi-Armed Bandits

There are several variations of the Bandit algorithm to maximize the rewards collected at each step. These are generally referred to as "action–value" functions.

- **Greedy algorithm:** The brute force application involves using the Greedy Exploitation algorithm. This involves storing the Q-value (value function) of the action for each iteration and choosing the maximum Q-valued action. This is a nonexploration strategy, as in many cases the rewards may not be the highest at the same arm/ location. Mathematically this can be seen as:

$$Q_t(a) = \sum 1_{(at=a)} \cdot (R_i) / \sum 1_{(at=a)},$$

choose the maximum Q-value:

$$\text{Argmax}_a \ Q_t(a)$$

- **Epsilon-Greedy algorithm**: In this kind of algorithm, the bandit exploits and explores new states based on certain probability values, denoted bye. The bandit explores a new state with probability e and exploits the best current reward state with probability 1-e, as shown in Figure 1-25.

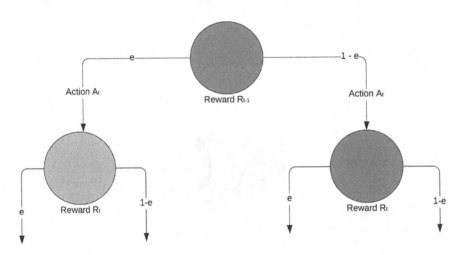

Figure 1-25. *Epsilon-Greedy algorithm*

- **Decayed Epsilon-Greedy algorithm**: This is a variation of the previous exploitation–exploration algorithm. Here, a logarithmic decay factor may be associated with the exploitation of previous states.

- **Nonstationary Weighted algorithm**: If the rewards acquired by the bandit change over time, then it is a nonstationary problem. In this case we apply a weighted average on the previous Q-value and current rewards. This can be shown as :

$$Q_{n+1} = Q_n + \alpha \left[R_n - Q_n \right],$$

where α is the average weighted factor.

- **Upper Confidence-Bound (UCB) algorithm**: This is a statistical distribution of exploration-exploitation of different rewards. The algorithm explores by measuring the expected variance in the rewards of previous action. This is an optimistic value approach to reduce the variance of a particular action of getting high rewards. Mathematically it can be described by the equation:

$$A_t= \text{argmax } [Q_t(a) + c\sqrt{(\ln(t)/N_t(a))}],$$

where $N_t(a)$ denotes the number of times the action a has been selected prior to time t and $\ln(t)$ is the natural logarithm of t.

- **Gradient Bandit algorithm**: This is a numerical preference algorithm that takes into account the preference of a particular state a over other states. The relative preference of one action over the other is recorded and can be sampled into a probabilistic distribution by including the softmax function. This is a very important function in general deep learning and will be using this in our deep RL algorithms.

$$\text{Softmax}(z) = e^z/(\sum e^z)$$

- **Thompson sampling**: It is a Bayesian sampling technique that is more sophisticated than Epsilon-Greedy algorithm and is based on posterior probability distribution of the actions and rewards.

Multi-Armed Bandit Simulation in Unity with UCB Algorithm

In this section, we will try to incorporate the Epsilon-Greedy, UCB with softmax gradient optimization. We will try to explore the different algorithmic approaches in Unity simulation, and then we can try to create an environment based on Python.

Open the scene "MAB-Unity." The scene consists of three cubes, each having a different probability of rewards. On selecting play in the editor, we see that the bandit chooses different rewards (i.e., cubes) and always tries to optimize its rewards. This is a purely action–reward-based, noncontextual bandit with feedback, and hence we can control the exploration-exploitation with the Epsilon-Greedy algorithm. By default the simulation runs in Epsilon-Greedy, and there is an option for activating the UCB algorithm as well. In the Console Tab, we can see the expected rewards. A preview of the environment is shown in Figure 1-26.

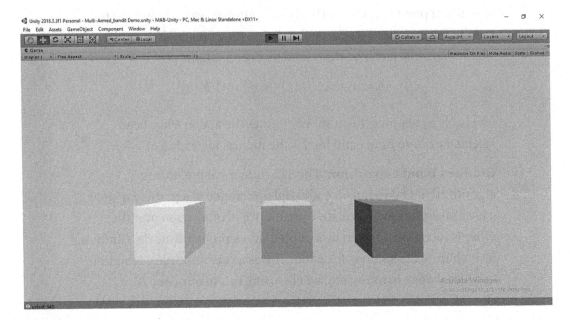

Figure 1-26. *Multi-Armed Bandit Scene in Unity*

Since by now we have gained some experience writing code in C# MonoBehaviour for Unity, let us open the "Agent" script. The first contains the variable setup; here it should be noted that if we want private variables to be rendered in the Inspector Window, we have to mention the [SerializeField] attribute over each of the private variables.

```
[SerializeField]
private int k = 3;
[SerializeField]
private float lr = 0.1f;
[SerializeField]
private float exp_rate = 0.3f;
    [SerializeField]
    private bool ucb = true;
    [SerializeField]
```

```
private float c = 2f;
[SerializeField]
private float time_lag = 0.1f;
List<int> actions = new List<int>();
public float total_reward = 0;
List<float> avg_reward = new List<float>();
List<float> true_val = new List<float>();
System.Random rnd = new System.Random();
private float time = 0.0f;
List<float> values = new List<float>();
List<float> action_times = new List<float>();
List<float> confidence_int = new List<float>();
// Start is called before the first frame update
[SerializeField]
private GameObject g0, g1, g2;
```

The initialization involves variables such as epsilon for the Epsilon-Greedy algorithm, Boolean trigger for UCB, and float arrays of rewards, values (Q-values), and action times (which signify to what extent an action "a" is repeated). The confidence interval is a float list that helps in the UCB algorithm. The actions list contains the indices of the relevant cubes during running of the application. The start method contains all the initializations of the variables and lists, which calls the Coroutine for the game control logic.

Let us explore the chooseaction method, which contains the implementation of Epsilon-Greedy UCB algorithm.

```
int action = 0;
if ((float)Random.Range(0.0f, 1.0f) <= exp_rate)
{
        int idx = rnd.Next(actions.Count);
        action = idx;

}
```

This part of the code segment randomly chooses float values and checks whether they are less than the exploitation rate. Then it tries to explore new cubes with the "rnd.Next()" method. This is an exploration strategy that is based on the randomized distribution of the samples.

If this option is not chosen, then the control passes to the else statement. If we want to use the UCB algorithm, we have to check the boolean variable to be true. The UCB code is as follows:

```
if (ucb)
        {
            if (time == 0f)
            {
                action = rnd.Next(actions.Count);

            }
            else
            {
   for (int i = 0; i < k; i++)
                    {
                        float x = (float)values[i];
   float r = c *  (Mathf.Sqrt(Mathf.Log((float)time) /
(action_times[i] + 0.1f)));
                        x += r;
                        confidence_int[i] = (float)x;

                    }
                    float max = 9999f;
                    action = 0;
                    for (int j = 0; j < k; j++)
                    {
                        if (confidence_int[j] > max)
                        {
                            max = confidence_int[j];
                            action = j;
                        }
                    }

            }
        }
```

The UCB code is divided into two statements. If the time period is not provided for UCB, then it is a random exploration algorithm. If the time period for past actions is taken into consideration, then the control goes to the "else" statement. The UCB then computes the Q-values of all the possible actions using the UCB formula. After attaining each of the Q-values, they are populated in the confidence interval list. The later part of the code segment then chooses the maximum Q-value from this confidence interval list and returns that particular cube.

We next move into the "take action" function and try to update the Q-values and reward values by adding a learning rate to aid in the UCB algorithm. The algorithm also computes the relative rewards at each step as well as the average rewards.

```
time++;
action_times[action] += 1;
float reward = Random.Range(0f, 1.0f) + true_val[action];
values[action] += lr * (reward - values[action]);
total_reward += reward;
avg_reward.Add(total_reward / time);
```

The "Play" method links the above two functions and runs them for the iterations provided in the Inspector Window. The Q-value of a particular action with the highest confidence interval values gets selected and passed to the "takeaction" method.

```
public void play(int n)
    {
        for (int y = 0; y < n; y++)
        {
            int act = chooseaction(exp_rate,
                                    c, values, action_times,
actions, time, ucb);
  takeaction(total_reward,
  avg_reward, action_times,
  time, act, true_val);
        }
    }
```

Let us enter into the IEnumerator code segment, where all the functions are called and the appropriate cube gets selected. The "Play" command gets called for 900 iterations, and for each iteration, we get the details of average rewards and total rewards in the Console Window. Then based on the selection of cubes, the highest valued cube per iteration is set active and the rest are deactivated. This signifies which cube is getting triggered at which iteration and provides the maximum Q-value.

```
yield return new WaitForSeconds(time_lag);

    play(900);
    //Debug.Log("Total REward " + total_reward);
    /*for (int t = 0; t < k; t++)
    {
        Debug.Log("True Values " + true_val[t]);
        Debug.Log("Estimated values " + values[t]);

    }
    */
    float thresh = 0.9f;
    for (int y = 0; y < avg_reward.Count; y++)
    {
        if (avg_reward[y] > thresh)
        {
            Debug.Log("select " + y + y % 3);
            if (y % 3 == 0)
            {
                g0.SetActive(true);
                g1.SetActive(false);
                g2.SetActive(false);
            }
            else if (y % 3 == 1)
            {
                g0.SetActive(false);
                g1.SetActive(true);
                g0.SetActive(false);
            }
```

```
        else if (y % 3 == 2)
        {
            g0.SetActive(false);
            g1.SetActive(false);
            g2.SetActive(true);
        }
    }
    yield return new WaitForSeconds(time_lag);
}
```

Thus we implemented an Epsilon-Greedy-UCB-based, multi-armed bandit
simulation. We can play with the settings by switching between Epsilon-Greedy and UCB
algorithms during gameplay to see how exploration–exploitation details are affected.
Once we have understood the code, we can click Play in the Unity Editor and see the
simulation running. After many iterations, we will observe that some of the cubes
are repeatedly being selected—a classic example of bandit exploitation. We can then
change the epsilon and learning rate values or change to UCB algorithm to have more
exploration. Figure 1-27 is a preview of the simulation.

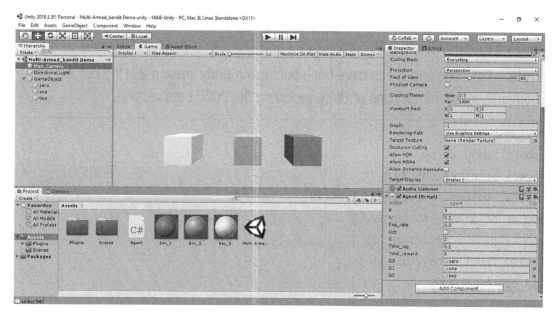

Figure 1-27. *Multi-armed bandit Inspector Window*

Building Multi-Armed Bandit with Epsilon-Greedy and Gradient Bandit Algorithms

Once we have verified our algorithm, we can try our hand at implementing a simpler version of Epsilon-Greedy environment in Python using Jupyter Notebook or Colab Notebook. Open the "Multi-Armed Bandit.ipynb" Notebook in Colab or Notebook. The code is pretty straightforward. We have an implementation of the classic 10-arm bandit, where we have an initial ground truth distribution of the probabilities of each arm (house in our case). We also initialize the probability of the arms and the agents' probabilities. The rest of the code represents a for loop that runs the number of epochs provided in "num_epochs" variable. If the value of epsilon is greater than random value, then we explore among the 10 different arms; otherwise we exploit. Once the rewards have been attained for a particular episode, we update the Q function by using an incremental approach given by the generic equation:

$$Q_{n+1} = \sum R_i / n,$$

where the Q-value for n+1-th iteration is the average of the previous rewards R_i collected over past n episodes.

The program is pretty much self-explanatory and contains all the details in the comments to generate a possible distribution and sampling of the arms.

Note   The code and scene have been built using Unity version 2018.3 but are compatible with all versions of Unity, including the 2020 beta version.

```
import numpy as np
np.set_printoptions(2)
initial_values = np.random.rand(10)
number_of_arms = np.zeros(10)
agents_prob = np.zeros(10)
reward_count = np.zeros(10)
num_epochs = 4000
e = 0.33
```

After the initialization, we enter into the for loop as follows:

```
for _ in range(num_epochs):

    # Either choose a greedy action or explore
    if e > np.random.uniform():
        which_arm_to_pull = np.random.randint(0,10)
    else:
        which_arm_to_pull = np.argmax(agents_prob)

    # now pull the rewarding arm
    if initial_values[which_arm_to_pull]
    >  np.random.uniform():
        reward = 1
    else:
        reward = 0
```

The Epsilon-Greedy sampling technique produces the rewards accordingly. Then we update the arm number that the bandit has to pull and update the reward count as follows:

```
# now update the lever count and expected value
number_of_arms[which_arm_to_pull] += 1
reward_count[which_arm_to_pull] =reward_count[which_arm_to_pull] + reward
```

The incremental approach is then applied to generate the Q-value for n+1-th iteration as follows:

```
#Incremental Approach to Update value of Q
#Q(t+1)=Q(t) + (1/n(R(n)-q(n)))

agents_prob[which_arm_to_pull] =agents_prob[which_arm_to_pull] + (1/number_
of_arms[which_arm_to_pull]) *
    (reward -agents_prob[which_arm_to_pull])
```

Finally we print the outcome of each epoch in terms of best rewards achieved, Q-values, and arm selected. The output should appear like Figure 1-28 after running.

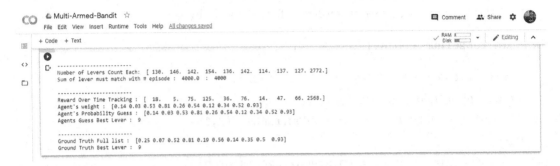

Figure 1-28. *Multi-armed bandit Epsilon-Greedy in Python*

In this section, we understood the simplest form of the RL algorithm called multi-armed bandits. We learned about the different optimization techniques of exploration and exploitation in MAB to have a greater Q-value or rewards at each action step. Unlike complex Markov Models, HMM, and Bellman equations, there is no concept of state here, and that is why it is a lightweight model for RL. We then created a MAB simulation environment in Unity using Epsilon-Greedy and UCB algorithm techniques and visualized the rewards in each stage of the process. In the next section, we will consider the final steps for introductory RL: value and policy iterations. This section was initialized in the Bellman equation and will continue from there.

Value and Policy Iterations

Since the introduction of the Bellman equation earlier in this chapter, we have been briefly introduced to the value and policy iteration functions. The policy iteration can be thought of as optimizing a policy $\pi^*(s \mid a)$ from a base policy $\pi(s \mid a)$, which would lead to an increase in the value function associated with that policy. A simple value update function can be mathematically simplified as :

$$V(s_t) = V(s_t) + \alpha \left[G_t - V(s_t) \right],$$

where alpha is a constant step size used in learning, $V(s_t)$ is the value attained at state t, and G_t is the expectation of rewards R_t introduced in the Bellman equation section. If we replace the value of G_t, with an iterative discount factor y (gamma) introduced in the Bellman equation, we can reframe the value equation as follows:

$$V(s_t) = V(s_t) + \alpha \left[R_{t+1} + yV(s_{t+1}) - V(s_t) \right]$$

This method of value optimization over a certain policy is known as temporal difference learning. Particularly, this equation signifies the TD(0) algorithm, since we concern ourselves with just one state ahead of the current state (i.e., step t+1).

The value iteration mechanism also has a definitive way to define the error term ∂ produced after each successive step of the learning process by assessing the values of t+1 and t states. This can be mathematically shown by the simplified equation:

$$\partial_t = R_{t+1} + yV(s_{t+1}) - V(s_t),$$

where ∂ is the error for timestamp t.

Now that we have the mathematical conception of value iteration technique, we can better realize what was happening in the "BellmanAgent, cs" script in Unity. The outcome of the value function is controlled by the policy function, which also gets updated. Based on the policy function, the agent has to maximize the value function, and if the policy fails to do that, then the policy gets updated as well. This can be explained simplistically by this equation:

$$\pi^*(s, a) = \text{argmax } V_\pi(s,a),$$

where symbols have their original meaning. Let us try to visualize how policy iteration can help attain maximum value function in Figure 1-29.

Value And Policy Functions

Abhilash Majumder | June 16, 2020

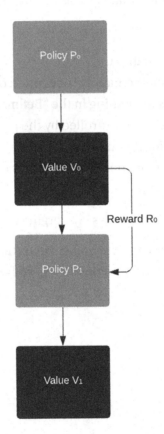

Figure 1-29. *Value policy iteration functions*

Now let us understand a fundamental concept involving value and policy iteration known as Q–learning. The Q-learning algorithm is an off-policy temporal difference learning algorithm that uses the Q function as the value function and tries to maximize the value. It can be simply written in accordance to generalized value iteration equation, replacing V(s) with Q(s,a) as follows:

$$Q(s_t, a_t) = Q(s_t, a_t) + \alpha \left[R_{t+1} + y \max Q(s_{t+1}, a_{t+1}) - Q(s_t, a_t) \right]$$

The Q–learning algorithm is a tabular discrete algorithm that uses the value and policy iteration equations and forms the baseline model in general RL. Let us first try to understand how Q-learning and policy updates work by understanding a tabular Gym environment.

Note   Q-learning was introduced by Chris Watkins in 1989.

Implementing Q-Learning Policy Using Taxi Gym Environment

Open the "Policy Iteration Function and Q Learning.ipynb" Notebook, and let us try to understand the environment. In this Notebook, we have used the Taxi environment (2D) from OpenAI Gym environment set, where the Taxi is shown with the help of a yellow box. The environment can be installed in the Notebook as follows:

```
#Policy Iteration by using Q-Learning
import numpy as np
import random
from IPython.display import clear_output
import gym
#Initialize the Taxi Gym Environment
enviroment = gym.make("Taxi-v3").env
enviroment.render()
#collect the details of observation and action space
print('Number of states: {}'.format(enviroment.observation_space.n))
print('Number of actions: {}'.format(enviroment.action_space.n))
```

Upon running the Notebook or Colab, we will be presented with the details of the Observation space and Action space, just like in the CartPole environment, as shown in Figure 1-30.

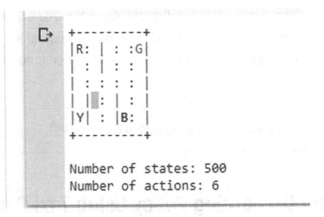

Figure 1-30. *Taxi-v3 Gym environment*

The next part of the Notebook contains the stepwise code for training using Q-learning based on observation states and rewards. We initialize the variables as

```
alpha = 0.1
gamma = 0.6
epsilon = 0.1
q_table = np.zeros([enviroment.observation_space.n, enviroment.action_
space.n])
num_of_epochs = 100000,
```

where "alpha" is the learning rate, "gamma" is the discount factor, "epsilon" is used for the exploration–exploitation strategy (used in the MAB algorithm), and "q_table" is the matrix containing the observation and action spaces.

We then run a for loop for the number of epochs we want to train with Q-learning as follows:

```
for episode in range(0, num_of_epochs):
    # Reset the enviroment
    state = enviroment.reset()

    # Initialize variables
    reward = 0
    terminated = False
```

We reset the environment before the start of each epoch. The next segment contains the different exploitation–exploration strategy of Q-learning and updates of the "q_table" by applying the Q-learning equation. The states, rewards, and action spaces are received from the Gym environment in each stage of the learning process.

```
while not terminated:
# Similar to epsilon-greedy algorithm for exploration-#exploitaion tradeoff
        if random.uniform(0, 1) < epsilon:
            action = enviroment.action_space.sample()
        else:
            action = np.argmax(q_table[state])

        # Return the current state, reward and action
        next_state, reward,
    terminated, info = enviroment.step(action)

    #Compute the q value of the state
    from the tabular    environment
        q_value = q_table[state, action]
        #Get the maximum Q value
        max_value = np.max(q_table[next_state])
        #update the Q-value based on the Q-learning Equation
    new_q_value = (1 - alpha) * q_value + alpha *
    (reward    + gamma * max_value)

        # Update Q-table
        q_table[state, action] = new_q_value
        state = next_state
```

The comments in each line describe the operation that is being performed in the subsequent step. After the training is complete, the Q-table contains the values of the most rewarding states. This can be represented by the updated Taxi environment, as shown in Figure 1-31.

Figure 1-31. Taxi Gym environment training in Q-learning

The next segment contains code for the evaluation of the model. For each epoch of the Q–learning agent, the Taxi attains a reward based on the Q-table. If the reward is negative, then we add a penalty value, which means that the Taxi has collided with another object in the environment.

```
state = enviroment.reset()
epochs = 0
penalties = 0
reward = 0

terminated = False
#Run epochs
while not terminated:
    action = np.argmax(q_table[state])
    state, reward, terminated, info = enviroment.step(action)
    #If reward is negative,penalty
    if reward == -10:
        penalties += 1

    epochs += 1

total_penalties += penalties
total_epochs += epochs
```

On running the segment, we get the penalty values and the epochs per episodes, as shown in Figure 1-32.

```
********************************
Results
********************************
Epochs per episode: 13.47
Penalties per episode: 0.0
```

Figure 1-32. *Taxi Gym environment evaluation*

Q-Learning in Unity

Let us now move to create a similar template for Q-learning in Unity. Open the scene named "Q-Learning" and click Play. The cylindrical object is the agent, which tries to move from top to bottom by avoiding the red planes and using only the green planes. The planes are the state samples, or the Observation space, as in Gym environments. Green planes have rewards associated with them, while red ones have negative rewards. The agent uses an iterative Q-learning algorithm as the policy to update the value function and to maximize its rewards. The scene should appear something as shown in Figure 1-33.

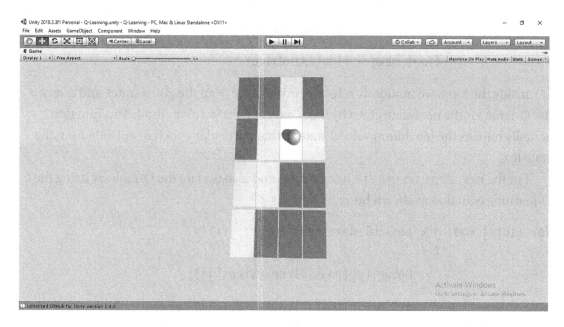

Figure 1-33. *Q-learning scene in Unity*

Open the attached script mentioned as "QLearning.cs," and let us have a brief walk-through of the important functions. Since most of the state initialization, tag allocation, and variable initialization are similar to previous projects, we will be skipping that in this section. The most important function in this context is the "train" function, which contains the core functionality of the Q-learning algorithm and also the updation of the Q-table by selecting the highest valued state (plane) in each timestamp.

```
for (int k = 0; k < max_epoch; k++)
    {
        int current_state = rnd.Next(0, reward.Length);
        while (true)
        {
            Debug.Log("training started");

            int next_state = GetProbNextState(current_state,
                                    transition_mat);
            List<int> possiblenextsteps = GetPossibleStates(next_state,
                                    transition_mat);
            Debug.Log("Current" + current_state);
            Debug.Log("Next" + next_state);
            //choose among the best probable
            state which gives the max reward

            float maxq = float.MinValue;
```

Inside the loop, we randomly select an initial state from the given states and query the Q-table for the next state given by the "GetProbNextState" method. This function actually returns the maximum valued state in that particular epoch or episode from the state list.

For the next steps, we use this information and also update the Q-table by using the Q-learning equation as shown here:

```
for (int j = 0; j < possiblenextsteps.Count; j++)
            {
                Debug.Log(possiblenextsteps[j]);

                int n_s = possiblenextsteps[j];
                float qs = quality_mat[next_state][n_s];
```

```
//update q value matrix
based on maximum value
if (qs > maxq)
{
    maxq = qs;
}
}
// update q matrix with
//Q-learning algorithmic formula
quality_mat[current_state][next_state] =
((1 - learning_rate) *   quality_mat[current_state]
[next_state])
+ ((learning_rate) * (reward[current_state][next_state] +
gamma * maxq));

current_state = next_state;
if (current_state == goal)
{
    //Agent.transform.position
    //= green_33.transform.position;
    //StartCoroutine(move_33());
    Debug.Log("Reached");

    break;
}
```

Note   The code and scene have been built using Unity version 2018.3 but are compatible with all versions of Unity, including the 2020 beta version.

After abstracting the states based on Q-policy, the code selects the location or transform of the plane that is being triggered. The agent is automatically shifted to that transform position. The rest of the code segment is a boiler plate code for the environment and the Coroutine "train" method that controls the entire workflow logic. Once we are satisfied with the understanding of the code base, we can run the scene and simulate it. The main idea of this simulation is to understand the importance of Q–learning in a discrete environment of rewards, states, and actions.

Summary

We are at the end of the first chapter, and here is the summary of what we have learned so far:

- We have tried to understand the basics of reinforcement learning (RL) and inclusion of states, actions, and rewards. RL is a different paradigm that involves interaction of an agent with an environment to maximize its goals.

- In order to understand the concept of states, rewards, and actions, we installed a Gym environment. Gym is an RL environment developed by OpenAI for research in deep RL as well as in robotics.

- We learned how to set up Anaconda and Jupyter Notebooks and how to initialize a Python kernel in Colab and Jupyter for RL.

- We tried to understand the logical problem of CartPole and tried to model it as an RL environment in Python. We saw the Observation and the Action space of the environment and also gained insight into Tensorflow, Tensorboard, and other deep learning libraries and frameworks.

- We learned of the Markov Process, Finite Decision Theory, Hidden Markov Models (HMMs) and how probabilistic distribution of states help in learning.

- We learned how to install Unity Engine from the Unity Hub.

- We developed a simulation using Puppo (Unity Berlin) based on Markov Models using transition matrix probabilities and another simulation using a cube agent for HMMs.

- We learned how to create Unity C# scripts and learned about Coroutinesand internal methods in Unity such as Start and Update.

- We extended our knowledge of Markov Models into reward-based learning by introducing the Bellman equation. We developed a Kart Racing simulation where a Kart Agent had to determine which Track section to choose based on the rewards and value maximization. We learned about value and policy iteration algorithms.

- We designed and learned about the multi-armed bandit problem and how different strategies like Epsilon-Greedy, upper confidence-bound, and gradient bandits affected the bandit's decision. We learned that bandit problems are the simplest form of RL algorithms without the concept of state and created a Bandit simulation in Unity.

- The last section relied on intensive discussion on value and policy iterative algorithms and how to maximize a particular value function based on a certain policy. We learned about temporal differencing and Q-learning, the most famous baseline learning algorithm for classic RL. We created a Gym Taxi environment to understand the Q-learning algorithm in Python and then created a simulation of a pathfinding agent based on reward maximization using Q-learning policy.

- In all these sections, we have tried to develop algorithms in parallel using Python as well as C# so as to get a better understanding at a core level regarding how these are represented.

- We have used Tensorflow libraries and also created bandit problems in Jupyter Notebooks or Colab for better understandability of the concepts.

This concludes the first chapter of the book. This chapter forms the base of RL concepts, and we have tried to gain insight into how development of RLc took place, from initial Markov Models to Bellman equations and then to value and policy iterations to maximize rewards.

All of these concepts fall under discrete classical RL and will be required extensively when we try to explore deep RL with the Unity ML Agents Toolkit, which converts the discrete action space to multi-discrete or continuous space for deep learning algorithms. In the next chapter we will be looking into Navigation Meshes, Pathfinding AI, and many more algorithms in automatic and heuristic pathfinding in Unity.

CHAPTER 2

Pathfinding and Navigation

Pathfinding is the algorithmic interpretation and implementation of attaining the shortest route(s) from a given source(s) to destination(s). While the paradigm falls under generic graph theory, there has been much research about different heuristic algorithms. The fundamental aspects of choosing the best-fit (least cost) route implies certain heuristics to be followed. In this section we will try to understand the different concepts of heuristic search algorithms, starting from basic Dijkstra Algorithm to variants of A* (A star). The need for different search algorithms is extremely essential since generic exhaustive algorithms such as breadth-first search (BFS) and depth first search (DFS) are not feasible for games, simulations, and robotics. As we proceed into the depths of each heuristic algorithm, we will encounter different trade-off metrics being employed, from time complexity to space complexity. We will also explore the fundamental aspects of navigation meshes and how to create an intelligent pathfinding agent that gets rewards when it reaches and finds the target object.

If we recollect from the previous chapter, we talked about how a reinforcement learning (RL) environment comprises states, actions, and rewards. We will continue on similar lines with the change in the concept of states and actions in generic pathfinding. The concept of states in pathfinding arises from the different planar coordinates where an agent places itself while it searches for a proper trajectory. If we consider the case of a GridWorld environment, where the agent can be placed anywhere in the grid, the position of the agent in a particular grid is a state. We have seen in the Bellman equation and in the Q-learning section in the last chapter, where the agent decides to go to a particular state (grid or "track section") for reward maximization. The similar concept is applied here as well. The action space includes the different directions the agent can move to check for alternative shorter paths to the destination. In the 2D GridWorld

A. Majumder, *Deep Reinforcement Learning in Unity*, https://doi.org/10.1007/978-1-4842-6503-1_2

environment, the agent may have the action space, which includes the eight directions comprising upper, lower, left, right, upper left, upper right, lower left, and lower right or may include a subset of them.

This concept of states and actions is very crucial for heuristic pathfinding algorithms. Since most of the pathfinding algorithms rely on centralized distance minimization techniques, there are certain modifications added to each of the algorithms in terms of dynamic weighting, edge selection, bidirectional minimization, and many more. A preview of how agents use pathfinding to reach their destination is shown in Figure 2-1.

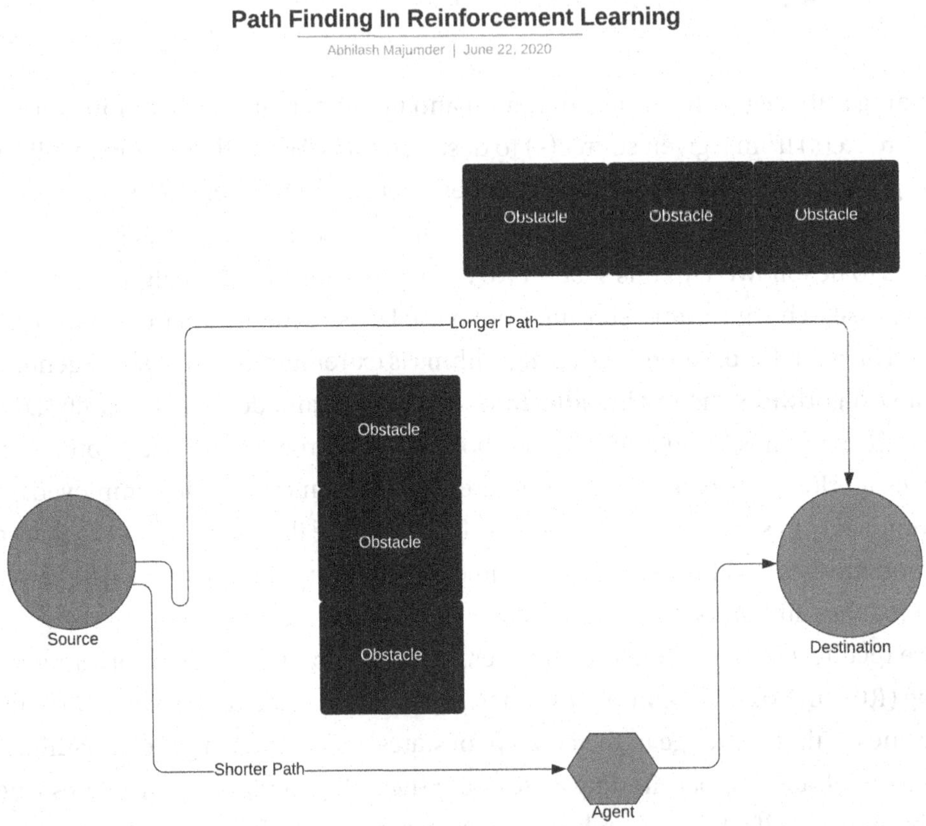

Path Finding In Reinforcement Learning

Abhilash Majumder | June 22, 2020

Figure 2-1. Path finding in RL environment

Generic pathfinding based on optimality is quite time-consuming when we use exhaustive search algorithms like Bellman Ford, which determines optimal trajectory from any source(s) to any destination(s) and takes into consideration negative weight edges. This is where Dijkstra, A*, B*, and many other algorithms come into the picture to strategically remove certain states in the trajectory of the agent that would lead to a suboptimal path. The metrics of optimization can include weight minimization, time minimization, reward maximization, and other strategies, and based on these constraints, different algorithms employ either dynamic programming or heuristic search to model the pathfinding problem. In the context of algorithmic complexity determination, we use the O() (big-oh) as the upper bound metric in complexity analysis. If we consider the grid environment to be a graph data structure where the nodes represent the states and source/destination nodes provided, we can emphasize the notation of V for the number of vertices and E as the number of edges in the graph. In general BFS and DFS techniques (basic search), the time complexity can be viewed as O($|V| + |E|$), which is of linear time complexity. This is due to the fact that Greedy exhaustive BFS algorithms rely on choosing all the vertices V and edges E during computation. For optimality, the different algorithms will have different big-O() values in terms of the runtime complexity, which we will see in the next section. This will be in accordance with the runtime of the algorithms implemented in Python. In general RL, these algorithms are used in robotics, autonomous vehicles, and self-searching agents as well as in different simulations based on nonplayer character (NPC) navigation. The RL environment in these cases may also involve certain obstacles or challenges that the agent has to avoid to reach the goal. This may include physical obstacles in the shortest path trajectory in a grid or virtual negative rewards-based obstacles (different coordinates in n-dimension planes where rewards are negative), which may prevent an agent from going to a particular state. The second example may be a scenario in robotics where a robotic agent is credited with negative reward when it tries to move away from the target.

Pathfinding Algorithms

Let us try to understand different algorithms involved in pathfinding. We will start to emphasize the algorithmic implementations and also view the contrast in time complexity of these algorithms. Initially we will start with generic exhaustive Greedy Search algorithm and then gradually we will venture into the depths of optimized heuristic family of A* algorithms.

- **Greedy algorithm:** This is an exhaustive search technique where an agent tries to venture all possible paths and states to choose an optimal trajectory to reach the destination, We consider a simplified GridWorld environment, where the agent starts from a particular

grid and has to reach another grid in an optimal path; this provides
a possible set of movable states for the agent in eight directions,
as mentioned in the previous section. Since it is an exhaustive
enumeration technique, all the possible states are explored, which
is pretty much similar to the BFS or DFS algorithm. If we are using
BFS, this can be visualized as an agent choosing all the possible states
from a particular state $S_{i,j}$ to $S_{i,j+1}$, $S_{i,j-1}$, $S_{i+1,j}$, $S_{i-1,j}$, $S_{i+1,j+1}$, $S_{i-1,j+1}$, $S_{i+1,j-1}$,
$S_{i-1,j+1}$. This can be visualized in Figure 2-2.

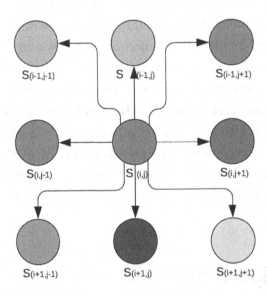

Figure 2-2. *Greedy search state space in grid*

Now, let us try to understand how the Greedy algorithm works
with the help of a sample gridWorld simulation in Python. We
create a simplified Gridworld mainly of 0 s and 1 s, where 0 s are
"walkable" grids and 1 s involve grids with obstacles. The agent
is provided a source grid and destination grid and has to greedily
search for the destination by exhaustively searching through
"walkable" grids.

Open the "Greedy.ipynb" Notebook in Jupyter or Colab and let us view the imports required for this program.

```
import numpy as np
import networkx as nx
import heapq
import sys
import time
```

We require the heapq library, which implements a priority queue (max heap data structure) for automatic sorting of a container (array, lists, tuples) that is helpful when updating the minimum distance from a particular state or grid. We then enter the Greedy function, which is the main part of the search algorithm.

```
def Greedy(maze,src,dest):
    pq=[(0,src)]
    while (len(pq)>0):
        dist_measure,node= heapq.heappop(pq)

    #If destination is reached
        if node==dest:

            print("Reached")
            break
```

The source state or grid ("src ") is inserted inside the priority queue, and the grid data structure (tuple) contains the position as one of the attributes in terms of x and y location of a particular grid in 2D plane. The search continues as long as the priority queue is not empty (a classic example of how BFS works).

Initially we check whether the currently extracted grid state from the priority queue is the destination grid state ("dest"). If the destination is reached, we break the loop.

```
#Look for child nodes (L,R,U,D,UL,UR,DL,DR)
for new_position in [(0, -1), (0, 1), (-1, 0), (1, 0), (-1, -1),
(-1, 1), (1, -1), (1, 1)]:
    new_node=(node[0] + new_position[0], node[1] + new_position[1])
```

```
#Check if new point is inside the maze
if new_node[0] > (len(maze) - 1) or new_node[0] < 0 or new_
node[1] > (len(maze[len(maze)-1]) -1) or new_node[1] < 0:

continue

#If not obstacle (maze index value==1)
  if maze[new_node[0]][new_node[1]] != 0:
    continue
#Update Distance
dist_temp=dist_measure+1
heapq.heappush(pq,(dist_temp,new_node))
path.append(new_node)

return path
```

In this part of the code segment, we iterate through the eight possible venturable grid states (upper, lower, left, right, upper left, upper right, lower left, and lower right) and add the grid positions to get the position of the new grid state.

Since Greedy is an exhaustive search, it places all the different grid positions again several times to get to the final destination. We then apply conditional logic to check if the maze or GridWorld is walkable by preventing the agent from going to grid states with a value of "1." We also check to see if the agent is inside the maze or grid environment and has not left the boundaries. Then we add the new distance as a unit value and add the new grid state to the priority queue to sort it again based on positional distance.

The Gridworld or maze is implemented as follows:

```
maze=[[0, 0, 0, 0, 1, 0, 0, 0, 0, 0],
      [0, 0, 0, 0, 1, 0, 0, 0, 0, 0],
      [0, 0, 0, 0, 1, 0, 0, 0, 0, 0],
      [0, 0, 0, 0, 1, 0, 0, 0, 0, 0],
      [0, 0, 0, 0, 1, 0, 0, 0, 0, 0],
      [0, 0, 0, 0, 0, 0, 0, 0, 0, 0],
      [0, 0, 0, 0, 1, 0, 0, 0, 0, 0],
```

```
         [0, 0, 0, 0, 1, 0, 0, 0, 0, 0],
         [0, 0, 0, 0, 1, 0, 0, 0, 0, 0],
         [0, 0, 0, 0, 0, 0, 0, 0, 0, 0]]
```

The main function calls the Greedy Search on this particular maze or GridWorld as follows:

```
src=(0,0)
    dest=(7,6)
    st=time.time()
    path=Greedy(maze,src,dest)
    print_path(path,dest)
    et=time.time()
    print("Time Taken for Computation of Greedy Path")
    print(et-st)
```

Here the source grid is chosen as (0, 0) and the destination grid is chosen as (7, 6); however, these can be changed according to our requirements. Then the Greedy function is called, and the time for computation of the path is calculated using the "time" library of Python. After running the code in the Notebook, we see a list of different grids, where the agent travels to reach (7, 6). Since Greedy is exhaustive, the number of searches may get repeated and the path can be really long. This can be correlated to the enormous runtime of the algorithm, as shown in Figure 2-3.

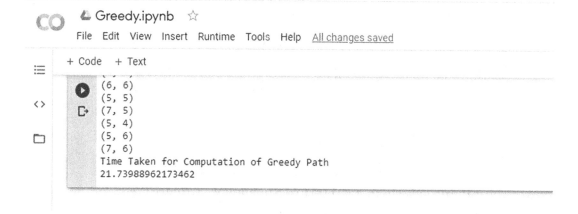

Figure 2-3. *Runtime of the Greedy Search algorithm*

Since the time complexity is quite large, we try to explore an optimized, single-source, shortest path algorithm called Dijkstra.

- **Dijkstra algorithm:** Dijkstra is a graph-based algorithm that provides the optimal, or the shortest, route from a source to a destination. The algorithm finds the optimal path by total reordering of the distance measures, and the generic ordering of the path lengths can be considered as monotonically increasing. The algorithm maintains two separate lists commonly referred to as open list and closed list. The open list contains the grid states or nodes that are currently being analyzed with the help of neighboring grids. The closed list contains the grid states that have been computed. The open list is implemented by using a priority queue, which stores the grid states based on the sorted nondecreasing order of their distance magnitudes from the source. Particularly since the Dijkstra algorithm always finds the shortest route between any grid state from the source, the algorithm stops when the grid state is the destination. This particular path is optimal, because had there been any other "optimal" path, the Dijkstra algorithm would have chosen that. This follows a general lemma in Graph Theory, where if an optimal path exists between a start and destination node, all the nodes along that particular path will have optimal distance from the start node or source. Mathematically, if $U(s)$ is the source node and $V(s)$ is the destination node, and if the path between them is optimal, then any node $U_1(s)$ on that path will also have an optimal distance from the source. This can be derived as follows:

$$V(s) = U(s) + d(u, v),$$

where $V(s)$ is the destination node, $U(s)$ is the source vode, and $d(u, v)$ is the optimal distance between the nodes. Then for any point $U_1(s)$ on that path:

$$V(s) = U(s) + d(u, u_1) + U_1(s) + d(u_1, v),$$

where $d(u, u_1)$ is the distance from source $U(s)$ to $U_1(s)$ and $d(u_1, v)$ is the distance from the $U_1(s)$ to destination $V(s)$. Hence the path $d(u, u_1)$ is the optimal path between source and the node $U_1(s)$. This completes the proof.

The Dijkstra algorithm uses this principle to find the optimal shortest path and keeps a history of the visited nodes or grid states so as to not backtrack. The algorithm, however, is suited for positive weight graphs and grids and does not provide an optimal solution for negative weight edges or grid paths (solved by Bellman Ford). The algorithm stores the distance of each grid state or node from the source or start node, and that is generally in nondecreasing order. This is shown in Figure 2-4.

Dijkstra SPF Algorithm

Abhilash Majumder | June 22, 2020

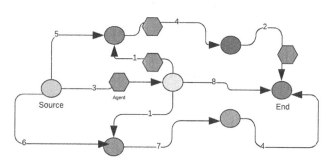

Figure 2-4. *Dijkstra Shortest Path First Algorithm*

In Figure 2-4, the agent (with the orange hexagon shape) finds the shortest route between the source(yellow circular shape) and destination(grey circular shape) in a graph.

Note   Dijkstra algorithm was designed by computer scientist Edsger W.Dijkstra in 1965.

The numbers on the "arrows" represent the edge weight or cost for traversing that edge (this can be compared to time taken to cover that edge). This unidirectional graph has a unique shortest path that involves a total cost of 10 units along the path, shown by the agent. This path also has the shortest distance from the source to any node on this path. We can try to create different graphs and then apply the Dijkstra algorithm and always check the validity of the proof.

Now that we have covered the important aspects of Dijkstra, let us try to implement this in Python so that we can visualize how the algorithm works. We will extensively create Unity Projects based on this algorithm in the next section and create an AI agent that uses this algorithm to reach a particular destination. Open the "Dijkstra.ipynb" Notebook in Jupyter or Colab. The code base has a common template using the same GridWorld environment (maze) like before, and we will concentrate ourselves with the actual "dijkstra" function that implements the logic.

We initialize the distance dictionary (containing two entities grid-Position.x and grid-Position.y) with the maximum value and use the function to minimize this dictionary to get minimum distance.

```
distance=dict()
#Initialization of Dictionary
# [(position.x,position.y),distance]

for i in range(0,9):
        for j in range(0,9):
                distance[(i,j)]=sys.maxsize
```

The next step involves including the start grid or source in the priority queue, which is our open list. This loop will continue as long as the priority queue has some elements (grids). Each grid is extracted from the priority queue or open list, and its distance is measured with the previously allocated distance. For the first iteration, since we included the distance with maximum value, the new value (1 unit) is smaller than the distance replaces it. For next steps, based on the different distance computations of neighboring nodes, this distance value for a particular grid will get changed. If the distance is more than the previously observed value, then it will not be taken into consideration. If the current grid is the destination, then the loop breaks and we have reached the target grid with a minimum cost path.

This is implemented by the following lines:

```
def dijkstra(maze,src,dest):
    pq=[(0,src)]
    while(len(pq)>0):
            dist_measure,node= heapq.heappop(pq)

            #If distance of the node is greater
            if(dist_measure>distance[(node[0],node[1])]):

                continue
            #If destination is reached
            if node==dest:

            print("Reached")
            break
```

The next segment deals with the surrounding states or grids along the eight directions for possible next grid positions. We have considered the distance between each grid as 1 unit in all the directions. We check for each of the eight possible grids and update the position of the new grid accordingly; also if the path contains obstacles (marked as "1") similar to the previous case, we will avoid those grids. We then add a cost value of 1 unit to the distance from the old grid to the new grid and check if the distance is less than the current distance of the new grid. If the condition of minimality is satisfied, we update the distance to the new grid with the additional value and add the new grid to the priority queue or open list for the next neighbor of grids. This process continues until the destination is reached. Once the destination is reached, all the grids along the path will have a minimum cost from the start grid or source.

```
#Look for child nodes (L,R,U,D,UL,UR,DL,DR)
for new_position in [(0, -1), (0, 1), (-1, 0), (1, 0),
(-1, -1), (-1, 1), (1, -1), (1, 1)]:
    new_node=(node[0] + new_position[0], node[1] +
    new_position[1])
```

```
#Check if new point is inside the maze
if new_node[0] > (len(maze) - 1) or new_node[0] < 0 or
new_node[1] > (len(maze[len(maze)-1]) -1) or new_node[1] < 0:
    continue

#If not obstacle (maze index value==1)
if maze[new_node[0]][new_node[1]] != 0:
    continue
#Update Distance
dist_temp=dist_measure+1
if(dist_temp<distance[(new_node[0],new_node[1])]):

    distance[(new_node[0],new_node[1])]=dist_temp
    heapq.heappush(pq,(dist_temp,new_node))
    path.append(new_node)

return path,distance
```

This is the entire control logic of the Dijkstra algorithm, and we will compare the runtime complexity of this with the previously created Greedy Search algorithm. On running this, we will get to see the runtime similar to the one shown in Figure 2-5.

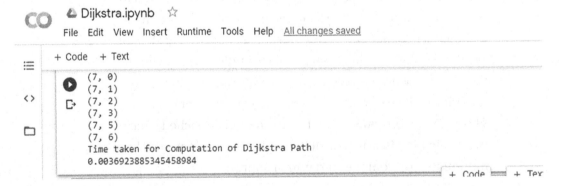

Figure 2-5. *Runtime of the Dijkstra algorithm*

In the next section of the notebook, we will observe creation of graphs and use Networkx library to create a Dijkstra path in a uniformly weighted graph with Euclidean distance as the metric of cost. Networkx is a Python library that contains several algorithms related to graph traversals and shortest pathfinding (SPF) algorithms and the one provided here is just an example of simulating Dijkstra algorithm with its help.

```
G=nx.grid_graph(dim=[4,5])
def eucli(a,b):
  (x1,y1)=a
  (x2,y2)=b
  return ((x1-x2)**2 + (y1-y2)**2)**0.5

paths=nx.dijkstra_path(G,(1,2),(4,3))
print(paths)
path_length= nx.dijkstra_path_length(G,(1,2),(4,3))
print(path_length)
nx.draw_networkx(G)
```

The simulated graph for this implementation looks like that shown in Figure 2-6.

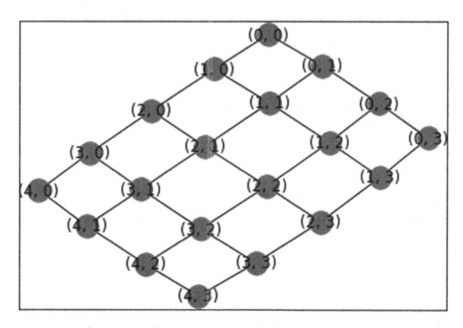

Figure 2-6. *Visualizing graph using Networkx library*

Now that we understand the Dijkstra algorithm, we will be creating a simulation of the same in Unity with an AI agent trying out the algorithm to reach the target in the next section. For the time being, we will concentrate on the fundamental aspects of a different class of pathfinding algorithms popularly called as A*. This is the most important class of algorithms when it comes to games, RL, and robotics, and since it is very closely related to the Dijkstra algorithm, we will understand the difference and also the variants of the algorithm.

- **A* algorithm:** A* is a path searching algorithm that is most extensively used in games and simulations owing to computational flexibility, robustness, and optimality. However, there is an expensive space complexity associated with a classic A* algorithm, mainly due to its nature to store previous grids or states (nodes in a graph). The fundamental aspect of A* is its heuristic nature. It combines information that the Dijkstra algorithm uses, which involves favoring grids or states closer to the destination along the optimal path. The algorithm uses the heuristic to rule out certain grids or states, which may increase the optimal trajectory of the path and only focuses on those states that provide the minimum cost. This requires processing and storing of a grid's information in terms of its neighbors' distances. There are certain important heuristics that are followed in A*, which relies on the weights associated with each grid or state (node). This may include Euclidean or Hamiltonian distance measures from that particular grid to the destination. The A* uses an optimization strategy based on the grid attributes. In addition to the grid position, each grid has three important attributes:

  - **g-Value:** This is the cost of the path from the start grid or source to that particular grid (node).

  - **h-Value:** This is the heuristic estimated cost from the current grid to the destination grid.

  - **f-Value:** This is the addition of the G- and H-values for a particular grid (state or node).

This can be mathematically simplified as :

$$F(n) = G(n) + H(n)$$

Now let us try to understand why the heuristic term plays a significant role in the A* algorithm.

- At one extreme, if the value of H(n) is 0, then F(n) = G(n). This implies that if no heuristic factor is considered, A* reduces to simplified the Dijkstra algorithm.

- If the H(n) value is always less than the cost of moving from grid 'n' to the destination, then A* is bound to find the shortest path. The less the value of H(n), the less the heuristic, which implies more exploration of different grids, which may cause greater time complexity.

- If the H(n) value is equal to the cost of moving from grid 'n' to the destination, then this is always the best or optimal path that A* chooses. However, this can be defined as a special case where the A* algorithm heuristic provides the exact value as that of the optimized path from grid to estination.

- If the H(n) value is greater than the cost of moving from grid 'n' to the destination, then exploitation along a certain path direction takes place. This would involve the A* algorithm to run significantly faster but produce suboptimal trajectories.

- At the other extreme, if the H(n) value is more than G(n), then only heuristics are involved in A* algorithm, which makes it similar to the Greedy algorithm.

- Generally H(n) is chosen as an admissible heuristic function, which never overestimates the actual cost. This makes the heuristic problem specific.

- H(n) can include distance metrics such as Euclidean, distance, Manhattan distance, or Squared Euclidean distance as the heuristic measure.

- A consistent or monotone heuristic is a heuristic where a particular grid 'n' has a value less than or equal to the distance between the grid to the next grid and the heuristic value of the next grid, which is shown as:

$$H(n) \leq d(n,n+1) + H(n+1)$$

Now that we understand the importance of heuristics in the A* algorithm, we can visualize the general propagation of an agent using A* in the form of a tree, as shown in Figure 2-7, where red nodes represent the closed list of grids and green nodes are in the open list.

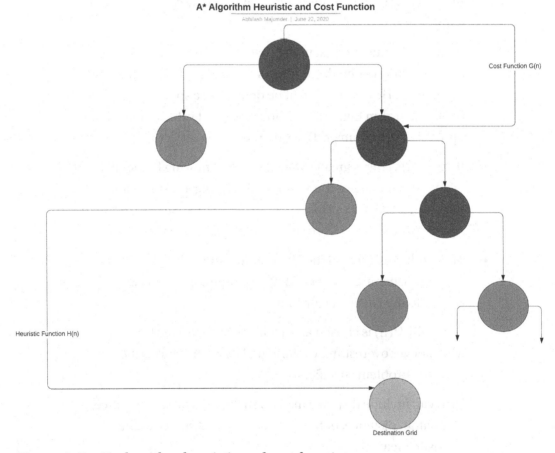

Figure 2-7. *A* algorithm heuristic and cost function*

Let us understand the implementation details in Python, and then we will be simulating the A* algorithm in Unity. Open the "A-star. ipynb" Notebook in Jupyter or Colab. We will be using the same template of GridWorld, as in all our previous Python simulations of search algorithms, such as the maze or GridWorld environment. At the start of the Notebook we initialize a node class that contains the distance, position in terms of x, y (in 2D grid environment), and f-, g- and h-values that will be used in the A* algorithm.

```python
class Node():
    """A node class for A* Pathfinding"""

    def __init__(self, parent=None, position=None):
        self.parent = parent
        self.position = position

        self.g = 0
        self.h = 0
        self.f = 0

    def __eq__(self, other):
        return self.position == other.position
```

The next segment involves the actual A* algorithm. We initiate two lists, as mentioned before: open and closed list. The open list will contain all the grids (nodes) that are currently being analyzed with the cost and the heuristic function, and the closed list consists of grids (nodes) that have already been analyzed.

```python
def astar(maze, start, end):

    """Returns a list of tuples as a path from the given start to
    the given end in the given maze"""

    # Create start and end node
    start_node = Node(None, start)
    start_node.g = start_node.h = start_node.f = 0
    end_node = Node(None, end)
    end_node.g = end_node.h = end_node.f = 0
```

```
# Initialize both open and closed list
open_list = []
closed_list = []

# Add the start node
open_list.append(start_node)
```

We include the source grid inside the priority queue or the open list. Both the source and the destination grids have f-, g-and h-values initialized to 0. Inside the loop, we will extract each grid. Then we will check the f-value of the extracted grid (node) with the f-values of the grids in the open list. If the value of the extracted grid is greater, then we assign it with the grid selected from the open list whose f-value is smaller than the extracted grid. We pop the extracted grid from the open list and add it to the closed list. If the extracted current grid is the destination grid, the search terminates and the variable "path" contains the optimal route from source to destination.

```
while len(open_list) > 0:

        # Get the current node
        current_node = open_list[0]
        current_index = 0
        for index, item in enumerate(open_list):
            if item.f < current_node.f:
                current_node = item
                current_index = index

        # Pop current off open list, add to closed list
        open_list.pop(current_index)
        closed_list.append(current_node)

        # Found the goal
        if current_node == end_node:
            path = []
            current = current_node
```

```
    while current is not None:
        path.append(current.position)
        current = current.parent
    return path[::-1] # Return reversed path
```

We then create a list of children grids or neighbors where the
heuristic will compute the Euclidean distance from the grid to the
destination. Like before, we analyze the state space in the eight
directions of a particular grid and make sure that it is "walkable"
(grid value is not 1) and it is inside the maze or the GridWorld
environment. We then add the new grid to the children list.

```
# Generate children
    children = []
    for new_position in [(0, -1), (0, 1), (-1, 0), (1, 0),
    (-1, -1), (-1, 1), (1, -1), (1, 1)]: # Adjacent squares

            # Get node position
    node_position = (current_node.position[0]
    +new_position[0], current_node.position[1]
    +new_position[1])

            # Make sure within range
if node_position[0] > (len(maze) - 1) or
    node_position[0] < 0 or node_position[1]
        > (len(maze[len(maze)-1]) -1) or
        node_position[1] < 0:
                continue

            # Make sure walkable terrain
        if maze[node_position[0]][node_position[1]] != 0:
            continue

        # Create new node
        new_node = Node(current_node, node_position)

        # Append
        children.append(new_node)
```

The next step is the computation of the f-, g-, and h-values. An initial check is made if the child grid in the children list is already on the closed list, which is then ignored. We add 1 unit as distance cost G (child; just like in Dijkstra), as we considered the distance between each grid to be 1 unit. We then compute the H (child) value based on the Euclidean square distance between the x and y coordinates of the current child grid and the destination grid to get the heuristic value. Finally we add the two values to get the F (child) value. If the current grid is on the open list, we check if the G (child) value is less than the g-values of the grids on the open list. If the g-value of the current child is greater, then we do not consider it, since we require the minimum cost value or optimized cost value. Finally we add the child grid to the priority queue or open list for the next iteration. This entire workflow is addressed in the following lines of code:

```
# Loop through children
    for child in children:

        # Child is on the closed list
        for closed_child in closed_list:
            if child == closed_child:
                continue

        # Create the f, g, and h values
        child.g = current_node.g + 1
        child.h = ((child.position[0]
        - end_node.position[0]) ** 2)
        + ((child.position[1] -
        end_node.position[1]) ** 2)

        child.f = child.g + child.h

        # Child is already in the open list
        for open_node in open_list:
            if child == open_node
            and child.g > open_node.g:
                continue
```

```
# Add the child to the open list
open_list.append(child)
```

This is the implementation of the A* algorithm, and if we run this simulation we will get to view the path followed as well as the runtime of the algorithm, similarly to the one shown in Figure 2-8.

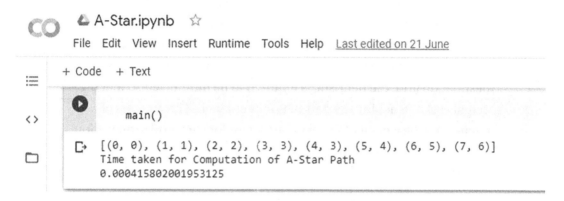

Figure 2-8. *Runtime of the A* algorithm*

Once we are comfortable with the implementation and the workflow of the algorithm, we can try out the A* implementation of the Networkx library, which has also been included in the same Notebook for interested readers.

We will utilize this algorithm when we are creating our simulations with Unity, and then we will see how the A* algorithm tries to find an optimal path using this algorithm. We discussed the classic A* algorithm in detail, and there are many variants of the A* algorithm that we will take a look at. These variations are based on different heuristic and algorithmic modifications, trading off memory for time optimization and vice versa. We will be working with the same maze template in our future class of A* algorithms.

Note   The A* algorithm was devised by N.J Nilsson, P.E Hart, and B Raphael.

Variants of the A* Algorithm

We discussed the details of the A* algorithm, but there are many modifications to increase memory optimization or reduce time complexity by following different methods. Some of the most popular algorithmic implementations are:

- **Dynamic weighted A* algorithm:** This is a weighted version of the classic A* algorithm. The weight-age is given to the heuristic part of the A* optimization function. This is done because at the start of the exploration, we generally require a stronger heuristic for more grid (node) exploration for an optimal path. As the agent approaches the destination grid, the heuristic is required to be minimized so that the actual cost of reaching the destination is attained. This process of decreasing the weight of the heuristic factor for each grid propagation toward the destination is known as dynamic weighted A*. The generic formulation follows as shown here:

$$F(n) = G(n) + w(n) * H(n),$$

where F(n), G(n), H(n) have their usual meaning, and w(n) is the dynamic weight part. Let us try to visualize its implementation in the maze environment in our Python Notebook. Open the "DynamicA-star.ipynb" Notebook, and we can observe that there is a weight attribute in the node class.

```
#Dynamic-A-Star Algorithm for Pathfinding
import time
class Node():

    def __init__(self, parent=None, position=None):
        self.parent = parent
        self.position = position

        self.g = 0
        self.h = 0
        self.f = 0

        self.w=1

    def __eq__(self, other):
        return self.position == other.position
```

Since we are using the same source template as the A* algorithm, there are only slight changes in the "dynamicastar" function. We initialize the weight decay, which is the decay factor, as the search continues toward the destination. This decay is essential to reduce the heuristic estimate.

```
def dynamicastar(maze, start, end):
    weight_decay=0.99
```

Most of the segment in the next section is similar to the A* algorithm involving putting the start grid in the open list and then iterating till the open list is not empty. Then we abstract the children grids in the eight directions and check for its distance, whether it is "walkable" and whether it is inside the maze. The only difference is in the cost function, which is as follows:

```
# Create the f, g, and h values
child.g = current_node.g + 1
```

```
#Compute distance towards end for dynamic weightmapping
child.h = ((child.position[0] - end_node.position[0]) **   2) +
((child.position[1] - end_node.position[1]) ** 2)
```

```
src_dest=((start_node.position[0]-end_node.position[0])**2) +
((start_node.position[1]-end_node.position[1])**2)
```

```
child.w= child.w*weight_decay*(child.h/src_dest)
```

```
 child.f = child.g + child.w*child.h
```

We first record the value of actual cost G (child) and heuristic estimate H (child), and then we update the W (child) factor by multiplying the depth of search with the decay factor. The depth of search indicates how far along the search trajectory the agent has visited the grids. Finally we update the F (child) value using the equation for dynamic weighted A*. The rest of the code segment is same as A*, which includes updating the closed list and adding child grid to the open list for the next iteration. Upon running the code, we can get an estimate of the time required for the algorithm, as in Figure 2-9.

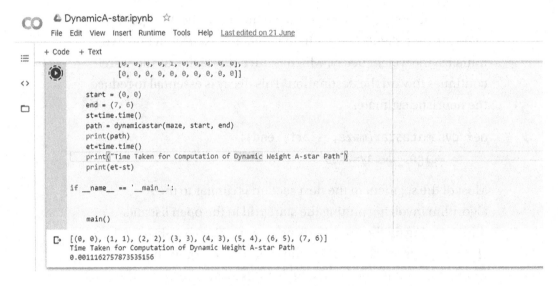

```
                        [0, 0, 0, 0, 1, 0, 0, 0, 0, 0],
                        [0, 0, 0, 0, 0, 0, 0, 0, 0, 0]]

        start = (0, 0)
        end = (7, 6)
        st=time.time()
        path = dynamicastar(maze, start, end)
        print(path)
        et=time.time()
        print("Time Taken for Computation of Dynamic Weight A-star Path")
        print(et-st)

    if __name__ == '__main__':


        main()
```

```
[(0, 0), (1, 1), (2, 2), (3, 3), (4, 3), (5, 4), (6, 5), (7, 6)]
Time Taken for Computation of Dynamic Weight A-star Path
0.0011162757873535156
```

Figure 2-9. *Runtime of dynamic weighted A* algorithm*

- **Iterative deepening A* (IDA*) algorithm:** This is another variation
  of the A* algorithm, which emphasizes memory optimization and
  performs recursion. The key feature of the IDA* algorithm is that it
  does not keep a record of the visited nodes as in the A* algorithm
  (open list). Instead it reiterates on the grid nodes from the start
  when a new grid node with greater f-score is reached. This algorithm
  uses a threshold value, and if a particular grid has an f-score greater
  than the threshold, the algorithm starts all over again from the start
  grid to the new grid (new depth). The implementation requires an
  infinite loop since we recursively track the grid nodes from the start
  whenever a higher F (grid) value is reached. During the recursion
  phase, whenever a higher F (grid) value is attained, the heuristic
  estimate does not explore along that grid node (as it is not likely on
  the optimal trajectory) but stores the F (grid) value. The recursion
  returns the minimum F (grid) value score, which is set as the new
  threshold since the reduction of f value would imply an optimal
  trajectory toward the destination. Let us explore a variation of this
  algorithm in the Notebook. Open the "IDA-star.ipynb" Notebook, and
  we will only look at the code changes, since the same maze template
  is being used. The node class is the same as A* node class with F(n),
  G(n), H(n), position, and distance attributes. The only difference is in

the "idastar" function, where there is an infinite loop. We initially set the threshold value as the maximum squared Euclidean distance or depth from the start grid to the destination grid given by:

```
threshold=((start_node.position[0]-
end_node.position[0])**2) + ((start_node.position[1]-
end_node.position[1])**2)
```

Inside the infinite loop, we observe most of the operations are the same, as a new children grid list is created, and for each new child grid, all possible eight directions are explored. The difference lies in the cost estimate update rule for each child grid.

```
child.g = current_node.g + 1
child.h = ((child.position[0] - end_node.position[0]) ** 2) +
((child.position[1] - end_node.position[1]) ** 2)
child.f = child.g + child.h
```

```
if(child.f<threshold):
#Restart again from the start to the path of the child node
  current_node=child
```

```
#check if child node is end node
if(child==end_node):
  break
```

The if condition verifies if the current child grid F (child) value is less than threshold, and if it is then the child grid becomes the next grid to be analyzed. This is a minimization technique that emphasizes selecting the lowest possible F (child) value among all the child grids as the new threshold. Similarly we break once the child grid is the same as the destination grid. We can run this program to generate the runtime efficiency of the algorithm. Since there is no memory in this algorithm, the path may contain multiple repeated grid nodes and is essentially useful in games and simulations where it is expensive to allocate memory for every NPC. In case of a single NPC or robotics, this algorithm may not provide a proper solution because reiteration provides time overhead. The complexity of IDA* relies mainly on the depth of the path, and it returns the optimal path like A*, provided the heuristic function is admissible (i.e., the h-value does not overestimate the true cost). Figure 2-10 shows the runtime of the algorithm.

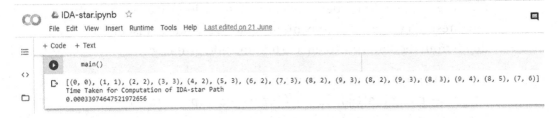

Figure 2-10. *Runtime of IDA* algorithm*

- **Lifelong planning A* (LPA*) algorithm:** This algorithm is an incremental A* algorithm, which is best suited for dynamic graphs or dynamic RL environments. This is most popularly used in games and simulations where no recalculation of the entire grid or graph nodes take place. There are certain additional components required to update the optimal trajectory in a dynamic environment. The LPA* algorithm maintains a list of predecessor and successor grid nodes. This helps in updating the neighbors of a particular grid node when its surrounding grids that lie on the optimal path are changed dynamically. The predecessor of a grid node n is any grid node that has an edge from it to n. The successor of a grid node n is the node to which an edge leads from n. The grid node has another attribute referred to as Rhs (node). This value is a lookahead based on the minimization of the G (node) value and can be written as:

$$Rhs(Node) = minimum(G(node_1) + d(node, node_1)),$$

where $d(node, node_1)$ is the distance between the grids N=node and $node_1$, with the former being the predecessor of the latter.

This plays an important factor, as if Rhs (n) equals the G(n), then the grid n is locally consistent. If all the grids are locally consistent, then an optimal trajectory is implied between those grids. Effectively the cost equation also changes and is a minimization of the following attributes:

$$F(n) = minimum((minimum (G(n), Rhs(n)) + H(n)),$$
$$(minimum(G(n), Rhs(n))),$$

where symbols have their usual meaning.

There are certain advantages of this optimization, as each grid node is visited at most twice for each iteration of the algorithm. Since the priority queue or the open list contains a larger set of attributes, the implementation of this data structure determines the runtime of the algorithm. The grid nodes are expanded in a monotonically increasing manner, and nodes that are not consistent locally are not explored. Since it is based on the A* algorithm, the heuristic should be admissible, and in dynamic graph changing environments, LPA* outperforms the A* algorithm. We will have a brief overview of how the algorithm works and is implemented in most game engines and simulations for dynamic RL environments. Open the "LPA-star.ipynb" Notebook and observe the changes in the node class.

```
class Node():
    """A node class for LPA* Pathfinding"""

    def __init__(self, parent=None, position=None):
        self.parent = parent
        self.position = position

        self.g = 0
        self.h = 0
        self.f = 0
        self.rhs=0

    def __eq__(self, other):
        return self.position == other.position
```

The Rhs (n) lookahead attribute has been added to the node class. We create predecessor and successor lists, as shown here:

```
predecessor_list=[]
successor_list=[]
```

The rest of the "lpastar" function is almost similar to previous algorithms, with the exception that for each child grid explored in the eight directions, they are entered into the successor list as shown here:

```
new_node = Node(current_node, node_position)
successor_list.append(new_node)
```

Next we go to the cost update method and try to understand how the cost is updated for the successor nodes. We update the G(n) and H(n) values for the current child grid. The Rhs(n) value is then updated for the child grid with the sum of the G(n) value and the distance from the predecessor of the child grid to the grid.

```
child.g = current_node.g + 1

child.h = ((child.position[0] - end_node.position[0]) ** 2) +
((child.position[1] - end_node.position[1]) ** 2)

for i in range(len(children)):
  if children[i]==child:
    break

#Do rhs calculation
child.rhs= child.g + children[i-1].h
if child.rhs<child.g:
  child.g=child.rhs
```

The next step involves updating the successor grid nodes of the child. This is done by using the "update_successor" function, which updates the Rhs(n) values of the successor grid node with the minimum value between the sum of G(n) and H(n) for the predecessor grid node, and the Rhs(n) of the successor grid node. If the successor grid is already in the open list, then it is removed from the list. If the G(n) and Rhs(n) values of the successor does not match, we set the F(n) as mentioned in the cost minimization equation for LPA*. This function updates all the successor grid nodes with the minimum cost value so that exploration continues along locally consistent successor grid nodes.

```
def update_successor(predecessor_list,successor,
successor_list,open_list,src):
  for pred in predecessor_list:
      successor.rhs=min(successor.rhs,pred.g+ pred.h)
  if successor!=src:
    successor.rhs=sys.maxsize
  if successor in open_list:
    open_list.remove(successor)
  if successor.g!=successor.rhs:
    successor.f=  min(min(child.g,child.rhs)
+ child.h,child.g + child.h)
    open_list.append(successor)
```

After all the successor grid nodes of the child grid have been updated, the F(n) value of the current child grid is updated as per the equation:

```
child.f = min(min(child.g,child.rhs) + child.h,child.g + child.h)
```

This algorithm has widespread applications in general pathfinding AI in any simulation engine. The reason can be attributed to the swift updates of the F(n), G(n), H(n), and Rhs(n) values whenever the grid environment changes. This is quite practical in dynamic environments, where faster optimal trajectory is returned at the expense of more memory consumption. We can run this in the Notebook or Colab to check the runtime of the algorithm, as shown in Figure 2-11.

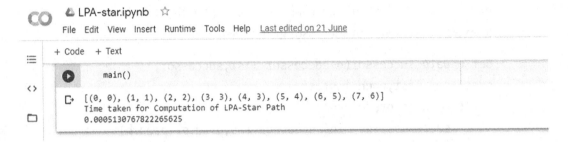

Figure 2-11. *Runtime of LPA* algorithm*

- **D* (D-star) algorithm:** This is another variation of A* that operates in a similar manner with respect to the classic A* algorithm. There are three variants of this algorithm:

  - Classical D* algorithm

  - Focused D* algorithm

  - D* lite

  For simplicity, we will be understanding the classical D* algorithm as the focued D* is based on this with certain heuristics. D* lite is a modification of the LPA* algorithm mentioned previously. This algorithm also has an open list and a closed list. Along with that, two attributes are required: raise and lower. The raise attribute of a grid indicates that its F(n) value is higher than the last time it was visited. The lower attribute of a grid indicates that the current F(n) value is lower than the last time the grid node was visited. In the "expansion" stage or path exploration stage, the algorithm updates a grid to the open list and updates the changes for all the neighboring grid nodes The major difference from A* is that unlike A*, which chooses the optimal path from the source grid to the destination grid, D* begins by searching backward from the destination grid. This can be understood where each grid node has a back pointer in the memory where it can store the previous grid in the path. When an obstacle is reached, the current grid node F(n) value is raised. This, in turn, raises all the neighboring grid nodes F(n) value. When the raised grid node can be lowered by choosing another trajectory (another neighboring

102

grid), this is also back-propagated to all the previously raised neighboring grid nodes. This is considered to be another variation of an incremental search and is most extensively used in games and simulations. We can try to understand a simplified variation of the D* algorithm using our Python Notebook. Open the "D-star.ipynb" Notebook in Jupyter or Colab. Since most of the code is similar to A*, we will only consider the important parts. We have a similar initialization of node class, and in the "dstar" function, we have the open and closed lists along with the successor and predecessor lists. The most important aspect is when an obstacle is encountered by the child grid node and the "is_raise" function is called to minimize the F(n) value of the child grid node based on the minimum F(n) value observed so far.

```
#Raise Function for neighbouring successor nodes
def is_raise(children,child_node,mini):
  if child_node.f < mini:
    mini=child_node.f
  return child_node
```

The next step involves checking the open list of grids for any value F(n) that is higher than the F(n) value of the current child grid. This implies that the open list grid nodes encountered an obstacle and have raised all the F(n) values of their nodes. Thus lowering is required.

```
#Recalculate distance based on the Raise value of node
for open_node in open_list:
    if child == open_node and child.g > open_node.g:
        continue
    if(open_node.f>child.f):
        open_node=child
        open_list.append(child)
```

Once we have understood this simplified variation of the D* algorithm, we can check for the runtime of this algorithm. Focused D* algorithm relies on heuristic estimation of raise and lower attributes. A preview of the runtime is shown in Figure 2-12.

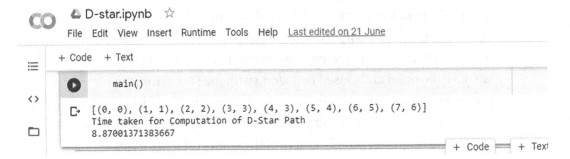

Figure 2-12. *Runtime of D* algorithm*

- **B* (B-star) algorithm:** This is a best first search algorithm, which is another variation of the A* algorithm. The concept of this search relies on proving or disproving whether the path through a particular grid node is the best path. The B* algorithm functions like a depth-first search tree, where it elongates from the root to the leaves, either proving or disproving. This enables the exploration to be limited to the grid nodes, where there is a chance of optimal path generation. This approach fine-tunes the A* algorithm as it creates a subspace of best fit grid nodes that are at optimal trajectory instead of iterating over all equally probable nodes. B* employs interval evaluations along with heuristic estimates. The algorithm performs by selecting nodes based on the upper and lower bounds of their F(n) values. This is a fairly simple algorithm, so let's try to understand its implementation in the "B-star.ipynb" Notebook. In most of the code segments, it is almost similar, except in the "bstar" function, where we initialize the minimum value with the lowest minimum value provided by Python.

```
mini=sys.maxsize
```

Inside the loop for the children grid nodes along the eight directions, we see that after the F(n) update function, we compare the "mini" value (the lower bound) among all the child grid nodes and update the F(n) value of the child grid with that lower bound minimum value. This ensures exploration continues along the proper child grid nodes.

```
child.f = child.g + child.h
    if(child.f<mini):
       mini=child.f
#Apply B-star logic
for child in children:
 if child.f==mini:
 # Child is already in the open list
    for open_node in open_list:
        if child == open_node and child.g > open_node.g:
            continue

    # Add the child to the open list
    open_list.append(child)
```

We can run this code and also get the runtime value of this algorithm as shown in Figure 2-13.

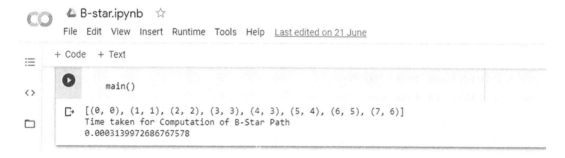

Figure 2-13. *Runtime of B* algorithm*

- **Simple memory-bound A* (SMA*) algorithm:** This is another algorithmic variation of A*, where it expands along most favorable grid nodes and prunes non-favourable nodes. It is completely optimal if the allowed memory is sufficient to store a shallow version of the simulation. In a given memory space, this algorithm provides the best solution than most A* variants. It does not revisit old grid nodes. Similarly as in A*, the expansion continues along with consideration of the F(n) heuristic. Most simplified, this can be thought of as a memory-constrained version of the B* algorithm with pruning. If sufficient memory is provided, this algorithm will best optimize the memory. A variation of the SMA* algorithm including a combination of B* with LPA* has been provided in the "SMA-star. ipynb" Notebook. Since the code has been previously discussed, we will just go through the linking of LPA* and memory-optimized B*.

```
child.rhs= child.g + children[i-1].h
if child.rhs<child.g:
        child.g=child.rhs
        #Update the successor nodes in the path
        for successor in successor_list:
          update_successor(predecessor_list,successor,
successor_list,open_list)
```

This is the LPA* variant of updating the successor, and the following code segment is the B* variant.

```
child.f = child.g + child.h
    if(child.f<mini):
      mini=child.f
#Apply B-star logic
for child in children:
 if child.f==mini:
 # Child is already in the open list
    for open_node in open_list:
        if child == open_node and child.g > open_node.g:
            continue

    # Add the child to the open list
    open_list.append(child)
```

Running this code segment provides us with the path as well as the runtime, as shown in Figure 2-14.

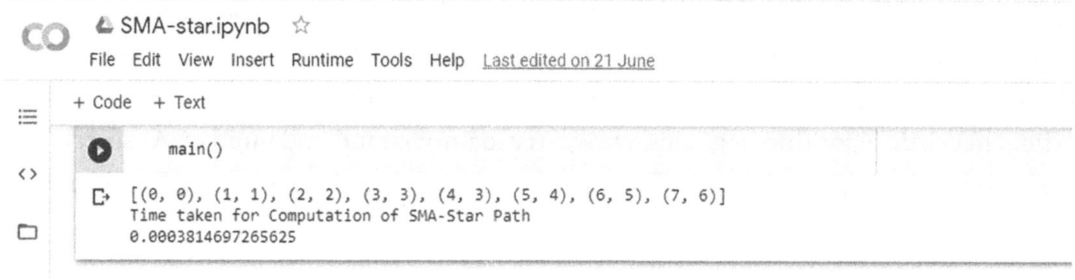

```
CO      SMA-star.ipynb  ☆
        File  Edit  View  Insert  Runtime  Tools  Help   Last edited on 21 June

        + Code   + Text

          ▶       main()

          ⌷   [(0, 0), (1, 1), (2, 2), (3, 3), (4, 3), (5, 4), (6, 5), (7, 6)]
              Time taken for Computation of SMA-Star Path
              0.0003814697265625
```

Figure 2-14. *Runtime for SMA* algorithm*

Other Variants of Pathfinding

By now, we are well-acquainted with heuristic estimates in generic pathfinding. These algorithms are implemented internally in several simulation engines and game engines and are the most extensively used in the field of heuristic pathfinding. Other algorithmic variations are also present, such as those listed here.

- **Jump search algorithm:** A modified A* algorithm where agents can jump from one grid to another for getting the optimal path. This can be thought of as follows: instead of choosing the eight possible directions at 1 unit apart, we consider eight or more directions that are 2 or 3 units apart. This greatly increases the search space and is used in games.

- **Alpha-Beta pruning algorithm:** A classical algorithm employed in Game Theory (2 person 0 sum game), where one agent has to maximize its rewards at the expense of the other agent. This algorithm tries to build a minimax tree—a tree that maximizes the rewards for one agent and that minimizes the rewards of the other.

- **Branch and bound:** This classic algorithm that involves generation of a search tree of all possible states. This is an exhaustive search algorithm used in combinatorial optimization problems.

- **Bellman Ford:** A variant of the Dijkstra algorithm involving negative weights in graphs and multisource shortest paths.

We have tried to understand all the variants of pathfinding algorithms and optimization techniques involved in games. The detailed description of A* pathfinding variants is a fundamental aspect of understanding how the Unity Game Engine internally optimizes search and AI pathfinding. While we provided a Python implementation of the different variants of heuristic algorithms, we will now concern ourselves with simulating Unity games with Dijkstra and A* algorithms. Since A* is considered as the primal heuristic algorithm in games, we will try to understand and build an A* search environment in Unity. Later we will focus on navigation meshes in Unity and build an enemy AI using NPC-based pathfinding.

Pathfinding in Unity

In this section, we will try to simulate the Dijkstra and A* algorithms in Unity, where an AI agent tries to reach the target. Since we have an understanding how the Dijkstra algorithm works, we will investigate the Unity simulation for the same.

Dijkstra Algorithm in Unity

We have to download the "DeepLearning" Unity Folder (from the Github Project associated with the book), and we will be using this for all our projects. Once downloaded, we will open the "Assets" Folder and navigate to the "HeuristicPathfinding" folder. This contains the setup scenes for Dijkstra and A* algorithmic simulations. Open the "DijkstraAgent" scene file in Unity Editor. The concept of the simulation is to let the purple agent cube reach the green target cube via a minimum cost path. The obstacles in the path are represented by the white cube blocks. We will be drawing our analogy from the GridWorld or menvironment with which we created in the Python implementation of the Dijkstra algorithm. The platform or the plane of the simulation is divided into grids (as can be seen in the Unity Scene). These grids are packed together to form a maze (matrix of grids). The dimension of the maze is 6X6, where we have six grids in the horizontal and vertical direction. Like before, for walkable grids, we initialize the value of the grid to be 0, and for non-walkable grid (those with the obstacles), we initialize a value of 1. We convert the Unity Scene into the maze simulation of Python by assigning the grids to the platform, the obstacles as the white cubes, and the target as the destination grid. A preview of the scene is provided in Figure 2-15.

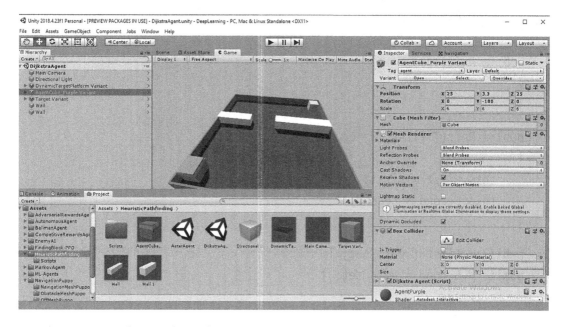

Figure 2-15. *Dijkstra algorithm Scene in Unity Editor*

Let us try to understand how the source code works for this simulation. Open the "Scripts" folder and open the "DijkstraAgent.cs" C# script. Since we will be trying to implement a C# version of the code segment of Python, we will go through certain data structures and collections (containers). We first initialize the "Pair" class, which is useful for storing the x and y coordinates of the grid platform (since it is 2D). This will be useful for filling the matrix or the grid platform with 0 and 1 values, depending on whether the grid is walkable or not. A grid coordinate is represented as a tuple or a container having x and y coordinates (x,y) such as (0,0), which signifies the start gridnode. Similarly, we have the destination gridnode as (5,5), which signifies the top-right corner of the platform. The numbering of the grid platform matrix starts from 0 to 5 (from left to right) in a particular row and from 0 to 5 (from bottom to top) for each column. Thus the bottom left coordinate where the agent cube is placed has a grid position coordinate of (0,0) as the x and y values, whereas the target agent is at position (5,5). The Obstacles can then be represented as grid positions [(0,3), (1,3)] on the left side and between [(3,3), (4,3), (5,3)] on the right side, only allowing movement though the (2,3) grid position. This is taken by following our rule that the numbering starts from left to right and from bottom to top. Once we are able to map the structure of the grid platform with the Unity Scene and the maze environment, we can create the class.

```
public class Pair<T, U>
{
    public Pair()
    {
    }

    public Pair(T first, U second)
    {
        this.First = first;
        this.Second = second;
    }

    public T First { get; set; }
    public U Second { get; set; }
};
```

We move to the main class "DijkstraAgent," and we initialize the variables like the agent GameObject, target GameObject, the grid matrix for the platform, and dictionary, which maps the matrix indices with the grid transform positions and an implementation of heap or priority queue data structure, which is extensively used in the sorting of the grid distances.

```
float[][] grid;
Dictionary<float, int> dictionary;
public GameObject agent;
public GameObject target;
Transform agent_transform;
Transform target_transform;
List<Pair<Pair<int, int>, float>> heapq;
```

Like before, in the start method, we initialize our GameObjects with tags and also fill the dictionary with the grid transform values based on the matrix grid coordinates. We initialize the grid matrix with 0's and obstacles as 1's and create an object of the heap data structure (priority queue). We then call the Coroutine function as a separate thread to start the simulation. This can be implemented as follows:

```
agent = GameObject.FindWithTag("agent");
target = GameObject.FindWithTag("target");
```

```
agent_transform = agent.GetComponent<Transform>();
target_transform = target.GetComponent<Transform>();
dictionary = new Dictionary<float, int>();
dictionary.Add(-25f, 0);
dictionary.Add(-15f, 1);
dictionary.Add(-5f, 2);
dictionary.Add(5f, 3);
dictionary.Add(15f, 4);
dictionary.Add(25f, 5);
//sample states (-25,-15,-5,5,15,25 for x and y axes)
grid = create_mat(6);
for (int i = 0; i < 6; i++)
{
    for (int j = 0; j < 6; j++)
    {
        grid[i][j] = 0;
    }
}

for (int i = 0; i < 6; i++)
{
    if (i != 2)
    {
        grid[i][3] = 1;
    }
}
heapq = new List<Pair<Pair<int, int>, float>>();
StartCoroutine(executeDijkstra(grid, dictionary, heapq, agent_transform,
target_transform));
```

We implement a multithreaded simulation in this case, as the Coroutine calls "executedijkstra" Enumerator method, which in turn passes the variables to another Coroutine named as "dijkstra." This is where the control logic is implemented, and a path container is created that stores the x and y coordinate positions of the grids that lie on the path the agent follows.

```
private IEnumerator executeDijkstra(float[][] grid, Dictionary<float,
int> dictionary, List<Pair<Pair<int, int>, float>> heapq,Transform agent_
transform, Transform target_transform)
    {

        yield return new WaitForSeconds(2f);
        List<Pair<int, int>> path = new List
   <Pair<int, int>>();
        yield return StartCoroutine(dijkstra(grid,
        dictionary, heapq, agent_transform,
        target_transform,   path));

    }
```

In the "dijkstra" method, we first create a collection or container called "distance." This container holds the grid x and y coordinates and a float value that signifies the distance of that particular grid node from the source grid node. We initialize this "distance" container with values from the grid matrix, which is a representative of the grid Transform positions (where grid.x = 0 and grid.y = 0 signify a coordinate on the platform as (0,0) or the start grid). In this case, we will manually place the target to grid location (5,5) on the platform matrix. We thus have the agent cube at the source (0,0) and target cube at the destination grid (5,5). We initialize the platform by following our platform rules.

```
List<Pair<Pair<int, int>, float>> distance = new List<Pair<Pair<int, int>,
float>>();

for (int i = 0; i < 6; i++)
{
    for (int j = 0; j < 6; j++)
    {
                    Pair<int, int> ps = new Pair<int, int>();
                    ps.First = i;
        ps.Second = j;
        distance.Add(new Pair<Pair<int, int>, float>(ps, float.MaxValue));

    }
}
```

Once we have built the "distance" container, we create another positional container called "states," which will be helpful when we consider the eight grid nodes in the neighborhood of a particular grid node (similarly to the children grid in the Python program). We create the source and destination grid and assign its positional values, with the exception of the source node; all other grid nodes have initial values set to the maximum float value of the system. This is similar to the one we used in Dijkstra, since we have to update the weights based on minimization algorithm. We then allocate the source node to the priority queue or heap.

```
Pair<int, int> src = new Pair<int, int>();
src.First = 0;
src.Second = 0;
Pair<int, int> dest = new Pair<int, int>();
dest.First = 5;
dest.Second = 5;
heapq.Add(new Pair<Pair<int, int>, float>(src, 0f));

List<Pair<int, int>> states = new List<Pair<int, int>>();

states.Add(new Pair<int, int>(0, -1));
states.Add(new Pair<int, int>(0, 1));
states.Add(new Pair<int, int>(-1, 0));
states.Add(new Pair<int, int>(1, 0));
states.Add(new Pair<int, int>(-1, -1));
states.Add(new Pair<int, int>(-1, 1));
states.Add(new Pair<int, int>(1, -1));
states.Add(new Pair<int, int>(1, 1));
```

The next part running a loop and iterating until the priority queue is not empty. We extract the grid node from the top of the queue and then check if the distance value of the grid is less than the previously observed value for the same grid. For the first iteration, since all the grid distance values are initialized as float.MaxValue (maximum float value), it will be replaced. We do not consider whether the current distance of the grid exceeds the previous distance value for the same grid, and if the destination and current grid positions are the same, we break out of the loop. This is the same algorithmic workflow that was implemented in the classic Dijkstra Python source code.

```
while (heapq.Count > 0)
{
            float dist = 0f;
            Pair<int, int> coord = new Pair<int, int>();
    foreach (Pair<Pair<int, int>, float> kv in heapq)
    {
        dist = kv.Second;
        coord = kv.First;
        break;
    }
    path.Add(coord);
    Debug.Log("heapsize");
    Debug.Log(heapq.Count);

    heapq.RemoveAt(0);
    float dist_measure = 0f;
    foreach (Pair<Pair<int, int>, float> kw in distance)
    {
        Pair<int, int> old_coord = kw.First;
        if (old_coord == coord)
        {
            dist_measure = kw.Second;
            break;
        }
    }
}
```

The next segment is similar to checking the grids in the eight directions of the current grid and adding the new grid position. Then we check whether the new position is inside the grid platform and also whether it is walkable(value not 1). We add a float value of 5f to the new grid distance. Then we check to see if the updated grid distance value is less than the previously observed value. If the value is less, we update the distance value for the current grid distance and add the new child grid to the priority queue and to the path container. This operation is similar to the child grid update code segment in the Python Notebook.

```
    Debug.Log("inside the loop");
    foreach (Pair<int, int> sample_pair in states)
```

```
{
    Debug.Log("inside the loop");
    Pair<int, int> new_coord = new Pair<int, int>();
    new_coord.First = coord.First + sample_pair.First;
    new_coord.Second = coord.Second + sample_pair.Second;
    int l = new_coord.First;
    int r = new_coord.Second;
    Debug.Log("inside the loop");
    if (l < 0 || l > 5 || r < 0 || r > 5)
    {
        Debug.Log("Checking neighbours");
        continue;
    }

    if (grid[l][r] == 1)
    {
        Debug.Log("notwalkable");
        continue;
    }
    float temp_dist = dist_measure + 5f;
    float dx = 0f;
    Pair<int, int> ps = new Pair<int, int>();
    ps = new_coord;
    foreach (Pair<Pair<int, int>, float> ds in distance)
    {
        if (ps.First == ds.First.First
        &&  ps.Second==ds.First.Second)
        {
            Debug.Log("changing the  values");
            dx = ds.Second;
            if (dx > temp_dist)
            {
                Debug.Log("changing values");
                ds.Second = dx;

                                #Add to heap
```

```
                    heapq.Add(new Pair<Pair<int, int>,
                    float>(ds.First, ds.Second));
                                        #Add the node to the path
                    path.Add(new Pair<int,
                    int>(ds.First.First, ds.First.Second));
            }
            break;
        }
    }
}
```

To visualize this in the Unity simulation, after the "dijkstra" function is completed, and the path container, which contains the (x, y) coordinates of the grids that are on the path from the source to the destination, is filled, another Coroutine is called. The "move_agent" Coroutine is pretty simple, as it retrieves each grid coordinate (x, y) from the path container and then maps the transform position of that particular coordinate using the dictionary. The agent's transform is then updated in accordance with the transform values of the grids on the Dijkstra path from this dictionary.

```
foreach (Pair<int, int> ps in path)
{
    int l = ps.First;
    int r = ps.Second;
    //Debug.Log(path.Count);
    Debug.Log("grid values");
    Debug.Log(l);
    Debug.Log(r);
    float x_vector = 0f;
    float z_vector = 0f;
    foreach (KeyValuePair<float, int> kv in dictionary)
    {
        if (kv.Value == l)
        {
            x_vector = kv.Key;
        }
    }
```

```
    if (kv.Value == r)
    {
        z_vector = kv.Key;
    }
     Debug.Log("Dictionary Values");
     Debug.Log(kv.Value);
    agent_transform.position = new
Vector3(x_vector,
agent_transform.position.y, z_vector);

    yield return new WaitForSeconds(1f);
     }

}
```

That completes the entire simulation code segment for the Dijkstra algorithm for pathfinding in Unity. After we are comfortable with our analysis of the code, we can try to run this in the Unity Editor. We will observe that for each iteration, the agent cube reaches the target through different grids. We have allowed a wait time for 1 second for each decision the agent makes based on the Dijkstra optimization. We can also go to the environments folder under the DeepLearning root folder to run the Unity executable simulation involving the Dijkstra algorithm. This forms a crude template for the readers, and different graph-searching algorithms can be implemented with this template. In the next part we will consider an implementation of the classic A* algorithm. Since we are now familiar with the original algorithm and also the Unity maze environment, which we created in this section, it will be fairly easy to understand the A* simulation concept in Unity. We will be using specialized node classes to store the F, G, H values, as in the algorithm, and use composite collection containers to update these values based on the heuristic estimate and the minimization cost function. Figure 2-16 provides a representation of the scene.

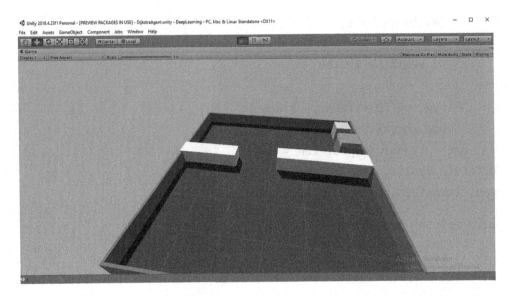

Figure 2-16. *Agent following the Dijkstra path toward the target cube*

A* Algorithm Simulation in Unity

Let us create the A* simulation on the same Unity maze environment or the grid environment. We have the similar architecture of the Unity Scene with the same agent and target at (0, 0) and (5, 5), respectively. Figure 2-17 provides a view of the scene.

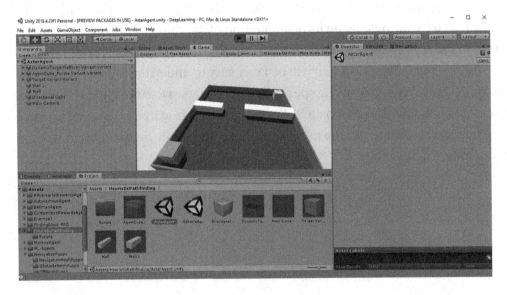

Figure 2-17. *A* algorithm simulation Unity Scene*

Since we have mentioned the workflow of the simulation in Dijkstra, we have followed a similar workflow in this algorithm as well. Initially we create the node class that contains the F, G, H values.

```
public class Node<T, U, V>
{
    public float f = 0f;
    public float g = 0f;
    public float h = 0f;

    public Node()
    {

    }
    public Node(T f, U g, V h)
    {
        this.F = f;
        this.G = g;
        this.H = h;
    }
    public T F { get; set; }
    public U G { get; set; }
    public V H { get; set; }
}
```

Under the monobehavior class, we have similar variables to the agent's transform, target's transform as well as the dictionary. There is a change in the data structure of the priority queue, since now we have to consider several attributes together to minimize the distance for optimal trajectory. So every entity inside the heap or priority queue (which is the open list, as in A* algorithm) will be a composite collection of different containers.

```
float[][] grid;
Dictionary<float, int> dictionary;
public GameObject agent;
public GameObject target;
```

```
Transform agent_transform;
Transform target_transform;
List<Pair<Pair<Pair<int, int>, Node<float, float, float>>
, float>> heapq;
//SortedDictionary<float, Pair<int, int>> heapq;
// Start is called before the first frame update
List<Pair<Pair<Pair<int, int>, Node<float, float, float>>
, float>> closed_list;
```

Each grid node entity in the open list heap has a position coordinate(x, y; given by a Pair<int, int>), followed by the grid node (F, G, H) and the distance from the start node. Therefore there is a substantial change in the information contained in an individual grid node. Unlike Dijkstra, it contains positions, node attributes, and distance. This start method contains the similar implementation and initialization of the grid platform and the GameObjects dictionary. The only additions are the open list (heap) and closed list composite containers, as shown here:

```
heapq = new List<Pair<Pair<Pair<int, int>,
    Node<float, float, float>>, float>>();
closed_list = new List<Pair<Pair<Pair<int, int>,
       Node<float, float, float>>, float>>();
StartCoroutine(executeAstar(grid, dictionary,
heapq,  closed_list, agent_transform, target_transform));
```

We then go to the Coroutine "executeAstar," where another Coroutine called "Astar," which implements the original algorithm, is called, and the path container is initialized and passed as argument like in Dijkstra.

```
yield return new WaitForSeconds(2f);
List<Pair<int, int>> path = new List<Pair<int, int>>();
yield return StartCoroutine(Astar(grid, dictionary, heapq, closed_list,
agent_transform, target_transform, path));
```

Inside the "Astar" function, we initialize the distance container, which holds the grid node position coordinates (x, y), and the distance from the start node. We also have the similar "states" container that contains the list of eight possible child grid node position coordinates for each grid node. We initially set the F, G, H values as 0 for the start grid and end grid. The position coordinate for the start grid is initialized to (0, 0), and that of the destination grid is (5, 5). The distance of the start grid is initialized as 0, and all other grids are initialized as float.MaxValue like in Dijkstra.

We then add the Start grid node to the open list or priority queue or heap.

```
Pair<int, int> src = new Pair<int, int>();
src.First = 0;
src.Second = 0;
Pair<int, int> dest = new Pair<int, int>();
dest.First = 5;
dest.Second = 5;
Node<float, float, float> src_node = new Node
<float, float, float>();
Node<float, float, float> dest_node = new Node
<float, float, float>();

src_node.F = src_node.G = src_node.H = 0f;
dest_node.F = dest_node.G = dest_node.H = 0f;
Pair<Pair<int, int>,
Node<float, float, float>> pair_dest =
new Pair<Pair<int, int>, Node<float, float, float>>
(dest, dest_node);

Pair<Pair<int, int>,
Node<float, float, float>> pair_src = new Pair
<Pair<int, int>, Node<float, float, float>>
(src,  src_node);
heapq.Add(new Pair<Pair<Pair<int, int>,
Node<float, float, float>>, float>(pair_src, 0f));
```

We then iterate as long as the open list is not empty and extract one grid node at a time. We then check if the F-value of the extracted grid node is greater than other grid nodes in the open list. Once a grid node with F-value less than the current grid node is found, we assign the node attributes (F, G, H) to the current grid node. If the current grid node is the destination node, we terminate the process and provide the path.

```
Pair<Pair<int, int>, Node<float, float, float>> current_node = new
Pair<Pair<int, int>, Node<float, float, float>>(coord, var_node);
Pair<Pair<Pair<int, int>, Node<float, float, float>>, float> current_
sample = new Pair<Pair<Pair<int, int>, Node<float, float, float>>,
float>(current_node, dist);
foreach (Pair<Pair<Pair<int, int>, Node<float, float, float>>, float> kv in
heapq)
{
    var_node = kv.First.Second;
    Node<float, float, float> cur_node = new
    Node<float, float, float>();
    cur_node = current_node.Second;
    if (var_node.F < cur_node.F)
    {
        cur_node.F = var_node.F;
        cur_node.G = var_node.G;
        cur_node.H = var_node.H;
        current_node.Second = cur_node;
    }
}
path.Add(coord);
if (current_sample.First.First == pair_dest.First)
{
    Debug.Log("Found");
    break;
}
```

In the next segment, we iterate over the eight neighboring grids and verify whether the new grid position lies inside the grid or maze platform and whether it is "walkable" (value not 1), like in Dijkstra. Then, like Dijkstra, we increment the distance of the new child grid by 5 units and compare whether this is the minimum distance value and add to the open list. This is the standard cost function for the distance update, similarly to Dijkstra.

```
List<Pair<Pair<Pair<int, int>, Node<float, float, float>>, float>>
children_list = new List<Pair<Pair<Pair<int, int>, Node<float, float,
float>>, float>>();
foreach (Pair<int, int> sample_pair in states)
```

```
{
    Debug.Log("inside the loop");
    Pair<int, int> new_coord = new Pair<int, int>();
    new_coord.First = coord.First + sample_pair.First;
    new_coord.Second = coord.Second + sample_pair.Second;
    int l = new_coord.First;
    int r = new_coord.Second;

    if (l < 0 || l > 5 || r < 0 || r > 5)
    {
        Debug.Log("Checking neighbours");
        continue;
    }
    if (grid[l][r] == 1)
    {
        Debug.Log("notwalkable");
        continue;
    }
```

Then we compare the distance metrics for the child grid, as shown here:

```
float temp_dist = dist_measure + 5f;
float dx = 0f;
Pair<int, int> ps = new Pair<int, int>();
ps = new_coord;
Node<float, float, float> temp_node = new
Node<float, float, float>(0f, 0f, 0f);
Pair<Pair<Pair<int, int>,
Node<float, float, float>>, float> new_node = new
Pair<Pair<Pair<int, int>, Node<float, float, float>>
, float>();
foreach (Pair<Pair<int, int>, float> ds in distance)
{
    if (ps.First == ds.First.First &&
        ps.Second == ds.First.Second)
```

```
        {
            Debug.Log("changing the  values");
            dx = ds.Second;
            if (dx > temp_dist)
            {
                ds.Second = dx;
                Pair<Pair<int, int>,
                Node<float, float, float>> temp_n =
                new Pair<Pair<int, int>,
                Node<float, float, float>>
                (ds.First, temp_node);

new_node = new
                Pair<Pair<Pair<int, int>,
Node<float, float, float>>, float>
(temp_n, ds.Second);

children_list.Add(new_node);
            }
            break;
        }
    }
}
```

In the next step for the current child grid node, we check whether it is present in the closed list. If the current child grid node is a part of the closed list, then the analysis is not done. The next step is the update of the minimization function of the A* algorithm. We update the value based on the distance cost G by adding a float value of 5. We then update the heuristic estimate value H, by comparing the square Euclidean distance from the current child grid to the destination grid node. Finally we combine the results of the cost function G and the heuristic H estimate values to get the F-value. This is the standard heuristic update rule of the A* algorithm, as mentioned in the Python implementation. This can be observed by the following lines.

```
foreach (Pair<Pair<Pair<int, int>, Node<float, float, float>>, float> child
in children_list)
{
    #Check in closed list
```

```
foreach (Pair<Pair<Pair<int, int>,
Node<float, float, float>>, float> closed_child
in closed_list)
{
    if (closed_child.First == child.First
    && closed_child.Second == child.Second)
    {
        continue;
    }
}
#Update G,H, and F values
Pair<Pair<Pair<int, int>,
Node<float, float, float>>, float> var_test =
new Pair<Pair<Pair<int, int>, Node<float, float, float>>
, float>();
var_test = child;
Pair<Pair<int, int>, Node<float, float, float>> dc =
new Pair<Pair<int, int>, Node<float, float, float>>();
dc = var_test.First;
dc.Second.G = dc.Second.G + 5f;
Pair<int, int> dist_pt = new Pair<int, int>();
dist_pt = dc.First;
float end_cur_dist = ((5f - dist_pt.First) *
(5f - dist_pt.First)) + ((5f - dist_pt.Second) *
(5f - dist_pt.First));
dc.Second.H = end_cur_dist;
dc.Second.F = dc.Second.G + dc.Second.H;
var_test.First = dc;
```

We also ignore the grid node if its G cost is greater than the G cost of the grid nodes in the open list. If all conditions pass, we add this child grid node to the open list for the next iteration.

```
foreach (Pair<Pair<Pair<int, int>, Node<float, float, float>>, float> open_
node in heapq)
    {
```

```
    if (var_test.First == open_node.First
    && var_test.Second == open_node.Second
    && var_test.First.Second.G > open_node.First.Second.G)
    {
        continue;
    }
}
heapq.Add(var_test);
}
```

That is the complete implementation of the A* algorithm in Unity. We then pass the path container in the "move_agent" Coroutine, as in Dijkstra, so that the agent transform can follow along those grid transforms that lie on the optimal path. We can run this code segment in the Unity Editor and check the path of motion of the agent. Figure 2-18 provides a representation of A* algorithm in work.

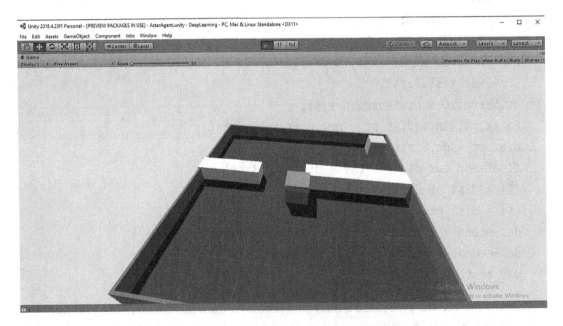

Figure 2-18. *Agent reaches toward target along the A* optimized path*

By now, we have a fair understanding of how pathfinding algorithms are built in game engines and simulation engines internally. An interested reader can use these templates to build their own efficient pathfinding algorithms that are under the A* class.

The core concept of these algorithms is very important to understand how the navigation system of Unity works, and we will be focusing on navigation meshes and enemy AI in the next section.

Navigation Meshes

Navigation meshes are considered meshes that control the area where the agent can walk and use optimized pathfinding algorithms to reach the target. Generally these are collections of convex polygons that divide the area into small triangles (simplest polygon) where the agent can walk. Generally in AI-based navigation, these are created with the help of data structures that contain the mesh information, such as the number of vertices and edges for a particular platform or model. Simplistically, if we divide the "walkable" areas into smaller triangular meshes, we can consider the agent as a point inside the triangle and the target as another point in a distant triangle. The approach now remains to find an optimized path between these two triangles, where the likes of A* algorithms are used. Since navigation meshes also can contain a diverse set of obstacles for the environment, these obstacles are considered separate points inside some of the triangles in the path from the source to the destination. When the agent or the agent point comes near the vicinity of the triangle containing the obstacle point, it detects that collision is likely to occur along that path based on distance measures. Thus collision detection is avoided. Since in most of the cases, these triangular meshes remain static, navigation meshes are used in level design to provide areas where the agent can traverse. However, we can also create dynamic navigation meshes that change according to the nature of obstacles and walkable path. Since we consider triangles as the fundamental components in a generic mesh data structure, we can generically define a mesh as a combination of three points along x, y, and z axes. There are two different ways to link different triangles (polygons) to create composite area meshes.

- **Edge sharing of triangle meshes**: The common edge of one triangle mesh is shared with another ad joint mesh.

- **Vertex sharing of triangle meshes**: This includes having a common vertex that connects 2 (two) triangle meshes.

A convex composite navigation can be made of different shapes, such as rectangular or rhomboid, but the fundamental part of any composite convex mesh is a triangle. Generally to reduce the level of detail (LOD) in complex gameplay scenes, navigation meshes are shown together as a big rectangle or convex polygon instead of individual triangles to reduce the computation cost during rendering. The illustration shown in Figure 2-19 tries to convey information regarding pathfinding in a navigation mesh. Each grid of the navigation mesh is made up of two triangles (yellow an black). Since the grid shape resembles a rectangle, each rectangle is made up of two triangles, which are the fundamental building blocks of any polygon. The source grid point on the mesh is the blue circle, and the destination is the green circle There is an obstacle (marked as red) in the center grid. We can see that most of the grids in the mesh are made up of triangles that share a common side, with the exception of one grid to the left of the obstacle. This grid is connected by the vertex sharing mode between the two triangles. When the agent encounters the obstacle, it redirects itself to the grid mesh along the diagonal, connected by the vertex sharing mode. This is how the agent reroutes its path to avoid the obstacle containing grid mesh. The arrow signs denote the direction of motion of the agent.

Note   The concept of navigation meshes was started around 1980's, where it was used mainly in robotics and games and was referred to as "Meadow Maps."

Abhilash Majumder | June 23, 2020

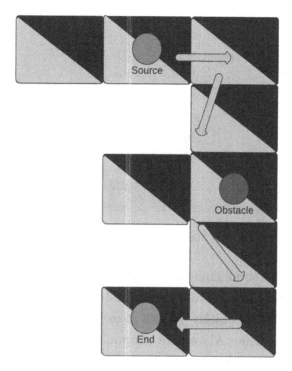

Figure 2-19. *Pathfinding in navigation meshes*

In the next section, we will see how to create navigation meshes in Unity using an AI module of Unity Engine. We will help our Puppo to collect the stick with the help of pathfinding in the navigation mesh.

Navigation Mesh and Puppo

Open the "DeepLearning" root folder and navigate to "environments." Then navigate to "NavigationPuppo" Unity executable file. Run the simulation or game. We can see that if we click anywhere in the green field (platform), Puppo will immediately go to that location. This is an example of an AI agent trying to find an optimal path from the current location to the location that is pointed out by us on the screen. Wherever we click on the ground, we see Puppo going to that particular location. Figure 2-20 provides a view of Puppo scene.

Figure 2-20. *Navigation Puppo Scene using Unity Navigation Mesh*

Let us try to create this simulation game. Open the "NavigationPuppo" folder inside the Assets folder and then click on the "NavigationMeshPuppo" scene. In Unity, we can create navigation meshes very quickly. We can go to the Windows Tab inside the Unity Editor and then select AI. Inside AI we have an option of "Navigation." This enables us to use the UnityEngine.AI component and change our RL platform environment into a navigation mesh. So the general way to add a navigation component inside the Unity Scene is to follow **Windows ➤ AI ➤ Navigation**. This can be shown as in Figure 2-21.

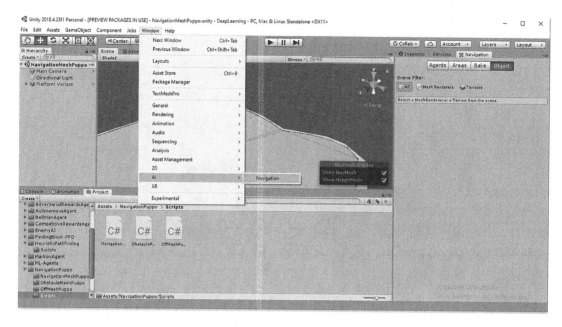

Figure 2-21. *Selecting the navigation component*

Then we select the terrain or ground environment where we want the navigation mesh to appear. This process is called as NavMesh Baking in Unity. The NavMesh Baking process collects the render meshes of all the convex meshes that are marked as navigation static. This implies the navigation mesh will remain static in the environment. After we select the "Platform Variant" in our scene, we go to the Navigation Tab in the Inspector Window (shown on the right in Figure 2-21) and click Bake. The navigation mesh then appears as a blue covering on the ground platform as shown in Figure 2-22. There are four main subtabs under the Navigation Tab, and we will explore each of these separately.

Figure 2-22. *Ground platform becomes blue, signifying navigation mesh creation*

We then explore the details of the four tabs placed under the Navigation Tab. The four main subtabs are discussed here.

- **Agent**: This tab contains the agent type, most generally humanoid is present by default. It also contains radius, height, step height, and max slope of the agent.

  - **Radius**: signifies the radius of the cylindrical collider surrounding the agent

  - **Height**: signifies the height of the agent

  - **Step height**: determines the height of the agent's steps during locomotion

  - **Max slope**: the permissible angle that the agent can detect and traverse in the environment

The Agent Tab can be visually observed and changed as well, as shown in Figure 2-23. This is required when we assign Puppo as the navigation mesh agent (NavMesh agent).

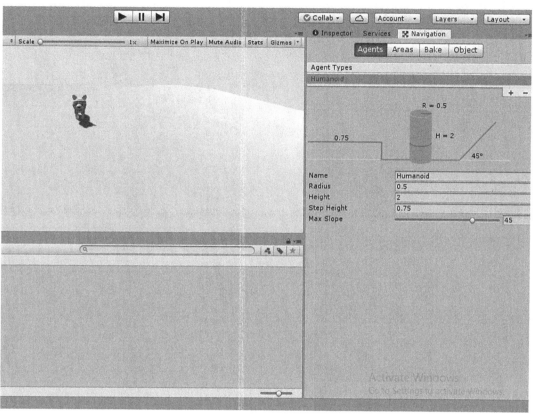

Figure 2-23. *Agents Tab under the Navigation Tab in Inspector Window*

- **Areas**: This tab focuses on the different segments of the navigation mesh. As we observe, we can see two parallel tabs, "Name" and "Cost." This can be useful if we are creating a diverse environment for our agent where certain parts of the terrain can be watery or muddy while other parts can be plain. We can associate different costs to the different mesh sections highlighted by their names. Since Unity Engine internally uses the A* algorithm, the cost factor determines the actual cost of the minimization function, which we saw in previous sections, denoted by the G(n) value. The higher the cost, the more difficult is for the agent to traverse along the path, since according to our discussion on A*, the lower value of G(n) is always taken into consideration (open list). Visually this can be shown as shown in Figure 2-24.

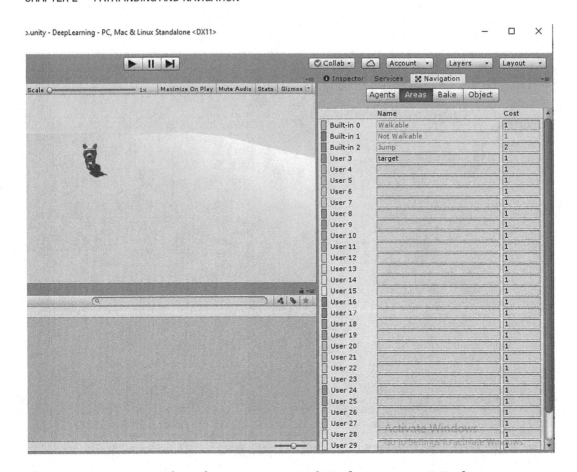

Figure 2-24. *Areas Tab under Navigation Tab in the Inspector Window*

- **Bake:** This tab controls the baking of the navigation mesh. Baking implies fitting the ground plane mesh with a convex polygonal navigation mesh. The accuracy of fitting can depend on several factors that are included in the list under the Bake Tab:

  - **Agent radius :**The cylindrical collider around the agent that determines how close the agent can get to a wall or obstacle

  - **Agent height:** determines the spaces the agent can use to reach the destination

  - **Max slope:** the maximum inclination of the ground terrain so that the agent can walk up

- **Step height:** the height of the obstacles on which the agent can step

  We also have additional settings under the Bake Tab that are included for off mesh links. We will look into this in the next section when we discuss off mesh links.

- **Drop height:** This is the maximum height the agent can drop from when it is moving from one navigation mesh to another via the off mesh links

- **Jump distance:** The maximum distance the agent can jump when crossing the off mesh link to go to adjacent navigation mesh.

  There are certain advanced settings under the Bake Tab as shown in Figure 2-25, which include:

- **Manual Voxel Size:** This allows us to change the accuracy of our Bake process. Voxelization is a process in which the screen is rasterized and the NavMesh is built to best fit the arbitrary level geometry. The Voxel size determines how accurately the navigation mesh fits the scene geometry. The default value is set to 3 voxels per agent radius (diameter = 6 voxels). We can manually change the value to trade off between the baking speed and accuracy.

- **Min Region Area:** This allows us to cull smaller areas that are not directly connected on the navigation mesh. Surfaces with an aggregate area less than the Min Region Area will get removed.

- **Height Mesh:** The height of the navigation mesh above the terrain.

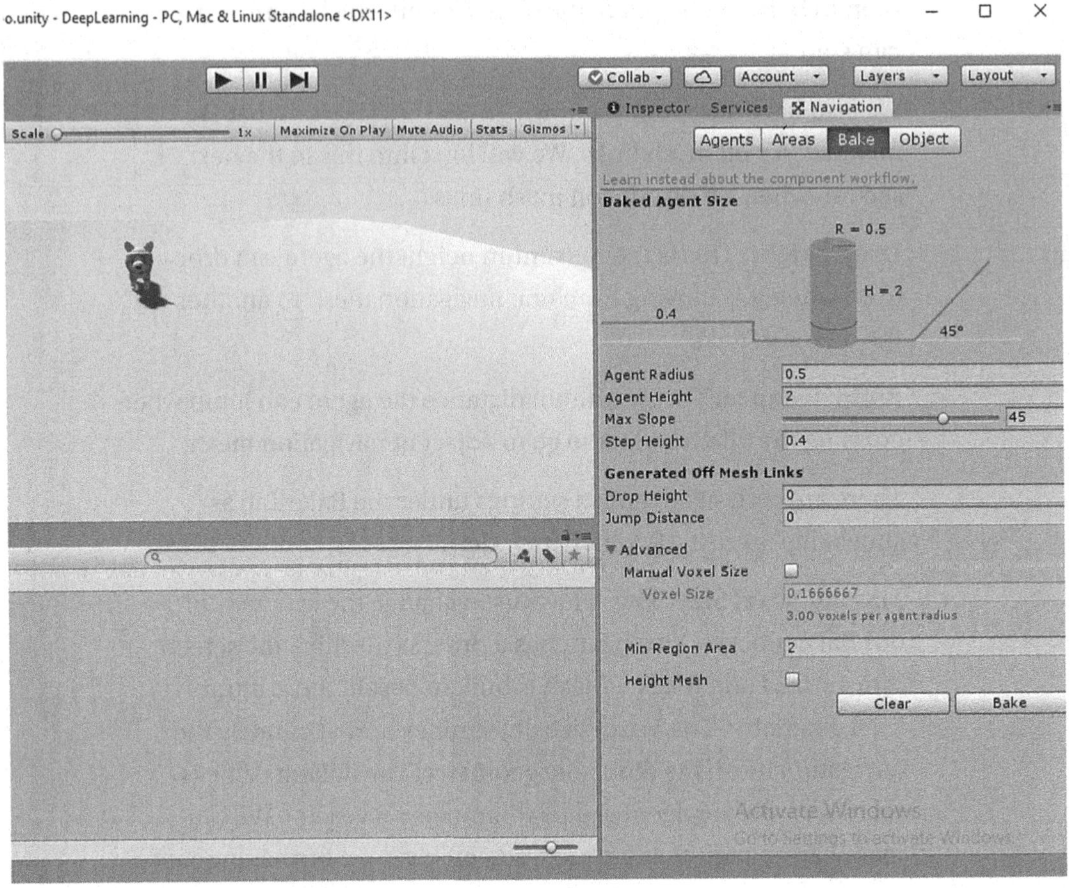

Figure 2-25. *Bake Tab under Navigation Tab in Inspector Window*

- **Object:** This tab contains the details about Prefabs, Mesh Renderers,
  and the Terrains in the scene, which contain the navigation meshes.
  We also have the navigation static, off mesh links, and navigation
  area, which is set to walkable in this tab, as shown in Figure 2-26.
  We will focus on the off mesh links in the subsequent sections to
  generate automatic off mesh links between navigation meshes.

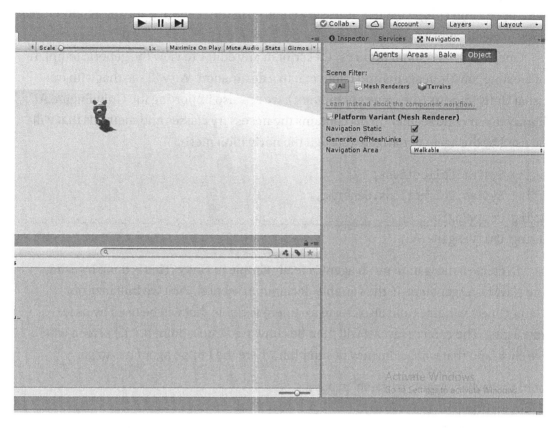

Figure 2-26. *Object Tab under Navigation Tab in Inspector Window*

Now that we have an overview of the navigation component in Unity, the next step is to attach the NavMesh agent component to Puppo. We initially set all the values as default. We have different components in this script that we have to add in order to make the agent follow the pathfinding algorithm to reach the destination. Components such as steering, obstacle avoidance, and pathfinding are present inside the component. Most of the steering and obstacle avoidance have modifiable values like angular speed, acceleration, stopping distance, height, radius, and so forth. The most important aspect is the pathfinding section, where auto repath and auto traverse off mesh is ticked by default. The auto repath automatically computes the new A* path from the current source to the destination when the destination changes its position (can be thought of as an extension to the LPA* algorithm we discussed). There is also an area mask component that indicates which section of the navigation mesh has which functionality (by default there are 3: walkable, non-walkable, and jump; there can be up to 29 custom). After we have added and completed the necessary changes in the scene, let us explore the source code to create our simulation game.

Open the "NavigationPuppo.cs" C# script in any editor to view the generic template of creating NavMesh agents and connect it to a destination. We will see that with our usual Unity imports (the using component); we are also importing the UnityEngine.AI library in our code segment. This contains the necessary classes and methods that will be used by the agent to navigate through the navigation mesh.

```
using System.Collections;
using System.Collections.Generic;
using UnityEngine;
using UnityEngine.AI;
```

To create a navigation mesh agent is really simple in Unity. This is done by using the NavMeshAgent type in the variable declaration section. First we initialize our GameObject variables and also create a camera variable that will be used by us for raycasting. The camera raycast will then be converted into a point on the screen where we click, and that will be the new destination where the Puppo agent has to go.

```
public NavMeshAgent navmesh_puppo;
Transform puppo_transform;
public Camera cam;
public GameObject puppo;
```

By now, we know that the start method is used for initialization of the varibles and the Gameobjects with the tags.

```
puppo = GameObject.FindWithTag("agent");
puppo_transform = puppo.GetComponent<Transform>();
```

In the update method, which is called per frame, we check whether we clicked the left mouse button via the command Input.GetMouseButtonDown(0), where 0 is the code for the left mouse button. Then we create a Raycast that is converted to a point on the screen by the camera using the ScreenPointToRay() function. Then based on where the ray hits on the screen, we update the new destination of the agent by using the SetDestination() function of NavMesh agent.

```
if (Input.GetMouseButtonDown(0))
{
    Ray ray = cam.ScreenPointToRay(Input.mousePosition);
    RaycastHit hit;
    if (Physics.Raycast(ray, out hit))
    {
        navmesh_puppo.SetDestination(hit.point);
    }
}
```

Once done, we can close the editor and assign the script to the Puppo (CORGI) game object. Then we can play the game when we run it in the editor. Figure 2-27 shows this scene.

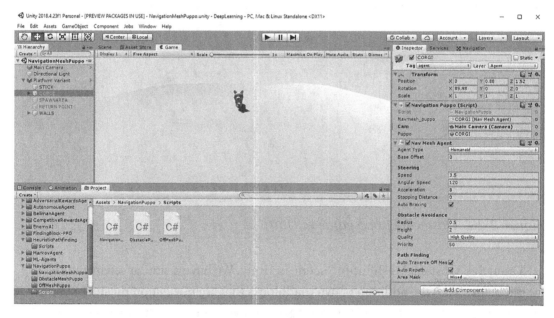

Figure 2-27. *Navigation Puppo Scene in the Unity Editor*

Obstacle Meshes and Puppo

In the previous section, we had an overview of the navigation component in Unity and how to create an AI agent that can move optimally to any point we click on the screen using A*. Now let us return to a classic RL environment of rewards and obstacles. In the "environment" folder, we will open the "ObstaclePuppo" Unity executable. When we run the game, we see that Puppo is now placed in the same ground, but there are certain obstacles in the form of roadblocks where Puppo cannot walk. But Puppo has to reach and collect all three sticks from the different locations on the ground and that, too, at following an optimal combines the path to the three sticks. When we play, we see how Puppo intelligently navigates through the scene and avoids the roadblocks and finally collects all three sticks. Figure 2-28 shows Puppo resting after collecting all three sticks.

Figure 2-28. *Obstacle Puppo game in Unity*

Open the "ObstacleMeshPuppo" scene in Unity. We have a similar environment as we did before, with the addition of two roadblocks that are navigation mesh obstacles and three sticks that are the rewards or targets. We bake the scene like before and visualize the blue covering of the navigation mesh. The difference here is that we have to initialize the obstacles that are present in the mesh. The Prefabs marked as "Fence" are the obstacles, and we have to add the NavMesh obstacle component to them. This lets Unity Engine know that the mesh contains obstacles at those particular transforms or positions. The rest of all the values and other components, such as the NavMesh agent or Bake properties, are same as the previous scene. Figure 2-29 shows Nav Mesh Obstacle Scene.

140

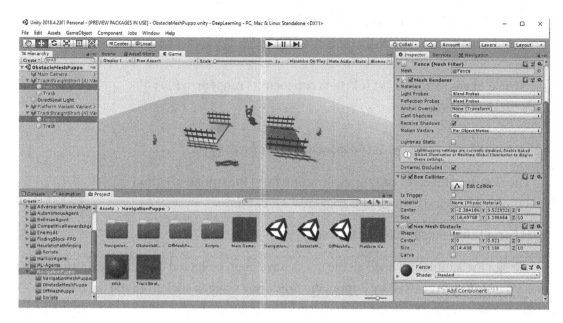

Figure 2-29. *Nav Mesh Obstacle added to the Obstacle Puppo Scene*

Let us open the "ObstaclePuppo.cs" C# script to create this simulation. Like before, we are using UnityEngine.AI module for our navigation mesh. We also initialize variables for the agent, target Gameobjects, and their transforms along with a NavMesh agent variable for Puppo (agent).

```
public GameObject puppo;
Transform puppo_transform;
public NavMeshAgent puppo_agent;
public float max_reward;
public List<GameObject> sticks;
public List<Transform> stick_transform;
public GameObject[] st;
float initial_reward = 0f;
```

Start method initializes the variables and also fills the list of the target sticks transforms as shown here:

```
float initial_reward = 0f;
puppo = GameObject.FindWithTag("agent");
sticks = new List<GameObject>();
```

```
st = GameObject.FindGameObjectsWithTag("target");
foreach (GameObject stick in st)
{
    stick_transform.Add(stick.GetComponent<Transform>());
    sticks.Add(stick);
}
puppo_transform = puppo.GetComponent<Transform>();
```

The next step involves calling a Coroutine from the update method called
"executeObstacleFind," which gets triggered every frame.

```
StartCoroutine(executeObstacleFind());
```

We run the simulation until all the sticks have been collected and the maximum
rewards have been received by Puppo. We randomly select a stick from the list based
on the transform positions and then assign its location as the new destination for agent
Puppo. This is controlled by the SetDestination, which takes the transform position
attribute of the stick GameObejct.

```
if (initial_reward < max_reward && sticks.Count > 0)
{
    int idx = Random.Range(0, sticks.Count);
    GameObject sample_stick = sticks[idx];
    Transform tf = sample_stick.GetComponent<Transform>();
    puppo_agent.SetDestination(tf.position);
```

Then we compute the distance between the agent and the stick. If the distance is less
than the given threshold, then it implies Puppo has reached the stick and collects the
stick. For every stick Puppo collects, a reward of 10 points is received by the agent Puppo.
To complete the simulation, Puppo needs to collect all three sticks, amounting to a total
of 30 points.

```
float distance = (float)Vector3.Distance(tf.position, puppo_transform.
position);
if (distance < 0.1f)
    {
        // Debug.Log(distance);
        initial_reward += 10f;
        Debug.Log("Stick Picked");
```

```
        Destroy(sample_stick);
        sticks.Remove(sample_stick);
        Debug.Log(initial_reward);
    }
}
if (initial_reward == max_reward)
{
    Debug.Log(max_reward);
    Debug.Log("Max Reward Picked");
}
yield return new WaitForSeconds(3.5f);
//After Episode Ends
yield return new WaitForSeconds(1f);
```

Finally we give rest to Puppo for each stick he collects and after collecting all the sticks. This is Puppo in the process of collecting the first stick, shown in Figure 2-30.

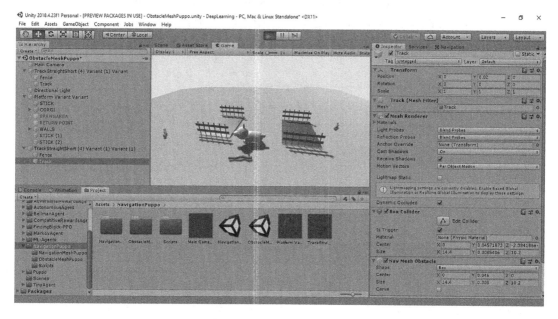

Figure 2-30. *Obstacle Puppo Unity Scene*

Off Mesh Links and Puppo

The final and the most interesting concept of navigation meshes are the off mesh links. These are links that allow motion of the navigation mesh agent outside the planar convex polygonal navigation meshes and also between different meshes. There are two ways to generate off mesh links to connect disjointed navigation meshes. Open the "OffMeshPuppo" Unity scene. The two ways to generate off mesh links are listed here.

- **Generate automatically**: This is controlled by clicking the Navigation Tab in the Inspector Window and then clicking on the Objects Tab. We have to click on "Generate OffMeshLinks" (ticked) to automatically generate links between the two navigation meshes. In this case, care must be taken on changing the "jump across" and "drop height" because the trajectory for drop height is designed such that horizontal travel by the agent is:

$$2* \text{agentRadius} + 4* \text{voxelSize}$$

and the trajectory for the "jump across" is defined such that the horizontal travel is more than 2* agentRadius and less than the jump distance. Figure 2-31 shows Off Mesh Links.

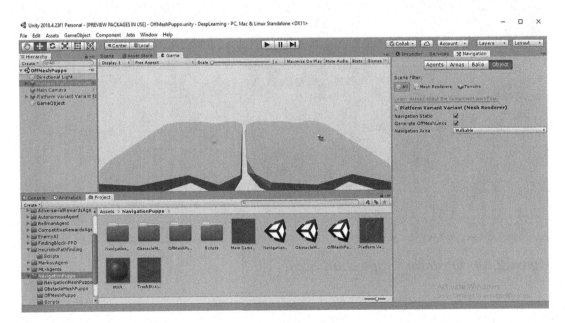

Figure 2-31. Automatic off mesh links between the two navigation meshes

- **Add off mesh link component**: This is another method of adding
  the off mesh link manually to the platform or terrains that need to be
  connected. Based on the width of the off mesh link, the agent always
  chooses the minimum path between the source and the destination,
  which are present in two different navigation meshes.

After adding the off mesh links, we will see that links are formed between the two
navigation meshes. This also shows us the path along which the agent Puppo can
traverse to reach the stick target in the next navigation mesh, as shown in Figure 2-32
and Figure 2-33.

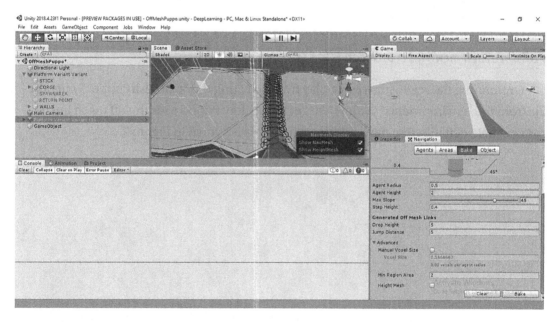

Figure 2-32. *Off mesh links in Editor Scene View*

Let us now create a very simple script to let Puppo use the off mesh link and reach
the stick target that is present in the next navigation mesh (the one on the left). Open the
"OffMeshPuppo, cs" C# script. Since most of the initialization and library inclusion is
similar to previous codes, we will concentrate ourselves on the "Offmesh" Coroutine. We
set the destination of the agent as the position of the target stick using the SetDestination
method, and then we check whether the distance between the target and Puppo is less
than a given threshold. If this condition is met, we reward Puppo with 10 points and the
stick is collected, giving puppo some time to rest.

```
nav_agent.SetDestination(target_transform.position);
if (Vector3.Distance(puppo_transform.position, target_transform.position) <
0.5f)
{
    initial_reward += 10f;
}
if (initial_reward == max_reward)
{
    Debug.Log("Reached");
    Debug.Log(initial_reward);
    target.SetActive(false);
}
yield return new WaitForSeconds(1f);
```

On running the scene (or we can play from selecting the "OffMeshPuppo" Unity.exe file from the "environments" folder), we get to see how Puppo uses the off mesh link to connect between different navigation meshes. This is shown in Figure 2-33.

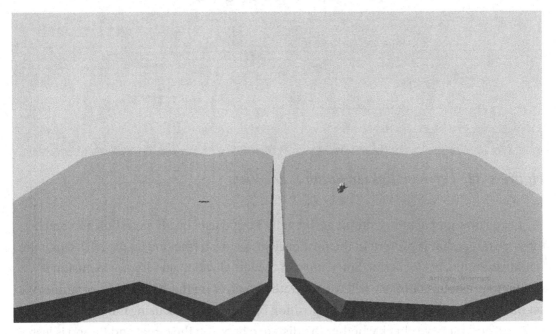

Figure 2-33.   Off Mesh links in Unity GamePlay Scene

We now proceed to the final section of the chapter, where we will create an enemy AI with the help of navigation meshes and pathfinding algorithms that we have learned so far.

Creating Enemy AI

Now that we have a fair understanding of how pathfinding works in sync with navigation meshes and the ease of use of the Unity NavMesh system, we will create a very simple enemy AI, where an agent cube has to find a target cube in an obstacle-filled environment. Once the target cube is in the line of sight of the agent cube (i.e., the agent can see clearly), then the agent starts firing at the target to destroy it. There is one catch, however—we have the ability to move the target anywhere we want in the scene to avoid getting shot by the agent. To play the game, go to the "environments" folder and just run the "EnemyAI" Unity.exe file. Click on the screen where we want the target to move to, and the target will move there. Once the agent finds the target, it starts firing and gets a reward once the agent destroys the target.

Figure 2-34 shows the Unity Scene for Enemy AI with Navigation Meshes.

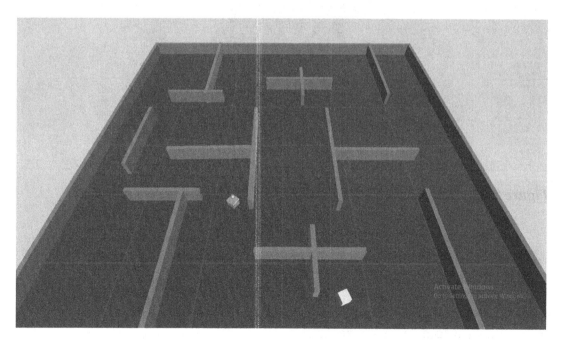

Figure 2-34. Enemy AI gameplay using NavMesh agent and pathfinding

Now let us open the "EnemyAI" folder in Assets to explore the scene and navigation mesh. We have the scene where the walls are the obstacles and platform serves as the navigation mesh. We create this using the Bake method mentioned earlier. Then we assign the NavMesh agent component to the purple agent cube. This is the enemy agent, which uses heuristic A* to find an optimal path to the target cube. The values of the settings of the navigation meshes as well the NavMesh agent are set as default. We have two different scripts for this particular use-case. The "PlayerAI" script controls the motion of the target (which is us), and the "EnemyAI" script, which controls the purple agent. We will explore the "PlayerAI" since it resembles the "NavigationPuppo.cs" script, which uses camera and raycast to determine a hit-point on the screen and makes the target move there accordingly. A preview of the scene is provided in Figure 2-33.

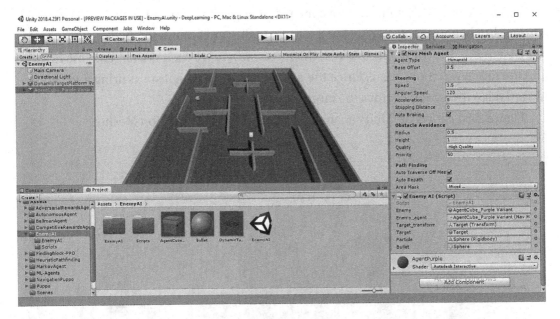

Figure 2-35. *Unity Scene View containing the NavMesh agent component*

Open the "PlayerAI" script. We see that we have the same initialization as before, containing the target Gameobject, target transform, a NavMesh agent variable, and the camera variable that converts the raycast to screen point like before.

```
public Camera cam;
public NavMeshAgent player_agent;
Transform player_transform;
public GameObject player;
```

We also have the start method initialized as:

```
void Start()
{
    player=GameObject.FindWithTag("target");
    player_transform=player.GetComponent<Transform>();
}
```

We then have the update method, similarly to before, where we check whether the user has clicked the left mouse button and then trigger a raycast that is transformed to a point using the ScreenPointToRay() function to get a new transform position. Then we set the destination as this new transform position.

```
if (Input.GetMouseButtonDown(0))
{
    Ray ray = cam.ScreenPointToRay(Input.mousePosition);
    RaycastHit hit;
    if (Physics.Raycast(ray, out hit))
    {
        player_agent.SetDestination(hit.point);
    }
}
```

Now let us view the "EnemyAI" script. We have certain variables to initialize, such as the target, agent GameObject, NavMesh agent, and a spherical GameObject called the "bullet." We assign the Rigidbody component to the "bullet" GameObject such that it uses collision detection when it collides with the target Gameobject.

```
public GameObject enemy;
Transform enemy_transform;
public NavMeshAgent enemy_agent;
public Transform target_transform;
public GameObject target;
public Rigidbody particle;
public GameObject bullet;
```

The start method then initializes those variables like so:

```
void Start()
{
    target=GameObject.FindWithTag("target");
    target_transform= GameObject.FindWithTag("target").
    GetComponent<Transform>();
    enemy=GameObject.FindWithTag("agent");
    enemy_transform= enemy.GetComponent<Transform>();
    bullet=GameObject.FindWithTag("bullet");
    particle= GameObject.FindWithTag("bullet").
    GetComponent<Rigidbody>();
}
```

We then have a OnTriggerEnter method that is triggered when collisions take place between the bullet and the target GameObject. The target is then desroyed by the bullet on collision.

```
void OnTriggerEnter(Collider col)
{
    if(col.gameObject.tag=="target")
    {
    //Destroy(gameObject);
        gameObject.SetActive(false);
        col.gameObject.SetActive(false);
}
```

Next we come to the update method. Here, we create a raycast that moves along the agent's z axis in the forward direction. This raycast is helpful to check if the target is present in the agent's line of sight. We also have the SetDestination() method, which updates the destination of the agent.

```
RaycastHit hit;
var dir= enemy_transform.TransformDirection(Vector3.forward);
enemy_agent.SetDestination(target_transform.position);
var dist=Vector3.Distance(enemy_transform.position,
target_transform.position);
```

If the Raycast hits the a GameObject, we check whether the hit object is the target with the help of the following lines of code:

```
Rigidbody clone=null;
        if(Physics.Raycast(enemy_transform.position,dir,
        out hit) && dist>4.5f)
        {
            if(hit.collider.gameObject.tag=="target")
                {
```

We then let the agent fire the bullets with the help of the Instantiate() method, which is used for instantiating prefabs or clones of the bullet GameObject. This hits the target Object and calls the OnTriggerEnter, and that method causes the target to get destroyed.

```
clone=Instantiate(particle,enemy_transform.position,enemy_transform.rotation);
clone.velocity= enemy_transform.TransformDirection(Vector3.forward*5);
```

We also have another condition that happens if the bullet misses the agent. This can happen when the agent is moving away from the line of sight of the target and is assigned to new location. In that case, if the agent cube is near the vicinity of the target cube, the latter gets destroyed.

```
else if(dist<=4.5f)
    {
        Debug.Log(dist);
        target.SetActive(false);
        //Destroy(target);
        bullet.SetActive(false);
            Destroy(clone);

    }
```

That is the entire code segment for this game. Let us return back to Unity and assign the "PlayerAI.cs" script to the target (green) and the "EnemyAI.cs" script to the agent (purple). Both of these GameObjects have the NavMesh agent attached to them. Click play in the Unity Editor, and we can play this AI-driven pathfinding game, as shown in Figure 2-35 and 2-36.

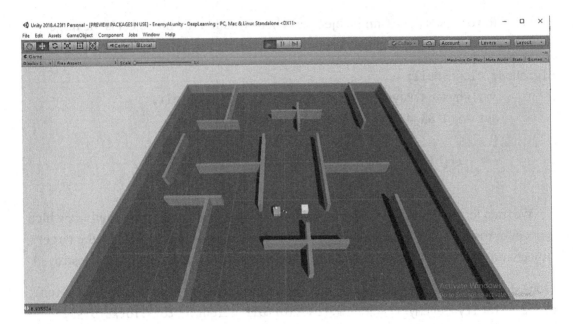

Figure 2-36. *Agent firing at the target during GamePlay using NavMeshes in Unity*

Summary

With that we come to the end of this chapter. We have explored briefly the core fundamentals of pathfinding algorithms in classic RL and autonomous control agents and also learned about navigation meshes.

- We started with the generic concept of pathfinding in a reinforcement learning (RL) environment. We understood the different scenarios where an autonomous agent must decide a proper optimal path from a source to a destination, even if there are obstacles in the path.

- We then went through the details of some popular pathfinding algorithms used in generic Graph Theory, such as Greedy breadth first search and Dijkstra.

- The next topic was on an improvisation of searching algorithms by adding a heuristic estimate. We introduced the concept of the A* algorithm for pathfinding and discussed Dijkstra as a special case of A* algorithms.

- We explored the different variants of A* algorithms based on time complexity and memory optimization, such as dynamic weighted A*, iterative deepening A*, lifelong planning A*, D*, B*, and small memory-bound A* algorithms. This helped us understand how different variations are used in simulations and game engines based on memory and speed.

- We then explored creating a simulation in Unity for both Dijkstra and A* algorithms and got to explore new fundamental concepts of classes and composite containers in C#.

- We tried to understand the fundamentals of navigation meshes and the convex polygons composing them.

- In Unity, we created navigation meshes and learned about the UnityEngine.AI component. This module is responsible for the navigation and pathfinding in Unity.

- We learned about off mesh links and obstacle avoidance with the help of NavMesh agents, NavMesh obstacles, and off mesh links and created games and simulations for the same.

- In the last section, we applied our knowledge and understanding to create an "EnemyAI" game, where the main task of the target is to avoid getting fired at by the NavMesh agent, which intelligently avoids the obstacles and finds the target through the most optimal trajectory.

Now we have an understanding of state-based RL as well as pathfinding in generic games and autonomous agents. This forms the basis of fundamental concepts of classic RL. In the next steps, we will start discovering slowly the depths of machine learning (ML) Agents and deep RL using Unity. The next chapter describes setting up and installing the Unity ML agents and configuring the system. We will look into the core concepts of Unity ML agents and why deep learning is required for RL.

Note   This is our Microsoft Word writing template, which includes brief guidelines for how styles should be applied to text. We would like you to use it. However, if you have a strong preference for another writing application, or your own Word template, let us know, and we'll work to accommodate you.

CHAPTER 3

Setting Up ML Agents Toolkit

We have seen in the previous chapters how states, actions, and rewards play a crucial role in driving an agent to reach its goal in a reinforcement learning (RL) environment. Now that we are familiar with the fundamentals of generic state-based RL, we will move ahead with the installation of all the libraries, frameworks, and extensions related to the usage of Unity ML agents as well as to further progress in the later modules of deep learning. Before we dive into the installation, let us try to understand the ML agents package made by Unity. Since its inception in 2017, the Unity ML Agents Toolkit has provided researchers, developers, and game programmers with a plethora of resources in the field of deep RL. The ML Agents Toolkit was initially created with the vision to assist researchers and developers in transforming games and simulations created with the help of Unity Editor into deep learning environments where the agents can be trained using state-of-the-art (SOTA) deep RL algorithms, evolutionary and genetic strategies, and other deep learning methods (involving computer vision, synthetic data generation) through a simplified Python API. With the latest release of package version 1.0 (at the time of writing this book), there have been huge advancements in the development of the Toolkit in terms of streamlining the C# SDK, Python API linking, robust compatibility with Tensorflow library, and huge advancements in areas of curriculum learning, self- and adversarial play, generative adversarial imitation learning, and pre-existing deep learning algorithms (Proximal Policy Optimization-PPO, Soft Actor Critic-SAC). There have been significant modifications of the core library that use the open AI Gym environment as a wrapper. The Unity ML Agents Toolkit version 1.0 has stable communicators linking Unity (C#) and the Python API (deep learning) and has provided game developers with the flexibility of writing deep learning agents and simulating their own aritificial intelligence (AI) in their games. Researchers, who are interested in modifying the core algorithms for their use-cases, are also provided with

© Abhilash Majumder 2021
A. Majumder, *Deep Reinforcement Learning in Unity*, https://doi.org/10.1007/978-1-4842-6503-1_3

a flexible Gym wrapper environment, which provides a template for writing their own deep learning algorithms. All of these can be done with the simple usage of the Unity Engine, Unity ML Toolkit, Jupyter Notebook, and Tensorflow framework. Now that we understand the scope and possibilities of Unity ML Agents, we will discuss the entire process of installing all the necessary libraries and frameworks in this chapter. The different agents in the Unity ML Agents Toolkit are presented in Figure 3-1.

Figure 3-1. *The Unity ML Agents Toolkit version 1.0.0*

Overview of the Unity ML Agents Toolkit

By now we have Unity already installed in our system (any version greater than 2018.3) and have had an overview of the MonoBehaviour C# environment. Before we dive into the installation guides, let us understand the ML Agents Toolkit components. The ML Agents Toolkit is a software development kit (SDK) that links the C# scripts made with Unity Engine with the Gym wrapper so that we can train our agents in deep learning algorithms. Therefore there are two fundamental aspects of the SDK:

- **The Unity Engine C# scripting**: This is the fundamental part of Unity that we have been using. Later we will see how we can include Tensorflow neural networks and train our model with just C# scripts for our games.

- **The OpenAI Gym Wrapper Python API**: This part is the communicator and the interface between the Unity Engine and the OpenAI environment. This module helps us to convert the Unity

Game Scene into a deep RL environment where we can use our own implementations of algorithms or use baselines provided by OpenAI to train our agents in the scene.

These are the main parts of the Unity ML Agents Toolkit, which enables us to create games in Unity and transform them into deep learning environments with the help of a Gym wrapper where we can apply our RL algorithms. Figure 3-2 shows the components of the ML Agents Toolkit.

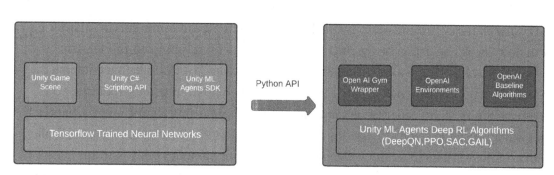

Figure 3-2. *Components of the Unity ML Agents Toolkit*

Now that we have an overview of the Unity ML Agents Toolkit, we can realize the importance of the Gym environment with which we played in the first chapter and analyzed the CartPole environment. In this section, we would install the prerequisites required for the ML agents to work seamlessly with our games. Since there are several instability issues between different versions of ML agents and Tensorflow frameworks, we will stick to a standard stable release of both of these. We have previously installed the Anaconda environment, which included installations of Jupyter Notebook, Spyder IDE, and the Python Console along with others. This will greatly help us in creating our models later and linking our scene with the Gym environment. We have previously installed Tensorflow version 1.7 using the following code in the Anaconda prompt:

```
pip install tensorflow==1.7
```

We had also installed TensorBoard for our visualization of model training with the command:

```
pip install tensorboard
```

Installing Baselines and Training A Deep Q-Network

The next step is to build our environment for Gym, which we will be using extensively in the later chapters. If we want to simulate our Gym in Colab or Jupyter Notebook, we have to install the Gym environment, which can be done using:

```
!pip install gym
```

Now let us try to build our previously created CartPole environment (in Chapter 1), but now we will be using the OpenAI Baselines library for training our model. The OpenAI Baselines library is an open source library created by OpenAI that contains the SOTA deep reinforcement learning algorithms applied on Atari games, robotics, and even games on Unity. Since we are familiar with the Q-learning algorithm (in Chapter 1), we will just use the Deep Q-Learning algorithm provided by Baselines on the CartPole Environment in a lucid manner. Deep Q Learning is an off policy deep learning implementation of Q-Learning algorithm over discrete/continuous spaces rather than only discrete states. It is recommended to try this out in Google Colab Notebook since we will be using a different version of tensorflow, which is stable with Baselines. First let us install the baselines from github in the Colab using the command:

```
!pip install git+git://github.com/openai/baselines
```

Now we will use this library to write a very simple deep Q-learning Model for the CartPole. This is just to test that our installation is correctly done and all the other libraries, such as Tensorflow, are compatible. We don't need to get into the details of the model just yet, since we will be exploring it in further chapters and hence this implementation will only use the SOTA deep Q algorithm implemented by OpenAI with only hyperparameters.

As before, we will import Baselines, Gym, and Tensorflow for our implementation:

```
import gym
from baselines import deepq, logger
import tensorflow as tf
```

deepq is the deep Q-learning implementation of OpenAI. With the installed version of Tensorflow, if issues arise due to "tf.contrib.layers:" incompatibility, we have to upgrade our Tensorflow version to a stable release of 1.14. However, this Baselines library is incompatible with Tensorflow version 2.0, as there are no "tf.contrib.layers" in that version. Now that we have complete stable libraries, we can simulate the CartPole environment using the following line:

```
env=gym.make("CartPole-v0")
```

This is the first step to set up our RL environment with actions, spaces, and rewards (Chapter 1). The next few lines contain the deep Q-network, which is created by OpenAI as the SOTA. Although there is no need to understand the implications and inner functionality of the model at this stage, we will go over the hyperparameters that are involved in creating the model.

```
act=deepq.learn(
    env,
    network='mlp',
    lr=1e-4,
    total_timesteps=1000,
    buffer_size=50,
    exploration_fraction=0.05,
    exploration_final_eps=0.001,
    print_freq=10,
)
```

We use the "deepq.learn" command from the Baselines library. The following are the hyperparameters associated with this model.

- "env": This is the CartPole environment we created in the previous step.

- "network": This is the type of neural network architecture the model will use. Based on the different aspects, the network can be "mlp," which signifies Multi-Layered Perception Model; "lstm," which is Long Short-Term Memory Model; or "cnn," which signifies Convolution Neural Network Model. There are other neural network architectures that are present, and we will cover all these in the deep RL chapter.

- "lr": This signifies the learning rate, which is used in generic ML for proper global convergence of the optimization function.

- "total_timesteps": the number of iterations we want to simulate the environment

- "buffer_size": the size limit of the memory buffer for recording previous states, actions, and rewards

- "exploration_fraction": the fraction of the timesteps; the model will try to explore new states

- "exploration_final_eps": exploration fraction for the final episode

- "print_freq": the frequency of printing the model logs on the screen

This is an overview of the deep Q model designed by OpenAI, which we are using to train the CartPole. We will be using variants of this model for our Unity games later. That is pretty much all that is required for simulating the environment and training the CartPole. Once this is done, we can be assured that the Baselines library has been properly imported in our system. Alternatively we can also test the installation by simply using the Python terminal or Anaconda prompt and typing:

```
python -m baselines.run --alg=deepq --env=CartPole-v0 --save_path=./
cartpole_model.pkl --num_timesteps=1e5
```

Once this is run, we will see the model is running in the Anaconda prompt environment and logs are getting captured in the user data (AppData in Windows), as shown in Figure 3-3.

```
| % time spent exploring | 76      |
| episodes               | 100     |
| mean 100 episode reward| 23.9    |
| steps                  | 2.37e+03|
-----------------------------------

| % time spent exploring | 37      |
| episodes               | 200     |
| mean 100 episode reward| 40      |
| steps                  | 6.37e+03|
Saving model due to mean reward increase: None -> 64.9000015258789
-----------------------------------
| % time spent exploring | 2       |
| episodes               | 300     |
| mean 100 episode reward| 87.5    |
| steps                  | 1.51e+04|

Saving model due to mean reward increase: 64.9000015258789 -> 96.69999694824219
-----------------------------------
| % time spent exploring | 2       |
| episodes               | 400     |
| mean 100 episode reward| 109     |
| steps                  | 2.6e+04 |
-----------------------------------
Saving model due to mean reward increase: 96.69999694824219 -> 124.69999694824219
```

Figure 3-3. *Training deep Q algorithm from Baseline for CartPole*

We have completely installed all the associated deep RL libraries and frameworks, including Tensorflow, TensorBoard, Anaconda environment, Gym, Baselines, Keras, and Unity Engine. For the next section we will go into the depths of installation of the ML Agents Toolkit in Unity and address the major errors and stability issues of the library, including compatibility with the deep learning frameworks of Python. For this session we will be using version 2018.4 of Unity, although it will work in later versions of Unity (2019 and 2020).

Installing Unity ML Agents Toolkit

The Unity ML Agents Toolkit is the official toolkit for deep learning in Unity. There are several steps to install the library on our system. The official Github page of the open source repository of Unity ML Agents can be found at `https://github.com/Unity-Technologies/ml-agents`.

This is the official repository of Unity ML Agents; let us see the details that are present on the Github page. On scrolling toward the "Readme" section, there are several details mentioned regarding the versions of the ML agents, the different built-in trained Unity Environments inside the repository (15+ in number), built-in support for proximal policy operation (PPO) and soft actor critic (SAC) algorithms and the cross-functional

161

flexibility of the SDK. If we head over to the releases page, given by the link https://
github.com/Unity-Technologies/ml-agents/releases, we will see all the releases of
the Unity ML Agents Toolkit. Each release version has package version details, major and
minor changes, bug fixes, and source files attached at the bottom. Since we are working
with version 1.0, the following versions of Python API, Gym wrapper, Unity C# SDK,
and other version details are mentioned. Figure 3-4 shows the Github page of Unity ML
Agents Release 1.

Figure 3-4. Unity ML Agents Release 1

There are two source files in "zip" and "tar.gz" format inside the assets, as shown
in Figure 3-5. This contains the precompiled binary of the version 1 release of Unity
ML Agents. The simplest way to get the ML Agents Toolkit in our local machine is to
download that particular version of the Unity ML Agents Toolkit. Once downloaded,
we can extract to a suitable location in our directory. There are several other ways to
download as well, and we can use git commands from the Windows command line or
Anaconda prompt to download the associated branch of ML agents.

```
git clone --branch release_1 https://github.com/Unity-Technologies/ml-
agents.git
```

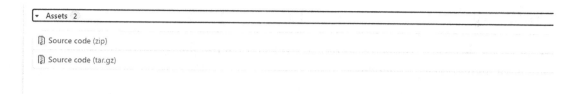

Figure 3-5. *Unity ML Agents version 1.0 source codes in zip format*

Cloning the Github Unity ML Agents Repository

Now that we have downloaded the official Unity ML Agents Repository from Github, either by using "git clone" or by manually downloading the source zip file, we have to make further modifications before we can use it. It is recommended not to clone the "master" branch of the ML Agents Repository; rather we can clone the "release_1" branch like the one shown in Figure 3-6.

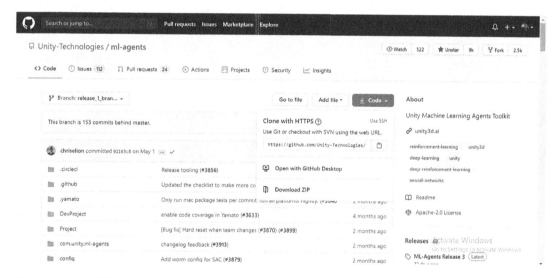

Figure 3-6. *Cloning the Unity ML Agents Release_1" branch on Github*

After we have downloaded and extracted the Unity ML Agents, we can create a new Unity project with the 3D template. To use the Unity ML Agents in this project, simply drag the Unity ML Agents extracted repository into the assets panel of the Unity Project. This will enable the Unity Engine to install all the dependencies, libraries, and frameworks, such as barracuda (the neural network link framework for Unity) provided by the ML Agents package.

Exploring the Unity ML Agents Examples

We can get a glimpse of the all the built-in Unity game templates present in the ML Agents folder when we can navigate to

Projects ➤ Assets ➤ ML-Agents ➤ Examples

Inside this folder, we have all the AI-trained game environments made with Unity ML Agents and that have pretrained deep RL algorithms like PPO and SAC. In older versions of ML Agents, in place of the "Projects" folder, there may be folders like "unity ml-agents" or "unity." As of now, we will concern ourselves with the contents of the Examples folder. Let us open the 3D Ball environment game made with Unity ML Agents. The environment is shown in Figure 3-7.

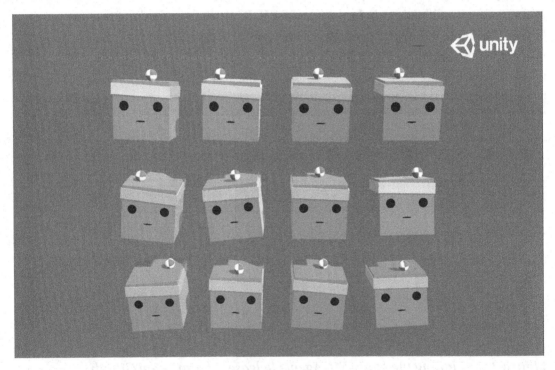

Figure 3-7. *3D ball environment Unity ML agents*

In this environment, we see 12 blue cubes balancing the little balls on the top of them. These blue cubes are the agents in the scene, and if the ball drops off from the "head" of the agents, a negative reward is given to the agent. So the agent has to continue balancing the balls on its head as long as possible to collect rewards and maximize its goal. This is the first example of the Unity ML Agents Toolkit that is trained with the help of PPO, a deep RL algorithm, which we will discuss later. As we can see from our concept from previous chapters, the agent is the blue cube, and the reward is balancing the ball (sphere) on its head.

- **States**: The observation space for this environment can be divided into two parts: stable and unstable. When the agent balances the ball, it is a stable space, whereas when the agent loses balance of the ball, it becomes an unstable space. Either the ball is on the head or it isn't.

- **Actions**: Each blue agent cube is free to rotate along x and z axes to balance the sphere on itself. Each ball has six degrees of motion along the x, y, and z axes. All of these fall into the action space for the environment. The cubes are fixed in their position and cannot undergo translational motion

- **Rewards**: The agent is rewarded for each timestep it balances the ball. The rewards are negative when the ball falls off from the "head" of the agent.

We will explore in depth when we try to build and train our own models using this environment. But for now, we can play around with other environments made with Unity ML Agents and try to identify the states, actions, and rewards for each environment. Here is another one named "basic," shown in Figure 3-8, where the agent has a choice to go to a bigger reward (shown by the big "green" ball) or the smaller reward (small "green" ball). This is a very simple game simulation using deep RL and Unity Engine, where the agent will try to maximize its reward by going toward the bigger sphere. Although initially the agent may go to either one of them, and as training progresses it finds that the bigger one has greater rewards, it will go in the direction of maximization of rewards. As an exercise we can try to identify the states, actions, and rewards spaces for this agent and environment. Once we are done playing around with built-in Unity games with ML Agents, let us try to understand other possible alternatives to install Unity ML Agents through the Unity Editor.

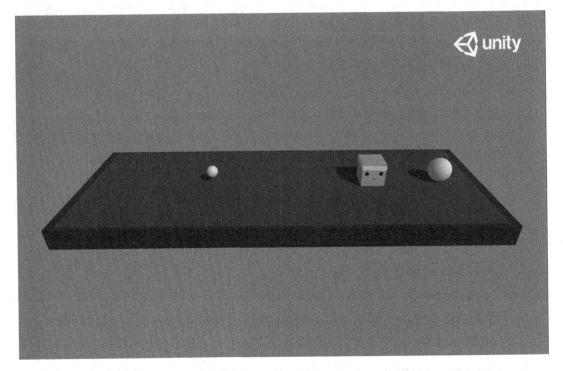

Figure 3-8. *Basic environment in Unity ML agents*

Let us open Unity, and as mentioned we have to drag in the ML Agents package we downloaded before. Then we will navigate to the Assets folder, and inside that the ML Agents folder contains all the environments we just viewed along with scripts and neural network models. Let us try to see an alternative way to install ML agents in our Unity Engine.

Local Installation of Unity ML Agents

Now we will locally install the Unity ML Agents. This is helpful when you do not require all the contents of the source repository except the essential ones, like the behavior scripts (brain), academy, and deep learning algorithms with the sample example scenes. Navigate to the Windows Tab and select the Packages option. The Packages Window contains all the packages that are currently present in that particular Unity project. These are "JSON" files that contain different packages, like Unity Ads, Physics, HRDP, and many more. A preview is shown in Figure 3-9.

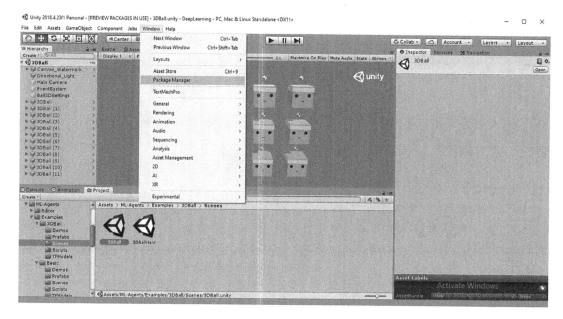

Figure 3-9. *Package option in Window Tab of Unity Editor*

The next step is to add the ML Agents Package that we downloaded (or cloned). This will install all the package details, including Barracuda, Python API, and certain C# scripts (namely, Behaviour scripts or Brains) without which ML Agents will not work. Since we have to add the package from our ML Agents installation directory, we select the "+" icon below to add it. We get an option "Add Package From Disk," and we have to click this to open a Windows pop-up. The next step is to navigate and select which package we want to include in the project. In my case, I am using the 2018.4 version of Unity, so the UI may differ for other later versions, but the steps remain the same. Figure 3-10 shows the Package Manager Window.

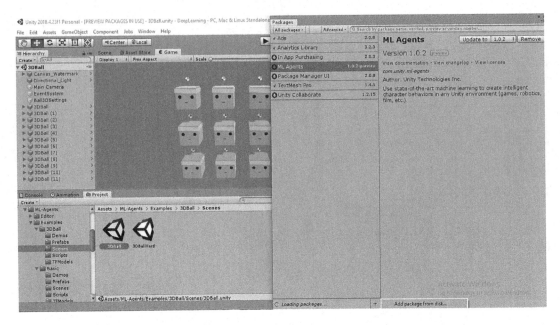

Figure 3-10. *Option to add ML Agents package from disk*

Next we have to navigate to our downloaded ML Agents folder and go to "com.unity. ml-agents" folder. This folder contains a JSON file named as "package.json," the contents of which are as follows:

```
{
  "name": "com.unity.ml-agents",
  "displayName": "ML Agents",
  "version": "1.0.2-preview",
  "unity": "2018.4",
  "description": "Use state-of-the-art machine learning to create
  intelligent character behaviors in any Unity environment (games,
  robotics, film, etc.).",
  "dependencies": {
    "com.unity.barracuda": "0.7.1-preview"
  }
}
```

The package file contains the details of the versions of ML Agents as well as the current version of Unity we are using, along with the Barracuda package version. The Barracuda package is extremely important, as it is a lightweight package for neural

168

networks in Unity, which enables us to run pretrained Tensorflow networks in our Unity games. Once we select this JSON package for import into Unity, we have to wait for some time until Unity completes building the dependencies and adding the necessary scripts for the ML Agents to work.

Installing ML Agents from Python Package Index

We can also install ML Agents from the Python Package Index (PyPI) site. This also allows downloading and installing any dependencies that may not have been installed previously. If errors and issues persist while downloading or installing ML Agents, this will help to remove those errors. This installation guide also aims to resolve issues if we have different versions of previously downloaded additional libraries such as Tensorflow or Pytorch, or Gym/Baselines. The command for installation is pretty simple and can be written from either command prompt or Anaconda prompt:

```
pip install mlagents
```

This downloads all the related libraries and provides logs as to which versions are getting downloaded. This does not download or clone from the Github repository but rather from the ML Agents PyPI page mentioned in the link https://pypi.org/project/mlagents/.

After the installation is completed in the Anaconda prompt, we can check by running the following command:

```
mlagents-learn -help
```

On running this command, all the related commands and information related to installed ML Agents would be displayed on the screen. Previously there used to be a Unity Logo along with the display; however, the newer versions have deprecated the logo in the "-help" command. The logo will be seen when we train ML Agents via Anaconda prompt later in this chapter. This installation would also install all the details mentioned in the "setup.py" file. The PyPI page may get updated with newer versions of ML Agents as time progresses, and running the aforementioned command ensures installation of the latest release. Figure 3-11 shows the mentioned steps.

```
(base) G:\>mlagents-learn --help
g:\anaconda\lib\site-packages\tensorflow\python\framework\dtypes.py:517: FutureWarning: Passing (type, 1) or '1type' as a synonym of type is deprecated; in a future ve
sion of numpy, it will be understood as (type, (1,)) / '(1,)type'.
  _np_qint8 = np.dtype([("qint8", np.int8, 1)])
g:\anaconda\lib\site-packages\tensorflow\python\framework\dtypes.py:518: FutureWarning: Passing (type, 1) or '1type' as a synonym of type is deprecated; in a future ve
sion of numpy, it will be understood as (type, (1,)) / '(1,)type'.
  _np_quint8 = np.dtype([("quint8", np.uint8, 1)])
g:\anaconda\lib\site-packages\tensorflow\python\framework\dtypes.py:519: FutureWarning: Passing (type, 1) or '1type' as a synonym of type is deprecated; in a future ve
sion of numpy, it will be understood as (type, (1,)) / '(1,)type'.
  _np_qint16 = np.dtype([("qint16", np.int16, 1)])
g:\anaconda\lib\site-packages\tensorflow\python\framework\dtypes.py:520: FutureWarning: Passing (type, 1) or '1type' as a synonym of type is deprecated; in a future ve
sion of numpy, it will be understood as (type, (1,)) / '(1,)type'.
  _np_quint16 = np.dtype([("quint16", np.uint16, 1)])
g:\anaconda\lib\site-packages\tensorflow\python\framework\dtypes.py:521: FutureWarning: Passing (type, 1) or '1type' as a synonym of type is deprecated; in a future ve
sion of numpy, it will be understood as (type, (1,)) / '(1,)type'.
  _np_qint32 = np.dtype([("qint32", np.int32, 1)])
g:\anaconda\lib\site-packages\tensorflow\python\framework\dtypes.py:526: FutureWarning: Passing (type, 1) or '1type' as a synonym of type is deprecated; in a future ve
sion of numpy, it will be understood as (type, (1,)) / '(1,)type'.
  np_resource = np.dtype([("resource", np.ubyte, 1)])
usage: mlagents-learn.exe [-h] [--env ENV_PATH]
                          [--curriculum CURRICULUM_CONFIG_PATH]
                          [--lesson LESSON] [--sampler SAMPLER_FILE_PATH]
                          [--keep-checkpoints KEEP_CHECKPOINTS] [--resume]
                          [--force] [--run-id RUN_ID]
                          [--initialize-from RUN_ID] [--save-freq SAVE_FREQ]
                          [--seed SEED] [--inference] [--base-port BASE_PORT]
                          [--num-envs NUM_ENVS] [--no-graphics] [--debug]
                          [--env-args ...] [--cpu] [--version] [--width WIDTH]
                          [--height HEIGHT] [--quality-level QUALITY_LEVEL]
                          [--time-scale TIME_SCALE]
                          [--target-frame-rate TARGET_FRAME_RATE]
                          [--capture-frame-rate CAPTURE_FRAME_RATE]
                          trainer_config_path

positional arguments:
  trainer_config_path

optional arguments:
  -h, --help            show this help message and exit
  --env ENV_PATH        Path to the Unity executable to train (default: None)
  --curriculum CURRICULUM_CONFIG_PATH
                        YAML file for defining the lessons for curriculum
```

Figure 3-11. Running "mlagents-learn --help" command in Anaconda prompt

Now we have successfully completed the installation of ML Agents with all the peripherals. Now let us try to understand how installation in a containerized environment, such as a virtual machine environment, can be done.

Installation in Virtual Environments

A virtual environment is a separate environment containing a root directory with its own set of libraries and frameworks that do not affect any other parts of the local system. It is a containerized environment, which has its own version of Python that may differ from the base or the locally installed Python. Working in a virtual environment is extremely helpful, as whenever any errors or crashes take place in the virtual environment, then other environments and local settings or libraries are not affected. While working in a production environment focused on game development with ML Agents, the virtual environment has two important aspects that make it helpful for development teams.

- **Easy dependency management:** Dependencies related to separate modules of Python can be managed easily without having to worry about crashing or making unwanted changes to the entire product.

- **Robust CI/CD pipeline:** CI/CD stands for continuous integration/
  continuous development, which generally refers to the production
  pipeline from development, building, testing, and analysis.
  With containerized environment, Agile methodologies can be
  implemented (based on sprints of development), which will
  definitely help in product growth.

For this particular case, we have to start with installation of the pip module, as it may
not be present in the virtual environment. This can be downloaded and installed using
the following command:

```
curl https://bootstrap.pypa.io/get-pip.py -o get-pip.py
```

The next step is to run the "get-pip.py" module by using:

```
python3 get-pip.py
```

Next, we check for the version of installed pip:

```
pip3 -V
```

The next step is to create our own virtual environment using the following command
in Anaconda prompt:

```
python -m venv python-envs\new-env
```

For activating the environment, the following command is used:

```
python-envs\new-env\Scripts\activate
```

That is all we have to do to set up our own virtual environment in Anaconda prompt.
The next steps for installation of ML Agents are similar to the previous section using
the pip command. The only difference here is that in this case, we are running the
ML Agents installation in a containerized environment rather than locally, and for
all the steps of model training, we can use the functions of ML Agents in this virtual
environment only. If ML Agents is not installed anywhere else, then these commands or
functions of ML Agents will not run unless it is in the associated virtual environment. We
can also deactivate our virtual environment and reactivate, which is similar to using the
activate command.

Advanced Local Installation for Modifying the ML Agents Environment

There is another aspect of installation of the "mlagents_envs" package that is required when we want to modify our training environments. Although this step is not compulsory, we should be able to install these modules separately as well. There are two ways to install the environments of the ML Agents.

- **Installation from PyPI:** The PyPI contains releases for the "mlagents_envs" package, which can be found in the link `https://pypi.org/project/mlagents-envs/`.

- The installation is done using the pip command:

  ```
  pip install mlagents-envs
  ```

- **Installation from ML Agents package:** For installing the environment from our cloned repository of ML Agents, we have to navigate to the root directory of the cloned repository in Anaconda prompt and then type:

  ```
  pip install  -e ./ml-agents-envs
  pip install  -e ./ml-agents
  ```

Installing them from the ML Agents cloned package has some prerequisites. The "-e" makes changes to all the dependencies of the ML Agents. If we are not using the pip command to install the environments, then we first have to install the "mlagetns-envs" before we install "mlagents." This is because mlagents depends on the "mlagents-envs" for its functionality. If we do it in the reverse order, then while we are installing "mlagents," the default mlagents-envs will be installed from PyPI.

This completes the entire installation process and also provides the different ways to install ML Agents. In the next section, we will take a look at the various components of this ML Agents package and how to link this with Python and Jupyter Notebooks.

Configuring Components of ML Agents: Brain and Academy

In this section, we will have an overview of the different components of the ML Agents package and try to understand the changes made in ML Agents from the previous and current version. The ML Agents package has three main parts that will be used for our deep learning:

- **mlagents**: This part contains the main source algorithms for deep RL for training our agents in Unity environments.

- **mlagents_envs**: This is essentially the Python API connecting the mlagents with the environment. Therefore, it is important to remember that Unity ML Agents relies on ML Agents environments.

- **gym_unity**: The wrapper over OpenAI's Gym environment that is used to convert our Unity Game Scenes into trainable deep learning environments

We can get into the details of each of the aforementioned folder structures and get to know each individual component, but without loss of generality, the mlagents folder will be extremely important to us for understanding the core PPO and SAC algorithmic implementation made by Unity and also how we can modify it. If we go to **mlagents ➤ trainers** folder, we can see several algorithms are present. Needless to say, this is the most important aspect, which we will be venturing later in the book. In the **mlagents-envs** folder, the most important part of the Python API linking is done by the **communicator_objects** folder. This particularly contains all the information related to connecting the local server to port 5004 while training ML Agents and also forms a bridge between the Tensorflow, Tensorboard, and C# Unity. Similarly, the **gym_unity** folder contains all the Unity environments and test folders that are converted to Gym environments during training of the RL Unity environment.

Now that we have installed and set up our ML Agents and had a brief overview of the three main parts, we will dive into the fundamental architecture of the ML Agents. This architecture pattern was initially released as a visualization of how the ML Agents works and has changed considerably in recent years. However fundamentally, though the architecture has been revamped into a more robust one, the core functionality runs on the baseline architecture: brain–academy architecture.

Brain-Academy Architecture

The fundamental concept regarding the initial build of ML Agents was to have agents that were controlled with the help of neural networks generally referred to as the brain of the agent. The academy was analogous to the environment, controlling the training of the brain as well as communicating with online models while running the agent or the simulation. Fundamentally, the brain architecture can be broadly classified as described here.

- **Internal brain:** This type of brain architecture contains pretrained models that have been trained using various deep learning algorithms. The internal brain does not require runtime communication with the Python API for training, as it already has been trained on a pre-existing set of observation-action space. All the example projects under Unity ML Agents have internal brain (pretrained network) associated with them.

- **Heuristic brain:** This type of brain normally does not contain any neural network model; rather, it contains a heuristic one. We discussed in Chapter 2 regarding heuristic pathfinding algorithms involving A*. These algorithms are included in this brain. Instead of using gradient descent-based deep learning, heuristic brains focus more on dynamic programming and state-based learning.

- **External brain:** The external brain is another brain that uses deep learning algorithms; however, this is used during training the agent in the Unity scene. The communicator object plays a significant role in communicating with the port 5004, where we train our model in Tensorflow. The external brain is used for training the agents in runtime through the communicator and the Python API. These trained models are then used as internal brains when passed as productionized and pretrained models for the agents.

The brain-academy architecture is shown in Figure 3-12.

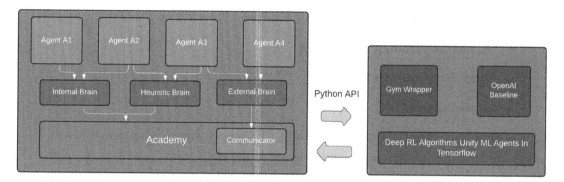

Brain - Academy Architecture Unity ML Agents
Abhilash Majumder | July 3, 2020

Figure 3-12. *Brain–academy architecture for Unity ML agents*

Academy: The Academy controls the collection of brains in the Environment and has access to the runtime environment. The scope of the environment that is controlled by the academy includes:

- **Unity Engine configuration:** This includes the speed, frames per second rate, and render pipeline associated with a particular game that is getting trained or running in Inference Mode.

- **Episode length:** This controls the episode length of the RL agent in the Unity GamePlay environment.

- **FrameSkip:** The number of Unity Engine sites to skip between each agent to make a new decision. This essentially factors out the number of frames that are not rendered, while the policy is getting updated in the training phase of the agent.

This is the central architecture model of the ML Agents that was present before the release of version 1.0. In the new release, the brain component (C# script) has been deprecated, and these are replaced with certain scripts that control the brain and the decision-making process of the agent.

Behavior and Decision Scripts in Unity ML Agents Version 1.0

The most important scripts that control the brain and the decision-making process are:

- **Behavior parameters C# script**
- **Decision requester C# script**
- **Model overrider C# script**

It is important to understand that in Unity ML Agents, there are sensors that are present to record any observation-action space in the environment. With the help of sensors, the agent will come to know about the different parts of the RL environment. These sensors are essentially rays (physics rays) that were used in our previous chapters to denote the position of an agent in the environment and also to check the distance between the agent and the reward.

To understand these changes, let us open the 3D Ball environment in Unity, and inside the 3D Ball Prefab, we will see two models: "Ball" and "Agent." The "Ball" prefab is the small sphere that the "Agent" prefab has to balance on its "head."

If we open the "Agent" prefab in the Inspector Window, we will see the different components and scripts associated with this prefab. Some of the details are generic, like transforms and box Cclliders; the other details require our attention. We can see that there are "Behavior Parameters," "Decision Requester," and "Model Overrider" C# scripts associated with this agent. There is also a "Ball 3D Agent" C# script attached as well, which we will see in a later section in this chapter. As mentioned, let us try to briefly understand these three different C# scripts.

- **Behavior parameters script:** The previous concept of brain architecture that had different types such as: internal, external, and heuristic are present in this script. The main purpose of this script is to determine whether the agent will run in Inference Mode (internal brain), in Heuristic Mode(heuristic brain), or in External Mode (external brain). This is shown in Figure 3-13.

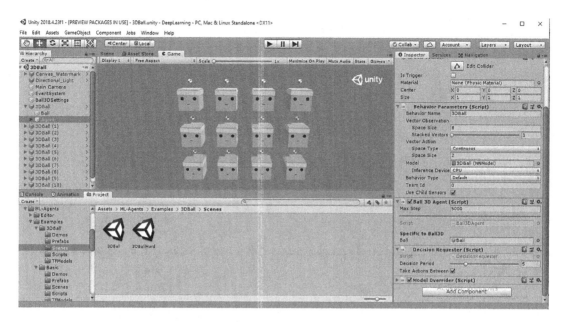

Figure 3-13. *Behavior parameter, decision requester, and model overrider scripts in the Inspector Window of "Agent" prefab in Unity*

It also controls the use of sensors, determines whether to use child sensors, and determines at a particular time-step which agent is searched for in a multi-agent training environment. We will explore more about this script in the next chapter when we will be considering the brain architecture in depth. For the time being, we can see that there are two important aspects inside this tab in the Inspector Window.

- **Model:** This contains the neural network model that is required during Inference Mode or during actual gameplay. This is the trained Tensorflow model that is placed in the internal brain. We can also select different pretrained models that are present in our scenes. This also contains the Inference Device—that is whether we want to run the model in CPU or GPU, as shown in Figure 3-14.

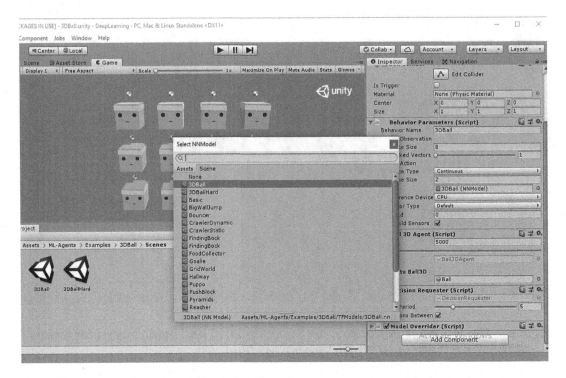

Figure 3-14. *Choosing the Neural Network model for the behavior parameters script*

- **Behavior type:** This controls the type of "Brain" we would want to use—internal, heuristic, or external. Depending on the behavior type, the agent tries to follow that particular policy for reward maximization. Fundamentally this can be thought of as the "Brain" architecture. It should be noted that in case there are no pretrained models for the internal brain to work upon, during the training stage of our model we will be using the external brain. Later this trained external brain can be stored in Unity and later used as the internal brain. The heuristic brain should be present if we don't want to use deep RL algorithms for our agents. Figure 3-15. represents the behaviors.

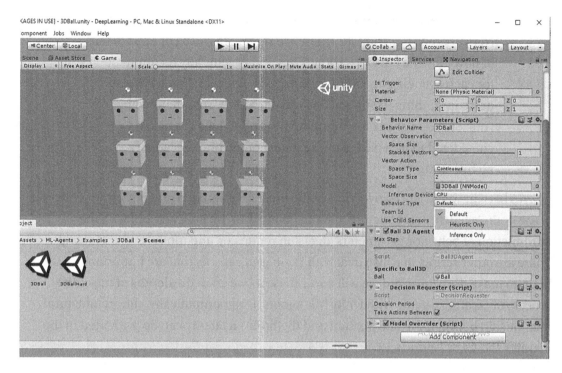

Figure 3-15. *Behavior types in the Inspector Window controlling brains*

There are several other attributes as well, and we will discuss all of these in depth in the next chapter. For now, it is important to understand the importance of behavior parameters as the fundamental brain of the ML Agents.

- **Decision requester script:** This script is associated with the decision-making process of the agent over its action space. This script also contains the frequency at which the decision is taken by the agent according to a particular policy and also moderates whether the agent can take actions in between decisions. This is related to the academy of the Brain-Academy Architecture Model, as it controls the decision-making process in academy steps. Again we will explore this further in the next chapter. It also contains variables such as "Decision Period," which defaults to 5, denoting the frequency of taking decisions and "Take Actions Between" (Boolean) variable, which allows the agent to take actions between decisions if checked.

179

- **Model overrider script:** This is used to override an existing Neural
  Network model during the inference stage. This also contains details
  of how long the episodes should run and is generally recommended
  for each agent having one behavior parameters (1:1 ratio). It also
  helps in running the neural network for a time-step denoted by
  "maxSteps" to check for failure in the model. This can also be
  considered to be a part of the academy of the brain–academy
  architecture.

We have now had a brief overview of the most fundamental and important concepts
of the brain–academy architecture and the changes in the new version, with the
introduction of behavior parameters, decision requester, and model overrider scripts.
There are other scripts that also deal with ray-based sensors that are important for the
brain to make decisions, and we will cover these as we go in the depths of the entire
process of creating a game with Unity ML Agents. Diagrammatically, the architectural
relationship between the new version and the brain-academy can be presented in the
manner shown in Figure 3-16.

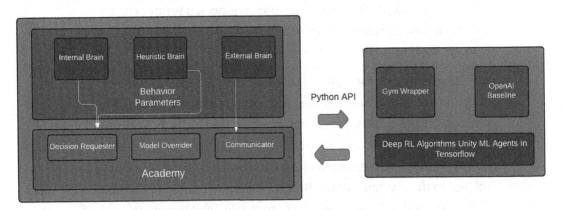

Figure 3-16. Relationship between the new and old architectures

Linking Unity ML Agents with Tensorflow

This section would mostly rely on linking the ML Agents Neural Network Model with Tensorflow, the deep learning framework that we will be using throughout. The link between the Unity C# ML Agents SDK code and the deep learning algorithms in Python is done with the help of the communicator object that we studied briefly at the start of this chapter. However, it is interesting to note that during training, we can use the implementations of the PPO and SAC algorithms provided by Unity in a very simplified manner through the Anaconda prompt environment. Inside the "trainers" folder in "mlagents" (discussed previously), we saw the different implementations of algorithms. However, currently we need to only understand how to refer these ML models with the prebuilt Unity ML Agents environments. For this, we require the "config" folder inside the ML Agents cloned repository. This contains several files with the extension "yaml." Essentially these are files that contain the hyperparameters required when we are training a neural network model in Tensorflow. But before training, let us understand something about Barracuda, the Unity Inference Engine.

Barracuda: Unity Inference Engine

The Unity ML Agents Toolkit is used for running pretrained neural network models using the Inference Mode (internal brain), as mentioned previously. This is done with the help of the Unity Inference Engine or Barracuda. This is a lightweight library that assists in converting neural network models (from Tensorflow) to serialized files with the extension ".nn." The Inference Engine is compatible with both C# Mono as well as Intermediate Language To C++ (ILCPP2). The ILCPP2 is a scripting backend that runs on C++ and is greatly helpful for reducing the size of the game; it works by performing bytecode stripping of the .NET DLL files from C# and produces a native binary file that is lightweight and faster. This choice is also present when we select the build settings for building our games. The Inference Engine supports two different formats, as described here.

- **Barracuda**: The ".nn" file format containing the trained neural network models. This is done by the "tensorflow_to_barracuda.py" Python script. We will be taking a look at this in the next chapters as well when we try to understand serialization of the neural network model.

- **ONNX**: This is "onnx" file format, which is an industry standard open
  format for cross-functional neural network model support produced
  by the "tf2onnx package."

The Inference Engine can be seen inside the behavior parameters script. We saw that
under the "Model" section there is an inference device attribute where we can select
CPU or GPU. This enables the Inference Engine to run on the device. Unless we are using
Resnet or VGG16 (Computer Vision models), we should be alright using CPU as our
Inference Engine device. Figure 3-17 shows the inference devices.

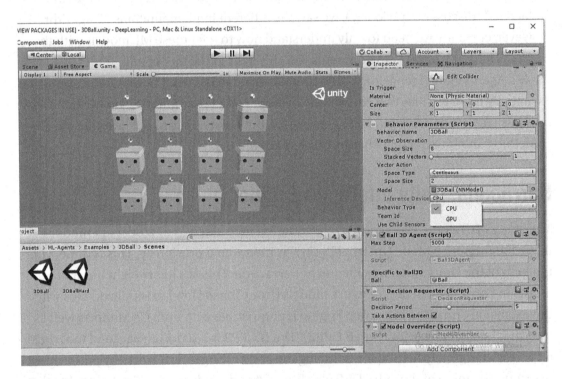

Figure 3-17. *The Inference device (CPU/GPU) for the Inference Engine to run*

Now that we have an idea how Tensorflow-trained networks are stored in Unity
through Barracuda, we can train a prebuilt model using the 3D Balls example.

Training 3D Ball Environment with Unity ML Agents

Let us navigate to the "config" folder in the repository and look inside its contents. We will be using the "trainer_config.yaml" file to train our model through Anaconda prompt. There are other several yaml files, like "gail_config.yaml" and "sac_trainer_config.yaml". However, for us, we will be using the "trainer_config.yaml" default file, which relies on the PPO algorithm for training. Let us take a look inside the "yaml" file.

On opening, we see a list of parameters (hyperparameters) that are used to train our neural network. For now let us think of these hyperparameters as certain attributes that will help in the training process. We have a default set of hyperparameters, which looks like the following:

```
default:
  trainer: ppo
  batch_size: 1024
  beta: 5.0e-3
  buffer_size: 10240
  epsilon: 0.2
  hidden_units: 128
  lambd: 0.95
  learning_rate: 3.0e-4
  learning_rate_schedule: linear
  max_steps: 5.0e5
  memory_size: 128
  normalize: false
  num_epoch: 3
  num_layers: 2
  time_horizon: 64
  sequence_length: 64
  summary_freq: 100
  use_recurrent: false
  vis_encode_type: simple
  reward_signals:
    extrinsic:
      strength: 1.0
      gamma: 0.99
```

As we see, there are several parameters like the "trainer: ppo," which signifies that the PPO model is used for this environment. Also we have several attributes, like memory size, max steps, number of epochs, batch size, and so on. All these have their own significance, which we will look at in depth in "Deep Learning" chapter. It is safe to assume that the training environment is governed with the help of these hyperparameters that specify what algorithm to use, the states and rewards, the memory size for holding the information of the observation space, how long the training will continue, and the time gap between the actions the agent chooses. This "default" module is used for training any environment where it is not specified which hyperparameters upon which to train. But in our case, we will be using the 3D Ball hyperparameter set, which looks like this:

```
3DBall:
  normalize: true
  batch_size: 64
  buffer_size: 12000
  summary_freq: 12000
  time_horizon: 1000
  lambd: 0.99
  beta: 0.001
```

In this case, we have a smaller set of hyperparameters compared to this one. We have the batch size, which controls the size of the batch for the training, and the buffer size, which contains the size of the replay buffer or memory. The "lambd" and "beta" are hyperparameters that govern the learning rate. Additionally we have another set of hyperparameters for the 3D Ball Hard environment, as shown here:

```
3DBallHard:
  normalize: true
  batch_size: 1200
  buffer_size: 12000
  summary_freq: 12000
  time_horizon: 1000
  max_steps: 5.0e6
  beta: 0.001
```

```
reward_signals:
  extrinsic:
    strength: 1.0
    gamma: 0.995
```

Therefore, for now we briefly have an idea of the hyperparameters contained inside the "trainer_config.yaml" file. Now let us open the Anaconda prompt environment, and then inside the Prompt, we have to navigate to the directory containing the "trainer_config.yaml" file. After that we have to type the command:

```
mlagents-learn trainer_config.yaml --run-id=new3DBall -train
```

The "trainer_config.yaml" is the yaml file that we mentioned before. This lets ML Agents know that we want to use the "3D Ball" module from the "trainer_config.yaml" file. The run-ID signifies the name of the new model that we are training. Generally the syntax for training can be written as:

```
mlagents-learn <path to trainer_config.yaml file> --run-id=<new name for
the trained model> --train
```

The –train command is optional in the new version and can be omitted as well. Now we are using the hyperparameters mentioned in the "trainer_config.yaml," but we know that there are other yaml files as well that contain a different training algorithm and different set of hyperparameters. For instance, if we are to train it with the help of the "sac_trainer_config.yaml" file, then the syntax would have been :

```
mlagents-learn <path to sac_trainer_config.yaml file> --run-id=<new name
for the trained model> --train
```

If we are in the "config" folder to run our command, then it can be simplified as:

```
mlagents-learn sac_trainer_config.yaml --run-id=sac3DBall --train
```

Once done, we will see that Unity ML Agents starts connecting to the Python API through port 5004 and then uses the Tensorflow library to start the training process.

After some time there will be an option that shows up in the Anaconda Prompt Window, noting that the 3D Ball environment has to be played in Unity Editor for external training to take place. If the Unity Editor environment is not in play mode then, the API times out, and the training is not done. Therefore, we need to go to Editor ➤

Project Settings ➤ Player. Inside the Player section, we have to go to the "Resolution and Presentation" section and check the "Run In Background" option. This will enable the Unity Engine Editor to run while we are training the model in the Anaconda Prompt Window, as shown in Figure 3-18.

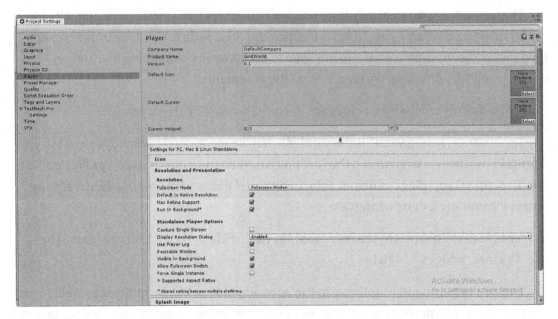

Figure 3-18. *Configuring Player (run in background) in project settings*

If we start our training process, it should appear something like Figure 3-19, plus this time there is a Unity logo to be displayed, as shown in Figure 3-19.

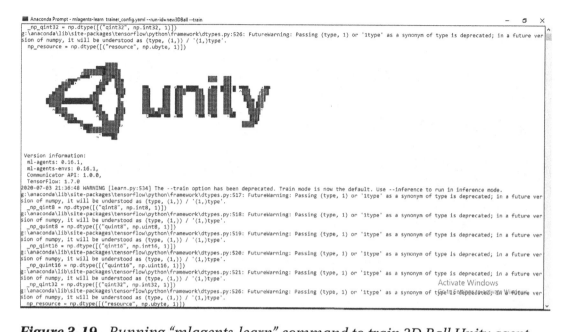

Figure 3-19. *Running "mlagents-learn" command to train 3D Ball Unity agent*

Once the training starts, we will see the version of "mlagents," "mlagents-envs," Python Communicator API, and Tensorflow. We will be prompted with the option to click Play in the Unity Editor scene to start the training process for external brain. This would look like the image shown in Figure 3-20.

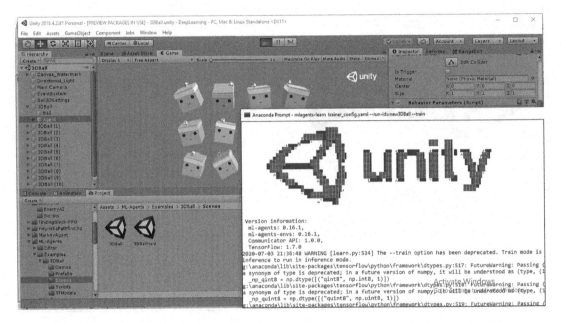

Figure 3-20. *3D Ball environment training with PPO deep learning algorithm in Unity ML agents and Tensorflow*

We will see that the agents try to balance the balls or spheres on their heads, and in many cases during the initial stages, the balls fall off their heads during training. This credits a negative reward to the agent, and as learning progresses we will gradually see the agents learning to balance the balls. Moreover, we have the hyperparameters displayed on the screen that are received from the "trainer_config.yaml" file. A preview of the training process is shown in Figure 3-21.

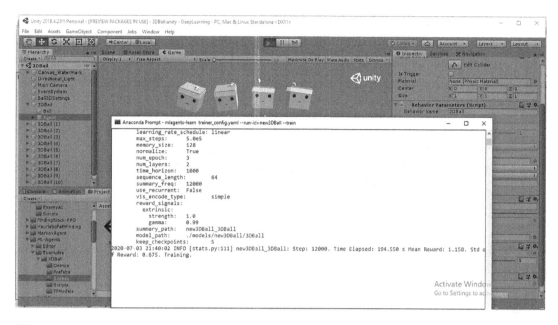

Figure 3-21. *Hyperparameters, rewards, and steps in the training process*

We now see that the agent learns gradually, and the logs in the Anaconda prompt also reveal the mean or average rewards and standard deviation of the rewards for every 12,000 steps, which is mentioned as a hyperparameter. If we let this train for a long time (let's say an hour, on average), we will see the rewards gradually increasing as the agent becomes more adept to balance the ball on it. Now let's visualize this learning in TensorBoard.

Visualization with TensorBoard

We know that TensorBoard is a visualization tool and have installed the same in Chapter 1, when we were trying out deep Q-learning in the CartPole environment. Now in this section, we will link the training that is happening in the Anaconda prompt with Unity ML Agents with Tensorboard for proper visualization of the rewards and other details. For this we have to open another Anaconda prompt terminal and navigate to the "config" folder like before in the ML Agents repository. Inside the folder, there is a "summaries" folder that holds the TensorBoard visualization statistics for the particular model being trained. The command for starting and linking with TensorBoard is:

```
tensorboard --logdir=summaries
```

Once this is done, we will have a message in Anaconda prompt showing the port number 6006 and also the http details to visualize. By default, TensorBoard operates from port 6006, and the link is of type http://<device-name>:6006, where device –name is the name of the computer system we are working on. This would be something like the image shown in Figure 3-22.

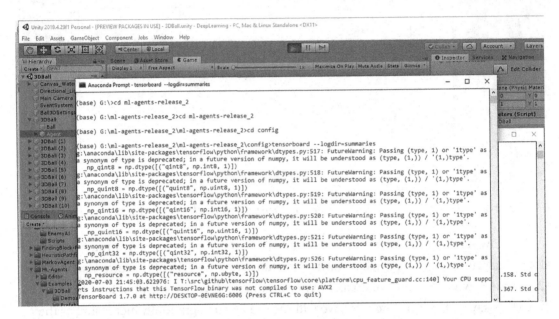

Figure 3-22. *Launching TensorBoard for Unity ML Agents*

The TensorBoard visualization shows the rewards and the steps completed in a particular epoch along with the loss of the deep learning algorithm (PPO). This is an interactive visualization tool, and as time progresses, we would see the values of the rewards increase. We will be exploring each of the TensorBoard modules separately, but in a nutshell, this dashboard provides an interactive view of the loss rate, the accuracy, rewards collected, mean rewards, standard deviation of the rewards, as well as the steps. This will be beneficial for us when we build our own agents in Unity and train them using ML Agents in the future chapters. The dashboard is presented in Figure 3-23.

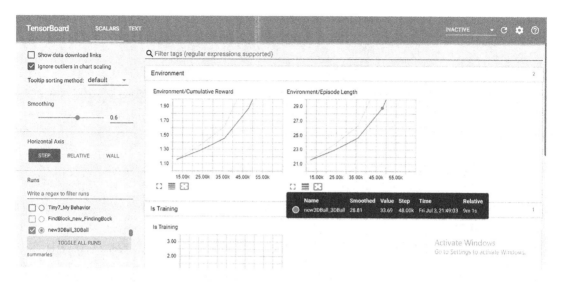

Figure 3-23. *The TensorBoard dashboard during training of the 3D Ball environment*

So we have now seen how to link Tensorflow to train our ML Agents in Unity and also how to link TensorBoard for interactive visualization during the training process. We can close the training whenever we like by stopping the Play mode in Unity.

Editor

Now if we want to visualize the trained new model (named "new3DBall") in the scene, we can navigate to the behavior parameters script in the "Agent" prefab, and in the place of "Model," we can select the ("new3DBall") model. We can then see, on playing in the Editor, that Unity Engine is now using the Unity Inference Engine and feeding the agent with the new trained model (Inference Mode). This is how a trained external brain is converted into an internal brain that can be used inside the Unity Editor. This brain is trained on PPO using the OpenAI Gym wrapper in Unity's environments to provide an actual AI agent that can balance the sphere. We can go ahead and also create a Unity executable simulation game with this trained neural network model by clicking on the Build Option after configuring the Build Settings from he Menu. On placing the newly trained model inside the "Model" section of the "Behavior Parameters" script, we should see something like that shown in Figure 3-24.

191

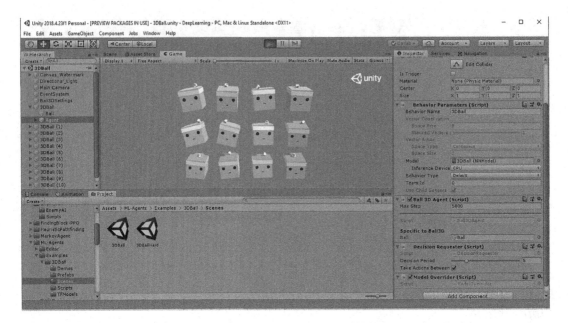

Figure 3-24. *Using a trained neural network as an internal brain for the 3D Ball agent*

By now, we have an idea of the scope of Unity ML Agents and have also trained a new neural network model with the help of ML Agents and Tensorflow and published a new simulation game based on the PPO algorithm of deep RL. In the further chapters, we will go into the depths of each of these separate modules of deep learning algorithms and also create simulations and games using the Unity ML Agents. We will also see how to harness the power of the Baselines Model of OpenAI to train our new games in Unity with the help of ML Agents and Python API. In the next section, we will play around with some of the sample examples of Unity scenes and get to know the diversity of the environments.

Playing Around with Unity ML Agents Examples

We have already seen the "3D Balls" environment and the "Basic" environment. Now let us have a brief overview of the other environments that are present inside the ML Agents Example folder. For each environment, we will have an overview of the agents, rewards, goals, and adversaries as well as the type of brain and Sensors used. One important thing to note is that in each of these environments we will notice the vector action space and whether it is discrete or continuous. This will help us to understand the diversity of the

environments and also the complexity of training each agent. We will be discussing 15
additional environments, so that for now we can train them by using the lessons learned
from the previous section.

- **Bouncer environment:** In this Unity environment, shown in
  Figure 3-25, the blue agent has to "jump" or "bounce" to reach the
  green target, which is at an elevated position from the ground. The
  agent is rewarded for each correct jump. Here we have the behavior
  parameters script, and it contains the bouncer neural network
  pretrained model. The vector observation-action space is continuous
  in this case, which is suitable for deep learning algorithms. For
  training in this environment using PPO or SAC (or ghost/GAIL),
  the process is very similar, as we have to run the "mlagents-learn"
  command in Anaconda prompt and pass the location of the "yaml"
  file for training.

```
mlagents-learn trainer_config.yaml --run-id=newBounce -train
```

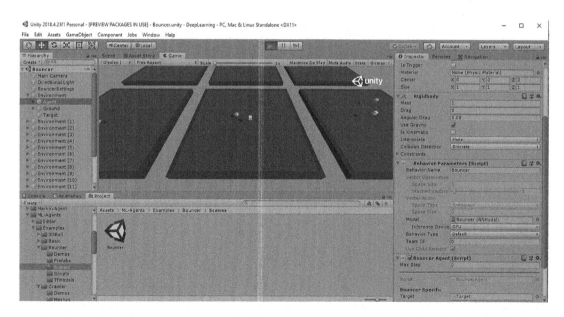

Figure 3-25. *Bouncer environment Unity ML Agents*

- **Crawler environment:** In this environment, shown in Figure 3-26, the crawler is a collection of joints. It resembles an insect that tries to find the green target (food). The crawler is rewarded for each correct finding; additionally, there are two variants: static and dynamic platforms. The crawler is a very complicated prefab, as the rewards here are driven by the motion and vector direction of the joints of the crawler system. While this may be intimidating at first to understand, we will be using this for training our Puppo, which also has a joint-based system. The vector space is continuous, and the details of the behavior parameters are also shown. The joint system comprises the joints in the legs of the agent, which helps it to move. The direction of the vector and the joint rotation play an important aspect in deciding the reward, as the nearer the crawler gets to the food, the greater the chances of getting rewarded. However, we can train this agent as well using our knowledge of the "mlagents-learn" command and can observe the way the crawler moves toward its target.

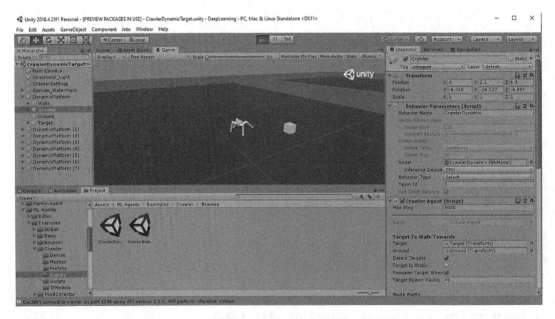

Figure 3-26. *Crawler environment in Unity ML Agents*

- **Food collector environment:** This is a different kind of a search environment, where the agent has to collect food (green target cubes) in a minefield filled with different prefabs and objects. This is shown in Figure 3-27. Here we can see a pink line that is effectively an extended sensor ray with which the agent It is important to note that in this case, the vector observation space is discrete, and to transform it into a deep learning model, this has to be converted into a multi-discrete vector space. Additionally, this can be trained in Unity ML Agents using the "mlagents-learn" command.

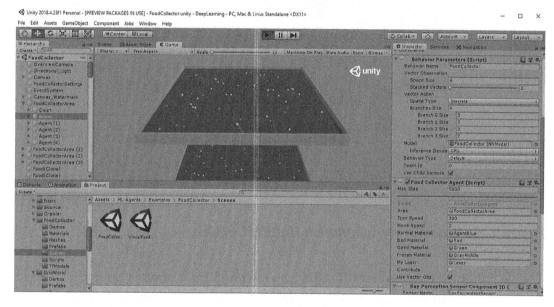

Figure 3-27. *GridWorld environment Unity ML Agents*

- **GridWorld environment:** This is an advanced environment, as it comprises computer vision and deep RL, shown in Figure 3-28. Here the agent is the "0" sign (blue-colored), whose goal is to reach toward the "+"(green sign). In this case we will be using Resnet, a SOTA computer vision model made with different Convolution Neural Networks. In addition to the behavior parameters script, we also have a camera sensor component script attached to the agent. This uses the compressed visual information in terms of pixels for Resnet deep network to train. Then the outcome of the computer vision model is passed on as the decisions used by the behavior script to navigate the agent ("0") toward the "+" green sign. Here, too, the vector space is discrete, and the model can be trained using the "mlagents-learn" command. This is an interesting environment, and we will use this when we try to understand computer vision models in deep RL.

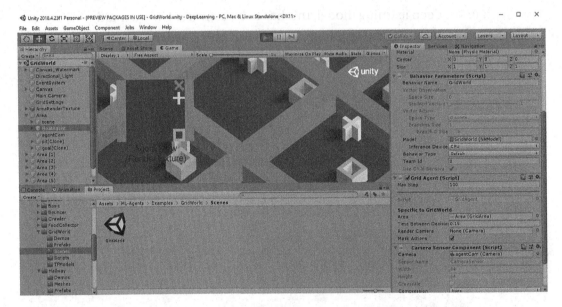

Figure 3-28. *GridWorld environment Unity ML Agents*

- **Hallway environment:** The Hallway environment is another unique environment where the blue agent has to navigate itself toward either the "X" or the "0" poles. There is a block in the center where, in each turn, a unique symbol (either "X" or "0") is shown. The agent has to remember what symbol was shown by the central block and should navigate itself automatically to the pole having the similar sign. If "X" is shown in the central block, the agent will go to the "X" pole and vice versa. It can be stated here that in this case, the agent should heavily rely on memory-based networks to store visual information regarding the symbol shown on the central block. Here, there are two variants, and one of them requires computer vision models, such as Resnet. However, there are certain other networks such as LSTM and recurrent neural networks (RNNs), that can be used to add more memory to the agent. We will be discussing this in more detail in the chapter on deep RL. In this case, we have a discrete vector observation space in the behavior parameters that can be trained by using the "mlagents-train" command and specifying the nature of the algorithm and the "yaml" file. Figure 3-29 shows a preview of the environment.

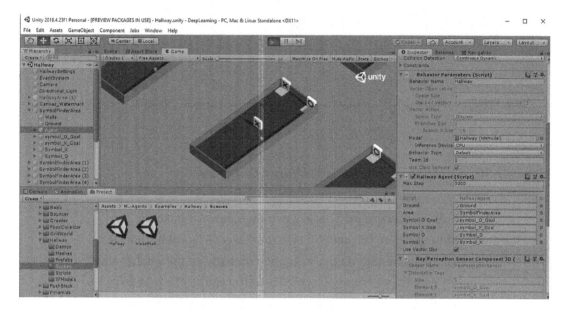

Figure 3-29. *Hallway environment Unity ML agents*

- **PushBlock environment:** This is a simple environment where the blue agent has to push the larger block toward the green checkpost. This is done by using sensor rays that collide with a collider and check whether the object in sight is the bigger cube, and then it pushes it toward the goal. Here also, the vector space is discrete, and we can train the model, as shown in Figure 3-30.

197

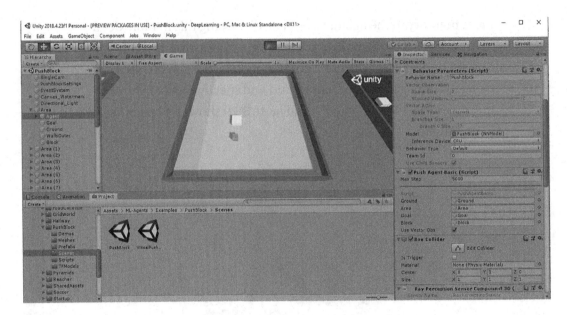

Figure 3-30. *PushBlock environment Unity ML Agents*

- **Pyramids environment:** This is a two-step, reward-based environment where the agent has to first target a "switch" placed inside an obstacle-laden environment. Once the agent reaches the switch, a new target emerges, which is in the shape of a pyramid. The agent then has to search for the pyramid. This is a simple twofold reward-validation environment, and we will be exploring it further in later chapters. Here, too, the vector space is discrete. This is presented in Figure 3-31.

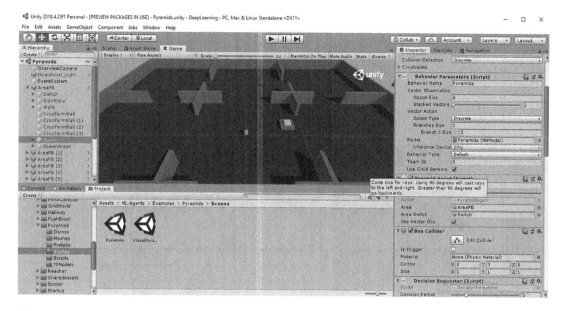

Figure 3-31. *Pyramid environment Unity ML Agents*

- **Reacher environment:** This is a rather challenging environment where the agent has to control robotic arms with the goal of keeping the ends of the arms within the green sphere, as shown in Figure 3-32. This is a deep RL problem that requires advanced learning algorithms so as to control the direction of motion of the arms. The 20 robotic arms in the environment are controlled by a single agent with a continuous vector space of actions. Later we will exclusively use this particular environment when we will learn about off policy deep deterministic policy gradients (DDPGs) and other advanced algorithms. However, for the time being, we can train this Reacher agent with the Unity ML Agents PPO algorithm and hyperparameters from the "trainer_config.yaml" file.

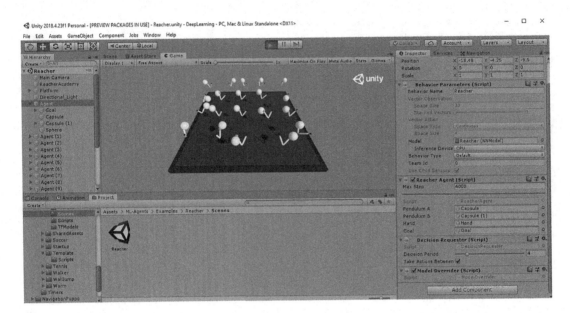

Figure 3-32. *Reacher environment Unity ML Agents*

- **Soccer environment:** This is a very popular and interesting environment that is extensively used in most of the games such as FIFA (Electronic Arts) and Google Dopamine Football playground. This is shown in Figure 3-33. This is actually a zero-sum game where adversarial teams have to play against each other to score a goal. This can be modeled into a football game where the goal scored by one team will negatively affect the other team. The rewards are provided to the winning teams, and negative rewards are provided to the teams that are unable to score the goal—the teams being the purple and blue agents. This will be used when we learn about adversarial self-play algorithms in RL, which operate on policies similar to mini-max (two-person, 0 sum) and alpha beta pruning algorithms. The space here is discrete, and here, too, we have sensor rays that are used to determine the location of the soccer ball (football) and the goal.

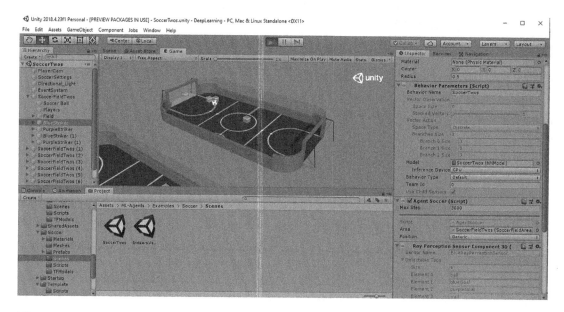

Figure 3-33. *Soccer environment Unity ML Agents*

- **Tennis environment:** This is a classic environment where two agents play a game of tennis, which is along similar lines to the game of soccer, as shown in Figure 3-34. Here we will see that if any of the agents miss hitting the tennis ball, negative rewards are credited. There are two different algorithmic paradigms that can be used here. Imitation learning with adversarial networks can help the agent to learn by a robust behavioral cloning policy. Again, we can use curriculum learning, which implies increasing the challenges step by step for a particular agent (continuous vector space).

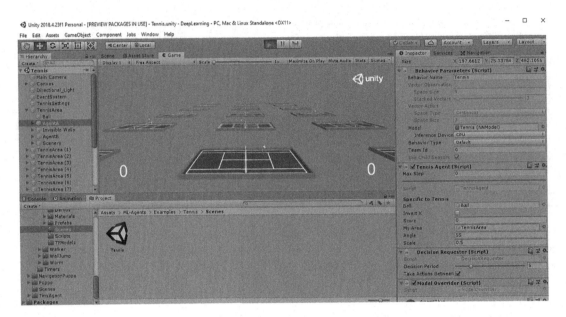

Figure 3-34. *Tennis environment Unity ML Agents*

- **Walker environment:** This is similar to the crawler environment,
  and the agent is a humanoid robot made up of a system of joints.
  However, unlike searching for targets, the main goal here is for the
  humanoid agent to walk with the help of its joints. This is also a
  complex challenge that relies on the joint-based system. Without
  loss of generality, the agent uses the direction vector of its joints to
  move forward and balance itself, collecting rewards for every time-
  step it is able to do so. Since all joint-based systems rely heavily on
  advanced deep RL techniques, the vector space is continuous. The
  environment is shown in Figure 3-35.

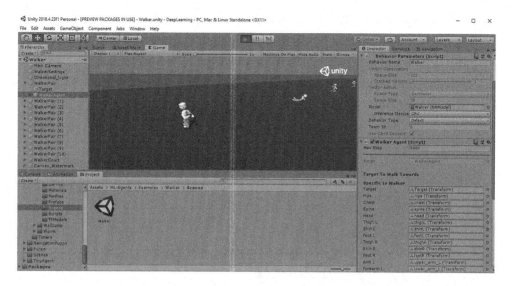

Figure 3-35. *Walker environment Unity ML Agents*

- **WallJump environment:** Similar to the PushBlock and Pyramid
  environments, the agent here has to jump over the wall to reach
  the target (green position), shown in Figure 3-36. This is a simple
  environment using sensor rays with continuous vector space
  observations. The agent is rewarded for every successful jump over
  the bigger cube ("wall").

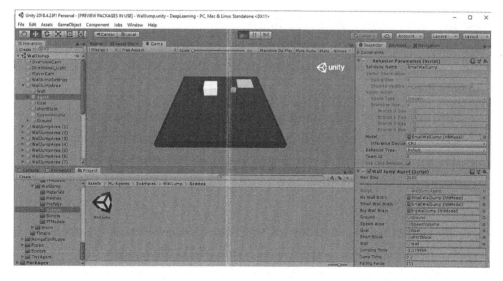

Figure 3-36. *WallJump environment Unity ML Agents*

- **Worm environment:** Similar to crawler, this joint-based agent resembles a worm that has to find green target cubes (food). It uses the similar policies of joint rotation and directions to calculate rewards and requires deep learning algorithms to train. Figure 3-37 shows a preview of the environment.

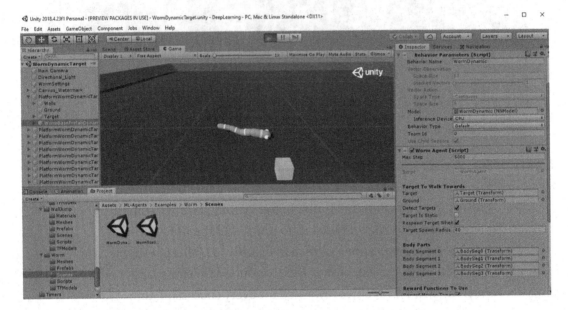

Figure 3-37. *Worm environment Unity ML Agents*

These are the various environments that are present inside the ML Agents Example folder. Needless to say, all these environments are very distinct and diverse in terms of observation-action space, rewards, environments, and adversaries. There are certain key points to note here:

- With our current understanding of training ML Agents, we can train all the environments by using the "mlagents-learn" command and specifying the "yaml" file we would like to use as hyperparameters for the training. We can also visualize each of the training agents in TensorBoard.

- There are certain environments, such as crawler, walker, and worm, that rely on a joint-based physics system, and in these cases, deep RL algorithms such as DDPG, TRPO, PPO, and AC can be used over continuous vector observation space. These will be taken up separately in later chapters of advanced deep RL. The training here relies on the joint dynamics and vector directions.

- Competitive environments such as soccer and tennis rely heavily on minimax strategy or zero-sum game with deep RL. With that, in the case of tennis, we will also investigate how adversarial imitation learning can help the agent as well as explain the core concepts of curriculum learning.

- Standard environments, such as Bounce, PushBlock, WallJump, pyramid, and food collector, rely on ray-based sensor data as information of the observation space of vectors and then use the external brain and RL algorithms to train. This will be used as a starting point to create deep RL games in Unity ML Agents.

- Computer vision and memory-based environments like GridWorld and hallway are very interesting, as these environments use Resnet models and deep convolution layers for retrieval of pixel information using the Unity camera. Then these are passed as continuous vector space observations to the brain or behavior scripts to make decisions. We also saw how LSTM-based memory networks play a significant role in the hallway environment and will be seeing it in later chapters.

Summary

With this we come to the end of this chapter, which mainly revolved around installing Unity ML Agents and other libraries and also providing a brief overview of the architecture of ML Agents, model training, and linking with the Tensorflow framework. To summarize:

- We installed Unity ML Agents from the Github repository as well as through the command line. We also had a glimpse of the "releases" link on Unity ML Agents. Installation from the Unity Package Manager was done, and we came to know about the importance of the "package.json" file.

- We then locally installed Unity ML Agents from PyPI as well as created virtual environments for robust CI/CD pipelines. Advanced installation was also conducted with the help of pip commands for "mlagents-envs."

- We understood the entire architecture of the fundamental components of ML Agents and how Unity C# SDK is linked to the Python API for deep learning models. We also installed Baselines from OpenAI and trained a deep Q-network. This will be helpful when we incorporate Baseline models in the Deep Reinforcement Learning chapter.

- The brain–academy architecture was visualized in depth with information regarding internal, heuristic, and external brains. The combination of brain and other hyperparameters are placed inside the academy, which also contains communicator objects. The communicator is responsible for linking ML Agents with the Python API for external training.

- We saw the new architecture design of ML Agents version 1.0 having behavior parameters, decision requester, and model overrider scripts. We understood the behavior parameters to be analogous to the brain of the agents and the other two scripts as part of the academy.

- Next we linked Tensorflow (port:5004) and TensorBoard (port:6006) with Unity ML Agents and trained the 3D Balls environment using the PPO algorithm. We used the "mlagents-learn" command and specified the "trainer_config.yaml" file, which contained the hyperparameters for training. We also saw the contents of the "yaml" file. We then linked TensorBoard with ML Agents to have a visualization of the rewards, loss, mean rewards, and time-steps of the training process.

- After training, we then used the trained model as the Inference Model (internal brain) for the 3D Ball agent and played the scene in the Unity Editor. We created a simulation game with the trained model using the build option.

- In the last section, we saw the 15 different environments apart from "Basic" and "3D Ball" environments. Each environment was distinct and had its own behavior parameters and brains. We came to know curriculum learning, computer vision models as well as memory-based models in deep RL. We will look into each of these in the next chapters based on the topics.

With that, we come to the end of this chapter. In the next chapter we will be learning about the brain architecture in more details and will also create a simulation game with the same.

CHAPTER 4

Understanding brain agents and academy

The brain architecture is an important aspect of the ML Agents Toolkit. In the previous chapter, we installed the ML Agents Toolkit and also learned briefly about this architecture. Internally the ML Agents Toolkit uses three different kinds of brains, with the addition of a player brain that is controlled by the user. We concern ourselves with understanding the inner workings of certain scripts in the ML Agents package, which uses the neural networks trained in Tensorflow in Unity Agents. Since we have tried to get a glimpse of deep Q-learning as the only deep RL algorithm as of now, we can also use this algorithm to train the brain of the agent. Whereas in Unity ML Agents, the default algorithm for the internal brain is proximal policy operation (PPO), which is robust and has a comfortable balance between ease of implementation, sample tuning, and complexity, we will explore different algorithms that will be used as the brain for the agent. In this section, we will have a deep insight into the brain architecture and all the associated C# scripts associated with it, including the different aspects of model training and hyperparameter tuning. We will be building games using ML Agents in Unity.

Before we dive into the associated scripts, let us recap certain aspects from the previous chapter where we emphasized the brain-academy architecture. Since the brain is primarily of three types—internal, heuristic, and external—we will concentrate mostly on certain aspects of the internal brain, which uses the Barracuda Inference Engine, and the xternal brain, which uses a communicator object to train the agent in real-time in Tensorflow. We mentioned the usage of certain scripts such as behavior parameters, which we will be exploring in-depth in this chapter. We would also look into how the engine configures itself when it is not connected to Python API via port 5004 for external training. The most important aspects of the brain architecture, in terms of C# scripts,

© Abhilash Majumder 2021
A. Majumder, *Deep Reinforcement Learning in Unity*, https://doi.org/10.1007/978-1-4842-6503-1_4

are found in the Runtime folder under the "com.unity.ml-agents" package. The building blocks of the entire brain architecture, which uses several policies, relies on Inference Engine, sensors, communicators, demonstrators, and model loaders. Each of these parts constitute a separate functionality for the brain, such as the Inference Engine, which helps to run trained Tensorflow models in Unity. Since all these components are C# scripts, the brain architecture can be visualized as shown in Figure 4-1.

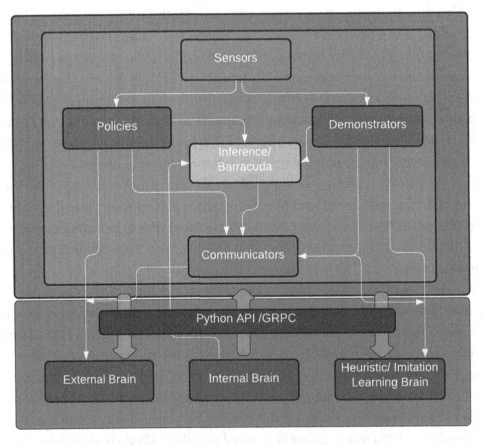

Parts of Brain Architecture in Unity ML Agents

Abhilash Majumder | July 10, 2020

Figure 4-1. *Parts of the brain architecture in Unity ML Agents*

The sensors are the most important aspects of the brain architecture, as it controls the observation space required by the agent to make its decision and choose its action. The sensors are physics rays, which collect information in the form of discrete and continuous vectors, and these are used in the model training part. The sensor data is then used by the policies that control the deep RL algorithms, like PPO and (soft actor critic) SAC, of Unity ML Agents. The policies along with the communicator are associated with the external brain. The external brain is trained in Tensorflow in run-time, like we trained our model in the last chapter. The demonstrations are a different set of algorithms that rely on imitation learning and behavioral cloning, and these too rely on sensor data. Through the communicator, the demonstrations can be trained as a sampled heuristic/external brain, which implements the family of imitation learning. Then we have the Inference Engine, which is used for the pretrained models. The Inference Engine receives the trained vector of observations/actions space. This is then used as the internal brain. The Inference Engine also has a choice to use sensor data processed using the deep RL algorithms in the policies as well as the observed data from the pretrained models. This final neural network model that is stored can be used for real-time game play in Unity. Now that we understand the important aspects of the brain, let us get into the details of its implementation as well as the communication with different Python APIs.

Understanding the Architecture of the Brain

To understand the different aspects of the brain architecture, we will try to understand the C# scripts associated with it. Since the sensors play a significant part in collecting observations for the agent, we will be discussing the different types of sensors that we can use in our scenes. The sensors are physics rays and are used for collecting observations when they collide with another GameObject in the scene. These control the distribution of the observation space, whether it will be discrete or continuous. We will explore the different types of sensors used for getting the observations required for the ML Agents training phase. This sensor data is then encoded to produce a tensor, such as one-hot encoding technique, and then passed on to deep learning layers for different policies. Inside the sensors folder, there are several types of sensors that are used by ML Agents: camera sensor, ray sensor, ray perception 2D sensor, and many others. Each sensor type has unique attributes, and we will be exploring all of these in this section. Then we will be looking into the policies that contain the training algorithms for deep RL. This will also contain the fundamental script of the brain architecture that we studied briefly in the Chapter 3, the behavior parameters C# script. We will also be exploring the inference module in-depth to understand how Barracuda performs inference for the Internal brain during running of the pretrained model.

Sensors

Sensors are the most important aspects in the entire ML Agents Toolkit package. This contains the observation space and controls the distribution of the space. Depending on these observations, the agent has to choose a policy and perform an action. These sensors are essentially ray sensors from the Physics Engine of Unity and collect information upon colliding with a tagged prefab. First we will look into the ISensor.cs script, as it contains the main methods that will be used by ray sensors as well as camera sensors. We will then look into some of the different sensor variants that are present in this folder. Essentially the pipeline of using sensors for collection of observations can be visualized as shown in Figure 4-2.

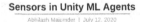

Sensors in Unity ML Agents

Abhilash Majumder | July 12, 2020

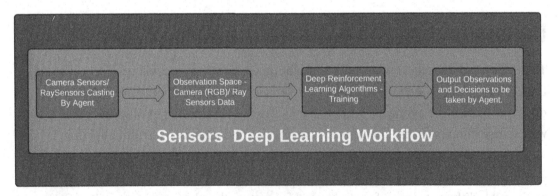

Figure 4-2. Sensors in Unity ML Agents

ISensor: The ISensor is an interface containing all the function declarations that are to be used for the different sensors in ML Agents. It contains functions that affect the camera sensor by changing the data type of the visual observations as well as the ray sensors by modifying the type of ray casts (2D or 3D). The ISensor script starts with an enum that defines the possibilities of storing visual information collected from camera sensors, whether it will be in the form of float arrays or in PNG format (binary format).

```
public enum SensorCompressionType
  {
    None,
    PNG
  }
```

The next segment has a method, "GetObservationShape," which controls the size of the observation space that will be used in RayPerceptionSensor script. As an example, in the case of ray sensors, if the sensor is observing the velocity vector of a RigidBody then its dimensions will be of size 3 (x, y, and z axes). However, in the case of a camera sensor, if an RGB pixel image is used, then the observation space would be 5 (height, width, and three channels for RGB). The latter will be discussed in detail how when we discuss how convolution neural networks (Conv2D) will be helpful in training these sampled images from the camera sensor. It also has a method, "Write," which writes the observations to the output container (array). The "GetCompressedObservation" method is useful for compressing the output array of results when the dimensions or the size of the output is considerably large. Apart from these, there are also "Update" and "Reset" methods, which specify the internal states of the sensor. The "Update" method updates the sensors at each decision taken by the agent, while the "Reset" method is triggered at the end of each episode of the agent. There are also "GetCompressionType" and "GetName" methods, which control the compression type and provide a deterministic sorted order of the sensors across all the agents, respectively.

```
int[] GetObservationShape();
int Write(ObservationWriter writer);
byte[] GetCompressedObservation();
void Update();
void Reset();
SensorCompressionType GetCompressionType();
string GetName();
```

It also contains helper functions inside the "SensorExtensions" class, which provides the number of elements in ISensor's observation space. This involves multiplying the shape elements of each input observation space as provided here:

```
public static int ObservationSize(this ISensor sensor)
{
    var shape = sensor.GetObservationShape();
    var count = 1;
    foreach (var dim in shape)
    {
        count *= dim;
    }
    return count;
}
```

That completes the ISensor interface script. and we will explore how this script is being used in camera and ray sensors for creating the observation space of the agent. Let us understand the ray sensors, and then we will explore the camera sensors.

Ray Sensors

RayPerceptionSensor: The first sensor that is important in the context of ML Agents is the RayPerceptionsensor.cs script, which is present inside the Runtime folder under "com.unity.ml-agents" package. This sensor essentially controls the dimensions 2D or 3D, in which the rays will be cast. This is done by the following lines:

```
namespace Unity.MLAgents.Sensors
{
    /// <summary>
    /// Determines which dimensions the sensor will perform the casts in.
    /// </summary>
    public enum RayPerceptionCastType
    {
        Cast2D,

        Cast3D,
    }
```

"RayPerceptionCastType" contains the type of the cast ray. The next part contains a data structure (struct) that contains the details that are contained inside "RayPerceptionInput" sensor. It contains details such as ray length, collision detection, offset, radius of cast, layer mask, angles, cast type, and transform. The layer mask is an important attribute, as it allows the ray to pass through certain layers to detect objects that are present in other layers. The offset allows the ray to be cast at a distance of a few units from the source. The collision detection attribute is used for checking whether the ray sensor has collided with the tagged object. The angle controls the direction of the rays, and generally 90 degrees is considered as the "forward" direction with respect to the object. The cast type is from the "RayPerceptionCastType" enum, which controls whether it is 2D or 3D. The transform signifies the positional transform of the object from which the ray is triggered: the agent. The cast radius determines the radius for spherical raycast, and generally if 0 or less value is provided, it signifies normal rays.

```
public struct RayPerceptionInput
    {
        public float RayLength;

        public IReadOnlyList<string> DetectableTags;

        public IReadOnlyList<float> Angles;

        public float StartOffset;

        public float EndOffset;

        public float CastRadius;

        public Transform Transform;

        public RayPerceptionCastType CastType;

        public int LayerMask;
```

There are certain methods inside this class, such as the "OutputSize" method, that control the size of the sensors. This size forms the size of the observation space, which is required by the behavior parameters script. This is presented as:

```
public int OutputSize()
    {
        return (DetectableTags.Count + 2) * Angles.Count;
    },
```

215

where the "DetectableTags.Count" controls the number of tagged GameObjects in the scene that the ray sensor from the agent can detect. The "Angle.Count" attribute returns the number of the different angles of the sensor rays that are fired from the agent.

We will next understand other methods, such as "PolarToCartesian3D" and "PolarToCartesian2D." These methods are useful for converting the ray transforms from polar coordinates in the Unity scene to Cartesian coordinates. Essentially this transforms the rays from local space to world space. The world space coordinates are then used for analyzing which detectable GameObjects the sensor rays hit. This can be done by using sine and cosine transforms of the transform positions. Diagrammatically this is shown in Figure 4-3.

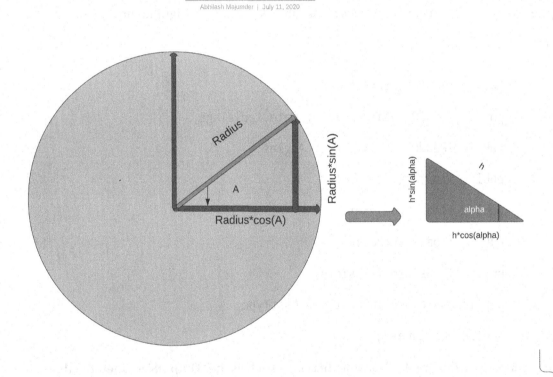

Figure 4-3. *Polar to Cartesian conversion of an n-D ray*

The "radius" signifies the ray length in polar coordinates. The concerned axes here in Unity are the x and z axes. For our reference, we consider the x axis as the horizontal plane and z axis as the vertical one. This is represented by the axes in the circle at 90 degrees apart. If the angle of the sensor ray is "A" with respect to the x axis, then the corresponding ray length along the x axis is "radius*cos(A)," and along the vertical z axis "radius*sin(A)." Now let us explore the 2D ray conversion in the "PolarToCartesian2D" method. This is very important, as we will be using angles to specify the gap between the rays in our scene.

```
static internal Vector2 PolarToCartesian2D(float radius, float
angleDegrees)
    {
        var x = radius *
  Mathf.Cos(Mathf.Deg2Rad * angleDegrees);
        var y = radius *
  Mathf.Sin(Mathf.Deg2Rad * angleDegrees);
        return new Vector2(x, y);
    }
```

In the case of 2D ray sensor conversion, we consider mutually perpendicular x and y axes. If we compare this with our previous diagram, the x axis is the horizontal line, and the y is the vertical line. The angle is converted to radians for sin and cosine angle calculation. Similarly if we look into the 3D counterpart:

```
static internal Vector3 PolarToCartesian3D
(float radius, float angleDegrees)
    {
        var x = radius *
  Mathf.Cos(Mathf.Deg2Rad * angleDegrees);
        var z = radius *
  Mathf.Sin(Mathf.Deg2Rad * angleDegrees);
        return new Vector3(x, 0f, z);
    }
```

In this case we have x-z as the mutually perpendicular axes, with y axis as 0. This is the part that we will be using in our scenes. For the next part, we have the "RayExtents" method, which controls the coordinates of the hitpoint of the sensor rays. This also estimates the distance from the ray source to the ray sensor and uses the polar to coordinate conversion to do this computation. Also here, we have the cases that decide if the ray is in 2D or in 3D.

```
var angle = Angles[rayIndex];
Vector3 startPositionLocal, endPositionLocal;
if (CastType == RayPerceptionCastType.Cast3D)
{
    startPositionLocal = new Vector3(0, StartOffset, 0);
    endPositionLocal = PolarToCartesian3D(RayLength, angle);
    endPositionLocal.y += EndOffset;
}
else
{
    // Vector2s here get converted to Vector3s (and back to Vector2s for
        casting)
    startPositionLocal = new Vector2();
    endPositionLocal = PolarToCartesian2D(RayLength, angle);
}
var startPositionWorld = Transform.TransformPoint(startPositionLocal);
var endPositionWorld = Transform.TransformPoint(endPositionLocal);
return (StartPositionWorld : startPositionWorld, EndPositionWorld :
endPositionWorld);
```

The next part contains the class "RayPerceptionOutput," which controls the different outcomes if the sensor ray has hit a tagged object. Inside this class, there is a struct "RayOutput" that contains several attributes such as "HasHit," "HitTaggedObject," "HitTagIndex," and "HitFraction." These contain the details about whether the sensor ray has hit the concerned object, the tag of the hit object, the index of the object's tag in the DetectableTags in the list (-1 if anything else was hit or nothing was specified), and the normalized distance to hit the object, respectively.

```
public struct RayOutput
        {
            public bool HasHit;

            public bool HitTaggedObject;

            public int HitTagIndex;

            public float HitFraction;
```

The "ToFloatArray" method writes the ray output information to a subset of the float array. The list contains the observation data, which can be the following:

- One-hot encoding data for the detectable tags. If "DetectableTags. Length" equals "n," the first n elements of the list will be a one-hot-encoding of the detectable tag that was hit or 0 if nothing was hit.

- "numDetectableTags" will be set to 1 if the sensor ray missed everything or 0 if it hit something (either "detectable" or not).

- "numDetectableTags + 1" signifies the normalized distance if the object was hit or 1.0 if nothing was hit.

There is also a float buffer array that controls the size of the output buffer, given by (numDetectableTags+2) * RayOutputs.Length.

```
public void ToFloatArray(int numDetectableTags, int rayIndex, float[]
buffer)
{
    var bufferOffset = (numDetectableTags + 2) * rayIndex;
    if (HitTaggedObject)
    {
        buffer[bufferOffset + HitTagIndex] = 1f;
    }
    buffer[bufferOffset + numDetectableTags] =
                                    HasHit ? 0f : 1f;
    buffer[bufferOffset + numDetectableTags + 1] =
                                    HitFraction;
}
}
```

There is an internal class called "DebugDisplayInfo" that is used for debugging the attributes of the drawn sensor ray on the screen and also shows the frame rates. It also displays the information whenever the ray hits any detectable tag and is used by the "RayPerceptionsensorComponent."

```
internal class DebugDisplayInfo
{
public struct RayInfo
```

```
{
    public Vector3 worldStart;
    public Vector3 worldEnd;
    public float castRadius;
    public RayPerceptionOutput.RayOutput rayOutput;
}
public void Reset()
{
    m_Frame = Time.frameCount;
}
public int age
{
    get { return Time.frameCount - m_Frame; }
}
public RayInfo[] rayInfos;
int m_Frame;
}
```

The next part is the implementation of the ray sensors, which inherits from the ISensor component. There are instantiated objects of "RayPerceptionInput" class and "DebugDisplayInfo" class. The public function RayPerceptionSensor sets the objects of the classes with initialized values and assigns sensor ray inputs.

```
float[] m_Observations;
int[] m_Shape;
string m_Name;
RayPerceptionInput m_RayPerceptionInput;
DebugDisplayInfo m_DebugDisplayInfo;
internal DebugDisplayInfo debugDisplayInfo
{
    get { return m_DebugDisplayInfo; }
}
public RayPerceptionSensor(string name, RayPerceptionInput rayInput)
{
    m_Name = name;
    m_RayPerceptionInput = rayInput;
    SetNumObservations(rayInput.OutputSize());
```

```
    if (Application.isEditor)
    {
        m_DebugDisplayInfo = new DebugDisplayInfo();
    }
}
```

The "SetNumObservations" method details the sizes of the observation array for the sensors. The "SetRayPerceptionInput" method checks whether the number of detectable tags, and the sensor rays are modified at runtime. It also checks if the size of the "RayPerceptionInput" array is the same as the "rayInput" array. This signifies that all the shapes related to sensor ray arrays are consistent and not modified at runtime.

```
void SetNumObservations(int numObservations)
{
    m_Shape = new[] { numObservations };
    m_Observations = new float[numObservations];
}
internal void SetRayPerceptionInput(RayPerceptionInput rayInput)
{
        if (m_RayPerceptionInput.OutputSize() != rayInput.OutputSize())
                {
                        Debug.Log(
                    "Changing the number of tags or
                    rays at runtime is not " +
                    "supported and may cause errors
                    in training or inference."
                );
            SetNumObservations(rayInput.OutputSize());
        }
    m_RayPerceptionInput = rayInput;
}
```

The next part writes the observations by collecting information from the collision of the sensor ray with the detectable objects. First it collects the information regarding the number of sensor rays fired from the agent and the detectable tags in the scene. If there is an inconsistency in the shape of the associated sensor arrays, it resets the information and resizes the buffer. Then it uses the "PerceiveSingleRay" method to trigger the casting of the ray and write the information to the buffer. The output of the cast is then written to the "rayOutput" array, which is an object of the "RayPerceptionOutput" class. It also returns the observation array length.

```
public int Write(ObservationWriter writer)
{
    using (TimerStack.Instance.Scoped("RayPerceptionSensor.Perceive"))
    {
        Array.Clear(m_Observations, 0, m_Observations.Length);
        var numRays = m_RayPerceptionInput.Angles.Count;
        var numDetectableTags
 = m_RayPerceptionInput.DetectableTags.Count;
        if (m_DebugDisplayInfo != null)
        {
            m_DebugDisplayInfo.Reset();
            if (m_DebugDisplayInfo.rayInfos == null
 || m_DebugDisplayInfo.rayInfos.Length != numRays)
            {
                m_DebugDisplayInfo.rayInfos =
new DebugDisplayInfo.RayInfo[numRays];
            }
        }
        for (var rayIndex = 0; rayIndex < numRays; rayIndex++)
        {
            DebugDisplayInfo.RayInfo debugRay;
            var rayOutput
 = PerceiveSingleRay(m_RayPerceptionInput,  rayIndex, out debugRay);
            if (m_DebugDisplayInfo != null)
            {
                m_DebugDisplayInfo.rayInfos[rayIndex]
 = debugRay;
            }
            rayOutput.ToFloatArray(numDetectableTags
, rayIndex, m_Observations);
        }
```

```
        writer.AddRange(m_Observations);
    }
    return m_Observations.Length;
}
```

We then address the "PerceiveSingleRay" static method. It takes an object of the "RayPerceptionInput" class, "rayIndex," which is the index of the particular ray in the ray array, and the DebugDisplayInfo object. It then assigns the variables such as ray length, cast radius, extents, start and end position, and direction of the ray. However, if the scale is not the same as the scale used in Unity, then the absolute value of the "rayDirection" variable will be different from "rayLength." There are also attributes that can transform the ray length for different cast lengths and hit fraction and also scale up or down the sphere or circle radius of the cast rays. There are also provisions to avoid division with 0 in case the unscaled ray length is 0.

```
var unscaledRayLength = input.RayLength;
var unscaledCastRadius = input.CastRadius;
var extents = input.RayExtents(rayIndex);
var startPositionWorld = extents.StartPositionWorld;
var endPositionWorld = extents.EndPositionWorld;
var rayDirection = endPositionWorld - startPositionWorld;
var scaledRayLength = rayDirection.magnitude;
var scaledCastRadius = unscaledRayLength > 0 ?
    unscaledCastRadius * scaledRayLength / unscaledRayLength :
    unscaledCastRadius;
bool castHit;
float hitFraction;
GameObject hitObject;
```

The next portion of the code segment checks whether the cast of the ray input ID of type 2D or 3D. It then checks if the cast radius is greater than 0, which signifies whether it will be a spherical cast or a ray cast. Then it uses the "Physics.RayCast" or "Physics. SphereCast" accordingly to fire the rays. It then checks whether the scaled ray length is 0 and also has checks to avoid division by 0.

```
if (input.CastType == RayPerceptionCastType.Cast3D)
{
    RaycastHit rayHit;
    if (scaledCastRadius > 0f)
    {
        castHit = Physics.SphereCast(startPositionWorld
            , scaledCastRadius, rayDirection, out rayHit,
                scaledRayLength, input.LayerMask);
    }
    else
    {
        castHit = Physics.Raycast(startPositionWorld
            , rayDirection, out rayHit,
                scaledRayLength, input.LayerMask);
    }
    hitFraction = castHit ? (scaledRayLength > 0
        ? rayHit.distance / scaledRayLength : 0.0f) : 1.0f;
    hitObject = castHit ? rayHit.collider.gameObject : null;
}
else
{
    RaycastHit2D rayHit;
    if (scaledCastRadius > 0f)
    {
        rayHit = Physics2D.CircleCast(startPositionWorld
            , scaledCastRadius, rayDirection,
                scaledRayLength, input.LayerMask);
    }
```

```
    else
    {
        rayHit = Physics2D.Raycast(startPositionWorld
          , rayDirection, scaledRayLength, input.LayerMask);
    }
    castHit = rayHit;
    hitFraction = castHit ? rayHit.fraction : 1.0f;
    hitObject = castHit ? rayHit.collider.gameObject : null;
}
```

After it has hit the target detectable tags, it uses the "CompareTag" method and
assigns the "HitTagIndex" with the proper index of the hit target. It also computes the
hit fraction and other attributes of the RayPerceptionOutput object. Once it has hit a
detectable object, the loop breaks. Finally it assigns the worldStart, worldEnd, rayOuput,
and castRadius variables with the computed values and returns the output ray to the
"Write" method.

```
var rayOutput = new RayPerceptionOutput.RayOutput
{
    HasHit = castHit,
    HitFraction = hitFraction,
    HitTaggedObject = false,
    HitTagIndex = -1
};
if (castHit)
{
    for (var i = 0; i < input.DetectableTags.Count; i++)
    {
        if (hitObject.CompareTag(input.DetectableTags[i]))
        {
            rayOutput.HitTaggedObject = true;
            rayOutput.HitTagIndex = i;
            break;
        }
    }
}
```

```
debugRayOut.worldStart = startPositionWorld;
debugRayOut.worldEnd = endPositionWorld;
debugRayOut.rayOutput = rayOutput;
debugRayOut.castRadius = scaledCastRadius;
return rayOutput;
```

However, the "Write" method also uses the "Perceive" method to call the "PerceoveSingleRay" method. This "Perceive" method takes the ray input array and the angles associated with the rays as input and passes them to the "PerceiveSingleRay" method to get the array of ray outputs and detectable tags. Then it is passed to the "Write" method to be written as the observation space.

```
RayPerceptionOutput output = new RayPerceptionOutput();
output.RayOutputs = new RayPerceptionOutput.RayOutput[input.Angles.Count];
for (var rayIndex = 0; rayIndex < input.Angles.Count; rayIndex++)
{
    DebugDisplayInfo.RayInfo debugRay;
    output.RayOutputs[rayIndex] = PerceiveSingleRay(input
        , rayIndex, out debugRay);
}
return output;
```

That completes the RayPerceptionsensor script, and it is the most important script that controls the rays being fired by the agent to get the observations of the detectable tags. The workflow of the RayPerceptionsensor script is shown in Figure 4-4.

Sensor Ray Perception Workflow

Abhilash Majumder | July 12, 2020

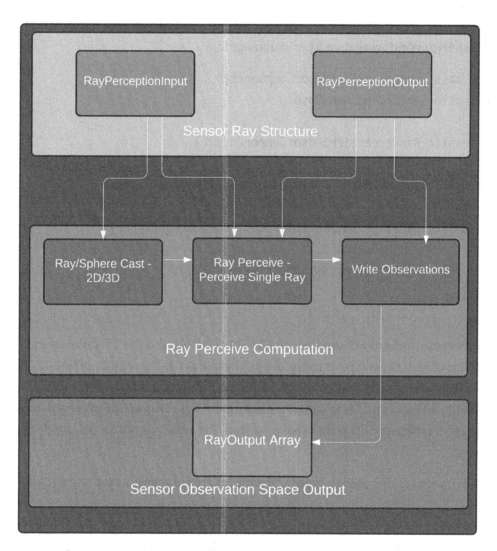

Figure 4-4. *"RayPerceptionSensor" script workflow*

There are variants of this script used for 2D ray perception as well as for 3D ray perception, which we will look into.

RayPerceptionSensorComponent2D: This script is used for adding the 2D ray perception sensor component to an agent in a scene. It also declares the cast type as 2D and uses the "Physics.2D" module to cast the rays. Though it uses the

RayPerceptionSensorComponentBase.cs script for its properties, the latter uses
RayPerceptionSensor script internally. So all the functionalities like drawing
spherical/ray casts along with perception of a single ray are done with the help of the
RayPerceptionSensor script, which we discussed in the previous section. This script
particularly declares that the type of the ray cast is 2D and can be added as a component
in the Inspector Window against a particular agent.

```
public class RayPerceptionSensorComponent2D :
RayPerceptionSensorComponentBase
{
        public RayPerceptionSensorComponent2D()
        {
            RayLayerMask = Physics2D.DefaultRaycastLayers;
        }
        public override RayPerceptionCastType GetCastType()
        {
            return RayPerceptionCastType.Cast2D;
        }
}
```

RayPerceptionSensorComponent3D: This is similar to the 2D component,
except that here 3D cast type is used for the rays. Initially there is an offset
provided to the start and end positions of the ray, as mentioned in the
"StartVerticalOffset" and "EndVerticalOffset" methods. This script inherits from the
"RayPerceptionSensorComponentBase" script. The offset declarations are declared
as follows:

```
[HideInInspector, SerializeField, FormerlySerializedAs("startVerticalOffs
et")]
[Range(-10f, 10f)]
[Tooltip("Ray start is offset up or down by this amount.")]
float m_StartVerticalOffset;
public float StartVerticalOffset
{
    get => m_StartVerticalOffset;
    set { m_StartVerticalOffset = value; UpdateSensor(); }
}
```

```
[HideInInspector, SerializeField, FormerlySerializedAs("endVerticalOffset")]
[Range(-10f, 10f)]
[Tooltip("Ray end is offset up or down by this amount.")]
float m_EndVerticalOffset;
public float EndVerticalOffset
{
    get => m_EndVerticalOffset;
    set { m_EndVerticalOffset = value; UpdateSensor(); }
}
```

The next code segment contains the type of the cast and assigns the values for the StartVerticalOffset and EndVerticalOffset variables.

```
public override RayPerceptionCastType GetCastType()
{
    return RayPerceptionCastType.Cast3D;
}
public override float GetStartVerticalOffset()
{
    return StartVerticalOffset;
}
public override float GetEndVerticalOffset()
{
    return EndVerticalOffset;
}
```

SensorComponent: This is a variant of the ISensor script, which is for the Unity Editor. For simplicity, a particular ISensor implementation should have a corresponding SensorComponent to build it. Internally it calls the different methods of the "ISensor" script, which is triggered when the agent starts to create ray sensors or camera sensors. The methods—"GetObservationShape" and "isVisual"—involve getting the observation shape of the sensor vector, checking whether the sensor type is visual (has five parameters) or a 3D vectorized attribute (example: velocity/position of RigidBody, which has three parameters,) respectively. The method "isVector" controls whether the output shape of the observation is vectorized or not (discrete or continuous).

```
public abstract ISensor CreateSensor();
public abstract int[] GetObservationShape();
public virtual bool IsVisual()
        {
                var shape = GetObservationShape();
                return shape.Length == 3;
        }
public virtual bool IsVector()
        {
                var shape = GetObservationShape();
                return shape.Length == 1;
        }
```

RayPerceptionSensorComponentBase: This script internally uses the functionality of the RayPerceptionSensor script and inherits from the SensorComponent script. This script is called when we assign a "RayPerceptionSensorComponent2D" or RayPerceptionSensorComponent3D component to our agent in the scene. It has the name of the sensor, which defaults to "RayPerceptionSensor."

```
[HideInInspector, SerializeField, FormerlySerializedAs("sensorName")]
 string m_SensorName = "RayPerceptionSensor";
public string SensorName
{
    get { return m_SensorName; }
    set { m_SensorName = value; }
}
```

There are certain important attributes of this script that controls the sphere cast radius, ray length, and angles. It defaults to an angle of 70 degrees between the rays fired from the agent; greater than 90 degrees would allow the rays to go behind the object and at 90 degrees would be strictly restricted to left and right. The default sphere cast radius is 0.5 float units, and the default ray length is 20 float units. It controls the number of rays fired per direction and defaults to three (left, right, and center). It lists the detectable tags that the sensor rays can detect and the layer mask that signifies which layers the ray can pass through.

```
[SerializeField, FormerlySerializedAs("detectableTags")]
[Tooltip("List of tags in the scene to compare against.")]
List<string> m_DetectableTags;
public List<string> DetectableTags
{
    get { return m_DetectableTags; }
    set { m_DetectableTags = value; }
}
[HideInInspector, SerializeField, FormerlySerializedAs("raysPerDirection")]
[Range(0, 50)]
[Tooltip("Number of rays to the left and right of center.")]
int m_RaysPerDirection = 3;
public int RaysPerDirection
{
    get { return m_RaysPerDirection; }
    set { m_RaysPerDirection = value;}
}
[HideInInspector, SerializeField, FormerlySerializedAs("maxRayDegrees")]
[Range(0, 180)]
[Tooltip("Cone size for rays. Using 90 degrees will cast rays to the left
and right. " +
    "Greater than 90 degrees will go backwards.")]
float m_MaxRayDegrees = 70;
public float MaxRayDegrees
{
    get => m_MaxRayDegrees;
    set { m_MaxRayDegrees = value; UpdateSensor(); }
}
public float SphereCastRadius
{
    get => m_SphereCastRadius;
    set { m_SphereCastRadius = value; UpdateSensor(); }
}
```

```
[HideInInspector, SerializeField, FormerlySerializedAs("rayLength")]
[Range(1, 1000)]
[Tooltip("Length of the rays to cast.")]
float m_RayLength = 20f;
public float RayLength
{
    get => m_RayLength;
    set { m_RayLength = value; UpdateSensor(); }
}
[HideInInspector, SerializeField, FormerlySerializedAs("rayLayerMask")]
[Tooltip("Controls which layers the rays can hit.")]
LayerMask m_RayLayerMask = Physics.DefaultRaycastLayers;
public LayerMask RayLayerMask
{
    get => m_RayLayerMask;
    set { m_RayLayerMask = value; UpdateSensor(); }
}
```

It also contains observation stacks, which signifies how many observations we would want to stack and pass it to the neural network (defaults to 1, signifying that no previous observations would be used for neural network training). It has other attributes, such as ray hit color, miss color, ray cast type (2D/3D), and start and end offset positions (inherited from the SensorComponent script). All of these components are editable in the Inspector Window when we will be assigning our RayPerceptionSensorComponent3D component/script to our agent in Unity in a later section.

```
[HideInInspector, SerializeField, FormerlySerializedAs("observationStacks")]
[Range(1, 50)]
[Tooltip("Number of raycast results that will be stacked before being fed
to the neural network.")]
int m_ObservationStacks = 1;
public int ObservationStacks
{
    get { return m_ObservationStacks; }
    set { m_ObservationStacks = value; }
}
```

```
[HideInInspector]
[SerializeField]
[Header("Debug Gizmos", order = 999)]
internal Color rayHitColor = Color.red;
[HideInInspector]
[SerializeField]
internal Color rayMissColor = Color.white;
[NonSerialized]
RayPerceptionSensor m_RaySensor;
public RayPerceptionSensor RaySensor
{
    get => m_RaySensor;
}

public abstract RayPerceptionCastType GetCastType();
public virtual float GetStartVerticalOffset()
{
    return 0f;
}
public virtual float GetEndVerticalOffset()
{
    return 0f;
}
```

The "CreateSensor" method overrides the "ISensor" script and initializes the sensor by using the methods in the "RayPerceptionSensor" script. It also stacks the observations if a value greater than 1 is used.

```
public override ISensor CreateSensor()
{
    var rayPerceptionInput = GetRayPerceptionInput();
    m_RaySensor = new RayPerceptionSensor(m_SensorName,
    rayPerceptionInput);
```

```
    if (ObservationStacks != 1)
    {
        var stackingSensor = new StackingSensor(m_RaySensor,
        ObservationStacks);
        return stackingSensor;
    }
    return m_RaySensor;
}
```

The next code segment contains the GetRayAngles float array method, which returns the angles of the sensor rays and the number of rays in each direction. The angular range between each ray is in arithmetic progression with a spacing of "delta." The delta variable is calculated by dividing the maximum ray angle with the value of the number of rays in each direction. Then it interpolates the rays in the form of { 90, 90 - delta, 90 + delta, 90 - 2*delta, 90 + 2*delta }.

```
internal static float[] GetRayAngles(int raysPerDirection, float
maxRayDegrees)
{
var anglesOut = new float[2 * raysPerDirection + 1];
var delta = maxRayDegrees / raysPerDirection;
anglesOut[0] = 90f;
for (var i = 0; i < raysPerDirection; i++)
{
    anglesOut[2 * i + 1] = 90 - (i + 1) * delta;
    anglesOut[2 * i + 2] = 90 + (i + 1) * delta;
}
    return anglesOut;
}
```

The next segment is GetObservationShape, which also overrides the same method from the "RayPerceptionSensor" and governs the number of detectable tags and number of rays, stack size of observations, and observation size.

```
public override int[] GetObservationShape()
        {
                var numRays = 2 * RaysPerDirection + 1;
                var numTags = m_DetectableTags?.Count ?? 0;
```

```
    var obsSize = (numTags + 2) * numRays;
    var stacks = ObservationStacks > 1
                ? ObservationStacks : 1;
    return new[] { obsSize * stacks };
}
```

In the last section of the segment, the "GetRayPerceptionInput" method is overridden and all the variables are assigned according to the "RayPerceptionInput" struct (structure), which we discussed before.

```
public RayPerceptionInput GetRayPerceptionInput()
{
    var rayAngles = GetRayAngles
                (RaysPerDirection, MaxRayDegrees);
    var rayPerceptionInput = new RayPerceptionInput();
    rayPerceptionInput.RayLength = RayLength;
    rayPerceptionInput.DetectableTags = DetectableTags;
    rayPerceptionInput.Angles = rayAngles;
    rayPerceptionInput.StartOffset = GetStartVerticalOffset();
    rayPerceptionInput.EndOffset = GetEndVerticalOffset();
    rayPerceptionInput.CastRadius = SphereCastRadius;
    rayPerceptionInput.Transform = transform;
    rayPerceptionInput.CastType = GetCastType();
    rayPerceptionInput.LayerMask = RayLayerMask;
    return rayPerceptionInput;

}
```

The "OnDrawGizmosSelectedMethod" script takes the input ray and calls the "PerceiveSingleRay" function from "RayPerceptionSensor" script for each of the rays along different directions. Depending on whether the rays are null or not, the color of the rays are displayed. Older observations are displayed in a lighter shade so as to de-emphasize the current training episode.

```
var rayInput = GetRayPerceptionInput();
for (var rayIndex = 0; rayIndex < rayInput.Angles.Count; rayIndex++)
{
    DebugDisplayInfo.RayInfo debugRay;
    RayPerceptionSensor.PerceiveSingleRay(rayInput, rayIndex, out debugRay);
    DrawRaycastGizmos(debugRay);
}
```

The "DrawRaycastGizmos" method uses the DisplayDebugInfo variable
(from RayPerceptionSensor script) to debug the variables such as offset positions,
ray direction, hit fraction, and hit radius. Figure 4-5 shows Ray Sensors using
"RayPerceptionSensorComponent3D" in "FindingBlock-PPO" Unity scene, which we
will study in a later section in this chapter.

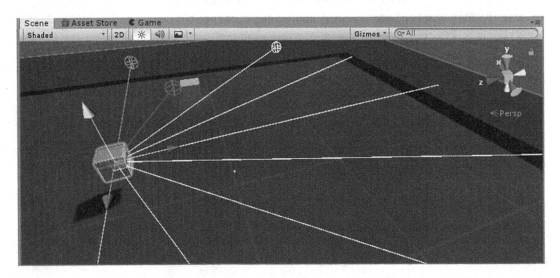

Figure 4-5. Ray perception sensor 3D in Unity using sensor rays

This completes the fundamental aspects of the ray sensors. There are associated
scripts, such as VectorSensor and StackingSensor.

VectorSensor: This script is a vector implementation of the ray sensors. It has
different variants of "AddObservation," a method overloading technique. This is useful
when the observation size can be a transform (Vector3/Vector2), quaternion(x, y, z, w),
Boolean, or an int. This will be used when we write our own agent script. If the expected

observation space size is not consistent with the received observation space size during training, then it shows a warning. It truncates the observations if excessive observations are received and pads with 0 if lesser observations than expected are received.

```
public int Write(ObservationWriter writer)
{
    var expectedObservations = m_Shape[0];
    if (m_Observations.Count > expectedObservations)
    {
        Debug.LogWarningFormat(
            "More observations ({0}) made than vector observation size
            ({1}). The observations will be truncated.",
            m_Observations.Count, expectedObservations
        );
        m_Observations.RemoveRange(expectedObservations, m_Observations.
        Count - expectedObservations);
    }
    else if (m_Observations.Count < expectedObservations)
    {
        Debug.LogWarningFormat(
            "Fewer observations ({0}) made than vector observation size
            ({1}). The observations will be padded.",
            m_Observations.Count, expectedObservations
        );
        for (int i = m_Observations.Count; i < expectedObservations; i++)
        {
            m_Observations.Add(0);
        }
    }
    writer.AddRange(m_Observations);
    return expectedObservations;
}
```

StackingSensor: This sensor is used for temporal stacking of the observations, and consecutive observations are stored in an array (1D) from left to right. The details of this particular sensor are cross-functional and are used in the deep RL algorithms, which require memory.

This completes the entire class of ray sensors. The agent uses the "RayPerceptionSensorComponent2D" or "RayPerceptionSensorComponent3D" in Unity. This script in turn calls the RayPerceptionSensorComponentBase script, which implements the SensorComponent script. The latter is an implementation of the ISensor script for the Unity Editor. The RayPerceptionSensorComponentBase script is displayed on the Inspector Window controlling the observations, rays, and their attributes. This script internally calls the "RayPerceptionSensor" script, which contains the structures "RayPerceptionInput" and "RayPerceptionOutput." This is one of the most important parts of the brain, which is used for collecting observations from sensor rays. Figure 4-6 shows this architecture.

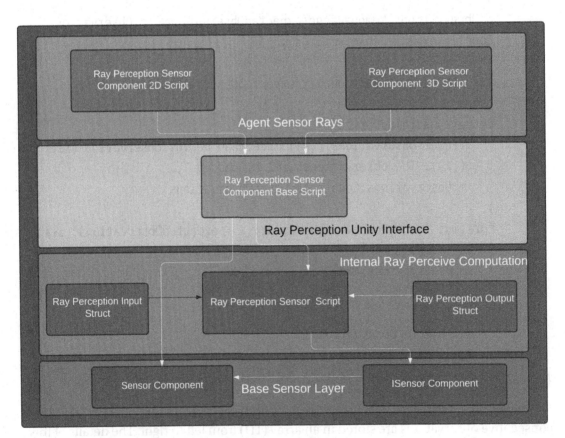

Figure 4-6. *Ray sensor scripts in Unity ML Agents*

Camera Sensor

In this section we will also explore the camera sensor, which is controlled by the CameraSensorComponent and CameraSensor scripts.

CameraSensorComponent: This script also inherits from the SensorComponent script like ray sensors and controls the different attributes of a visual observation space. Since environments like GridWorld rely on visual observations in a compressed form (PNG), which is then passed into deep learning computer vision algorithms, this script is used for assigning the height, width, compression, and the vectorized distribution of the input observation space. The script is assigned to an agent that controls the visual observation with the help of a camera present in the Unity scene. It assigns the camera as the default visual observation too. The width and height of the generated image is also an attribute that defaults to 84 units.

```
[AddComponentMenu("ML Agents/Camera Sensor", (int)MenuGroup.Sensors)]
public class CameraSensorComponent : SensorComponent
{
    [HideInInspector, SerializeField
    , FormerlySerializedAs("camera")]
    Camera m_Camera;
    CameraSensor m_Sensor;
    public Camera Camera
    {
        get { return m_Camera;  }
        set { m_Camera = value; UpdateSensor(); }
    }
    [HideInInspector, SerializeField
    , FormerlySerializedAs("sensorName")]
    string m_SensorName = "CameraSensor";
    public string SensorName
    {
        get { return m_SensorName;  }
        set { m_SensorName = value; }
    }
    [HideInInspector, SerializeField
```

```
, FormerlySerializedAs("width")]
int m_Width = 84;
public int Width
{
    get { return m_Width;  }
    set { m_Width = value; }
}
[HideInInspector, SerializeField
, FormerlySerializedAs("height")]
int m_Height = 84;
public int Height
{
    get { return m_Height;  }
    set { m_Height = value;  }
}
```

The script also has attributes that control whether the images are received in RGB (three channels) or in grayscale (one channel) format. It also contains the compression type of the image defaulting to "PNG." This camera sensor object can then be used for collecting visual information (visual sensor). This object is of type ISensor, which governs all the sensors in the Unity ML Agents.

```
[HideInInspector, SerializeField, FormerlySerializedAs("grayscale")]
bool m_Grayscale;
public bool Grayscale
{
    get { return m_Grayscale;  }
    set { m_Grayscale = value; }
}
[HideInInspector, SerializeField, FormerlySerializedAs("compression")]
SensorCompressionType m_Compression = SensorCompressionType.PNG;
public SensorCompressionType CompressionType
{
    get { return m_Compression;  }
    set { m_Compression = value; UpdateSensor(); }
}
```

```
public override ISensor CreateSensor()
{
    m_Sensor = new CameraSensor(m_Camera, m_Width, m_Height, Grayscale,
    m_SensorName, m_Compression);
    return m_Sensor;
}
```

It also has overridden the method "GetObservationShape," like in the case of ray sensor, which returns the observation vector (container), whose shape is controlled by the height, width, and the channels of the image (RGB/grayscale). It also has another method "UpdateSensor," which assigns the name of the camera sensor and the compression type (none/PNG).

```
public override int[] GetObservationShape()
        {
            return CameraSensor.GenerateShape(m_Width
                    , m_Height, Grayscale);
        }
internal void UpdateSensor()
        {
            if (m_Sensor != null)
            {
                m_Sensor.Camera = m_Camera;
                m_Sensor.CompressionType = m_Compression;
            }
        }
```

CameraSensor: This inherits from the ISensor script and overrides its methods. The basic functionality of this script is to wrap a camera object to generate visual observations for the agent. It has the attributes that are present in the CameraSensorComponent script such as height, width, grayscale, name shape, and compression type and has associated functions to assign them. The "GetCompressedObservation" method encodes the image in PNG binary format.

```
public byte[] GetCompressedObservation()
{
    using (TimerStack.Instance.Scoped("CameraSensor.
    GetCompressedObservation"))
    {
        var texture = ObservationToTexture(m_Camera, m_Width
                        , m_Height);
        // TODO support more types here, e.g. JPG
        var compressed = texture.EncodeToPNG();
        DestroyTexture(texture);
        return compressed;
    }
}
```

The important methods include the override "Write" method, "ObservationToTexture" method. The latter is important because the camera captures the image presented on a render texture (Texture 2D). This function assigns the variables with the Texture 2D properties such as the width, height, and texture format (RGB24) and also controls the transform of the camera and its depth of view. This script can also help in rendering to offscreen texture, which is useful when training Resnet model in CPU. For each timestamp, the image is captured and activated so that it can be processed by the neural network. After it is processed, the RenderTexture variable is released, and a new image is assigned to it for the next time step.

```
var texture2D = new Texture2D(width, height, TextureFormat.RGB24, false);
var oldRec = obsCamera.rect;
obsCamera.rect = new Rect(0f, 0f, 1f, 1f);
var depth = 24;
var format = RenderTextureFormat.Default;
var readWrite = RenderTextureReadWrite.Default;
var tempRt =RenderTexture.GetTemporary(width, height, depth, format,
readWrite);
var prevActiveRt = RenderTexture.active;
var prevCameraRt = obsCamera.targetTexture;

RenderTexture.active = tempRt;
obsCamera.targetTexture = tempRt;
```

```
obsCamera.Render();
texture2D.ReadPixels(new Rect(0, 0, texture2D.width, texture2D.height),
0, 0);
obsCamera.targetTexture = prevCameraRt;
obsCamera.rect = oldRec;
RenderTexture.active = prevActiveRt;
RenderTexture.ReleaseTemporary(tempRt);
return texture2D;
```

The "Write" method then calls this "ObservationToTexture" method to the observation space of the agent. However, in this case, the observation space is written over a Tensor (which we will discuss in next chapter), which can be assumed as a dense matrix suitable for performing deep learning algorithmic computations. Once the visual information from the observation space is processed by the network running on the external brain, the associated texture is destroyed. The script does this with the help of the following lines:

```
using (TimerStack.Instance.Scoped("CameraSensor.WriteToTensor"))
    {
        var texture = ObservationToTexture(m_Camera,
                        m_Width, m_Height);
        var numWritten = Utilities.TextureToTensorProxy(texture
                        , writer, m_Grayscale);
        DestroyTexture(texture);
        return numWritten;
    }
```

The "GenerateShape" method returns the shape of the image and its associated channels: one for grayscale, three for RGB.

```
internal static int[] GenerateShape(int width, int height, bool grayscale)
        {
            return new[] { height, width, grayscale ? 1 : 3 };
        }
```

In the GridWorld environment, there is a use of the camera sensor component. These two important scripts control the visual observation input from the camera and pass this information to the neural network for training. This is shown in Figure 4-7.

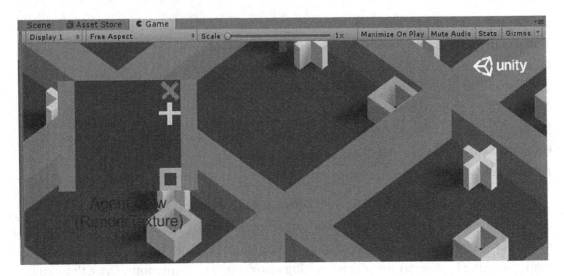

Figure 4-7. *Camera sensor in GridWorld*

There is another class called as "RenderTextureSensor," which contains the initialization of the functions and methods used in the CameraSensor script, such as creating Texture 2D format and assigning the height, width, channels, name, and compression for training. The sensor part controls the centralized observation space of the agent and provides all the details for the agent to take its next decision base on the runtime policy. We have explored the two distinct variants of sensors in depth: the ray sensors and the camera sensors. The important conclusion is that both these sensors inherit from "ISensor" and "SensorComponent" script at the lower level and have their own individual functionality. In contrast to the ray sensors workflow, the camera sensor workflow can be visualized as shown in Figure 4-8.

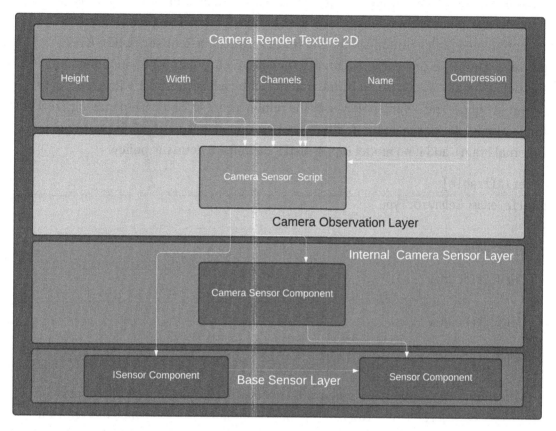

Figure 4-8. Camera sensor workflow in Unity ML Agents

Policies

In this section, we will explore the policies that the agent follows while taking decisions. We will explore the BehaviorParameters script, which we mentioned briefly in the last chapter, and we will get to know how this script relates to the sensor components to get the observation space for the agent. The BarracudaPolicy script provides information related to the Inference Engine policy while running the internal brain. The HeuristicPolicy script is involved in making heuristic policies when no specific brain (Internal/External) is applied on the agent.

BehaviorParameters: As mentioned in the last chapter, this script is associated with the decision-making process of the agent after receiving the observation from the sensors. The agent has a choice to choose its decision as default, internal, or heuristic. If the default policy is chosen, the script tries to attain the current policy. This can be a pretrained policy running in the Inference Engine or a heuristic policy. If no pretrained model is present (no inference) and heuristic policy is not implemented, this default policy is used for real-time training of the neural network with Tensorflow (external brain). The default policy uses the remote process for decision making: (real-time training). If external brain training is not present, it will use the Inference Engine (internal brain), and if no model is provided it defaults to heuristic policy.

```
[Serializable]
public enum BehaviorType
{
    Default,

    HeuristicOnly,

    InferenceOnly

}
```

The next code segment implements the policies at runtime and also generates the agent's policy objects. This script uses the BrainParameters script, which has attributes such as observation size, stacked observations, vector action size, and discrete or continuous distribution of observations. The segment also contains a neural network model variable that is used if internal policy is chosen for inference. It also has attributes that specify the inference device, such as CPU or GPU, on which the pretrained model will run during game play in Unity.

```
[HideInInspector, SerializeField]
BrainParameters m_BrainParameters = new BrainParameters();
public BrainParameters BrainParameters
{
    get { return m_BrainParameters; }
    internal set { m_BrainParameters = value; }
}
```

```
[HideInInspector, SerializeField]
NNModel m_Model;

public NNModel Model
{
    get { return m_Model; }
    set { m_Model = value; UpdateAgentPolicy(); }
}

[HideInInspector, SerializeField]
InferenceDevice m_InferenceDevice;

public InferenceDevice InferenceDevice
{
    get { return m_InferenceDevice; }
    set { m_InferenceDevice = value; UpdateAgentPolicy();}
}
```

It also controls the behavior type, the name of the behavior, and Boolean variable, which controls whether child sensors would be used and also assigns a team ID for the behavior, which is represented as "FullyQualifiedBehaviorName." The child sensors signify the sensors attached to the children GameObjects of the agent.

```
[HideInInspector, SerializeField]
BehaviorType m_BehaviorType;

public BehaviorType BehaviorType
{
    get { return m_BehaviorType; }
    set { m_BehaviorType = value; UpdateAgentPolicy(); }
}

[HideInInspector, SerializeField]
string m_BehaviorName = "My Behavior";

public string BehaviorName
{
    get { return m_BehaviorName; }
    set { m_BehaviorName = value; UpdateAgentPolicy(); }
}
```

```
[HideInInspector, SerializeField, FormerlySerializedAs("m_TeamID")]
public int TeamId;

[FormerlySerializedAs("m_useChildSensors")]
[HideInInspector]
[SerializeField]
[Tooltip("Use all Sensor components attached to child GameObjects of this
Agent.")]
bool m_UseChildSensors = true;

public bool UseChildSensors
{
    get { return m_UseChildSensors; }
    set { m_UseChildSensors = value; }
}

public string FullyQualifiedBehaviorName
{
    get { return m_BehaviorName + "?team=" + TeamId; }
}
```

The next method is "GeneratePolicy," which is of type "IPolicy." It takes arguments as the brain parameters and the behavior type. Based on the type of the behavior, a switch case is applied. If "HeuristicOnly" type is chosen, then it draws its behavior from the "HeuristicPolicy" (which we will discuss). If "InferenceOnly" policy is used, then there is a check to make sure that a valid pretrained model is available for inference through Barracuda. If not, then a warning is provided to change the behavior type. If a pretrained model is present, then it is passed to "BarracudaPolicy" script to run the inference.

```
case BehaviorType.HeuristicOnly:
    return new HeuristicPolicy(heuristic
    , m_BrainParameters.NumActions);
case BehaviorType.InferenceOnly:
{
    if (m_Model == null)
    {
        var behaviorType = BehaviorType.InferenceOnly.
        ToString();
```

```
        throw new UnityAgentsException(
            $"Can't use Behavior Type {behaviorType} without a model. " +
            "Either assign a model, or change to a different Behavior
            Type."
        );
    }
    return new BarracudaPolicy(m_BrainParameters, m_Model,
    m_InferenceDevice);
}
```

Then we have the "Default" policy, which initially checks whether the communicator
is on. This implies the port 5004 is connected for real-time Python training of the model
using Tensorflow. This is the external brain training taking place. In the event of the
port being not connected, the policy checks for an available valid pretrained model for
"Inference" policy. Otherwise it defaults to "Heuristic" policy.

```
case BehaviorType.Default:
    if (Academy.Instance.IsCommunicatorOn)
    {
            return new RemotePolicy(m_BrainParameters,
            FullyQualifiedBehaviorName);
        }
        if (m_Model != null)
        {
            return new BarracudaPolicy(m_BrainParameters, m_Model, m_
            InferenceDevice);
        }
        else
        {
            return new HeuristicPolicy(heuristic, m_BrainParameters.
            NumActions);
        }
    default:
        return new HeuristicPolicy(heuristic, m_BrainParameters.
        NumActions);
}
```

The last method of this script "UpdateAgentPolicy" updates the policy of the agent if the agent is not null.

```
internal void UpdateAgentPolicy()
{
    var agent = GetComponent<Agent>();
    if (agent == null)
    {
        return;
    }
    agent.ReloadPolicy();
}
```

This BehaviorParameter script uses certain adjoining scripts such as BrainParameters, BarracudaPolicy, "HeuristicPolicy," and "IPolicy" scripts, which are fundamental for its functionality. In the next sections of this chapter, using the Unity Editor, we will assign a "BehaviorParameters" script to the agent.

If we open any scene in the DeepLearning Assets folder and navigate to any agent in the scene, we will see the behavior parameters script attached to it. For instance, in this case the "BehaviorParameter" script for "Hallway" is shown in Figure 4-9.

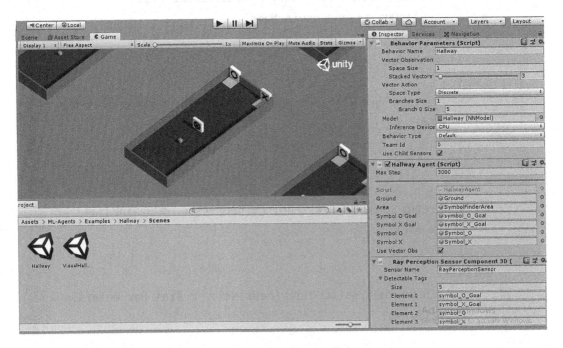

Figure 4-9. *BehaviorParameters script in the Hallway scene*

250

Some of the parameters such as VectorObservation and VectorAction are derived from the BrainParameters script, and we can see variables such as Model (controls the neural network model), Inference Device (CPU/GPU), Behavior Type (HeuristicOnly, InferenceOnly, Default), Team ID, and Boolean Use Child Sensors, which we discussed in this script.

BrainParameters: This controls the observation input and output spaces. It determines whether the action space is discrete or continuous inside the "BrainParameter" class, and it holds data related to the size of the vector observation space (defaults to 1). It also has attributes such as "stacked vectors," which refers to the concatenation of observations across different frames to be used for training.

```
public enum SpaceType
{
    Discrete,

    Continuous
}
[FormerlySerializedAs("vectorObservationSize")]
 public int VectorObservationSize = 1;

[FormerlySerializedAs("numStackedVectorObservations")]
 [Range(1, 50)] public int NumStackedVectorObservations = 1;
```

The "VectorActionSize" variable defines the size of the action space. If the space is continuous, the size is simply defined as the size of the vector. For discrete action spaces, the size depends on the branching of the action space. It also has "VectorActionDescriptions," which describe the action space and "VectorActionSpaceType," which is continuous or discrete.

```
[FormerlySerializedAs("vectorActionSize")]
public int[] VectorActionSize = new[] {1};

[FormerlySerializedAs("vectorActionDescriptions")]
public string[] VectorActionDescriptions;

[FormerlySerializedAs("vectorActionSpaceType")]
public SpaceType VectorActionSpaceType = SpaceType.Discrete;
```

The "NumActions" returns the number of actions inside the vector action space. If it is discrete, the length of the "VectorActionSize" array is returned (depending on branching factor). For continuous spaces, the value at the first index of the "VectorActionSize" array is returned as the observations are stacked.

```
public int NumActions
{
    get
    {
        switch (VectorActionSpaceType)
        {
            case SpaceType.Discrete:
                return VectorActionSize.Length;
            case SpaceType.Continuous:
                return VectorActionSize[0];
            default:
                return 0;
        }
    }
}
```

The last method in this script, Clone, initializes the BrainParameter object with the values discussed in this context. These attributes are then passed into the BehaviorParameters script, which appears on the Editor.

```
public BrainParameters Clone()
{
    return new BrainParameters
    {
        VectorObservationSize = VectorObservationSize,
        NumStackedVectorObservations
        = NumStackedVectorObservations,
        VectorActionSize = (int[])VectorActionSize.Clone(),
        VectorActionDescriptions
        = (string[])VectorActionDescriptions.Clone(),
        VectorActionSpaceType = VectorActionSpaceType
    };
}
```

BarracudaPolicy: This is used for the Inference Engine for running a pretrained neural network in Unity. Internally this script uses the "ModelRunner" class. The first stage of this script contains the enum for the different types of "Inference Device," which is CPU or GPU (0 or 1, respectively.) The "BarracudaPolicy" inherits from the "IPolicy" interface. It contains attributes such as the agent ID and the list of sensor shapes. The "ModelRunner" script is used across all the policies that have the similar deep learning model and the same inference device.

```
public enum InferenceDevice
{
    CPU = 0,

    GPU = 1
}
protected ModelRunner m_ModelRunner;
int m_AgentId;
List<int[]> m_SensorShapes;
```

This script also has a method BarracudaPolicy, which takes as arguments the attributes from the BrainParameters class, the neural network model to be used, and the inference device to run the model. This method uses the "GetOrCreateModel" method from the Academy class, which implies that if the model has been used previously for inference, it will continue using that. In the event that no pretrained model has been used for that agent before, it will get the built model assigned from the assets folder.

```
public BarracudaPolicy(
    BrainParameters brainParameters,
    NNModel model,
    InferenceDevice inferenceDevice)
{
    var modelRunner = Academy.Instance.GetOrCreateModelRunner(model,
    brainParameters, inferenceDevice);
    m_ModelRunner = modelRunner;
}
```

It contains a "RequestDecision" method that makes decisions for the agent based on the trained model. It takes as input the list of sensors (ray/camera) and has an associated episode ID for each stage of the decision-making process.

```
public void RequestDecision(AgentInfo info, List<ISensor> sensors)
{
    m_AgentId = info.episodeId;
    m_ModelRunner?.PutObservations(info, sensors);
}
```

The "DecideAction" method uses the "GetAction" method from the ModelRunner script to allow the agent to take corresponding action against a particular decision.

```
public float[] DecideAction()
{
    m_ModelRunner?.DecideBatch();
    return m_ModelRunner?.GetAction(m_AgentId);
}
```

HeuristicPolicy: This is used when neither Default nor InferenceOnly options are provided in the BehaviorParameters script. This is a rather hard-coded implementation of the heuristic policies, which makes the agent take action each time the "RequestDecision" method is called. It does not use the BrainParameters script attributes and uses the input list of sensors from the agent directly to make its decisions. The methods that are important in this context are "RequestDecision" method, which takes the list of sensors as input, and the "DecideAction" method, which takes the previous decision made by the policy.

```
public HeuristicPolicy(ActionGenerator heuristic, int numActions)
{
    m_Heuristic = heuristic;
    m_LastDecision = new float[numActions];
}
public void RequestDecision(AgentInfo info, List<ISensor> sensors)
{
    StepSensors(sensors);
    m_Done = info.done;
    m_DecisionRequested = true;
}
```

```
public float[] DecideAction()
{
    if (!m_Done && m_DecisionRequested)
    {
        m_Heuristic.Invoke(m_LastDecision);
    }
    m_DecisionRequested = false;
    return m_LastDecision;
}
```

The StepSensors function uses the ISensor.GetCompressedObservation, which makes the sensor usage consistent between training and inference. If no compression is used, then the observation space data from the sensors is used (written to ObservationWriter class); otherwise, it is passed as compressed data.

```
void StepSensors(List<ISensor> sensors)
{
    foreach (var sensor in sensors)
    {
        if (sensor.GetCompressionType()
            == SensorCompressionType.None)
        {
            m_ObservationWriter.SetTarget(m_NullList
              , sensor.GetObservationShape(), 0);
            sensor.Write(m_ObservationWriter);
        }
        else
        {
            sensor.GetCompressedObservation();
        }
    }
}
```

IPolicy: This interface is used across all the policy scripts we studied, as it is connected to a single agent. It provides the methods that are required by other policy scripts described in this section, to provide decisions that the agent can take. It has two unique declarations: the "RequestDecision" method, which signals the brain that

255

the agent needs to make a decision based on the policy on which it is running, and the "DecideAction" method, which implies that the decision has to be taken at that particular time step this method is called.

```
void RequestDecision(AgentInfo info, List<ISensor> sensors);
float[] DecideAction();
```

The brain is expected to update its decisions once the "DecideAction" method is called.

That completes the policies section, which involves the decision-making steps of the agent. This part takes as input the sensor data and acts as an interface for the different types of brain—internal, external, and heuristic—to work upon and provides the decisions to the agent. This is the C# part of the brain that internally links with the deep learning networks in Tensorflow (which we will discuss in the Chapter 5). The entire policy architecture can be summarized in Figure 4-10.

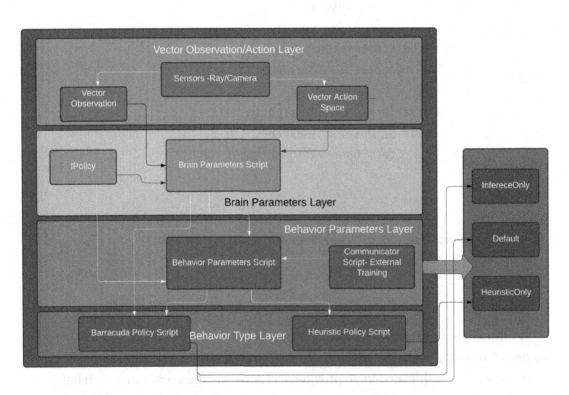

Figure 4-10. *Sensor-Policy architecture in the brain of agents*

By now we have a good understanding of the two major parts of the brain: sensors and policies. This is, however, restricted only to the C# layer of the ML Agents software development kit (SDK). The other important parts of the brain include the inference, communicators, and demonstrations. Of these the inference module is related to the Barracuda Engine and procedure of using Tensorflow pretrained model on stacked observation data. The demonstrators are an important aspect of the imitation learning set of algorithms. These two will be briefly discussed here since they have more to do with the Python side of ML Agents. The communicators is an interesting module that deals with how the connection takes place between the policy and Tensorflow/Python API.

Inference

This part is used for the Inference Engine for running the pretrained models in Unity. Essentially this deals with the compressed Tensor data that has been received as an output from the Tensorflow training. The Barracuda policy that we learned about previously uses this module to link the observations and action spaces and provides the decisions during gameplay. There are certain important aspects of this module, such as the "ModelRunner" script and "BarracudaModelParamLoader" script. The associated scripts that deal with the Tensor-processed data are TensorApplier, TensorGenerator, TensorProxy, and the TensorNames script. We will be learning about some of the aspects of this module—namely, the ModelRunner script—to understand how the Barracuda policy uses this script to make decisions.

ModelRunner: The attributes of this script include the agent information, sensors, and dictionary containing the last action performed by the agent. It also contains properties like the neural network model, which is to be used for inference, inference device, inference inputs and outputs, and validation of the sensor shape. The "ModelRunner" method uses the parameters from the "BrainParameter" script and also has a "TensorAllocator" attribute for intermediate caching of the Tensor result of each episode of training. It then loads the model to be used by using the ModelLoader.Load syntax and assigns it as a Barracuda model. In the event of no model being present for inference, a null value is assigned.

```
public ModelRunner(
    NNModel model,
    BrainParameters brainParameters,
    InferenceDevice inferenceDevice = InferenceDevice.CPU,
```

```
    int seed = 0)
      {
    Model barracudaModel;
    m_Model = model;
    m_InferenceDevice = inferenceDevice;
    m_TensorAllocator = new TensorCachingAllocator();
    if (model != null)
      {
#if BARRACUDA_VERBOSE
        m_Verbose = true;
#endif

        D.logEnabled = m_Verbose;
        barracudaModel = ModelLoader.Load(model);
        var executionDevice = inferenceDevice == InferenceDevice.GPU
            ? WorkerFactory.Type.ComputePrecompiled
            : WorkerFactory.Type.CSharp;
        m_Engine = WorkerFactory.CreateWorker(executionDevice,
        barracudaModel, m_Verbose);
      }
    else
    {
        barracudaModel = null;
        m_Engine = null;
    }
```

The next part involves abstracting the inference inputs from the loaded Barracuda model with the help of BarracudaModelParamLoader.GetInputTensors command. Likewise, the inference outputs are also received from the Barracuda model. However, for running the inference, there are certain other attributes such as TensorGenerator and TensorApplier classes, which are required. The TensorGenerator is actually a dictionary, mapping between the Tensor Names and the generators. Generators can be considered as specialized functions that can help to analyze large data sets by passing it as an iterator. Instead of loading the entire data set during training or during use of a pretrained model, the generator helps to partition the data according to a function that allows better data inflow for processing. We will understand the use of a generator in depth when we study convolution neural networks in the next chapter. For the time being, it is safe to assume that the "TensorGenerator" class is a mapping that allows a proper data flow pipeline for inference. Similarly, the TensorApplier is a mapping between output Tensor names and the methods that will use that particular output Tensor. It also stores the model information and actions and updates the memory (buffer) of the agent.

```
m_InferenceInputs = BarracudaModelParamLoader.GetInputTensors(barracudaModel);
m_OutputNames = BarracudaModelParamLoader.GetOutputNames(barracudaModel);
m_TensorGenerator = new TensorGenerator(
    seed, m_TensorAllocator, m_Memories, barracudaModel);
m_TensorApplier = new TensorApplier(
    brainParameters, seed, m_TensorAllocator, m_Memories, barracudaModel);
```

The PrepareBarracudaInputs initializes the inference inputs from Barracuda and also creates a mapping in a dictionary between the names and the inference inputs.

The FetchBarracudaOutputs fetches the output depending on a particular "name" provided. This is important to get the correctly mapped inference input associated with a particular name so that it can be processed.

```
static Dictionary<string, Tensor> PrepareBarracudaInputs(IEnumerable<Tensor
Proxy> infInputs)
{
    var inputs = new Dictionary<string, Tensor>();
    foreach (var inp in infInputs)
    {
        inputs[inp.name] = inp.data;
    }
    return inputs;
}

List<TensorProxy> FetchBarracudaOutputs(string[] names)
{
    var outputs = new List<TensorProxy>();
    foreach (var n in names)
```

```
    {
        var output = m_Engine.PeekOutput(n);
        outputs.Add(TensorUtils.TensorProxyFromBarracuda(output, n));
    }

    return outputs;
}
```

The PutObservations validates the shape of the sensor and associates an episode ID
with each episode such that the decisions taken by the agent are in a sorted manner. If
the agent reaches the goal by following the Inference Engine model, then the last action
is removed from the dictionary, as no further steps should be taken for that episode.

```
public void PutObservations(AgentInfo info, List<ISensor> sensors)
{
#if DEBUG
    m_SensorShapeValidator.ValidateSensors(sensors);
#endif
    m_Infos.Add(new AgentInfoSensorsPair
    {
        agentInfo = info,
        sensors = sensors
    });
    m_OrderedAgentsRequestingDecisions.Add(info.episodeId);
    if (!m_LastActionsReceived.ContainsKey(info.episodeId))
    {
        m_LastActionsReceived[info.episodeId] = null;
    }
    if (info.done)
    {
        m_LastActionsReceived.Remove(info.episodeId);
    }
}
```

The "DecideBatch" method actually runs the pretrained model in batches in
Inference Engine. The current batch size is checked and passed through the generator
function in "TensorGenerator" script to produce a Tensor that can be passed as

information to the agent. As mentioned the generator allows the data to be passed in the form of sequentially partitioned and processed data in batches rather than passing the entire data. This improves performance and also can assist if a large amount of memory is taken up while passing the processed data. The "BeginSample" method associates the sampled Tensor names with the inference input. The input tensors are then fed to the Inference Engine using the "GenerateTensor" method. This method is the initial pipeline for batch processing, which involves passing the Tensor data to the Inference Engine using the generator function.

```
if (currentBatchSize == 0)
{
    return;
}
if (!m_VisualObservationsInitialized)
{
    var firstInfo = m_Infos[0];
    m_TensorGenerator.InitializeObservations(firstInfo.sensors,
    m_TensorAllocator);
    m_VisualObservationsInitialized = true;
}

Profiler.BeginSample("ModelRunner.DecideAction");
Profiler.BeginSample($"MLAgents.{m_Model.name}.GenerateTensors");
m_TensorGenerator.GenerateTensors(m_InferenceInputs, currentBatchSize,
m_Infos);
Profiler.EndSample();
```

The next stage involves preparing the Barracuda inference inputs corresponding to the prepared Tensor data. Here the TensorGenerator script becomes useful, which contains a mapping between the Tensor names (data) and the inference inputs.

```
Profiler.BeginSample($"MLAgents.{m_Model.name}.PrepareBarracudaInputs");
var inputs = PrepareBarracudaInputs(m_InferenceInputs);
Profiler.EndSample();
```

Then the Barracuda/Inference Engine executes the model. For this it uses the WorkerFactory class internally to execute the model. The m_Engine variable uses the inference inputs and assigns a particular action in a time-step to be performed by the agent, such as 3D motion. This, in turn, returns the output of the executed model, in the form of memories, actions, and decisions taken by the agent. Here the TensorApplier script becomes useful; it controls the mapping between the associated inference output and the memories and actions taken by the agent.

```
Profiler.BeginSample($"MLAgents.{m_Model.name}.ExecuteGraph");
m_Engine.Execute(inputs);
Profiler.EndSample();

Profiler.BeginSample($"MLAgents.{m_Model.name}.FetchBarracudaOutputs");
m_InferenceOutputs = FetchBarracudaOutputs(m_OutputNames);
Profiler.EndSample();

Profiler.BeginSample($"MLAgents.{m_Model.name}.ApplyTensors");
m_TensorApplier.ApplyTensors(m_InferenceOutputs, m_
OrderedAgentsRequestingDecisions, m_LastActionsReceived);
Profiler.EndSample();

Profiler.EndSample();


m_Infos.Clear();


m_OrderedAgentsRequestingDecisions.Clear();
```

The method "HasModel" checks whether a valid pretrained model is present for inference along with an associated inference device. The method "GetAction" retrieves the last action taken by the agent in a sorted order of the decisions vector.

To summarize this particular script is associated with using the inference mode for the agent. The pipeline involves acquiring the processed data from the pretrained model, partitioning it into Tensor data according to a generator function for smoother batch processing, passing this Tensor data along with its Tensor name as inference input to the Barracuda Engine ("TensorGenerator"), executing the model, extracting the results in the form of memory, assuming actions taken by the agent in an inference output format, associating the inference output with the results of each episode with the help of TensorApplier, and extracting the latest output for the next episode. This continues as long as the agent has reached the goal in inference training or the episode is terminated. This can be illustrated in Figure 4-11.

Inference Module Of Brain

Abhilash Majumder | July 14, 2020

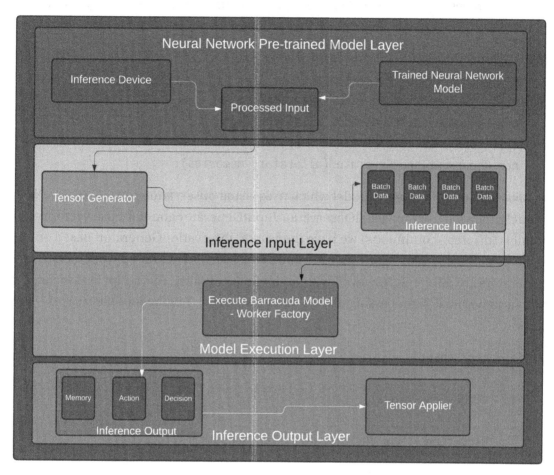

Figure 4-11. *Inference module workflow in ML Agents brain*

The other scripts associated with this inference module include those mentioned here.

TensorGenerator: This script, as mentioned earlier, maintains a mapping between the Tensor name and the generator function for batch processing of the preprocessed data. This is important because in ML Agents, we will look into a variety of models using both discrete/multi-discrete and continuous observation spaces. Depending on the nature of the Tensor pretrained data, the generator function is different for each model. There can be different generators that can be used for this case, such as for batch processing, sequence length, or recurrent input (used in recurrent neural network):

```
m_Dict[TensorNames.BatchSizePlaceholder] =
    new BatchSizeGenerator(allocator);
m_Dict[TensorNames.SequenceLengthPlaceholder] =
    new SequenceLengthGenerator(allocator);
m_Dict[TensorNames.RecurrentInPlaceholder] =
    new RecurrentInputGenerator(allocator, memories);
```

For instance, if we use a model which uses visual observation data (ConvD NN model), then we use the VisualObservationInputGenerator and if we use vectorized models (discrete/continuous) we have the VectorObservationGenerator. Based on the type of the deep RL algorithm used and the associated neural network model, the generators are different. However, without loss of generality, this script is associated with a smooth batch processing of data for the Inference Engine module to work upon.

```
if (isVectorSensor)
{
    if (vecObsGen == null)
    {
        vecObsGen = new VectorObservationGenerator(allocator);
    }
    vecObsGen.AddSensorIndex(sensorIndex);
}
else
{
    m_Dict[TensorNames.VisualObservationPlaceholderPrefix
            + visIndex] =
        new VisualObservationInputGenerator(sensorIndex
            , allocator);
    visIndex++;
}
```

Along with this, Barracuda also has its own generator function associated with the Inference Model that can be used.

TensorApplier: This script is a mapping of the Tensor output with the memory and actions of the agent. Depending on the type of distribution—continuous or discrete—the mapping is different. For continuous action space, ContinuousActionOutputApplier is used, while DiscreteActionOutputApplier is used for discrete spaces. It also updates the memory with execution of each episode of the agent and uses the BarracudaMemoryOutputApplier method to hold the memory contents of each episode. The script also updates the agent based on the actions taken by it.

Demonstrations

Another fundamental part of the brain that involves imitation learning through heuristic policy and records the user's gameplay for training the agent is the demonstrations module. This module does not require neural network training or Inference Engine to allow the agent to make decisions. Rather this is a separate module that is devoted to making the agent learn by imitating human control. The most important script that we will be exploring in this section is the DemonstrationRecorder script.

DemonstrationRecorder: In order to record demonstrations from an agent by heuristic control, we have to add this script to the agent. When the "Record" option is checked during the gameplay, the demonstrations are recorded in a .demo file located in the assets folder. This particular demo file contains the details of the demonstrations of executing the imitation learning algorithm, which may take a few minutes to many hours based on the complexity of the environment. Figure 4-12 shows the demonstration file in 3D Ball environment in Unity.

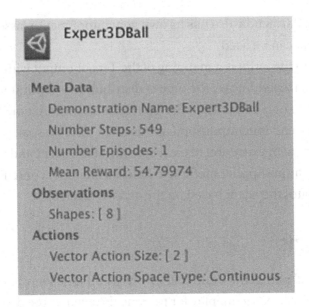

Figure 4-12. *Sample demonstration file (.demo) in Unity*

This script has certain attributes, such as the demonstrator name, the maximum length of the name, extension type of the file (.demo), and the default storage directory (Assets/Demonstrations).

```
[FormerlySerializedAs("demonstrationDirectory")]
 [Tooltip("Directory to save the demo files. Will default to " +
            "{Application.dataPath}/Demonstrations if not
            specified.")]
     public string DemonstrationDirectory;

     DemonstrationWriter m_DemoWriter;
     internal const int MaxNameLength = 16;

     const string k_ExtensionType = ".demo";
     const string k_DefaultDirectoryName = "Demonstrations";
     IFileSystem m_FileSystem;

     Agent m_Agent;
```

On initialization, rather during lazy initialization, the behavior parameters of the agent are taken as inputs and an associated file path and file name is provided for the demonstration file.

```
internal DemonstrationWriter LazyInitialize(IFileSystem fileSystem = null)
    {
        if (m_DemoWriter != null)
        {
            return m_DemoWriter;
        }

        if (m_Agent == null)
        {
            m_Agent = GetComponent<Agent>();
        }

        m_FileSystem = fileSystem ?? new FileSystem();
        var behaviorParams
        = GetComponent<BehaviorParameters>();
        if (string.IsNullOrEmpty(DemonstrationName))
        {
            DemonstrationName
            = behaviorParams.BehaviorName;
        }
        if (string.IsNullOrEmpty(DemonstrationDirectory))
        {
            DemonstrationDirectory
            = Path.Combine(Application.dataPath
            ,  k_DefaultDirectoryName);
        }

    DemonstrationName
     = SanitizeName(DemonstrationName, MaxNameLength);

    var filePath = MakeDemonstrationFilePath
    (m_FileSystem, DemonstrationDirectory,
    DemonstrationName);
```

```
        var stream = m_FileSystem.File.Create(filePath);
    m_DemoWriter = new DemonstrationWriter(stream);

    AddDemonstrationWriterToAgent(m_DemoWriter);

    return m_DemoWriter;
}
```

The "SanitizeName" method removes all characters, with the exception of alphanumeric characters, from the demonstration name. It can be considered analogous to regular expressions used for removing the characters.

```
internal static string SanitizeName(string demoName, int maxNameLength)
    {
        var rgx = new Regex("[^a-zA-Z0-9 -]");
        demoName = rgx.Replace(demoName, "");

    if (demoName.Length > maxNameLength)
    {
        demoName = demoName.Substring
            (0, maxNameLength);
    }
    return demoName;
}
```

The MakeDemonstrationFilePath is important for saving the demonstration file after the observations are complete. It uses a timestamp to save the demonstrations files. After the training episode is over, the "AddDemonstratorWriterToAgent" method is called. It calls the behavior parameters of the agent and associates the trained observation file (.demo) file with it. The agent then runs this trained demonstrations file and uses imitation learning. The important part is that during the recording phase (training phase of imitation learning), the behavior parameter type can be set to HeuristicOnly, since in this case there are no associated internal/external brain to choose from. This heuristic brain runs on the HeuristicPolicy, which we discussed in the policy section of the brain. However, another modification can be using a player brain, that can record the actions through the user's gameplay.

```
var behaviorParams = GetComponent<BehaviorParameters>();
        demoWriter.Initialize(
            DemonstrationName,
```

```
        behaviorParams.BrainParameters,
        behaviorParams.FullyQualifiedBehaviorName
    );
    m_Agent.DemonstrationWriters.Add(demoWriter);
```

This concludes the demonstrations part and the associated script, which are very important to understand. The related scripts will be discussed separately when we will explore generative adversarial imitation learning (GAIL) in depth in later chapters. The workflow of imitation learning can be viewed, as shown in Figure 4-13.

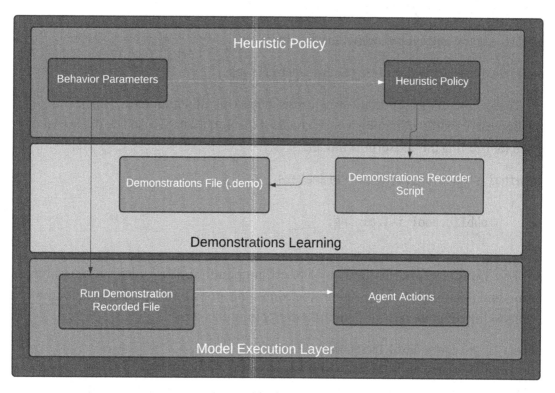

Figure 4-13. *Demonstrations module for imitation learning in brain*

Communicators

The communicators module is associated with linking the brain with the Python API. Since this module is important for real-time training, it can be considered to be a part of the academy. Since this module controls the linkage between the C# and Python API for training, we will look into the ICommunicator script.

ICommunicator: The ICommunicator script contains the important attributes, such as the port number, for connecting to Python, the Unity Package Version, Unity Communication Version, name, and the RL capabilities of the C# framework.

```
public int port;
public string name;

public string unityPackageVersion;

public string unityCommunicationVersion;

public UnityRLCapabilities CSharpCapabilities;
```

These contain the important structures such as UnityRLParameters, which contain the Boolean variable isTraining, which checks if the port (5004) is used by the external brain for running the Tensorflow model.

```
internal struct UnityRLInputParameters
    {
        public bool isTraining;
    }
```

The "QuitCommandHandler" and "ResetCommandHandler" quits and resets the events and parameter updates sent by the communicator. The script also handles the "UnityRLInputParameters" updates from the communicator.

```
internal delegate void QuitCommandHandler();
internal delegate void ResetCommandHandler();
internal delegate void RLInputReceivedHandler(UnityRLInputParameters
inputParams);
```

The next part is important because in communicators there are two types: Unity communicator and external communicator. The flow of information (packets) between the two communicators is purely sequential. An initialization message packet is exchanged between the two communicators once a connection is established. This is analogous to the handshaking technique in computer networks. As a convention, the Unity input is a message from external to Unity and Unity output is a message from Unity to external. Message packets are sent sequentially one after another for each information exchange, except for the first time where the external communicator sends two messages for establishing the connection. The structure of the message can be presented as follows:

```
UnityMessage
    ...Header
    ...UnityOutput
    ......UnityRLOutput
    ......UnityRLInitializationOutput
    ...UnityInput
    ......UnityRLInput
    ......UnityRLInitializationInput
```

The "ICommunicator" interface contains all the declarations of the previous functions such as quit/reset the command received. It also sends the academy parameters through the communicator using the "Initialize" method:

```
UnityRLInitParameters Initialize(CommunicatorInitParameters
initParameters);
```

The "SubscribeBrain" puts a new brain for communication:

```
void SubscribeBrain(string name, BrainParameters brainParameters);
```

The PutObservation sends the observations to the agent at each time step of external training through communicators. The DecideBatch signals the ICommunicator that the agents are ready to receive the action, and if the communicator has not received an action for its agents, then it needs to get an action at this point. The "GetActions" method gets the agent actions based on the batching procedure(key).

```
void PutObservations(string brainKey, AgentInfo info, List<ISensor>
sensors);
void DecideBatch();
float[] GetActions(string key, int agentId);
```

There are other scripts associated with the communicator, such as the rpccommunicator and UnityRLCapabilities script, which internally implements this Icommunicator interface. The most important functionalities of the communicators involve exchange of message packets between the Unity brain and the external communicator via port number 5004.

This concludes the in-depth analysis of the five main parts of the brain architecture: sensors, policies, communicators, inference/Barracuda, and demonstrations. Associated folders that are present in the brain architecture include "Editor" and Grpc. The Editor folder contains scripts that inherit/implement the four major parts of the brain for display in the Editor. The Grpc is a routing protocol that is used as a part of the communicator. In the next section, we will understand the academy architecture, which involves three major scripts: Agent, Academy, and DecisionRequester. These control and coordinate the training activities of the agent and its relationship with the environment.

Understanding the Academy and Agent

Now that we have an idea of the brain architecture, we can understand the different aspects of the academy, which works in sync with the brain. The academy can be considered to be part of the RL environment in Unity, which is responsible for controlling the training, episodes, epochs, and the environment variables for the agent brain. Accordingly the academy, agent, communicator, and Python API are the four major peripherals of the brain that assist the brain with its decision-making process. We studied the communicator object in the previous section, and here we will see how the academy is also related to the communicator. We will study the Academy script, which is associated with the academy architecture. In the later sections we will be looking at the "Agent" script and the DecisionRequester script.

Academy: The academy, along with the learning brain, is part of the environment, while the communicator is used for exchanging message packets between the former and the Python API. In the "FixedUpdate" method, the "Academy.Instance. EnvironmentStep()" method is called, which is used for setting up the environment for each episode of training.

```
void FixedUpdate()
        {
            Academy.Instance.EnvironmentStep();
        }
```

The academy class is a singleton design pattern. The instance is initialized the first time it is accessed. After it is initialized, the academy attempts to connect to the Python API through the external communicator. In the event that no port is available or no message packets are exchanged between the external communicator and academy, the external brain will not function. In this case, the academy defaults the environment to run in Inference Mode or in Heuristic Mode. The communicator interaction is very important, as it interacts directly between the Python API and the academy. The script contains some important attributes such as the API version, which has to be compatible with the "UnityEnvironment.API_VERSION," the package version, the training port (5004), and the flag for signaling the training port ("—mlagents-port").

```
const string k_ApiVersion = "1.0.0"
internal const string k_PackageVersion = "1.0.0-preview";

const int k_EditorTrainingPort = 5004;
 const string k_PortCommandLineFlag = "--mlagents-port";
```

The academy script then follows a lazy initialization procedure, and once initialized, the connection remains open for message exchange between the communicator and the academy. It then checks whether the communicator is on by using the Boolean variable IsCommunicatorOn.

```
static Lazy<Academy> s_Lazy = new Lazy<Academy>(() => new Academy());
public bool IsCommunicatorOn
        {
            get { return Communicator != null; }
        }
```

It controls the number of episodes completed, the total episode count of the training phase, the total steps completed in a single episode, and the total steps completed during the entire simulation. It uses the "ModelRunner" class (discussed), to store the neural network model trained in run-time for inference. It also has a random seed value for the inference to work.

```
int m_EpisodeCount;
int m_StepCount;
int m_TotalStepCount;

        internal ICommunicator Communicator;
```

```
bool m_Initialized;
List<ModelRunner> m_ModelRunners = new List<ModelRunner>();

bool m_HadFirstReset;
int m_InferenceSeed;

public int InferenceSeed
{
    set { m_InferenceSeed = value; }
}
```

The important aspect of the academy class is that in the event of a multi-agent environment, it maintains a synchronization in communication. This implies that the agents perform their steps in a consistent manner and an agent has to act based on a particular decision before another agent can request a decision. It also has variables such as DecideAction, AgentIncrementStep, and Destroy methods to control this synchronization. It controls the reset, action, pre-step, and other decisions taken by the agent.

```
internal event Action DecideAction;
internal event Action DestroyAction;
internal event Action AgentIncrementStep;
public event Action<int> AgentPreStep;
internal event Action AgentSendState;
internal event Action AgentAct;
internal event Action AgentForceReset;
public event Action OnEnvironmentReset;
AcademyFixedUpdateStepper m_FixedUpdateStepper;
GameObject m_StepperObject;
```

It then initializes the agent ("Academy" method) to make sure at least a valid agent is present in the scene. The "EnableAutomaticStepping" involves the use of "Academy/.EnvironmentStep" method to control the actions and decisions taken by the agent and also the environment for training. It is present in a Fixed Update method, as it is called for each frame for the agent to take an action, and attaches the "AcademyFixedUpdateStepper" component to the agent for this task.

```
void EnableAutomaticStepping()
```

```
{
    if (m_FixedUpdateStepper != null)
    {
        return;
    }

    m_StepperObject = new GameObject("AcademyFixedUpdateStepper");
    m_StepperObject.hideFlags = HideFlags.HideInHierarchy;
    m_FixedUpdateStepper = m_StepperObject.AddComponent
                                    <AcademyFixedUpdateStepper>();
    try
    {
        GameObject.DontDestroyOnLoad(m_StepperObject);
    }
    catch {}
}
```

The "DisableAutomaticStepping" method is used for manually controlling the
academy training steps rather than updating it at each frame. Contrary to the Fixed
Update method, to utilize academy training, we have to manually set the stepping using
the "Academy.EnvironmentStep" method. It is not recommended generally to disable
the automatic update for best performance measures during online training with
academy.

```
void DisableAutomaticStepping()
    {
        if (m_FixedUpdateStepper == null)
        {
            return;
        }

        m_FixedUpdateStepper = null;
        if (Application.isEditor)
        {
            UnityEngine.Object.DestroyImmediate(m_StepperObject);
        }
```

```
        else
        {
            UnityEngine.Object.Destroy(m_StepperObject);
        }

        m_StepperObject = null;
    }
```

The "AutomaticSteppingEnabled" is used for automatic stepping during academy training. It chooses between the "DisableAutomaticStepping" and "EnableAutomaticStepping" depending on fixed updates are present in the training phase. The next method, "ReadPortFromArgs," reads the port and the associated flag for training. The "EnvironmentParameters" are very important in this context as, if curriculum learning (which will be discussed later) is used, then the values of the parameters generated from the training process can be passed to the academy.

```
public EnvironmentParameters EnvironmentParameters
    {
        get { return m_EnvironmentParameters; }
    }
```

The "StatsRecorder" method records the statistics of a particular academy being trained in Unity. The "InitializeEnvironment" method is used for initializing the environment and registering the side channels (part of communicators) for information exchange. The side channels will be particularly useful when we see how to pass information between the Jupyter Notebook and Unity when training a model. It allows us to register the observation and action space and has certain attributes to control the simulated training. The next step involves starting the port and establishing the connection with the external communicator ("rpcCommunicator").

```
TimerStack.Instance.AddMetadata("communication_protocol_version",
k_ApiVersion);
TimerStack.Instance.AddMetadata("com.unity.ml-agents_version",
k_PackageVersion);

EnableAutomaticStepping();
```

```
SideChannelsManager.RegisterSideChannel(new EngineConfigurationChannel());
m_EnvironmentParameters = new EnvironmentParameters();
m_StatsRecorder = new StatsRecorder();

var port = ReadPortFromArgs();
if (port > 0)
{
    Communicator = new RpcCommunicator(
        new CommunicatorInitParameters
        {
            port = port
        }
    );
}
```

If the communicator is not connected, a new attempt to start the link between the UnityRLParameters and the communicator is started. Based on the outcome, if the communicator fails to respond due to no Python process being in the training state, then the academy defaults to "Inference" mode of learning. It also issues a warning stating that in the event of not being able to connect with the trainer on port 5004, with the current "API_VERSION," the academy forces the brain to use the inference module and its associated policies.

```
if (Communicator != null)
{
    try
    {
        var unityRlInitParameters = Communicator.Initialize(
            new CommunicatorInitParameters
            {
                unityCommunicationVersion = k_ApiVersion,
                unityPackageVersion = k_PackageVersion,
                name = "AcademySingleton",
                CSharpCapabilities = new UnityRLCapabilities()
            });
```

```
        UnityEngine.Random.InitState(unityRlInitParameters.seed);
        m_InferenceSeed = unityRlInitParameters.seed;
        TrainerCapabilities = unityRlInitParameters.TrainerCapabilities;
        TrainerCapabilities.WarnOnPythonMissingBaseRLCapabilities();
    }
    catch
    {
        Debug.Log($"" +
            $"Couldn't connect to trainer on port {port} using API version
            {k_ApiVersion}. " +
            "Will perform inference instead."
        );
        Communicator = null;
    }
    if (Communicator != null)
    {
        Communicator.QuitCommandReceived += OnQuitCommandReceived;
        Communicator.ResetCommandReceived += OnResetCommand;
    }
```

The next few code segments are related to recording the different statistics of the training environment, such as episodes, number of episodes, resetting the environment, steps completed in a particular episode, and others. Another interesting aspect is that the Academy script uses the "GetOrCreateModel" method from the ModelRunner class, which we talked about in the inference module of the brain. This is required because in case the communicator is not connected, the academy resorts to the inference module, which runs on the Barracuda Engine and uses the ModelRunner script. Internally as we have studied, this script uses the BrainParameters script to make the decisions depending on the pretrained neural network, inference policy, and the inference device. The "Dispose" method disposes the connection if the training is completed by closing the communication and side channels with the communicator. Once the training/ inference is completed, the academy resets itself, so that when we would want to train again using the internal or the external brain, it should connect with the inference or communicator module, respectively.

The entire workflow of the academy involves controlling the package versions, port number, API compatibility with Python along with controlling the episodes and steps in an episode during training. It also plays an important role in connecting the communicator with the brain for real-time training and also provides selection between the enable or disable environment steps option. It also controls the choice of brain to run the model based on whether the communicator sends a feedback message packet ensuring connection establishment. If connection is made, the online training procedure is triggered, which trains the external brain of the agent with Tensorflow through the Python API. If connection is not made, then the inference model is assigned to the brain. To conclude, this architecture controls all the environmental attributes required by the brain to train its policies. This is shown in Figure 4-14.

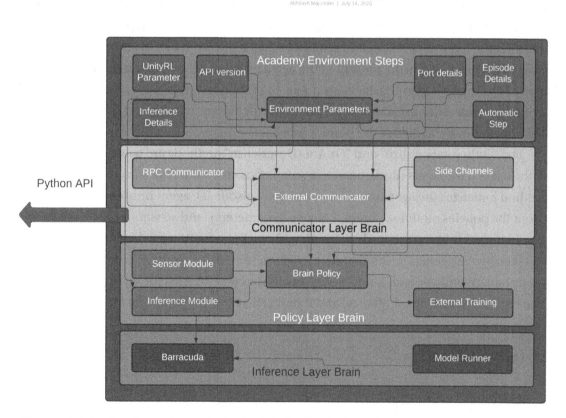

Figure 4-14. *Academy layer linked with the brain in ML Agents*

Agent: Since this script is particularly large, we will look into the important aspects of it. As mentioned, the agent uses the brain–academy architecture to make its decisions and corresponding actions. It has certain parameters that control the action space, whether continuous or discrete. For discrete spaces, the DiscreteActionMasks Boolean array controls the decision branches the agent will not take. It has the rewards, maximum steps reached in a training simulation period, and a corresponding episode ID. The AgentActions struct contains the float array vectorActions. As mentioned before, the agent receives the observation inputs through the sensor layer of the brain (ray/sphere/camera) and passes it to the different policies present in the policy layer of the brain to make corresponding decisions. Based on the availability of the communicator and the associated port, the academy decides whether to train the agent on external policy (real-time Tensorflow training) or in inference policy. The academy then passes this information to the BehaviorParameters script of the brain with an associated behavior type (default, inference only, heuristic only). There are also certain important variables that control the cumulative reward, completed episodes, step count, agent information, request decision, and request action. It also contains observation sensors and a list of sensors present in the agent prefab for the sensor module of the brain. For imitation learning, it also contains the DemonstrationWriters variable for writing the observations(heuristic policy) in the .demo file, which we studied in the "demonstrations" module of the brain.

The "OnBeforeSerialize" and "OnAfterDeserialize" methods are used for serialization of the agent parameters (decisions, steps, max steps, actions). The "LazyInitialize" method initializes the agent with the associated episode ID, agent information, policy (from the policies module of brain, BehaviorParameters), and sensors. It also initializes step increments in each episode of training (AgentIncrementStep), the decision that is to be taken by the agent (DecideAction), the action step of the agent (AgentAct), the agent send state (AgentSendState), and AgentForceReset, which resets the agent parameters. The methods ResetData, Initialize, and InitializeSensors are important for the workflow of the agent.

```
if (m_Initialized)
{
    return;
}
m_Initialized = true;
```

```
m_EpisodeId = EpisodeIdCounter.GetEpisodeId();
m_PolicyFactory = GetComponent<BehaviorParameters>();

m_Info = new AgentInfo();
m_Action = new AgentAction();
sensors = new List<ISensor>();

Academy.Instance.AgentIncrementStep += AgentIncrementStep;
Academy.Instance.AgentSendState += SendInfo;
Academy.Instance.DecideAction += DecideAction;
Academy.Instance.AgentAct += AgentStep;
Academy.Instance.AgentForceReset += _AgentReset;
m_Brain = m_PolicyFactory.GeneratePolicy(Heuristic);
ResetData();
Initialize();
InitializeSensors();

if (Academy.Instance.TotalStepCount != 0)
{
    OnEpisodeBegin();
}
}
```

The "DoneReason" enum contains details such as DoneCalled, MaxStepReached, and Disabled, which signals the agent that the goal is reached or the training has stopped, the maximum steps that the agent reached, and whether the agent is disabled. The next important method is "NotifyAgentDone," which marks the agent as done; this implies that the agent has reached a goal or the training has been terminated. This contains the rewards attained by the agent, the episode ID of the completed episode, and also collects decisions with the "CollectObservations" method. Since we mentioned that the last action is taken up by the agent in the successive training step, this is achieved by the "m_Brain?.RequestDecision" method. After the decision taken by the agent, the sensors are reset using the "ResetSensors" method. Now along with inference and external training, we also have demonstrators that rely on heuristic control. For that the agent selects the decision based on the contents of the ".demo" file and also writes the new set of rewards and actions through the "Record" method. For each episode, the rewards are calculated along with the decisions, and at the end of the episode, the

array containing the details of that particular episode is cleared. The rewards are set
to 0, and the request decision/request action variables are set to false. This method
actually signals the agent to write the observations once the goal is reached by following
a particular policy.

```
if (m_Info.done)
{
            return;
}
m_Info.episodeId = m_EpisodeId;
m_Info.reward = m_Reward;
m_Info.done = true;
m_Info.maxStepReached = doneReason == DoneReason.MaxStepReached;
if (collectObservationsSensor != null)
{
    collectObservationsSensor.Reset();
    CollectObservations(collectObservationsSensor);
}
m_Brain?.RequestDecision(m_Info, sensors);
ResetSensors();

 foreach (var demoWriter in DemonstrationWriters)
{
    demoWriter.Record(m_Info, sensors);
}

if (doneReason != DoneReason.Disabled)
{
    m_CompletedEpisodes++;
    UpdateRewardStats();
}

m_Reward = 0f;
m_CumulativeReward = 0f;
m_RequestAction = false;
m_RequestDecision = false;
Array.Clear(m_Info.storedVectorActions, 0, m_Info.storedVectorActions.
Length);
```

The "SetModel" method is similar to BehaviorParameters, which decides which model to use based on inference, external training model, or heuristic policy. The "ReloadPolicy" method reloads the current policy that the agent is using at the start of a particular episode. The "SetReward" method offers an implementation of the rewards attained by the agent during training. It is important to note that the rewards are used only during external brain training state in RL and not in inference mode. This method replaces any rewards added to the agent during the current training time step.

```
public void SetReward(float reward)
        {
#if DEBUG
        Utilities.DebugCheckNanAndInfinity(reward, nameof(reward),
nameof(SetReward));
#endif
        m_CumulativeReward += (reward - m_Reward);
        m_Reward = reward;
        }
```

It is recommended to use a positive reward to reinforce learning (during training) and a negative reward to penalize mistakes. We will be using this in our scripts. The "AddReward" method is used for adding the Rewards for all the stages of the training (cumulative rewards across episodes).

```
public void AddReward(float increment)
        {
#if DEBUG
        Utilities.DebugCheckNanAndInfinity(increment,
nameof(increment), nameof(AddReward));
#endif
        m_Reward += increment;
        m_CumulativeReward += increment;
        }
```

The "GetCumulativeReward" method is used to get the cumulative rewards for the episode. The "UpdateRewardStates" method is used to update the rewards based on the policy used by the agent and depends on the BehaviorType. The "RequestAction" method is used to repeat the previous action taken by the agent according to the decision (latest) from its policies. In many cases a new decision may not be requested—for example, an agent may use the previous decision to translate along an axis. Here the agent uses the "RequestAction" method to stay on its course, the decision is called when the agent wants to change its course or its velocity/acceleration/force. The "ResetData" method resets the brain parameters, the observation/action spaces, and the vectors (discrete/continuous). Inside the "Initialize" method, there is a heuristic method that uses the "Input.GetAxis" to maneuver the agent along different axes. This is more or less a use-controlled heuristic policy that is used in case the demonstrations policy (imitation learning) is triggered by the brain.

```
public override void Heuristic(float[] actionsOut)
            {
                    actionsOut[0] = Input.GetAxis("Horizontal");
                    actionsOut[1] = Input.GetKey(KeyCode.Space) ? 1.0f : 0.0f;
                    actionsOut[2] = Input.GetAxis("Vertical");
            }
```

The "IntializeSensors" method relies on the sensor module of the brain and uses its methods such as acquiring the child sensors of the agent, controlling the stacked observations of vectors (VectorSensor and BrainParameter scripts)and other attributes. This method is like an interface that signals the sensor module of the brain to record the observations in the vector container(float array). The SendInfoToBrain sends the sensor information taken by the agent to the brain, which can then work on this data. As mentioned, this information is passed to the policies module of the brain. Here the academy plays a role—if the communicator is connected, external real-time training policy is taken up and the agent is trained using that policy. If not, the information is sent to the inference module of the brain, where the Barracuda Engine runs an associated pretrained neural network model. The "RequestDecision" method (discussed) then uses these observations from sensors and the policy of the brain to let the agent make a particular decision

```
m_Brain.RequestDecision(m_Info, sensors);
```

The other methods, "GetAction" and "ScaleAction," are used by the agent to convert those decisions taken into actions. The "CollectDiscreteActionMasks()" method is used to mask certain discrete actions, which the agent will not perform. Lastly, the "OnActionReceived" method signifies the actions taken by the agent based on the decision policy. For continuous cases, a float array is returned and this should be clamped to increase stability in training, and for discrete cases, the action space consists of the branches (e.g., input up arrow key signifies agent moving forward and vice versa).

To summarize, the agent script relies on the brain and academy to choose its decision and accordingly takes its action and gets rewards. The initialization stage includes assigning the values of brain parameters, agent parameters and setting up the reward functions for the environment. The agent attains the input information from the sensor module of the brain and passes it to the brain for processing. The academy then confirms whether to use external brain or internal brain, depending on the connection established by the communicator module. Based on that, respective policies are applied to the agent to make its decisions. The decision aspect invokes the agent to take actions. The results of the actions can be either a credit of positive or negative reward for the agent. Depending on whether the goal is reached or the rewards are attained, this process of requesting sensor information and processing it with the policies and providing actions continues. At the end of each episode, the agent is reset and all the agent parameters are reset.

The last script that we will discuss is the "DecisionRequester" script.

DecisionRequester: This script automatically requests decisions for an agent. This is a script that is required to be attached to an agent in our scene. It controls the frequency at which the agent will request the decisions, in units of academy time-steps. For instance, a value of 5 implies that the agent will request the decision after 5 academy time-steps. It controls the choice about whether the agent will take actions between decisions in academy time-steps, such as the example mentioned in the "agent" script. It also initializes the agent class.

```
[Range(1, 20)]
[Tooltip("The frequency with which the agent requests a decision. A
DecisionPeriod " +
                "of 5 means that the Agent will request a decision every 5
                Academy steps.")]
public int DecisionPeriod = 5;

[Tooltip("Indicates whether or not the agent will take an action during the
Academy " +
                "steps where it does not request a decision. Has no effect
                when DecisionPeriod " +
                "is set to 1.")]
```

```
[FormerlySerializedAs("RepeatAction")]
public bool TakeActionsBetweenDecisions = true;

[NonSerialized]
Agent m_Agent;
```

The method "MakeRequests" uses the decisions from the academy to inform the agent about whether or not it should request a decision or take actions between decisions.

```
void MakeRequests(int academyStepCount)
    {
        if (academyStepCount % DecisionPeriod == 0)
        {
            m_Agent?.RequestDecision();
        }
        if (TakeActionsBetweenDecisions)
        {
            m_Agent?.RequestAction();
        }
    }
```

That completes the entire architecture of the brain, academy, and agent in depth. We now have a fair understanding about the different scripts in the brain/academy section and have also studied the interactions between them. The link between the different parts of the brain, academy, and agent can be illustrated as shown in Figure 4-15.

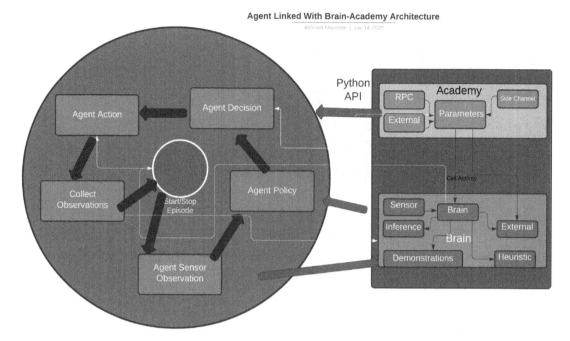

Figure 4-15. *Brain academy architecture linked with agent*

There are certain scripts that require knowledge of deep learning in this module and will be discussed later, especially the ModelOverrider script. In the next section, with this knowledge, we will build a small deep learning agent in Unity and train it with Unity ML Agents.

Training an ML Agent with a Single Brain

In this section, we will create a simple agent whose task is to find the target object present in the scene. Only this time we will be using our own agent script implementation to train it with Unity ML Agents. For this, we have to navigate to the Assets folder under the DeepLearning folder and navigate to FindingBlock-PPO folder. We have to open up the findingblock Unity scene file. In this scene, the blue agent has to locate the green target with the help of ML Agents and sensors. It is surrounded in a bounding box platform. A sample preview of the scene looks similar to Figure 4-16.

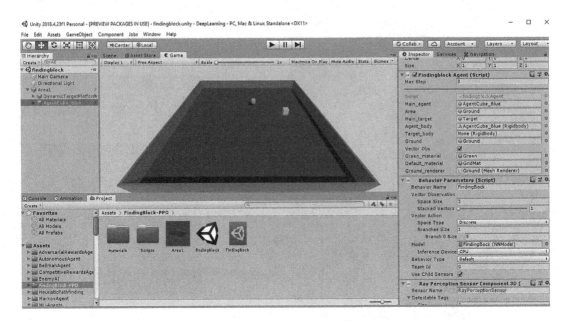

Figure 4-16. *Finding block scene in Unity ML Agents*

Attach Behavior Parameters Script

Behavior Parameters: Now in this case, since we have to use external brain for training our agent in ML Agents, the first objective is to attach all the necessary components to the blue agent. For this the most important part is to associate a brain for the agent, and in this case we will attach the "BehaviorParameters" script to the blue agent. Now as we have mentioned, this controls all the vector observations, stacked vectors, the action space, inference device, and child sensors. For our case, we will keep most of the details with the default values except the space size of the vector observation. This is because in our case, the agent can move along x and z axes. For each axis, the agent can move in the positive and negative direction—hence the possible space of observation is two along a single axis. For both x and z axes, the total vector observation space becomes 2*2, which is 4. We know internally there is a float array that is present in the vector observations section, numbered from 0 to 3.

    Ray Perception Sensor Component 3D: We will attach this script, as it is associated with the Sensors module of the brain and is used for collecting observations in the scene. We will keep most of the default values as it is, such as angles, rays in each direction, ray length, and so forth, or we can change them accordingly. We have to define the detectable tags that the agent has to observe. In this case, the agent should only observe the target and the wall boundary of the platform; and those detectable tags are mentioned accordingly. Figure 4-17 shows this setup in Unity.

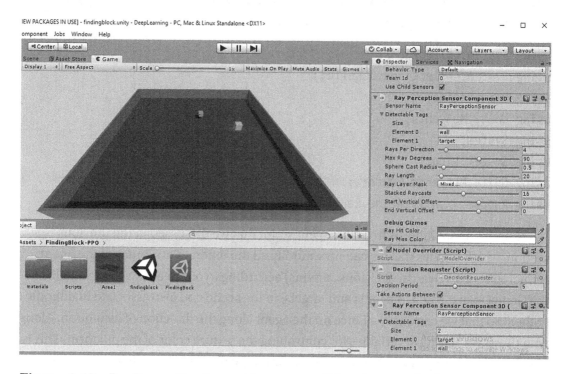

Figure 4-17. *RayPerceptionSensorComponent3D script attached to agent*

Decision Requester: This script is also attached to the agent, as it helps in the decision-making process, as discussed before. We will keep the default values here.

Model Overrider: We have to attach this script to override our training model in run-time or during Inference. We will study this script in the next chapter.

That was all the associated scripts we had to attach to associate a brain to the agent. Now we have to write our own script to handle the agent and also design a reward function for our RL problem.

Writing Agent Script

For this context, we will open the findingblockAgent script. Since in this script we will be using dependencies from the ML Agents framework, we have to include some libraries, particularly the Unity.MLAgents and Unity.MlAgents.Sensors:

```
using System.Collections;
using System.Collections.Generic;
using UnityEngine;
using Unity.MLAgents;
using System;
using System.Linq;
using Unity.MLAgents.Sensors;
using Random = UnityEngine.Random;
```

Now this script inherits from the Agent script that we discussed in the previous section, which implies that we can now modify all the different attributes of the Agent script (episodes, rewards, decisions, actions) according to our needs. We will initialize the GameObjects, such as agents and targets, in the scene and also associate Rigidbodies to them so that we can apply a Force on the agent along the direction of its motion. Along with these, we also have variables for controlling the texture color of the platform. This is because once the agent reaches the goal, we want the platform to be lit in green color.

```
float rewards = 0f;
public GameObject main_agent;
public GameObject area;
public GameObject main_target;
private int target_hit_count = 0;
private findblockArea my_area;
public Rigidbody agent_body;
public Rigidbody target_body;
public GameObject ground;
public bool vectorObs;
public Material green_material;
public Material default_material;
public Renderer ground_renderer;
```

Now there are certain override methods that we will use in our script. The first overridden method is Initialize. In this method, we will initialize the agent, target, and the platform

```
public override void Initialize()
{

    agent_body = GetComponent<Rigidbody>();
    my_area = area.GetComponent<findblockArea>();
    target_body = GetComponent<Rigidbody>();
}
```

The next overridden method is "CollectObservations," which takes as input the sensors from the "VectorSensor" class. Since, in our case, we will be using ray sensors module of the brain, the Boolean variable "vectorObs" results in true. The "sensor. AddObservation" method collects the sensor information in the form of a float vector.

```
if (vectorObs == true)
{
    sensor.AddObservation(transform.InverseTransformDirection(agent_body.
    velocity));
}
```

Since, we also require a default heuristic policy for our brain, we override the Heuristic method. This is a straightforward heuristic implementation where we use the W, A, S, and D keys to control our agent. For this we use the "Input.GetKey" method from Unity, and fill in the "actionOut" float array(contains the action spaces).

```
public override void Heuristic(float[] actionsOut)
{
    actionsOut[0] = 0;
    if (Input.GetKey(KeyCode.D))
    {
        actionsOut[0] = 3;
    }
    else if (Input.GetKey(KeyCode.W))
    {
        actionsOut[0] = 1;
    }
```

```
    else if (Input.GetKey(KeyCode.A))
    {
        actionsOut[0] = 4;
    }
    else if (Input.GetKey(KeyCode.S))
    {
        actionsOut[0] = 2;
    }
}
```

The next overridden method is MoveAgent script that controls the motion of the agent. Since we are using the discrete action space, the agent can take decisions based on branching. As mentioned, the agent can move along both directions in the x and z planes, and for each action the agent takes, a force is applied to it. This helps the agent to move along the direction, rotation proposed by the action vector.

```
public void moveAgent(float[] acts)
    {
        var direction = Vector3.zero;
        var rotation = Vector3.zero;
        var action = Mathf.FloorToInt(acts[0]);
        switch (action)
        {
            case 1:
                direction = transform.forward * 1.0f;
                break;
            case 2:
                direction = transform.forward * (-1.0f);
                break;
            case 3:
                rotation = transform.up * 1.0f;
                break;
            case 4:
                rotation = transform.up * (-1.0f);
                break;

        }
```

```
    transform.Rotate(rotation, Time.deltaTime * 100f);
    agent_body.AddForce(direction * 1f
    , ForceMode.VelocityChange);
}
```

The next overridden method is "OnActionReceived," which is used to credit the agent with rewards based on whether the agent has reached the target in that episode of training or not. Correspondingly, we call the "MoveAgent" method here for each step of the episode. The "AddReward" method adds the rewards. We can also use "SetRewards" to replace the rewards received with a single reward that the agent will receive on reaching the target.

```
public override void OnActionReceived(float[] vectorAction)
    {
        moveAgent(vectorAction);

        AddReward(-0.0001f);
        Debug.Log("Choosing action");
        rewards += -0.0001f;
        Debug.Log(rewards);
    }
```

The last overridden method is "OnEpisodeBegin," and as the name suggests, this controls the events that are required at the start of a particular training episode. This calls the reset() method, which is used to set the position of the target and the blue agent to a random start position within the platform. If in any case the blue agent goes below the surface of the platform, the "EndEpisode" method is signaled. This instructs the ML Agents architecture to start the next episode of training.

```
public override void OnEpisodeBegin()
    {
        Debug.Log("Resetting");

        reset();
        if (main_agent.transform.position.y <= -2.0f
            || main_agent.transform.position.y >= 3.0f)
```

```
    {
        Debug.Log("Down");
        reset();
        EndEpisode();
    }

}
```

Those are all the overridden methods that are required in any traditional sensor(ray sensor)-based ML Agents agent in Unity. There are associated functions such as "OnCollisionEnter," which checks if the agent has reached the green target and uses the "SetReward" method to set the agent rewards or if it has collided with the wall in which case the SetReward method credits a negative reward to simulate punishment.

```
void OnCollisionEnter(Collision collision)
    {
        if (collision.gameObject.CompareTag("target"))
        {
            SetReward(5.0f);
            target_hit_count++;
            rewards += 5.0f;
            Debug.Log(rewards);
            StartCoroutine(Lightupground());
            EndEpisode();

        }
        else if (collision.gameObject.CompareTag("wall"))
        {
            SetReward(-0.02f);
            rewards += -0.02f;
            Debug.Log(rewards);
            Debug.Log("Failed");
            EndEpisode();
        }

    }
```

The reset method resets the agent by choosing any angle in range (0-360 degrees) for its direction and a random transform location along the x and z axes. Similarly the green target is also initialized at a random transform position at the start of each episode.

```
public void reset()
    {
        var rotate_sample = Random.Range(0, 4);
        var rotate_angle = 90f * rotate_sample;
        main_agent.transform.Rotate(new Vector3(0f
          , rotate_angle, 0f));

        var loc_random_x = Random.Range(-30f, 34f);
        var loc_random_z = Random.Range(-29f, 50f);

        main_agent.transform.position =
          new Vector3(loc_random_x, 2.5f, loc_random_z);
        agent_body.velocity = Vector3.zero;
        agent_body.angularVelocity = Vector3.zero;
        target_reset();

    }
```

The "Lightupground" Enumerator lights up the platform surface by changing the material of the ground renderer to green, which asserts that the agent has reached the green target.

```
private IEnumerator Lightupground()
    {
        ground_renderer.material = green_material;
        Debug.Log("Success");
        yield return new WaitForSeconds(0.1f);
        ground_renderer.material = default_material;

    }
```

That concludes the findingblockAgent script, which is required for our blue agent to reach the green target or to find it. We will attach this script to the blue agent, and now we have to train this agent in Tensorflow and Unity ML Agents. To summarize we just have to override certain methods of the "Agent" script to make our own RL environment and agent in it. This is the ease of creation of a simulated RL environment which leverages the deep learning algorithms of Unity ML agents and the OpenAI Gym wrapper.

Training Our Agent

By now, we are familiar with training agent using the default PPO algorithm implemented in Unity ML Agents. So we will open our Anaconda prompt and type the mlagents learn command. We will use the "trainer_config.yaml" file (like in the last chapter), and since we have not created any hyperparameters particular to this "FindingBlock-PPO" Unity scene, we will use the default hyperparameter set present in the "yaml" file.

```
mlagents-learn <path to trainer_config.yaml> --run-id=
"newFindingblockagent" --train
```

On writing this command, we will see the Unity logo with the Tensorflow API version, Unity package version, and Python API version. When prompted, we have to click the Play button in the Unity Editor to start the training process, as shown in Figure 4-18.

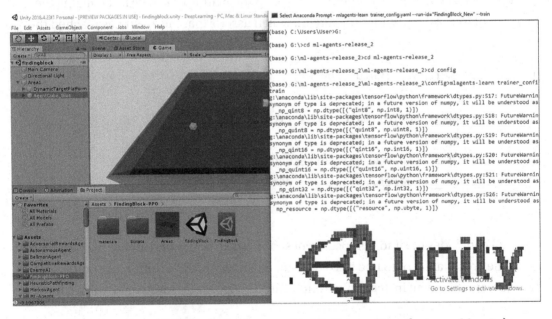

Figure 4-18. *Training "FindingBlockAgent" with Tensorflow (external brain)*

We will also see the list of the default hyperparameters and the outcome of each training episode. Now we internally can connect that the academy exchanges information packets with the communicator (port: 5004) to allow the training process. We can also connect with how the external brain is now training with the default policy of the "BehaviorParameters" script attached to the agent, as shown in Figure 4-19.

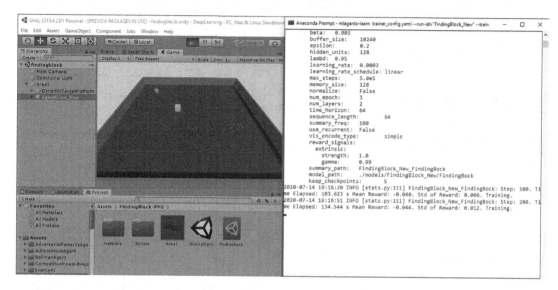

Figure 4-19.   *Training episodes with PPO algorithm in ML Agents*

During training, we can also move over to the Scene View to see how the ray sensors are detecting the tagged objects in the scene, as shown in Figure 4-20.

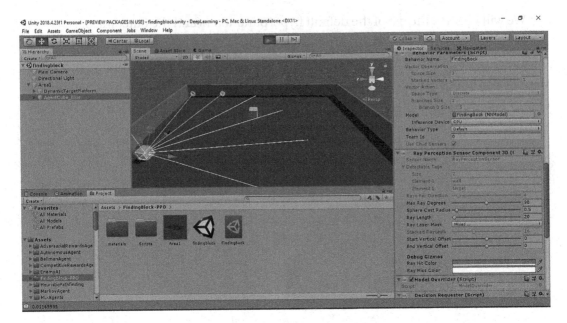

Figure 4-20. *Ray sensors detecting tags during Tensorflow training*

Visualize with TensorBoard

Now we will visualize this learning in TensorBoard. We have already explored how to do that in the previous chapter. We have to navigate to the "config" folder of ML Agents and then we have to type the command:

```
tensorboard -logdir=summaries
```

This lets TensorBoard know that the logs and details of the training phase will be recorded in the "summaries" folder. Connection is made on port 6006 and a corresponding "http" address is provided which contains the device name of our system. When we open Tensorboard we will see the environment cumulative rewards and the episode length, as shown in Figure 4-21.

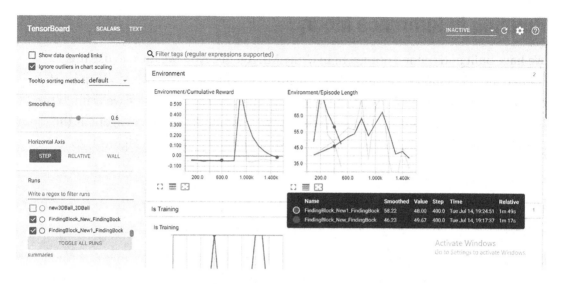

Figure 4-21. *Environment parameters with TensorBoard*

We will also visualize the loss, policy entropy, policy extrinsic reward, and value estimate details that are an important metric for learning, as shown in Figure 4-22.

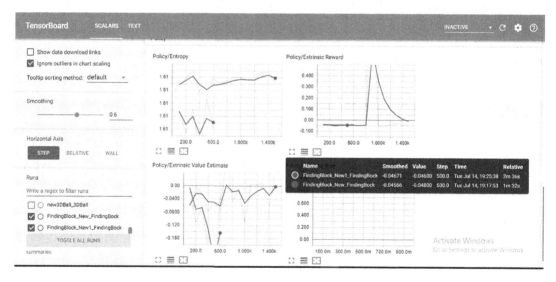

Figure 4-22. *Policy parameters with TensorBoard*

Running in Inference Mode

We have built and trained our agent in Unity ML Agents. Now we have to use this trained model in Inference Mode. We can attach this model to the NNModel part of the "BehaviorParameters" script and select the inference device where we want to run. Finally, we can build this Unity scene with the trained model placed in agent as the internal brain (for inference) and watch the simulation, as shown in Figure 4-23.

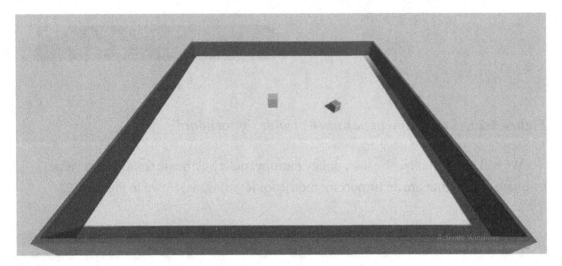

Figure 4-23. *Finding block agent simulation using ML Agents*

Generic Hyperparameters

Since we used the default hyperparameters for our training according to the "trainer_config.yaml" file, we can play around with those hyperparameters accordingly to have a better outcome. The default set of hyperparameters can be presented as :

```
default:
  trainer: ppo
  batch_size: 1024
  beta: 5.0e-3
  buffer_size: 10240
  epsilon: 0.2
```

```
hidden_units: 128
lambd: 0.95
learning_rate: 3.0e-4
learning_rate_schedule: linear
max_steps: 5.0e5
memory_size: 128
normalize: false
num_epoch: 3
num_layers: 2
time_horizon: 64
sequence_length: 64
summary_freq: 100
use_recurrent: false
vis_encode_type: simple
reward_signals:
  extrinsic:
    strength: 1.0
    gamma: 0.99
```

This signifies that PPO algorithm is used as the deep RL algorithm (we will study this in the next chapter). We can control the epochs, episodes, and other attributes. If we are facing performance issues related to the system memory, we can change the batch size attribute. Changing the hidden units, learning rate can also help in faster convergence to a global minima. If we set the "use_recurrent" attribute to true, then we will be using a recurrent neural network for holding information inside the agent's memory. We can increase the memory size attribute and also check the corresponding performance. However, for best practices, it is regarded that a hidden layer depth of around 128 with a batch size of 512 can perform fairly well in most of the use-cases. However, based on complex environments, these can be changed as well. We can play around with these hyperparameters and visualize it on TensorBoard. The implications associated with changing these parameters will be discussed in more depth in the next chapter.

Summary

We are at the end of this chapter, which details the entire architecture of the ML Agents in depth. Certain key takeaways from this chapter include:

- We learned about the fundamental architecture of the brain in ML Agents. We studied about the different types of sensors for collecting information as well as the policies required to train those observations. We then learned about the inference module of the brain, which uses the Barracuda Engine. The demonstrations module, which is important for imitation learning was understood. Lastly we visited the communicators, which are also a part of the academy framework controlling the real-time Python API training process.

- The next part revolved around understanding the academy architecture, where we saw how environment parameters are controlled by the academy. Based on the communicators' response, the academy chooses the type of brain (inference, external, heuristic) for the agent.

- We explored the Agent script, which we have also used for training our own "FindingBlock" agent. We understood how the agent links itself with the brain and the academy and takes actions based on the decisions provided by them. We observed the distinction between the discrete and continuous action spaces.

- The Decision Requester script was explored, which controlled the agents' decision-making process. We also went in depth on the Behavior Parameters script, which is a fundamental part of the brain.

- In the next phase we create a simulation based on the PPO algorithm where an agent has to find a target in a constrained environment. We used RayPerceptionsensorComponent3D, behavior parameters, decision requester, and model overrider scripts to set up the brain-academy architecture for our agent. We then wrote the overridable method of the Agent script to create our own reward functions, observations, and action spaces.

- We trained our agent using the mlagents-learn command, which we explored in the last chapter, and visualized the ray sensors, rewards, actions in real-time external training through Python API.

- Visualization was done in Tensorboard regarding the policy rewards, cumulative rewards, and loss and then we used the trained brain for inference and built a Unity executable file containing the agent with the trained internal brain.

- Lastly we briefly studied the default hyperparameters present in the "trainer_config.yaml" file. We will be discussing how changing a hyperparameter can affect the learning process in the next chapters.

With that we come to the end of this chapter. In the next chapter, we will learn about the different deep RL algorithms made in Unity ML agents as well as create our own deep learning models using the Gym Wrapper. We will look into the Python side of the ML Agents and also create vision-based neural networks for our agents.

CHAPTER 5

Deep Reinforcement Learning

In the last chapter, we studied the various aspects of the brain-academy architecture of the ML Agents Toolkit and understood certain scripts that are very important for the agent to make a decision according to a policy. In this chapter, we will be looking into the core concepts of deep reinforcement learning (RL) through Python and its interaction with the C# scripts of the brain-academy architecture. We have had a glimpse of a part of deep RL when we briefly discussed the deep Q-learning algorithm using the OpenAI Gym environment (CartPole) and also when we were discussing the Baselines library of OpenAI. Through the course of training the ML Agents in Tensorflow through external brain, we have also used the proximal policy optimization (PPO) algorithm with the default hyperparameters present in the trainer_config.yaml file. We will be discussing these algorithms in depth along with several other algorithms from the actor critic paradigm. However, to fully understand this chapter, we have to understand how to build deep learning networks using Tensorflow and the Keras module. We also have to understand the basic concepts of deep learning and why it is required in the current context. Through this chapter we will also create neural network models for computer vision methods, which will be extremely important when we will be studying the GridWorld environment. Since we primarily have ray and camera sensors that provide the observation space to the agent, in most of the models, we will have two variants of policies: multi-layered perceptron (MLP-based networks) and convolution neural networks (CNN-2D-based networks). We will also be looking into other simulations and games that are created using the ML Agents Toolkit and will also try to train our models based on the Baseline implementations by OpenAI. However, let us first understand the fundamentals of generic neural network models in deep learning.

© Abhilash Majumder 2021
A. Majumder, *Deep Reinforcement Learning in Unity*, https://doi.org/10.1007/978-1-4842-6503-1_5

Fundamentals of Neural Networks

Since we have been training our agents and have also applied certain deep learning algorithms, we should understand how a neural network performs. The simplest form of a neural network is a perceptron model, which consists of an input layer, certain "hidden" layers, and an output layer. The generic requirement of deep learning or neural network-based models is to iteratively optimize a cost function, prominently referred to as a "loss" function based on certain constraints. In many cases, whenever we apply neural networks, it is assumed that the concerned function must be a continuously differentiable function, having nonlinearity. This also implies that the curve of the function will contain certain trajectories that are called "maxima" and "minima." The former refers to the highest value of the function, while the later refers to the lowest one. In generic machine learning (ML), we are interested in finding a global minima of the curve with the assumption that the corresponding weights or coefficients of the function will be optimal and consistent to produce minimum error. However, in RL, we will see that both global minima as well as global maxima plays a significant role in policy gradients.

Perceptron Neural Network

For simplicity let us take a function where the value y depends on a value x in a two-dimensional plane. We will associate weights or coefficients with x and also add biases. In the context of Perceptron model, weights are the most important aspects, and we will be optimizing these weights iteratively using simple MLP networks. If we signify w to be the set of weights and b to be the set of biases for our model, we can write:

$$y = \sigma\,(w.x + b),$$

where σ is a nonlinear function that relies on e (natural log), which is most commonly known as a sigmoid function. This nonlinear sigmoid function is represented as:

$$\sigma(x) = 1/(1 + e^{(-x)})$$

Now, the importance of this particular nonlinear function is that it aids in the convergence of the loss function toward the global minima. These nonlinear functions are generally referred to as activation functions. The sigmoid function generally represents an S-shaped curve. There are several other functions that we will explore in our next sections, such as Softmax, Relu, and others. It is important to understand that these nonlinear transformations to the weighted function assist in the global convergence. We can create this simplified formulation of the sigmoid curve using Python through Jupyter Notebooks. We will import the math and matplotlib libraries for creating a scaled sigmoid graph. Let us open the Sigmoid-Curve.ipynb notebook. We will see that the sigmoid function implements the exponential equation of the sigmoid curve by using an array.

```
def sigmoid(x):
    a = []
    for item in x:
        a.append(1/(1+math.exp(-item)))
    return a
```

After this we plot the curve using matplotlib and specify a uniform distribution of points from -10 to +10 along the x axis with a difference of 0.2 between any two points.

```
x = np.arange(-10., 10., 0.2)
sig = sigmoid(x)
plt.plot(x, sig)
plt.show()
```

Upon running this, we will have a scaled sigmoid curve in our Jupyter Notebook, as shown in Figure 5-1, and we have created an activation function. This is a very important function when it comes to binary classification in generic ML, as we will be exploring briefly.

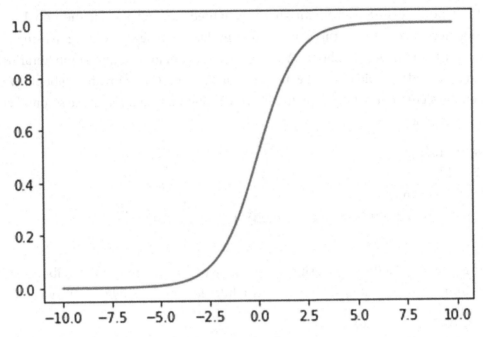

Figure 5-1. *Sigmoid curve in Jupyter Notebook*

In general iterative gradient-based learning, there are three fundamental steps:

- forward pass
- error computation
- backward pass

Forward pass: This is the first stage in which the value of y is computed after multiplying the input vectors (inputs) with the weight vector (weights) and adding bias vector(bias), if required. It is to be kept in mind that in ML, we will be dealing with tensors, which are matrices effectively for all the input and outputs. Hence the letters y, w, and x represent vectors or matrices rather than a single valued function. We saw this in the section where the following equation was shown:

$$y = \sigma\,(w.x + b)$$

Error computation: Since we will be running our perceptron neural network against a certain "ground truth" data set to be validated as to what extent the network is predicting correct outputs based on the input tensors, weight matrices, and biases.

Here lies an important concept of error computation between each iterative learning phase. Effectively the error in each epoch is considered to be the absolute difference between the predicted output tensor and the actual output tensor.

$$\Delta = |y' - y|,$$

where Δ is the error term. Now we will be considering an important metric, referred to as the mean-squared-error, which is given by the formulation:

$$\Delta_{mse} = 0.5\,(\,y' - y)^2$$

This equation, referred to as the loss function or quadratic cost function, is extremely important in generic learning because we will be using it in the next step to compute the gradients.

Backward pass: This is a very important step that deals with the following updates.

- **Compute gradients:** The mean-squared-error computed in the previous equation needs to be partially differentiated to update the weights for the next epoch and also to find a proper convergence of the algorithm. This implies that we have to differentiate the error in the previous step with respect to the weight matrix. Mathematically this can be shown as:

$$J = \partial\,\Delta_{mse}\,/\partial w,$$

which effectively implies that we have to partially differentiate the error term with respect to the weight matrix by using chain rule of differentiation. The chain rule can be stated as :

$$d(xy) = [y(dx) + x(dy)]\,(dx),$$

where xy is a continuously differentiable function of f(x, y).

We have to partially differentiate the function y, with respect to w. In generic partial differentiation technique, we have to compute the derivative of the term with which the derivative can be computed and keep the rest as constant. For instance, if an equation is of form f(x, y)=xy, then if we are required to partially differentiate f with respect to x, we would have:

$$\partial(f(x, y)) = [y\,(d(x)/dx) + x(d(y)/dx)]\partial x,$$

where $d(f(x))/dx$ represents normal differentiation of a function. By rules of calculus, this yields:

$$\partial(f(x, y)) = [y]\partial x,$$

as differentiation of a constant is computed as 0; hence, the second term vanishes. Now since we used a sigmoid curve as our activation, we have the partial derivative of the loss function as follows:

$$\partial(y) = [\ [d(\sigma(y))/d(y)][d(y)/dw]\ ]\partial w,$$

by the laws of chain rule in differentiation. Now the derivative of a sigmoid curve is simply given by:

$$d(\sigma(\theta)) = \theta(1\text{-}\theta)\ d(\theta),$$

where θ is any polynomial function, which in this case is y. The derivative of the second part can be computed by following the chain rule:

$$d(y)/dw = w(d(x)/dw) + x(d(w)/dw) + (db/dw)$$

Now since this is partial differentiation, we will be removing derivatives of constants $(d(x)/dw$ and $d(b)/dw)$, which effectively reduces our final equation, which can appear like this:

$$\partial(y) = [[y(1\text{-}y)]\ (x)(d(w)/dw)]\partial w$$

Now we have used the Δ_{mse} as the error function, and if we have to compute the partial derivative of Δ_{mse}, then we can write:

$$\partial(\Delta_{mse}) = [0.5^* 2(d|y'\text{-}y|/dw)]\partial w$$

Now y' is the actual value for validation and y is the predicted value; hence, effectively we have to do a partial derivative of y, which has already been computed. This entire process is used to find the gradients of the loss function at each step of the learning process.

- **Back propagation:** The most important part of the weight update rule in generic ML. After we compute the gradients, we then propagate those gradients along the way from the output tensors

to the input tensors. Since in our case, we used a simple sigmoid
Perceptron model without any hidden layers, in many complex
neural networks, we will be having many hidden layers. This implies
each and every hidden layer will consist of individual perceptron
units like the one we used. For our case, since there are no hidden
layers, we simply update the weight tensor using the rule:

$$w = w - \alpha(J),$$

where $J = \partial \Delta_{mse} / \partial_w$, α is the learning rate. In this context, this
weight update rule is associated with the gradient descent
algorithm. As mentioned before, the major backbone of
supervised ML is to optimize a loss function by updating the
weights and converging to a global minima. Keeping this in
mind, it is considered in gradient descent that the trajectory of
the weight update policy should be along the steepest slope of
convergence. However in many cases, gradient descent may
not be useful, as it may overfit the data set. This implies that the
policy may oscillate along the vicinity of the global minima and
never converge, or it may be stuck in a local minima. That is
where the symbol α comes into the picture. The α is termed as the
learning rate, which modulates the step size to be taken by the
policy to reach the global minima. But it has been observed that
this does not solve the issue of local oscillation of the converging
algorithm; hence, there have been several developments to
optimize the gradient descent algorithm by using certain
momentum. Throughout the deep learning module, we will be
using optimizers exhaustively while writing our neural networks
for different deep RL algorithms. Some of the most prominent
optimizers include Adam, Adagrad, and Adadelta, while older
variations include RMSProp and SGD. These optimizers use
momentum coupled with stochastic gradient convergence
algorithms to modulate the step size. We can visualize a simple
gradient descent convergence using the Stochastic Gradient
Descent (SGD) algorithm, as shown in Figure 5-2.

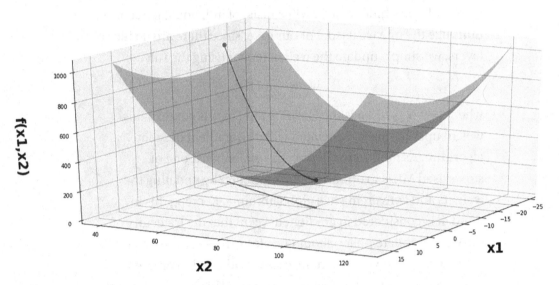

Figure 5-2. Gradient Descent algorithm in BackPropagation

This can be visualized by running the Plotting Gradient Descent.ipynb Notebook. Effectively we studied backpropagation using a simple Perceptron model, and this completes the introductory part of a fundamental neural network, which includes sigmoid activation, error computation, and weight update policy using gradient descent algorithm and backpropagation to the input layer. This model can be illustrated as shown in Figure 5-3.

Perceptron Neural Network Model

Abhilash Majumder | July 24, 2020

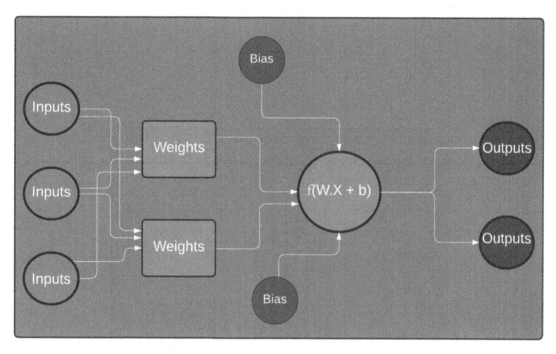

Figure 5-3. *Feed-forward perceptron neural network model*

In the next section, we will study a comparatively dense network and understand the concept of backpropagation for that model. Without loss of generality, all the layers involved in a particular neural network are based on certain matrices/tensors for computation, and in most of the cases, multiplication is called "dot" operation of product between two or more tensors. Since all these partial differentiation rules will be applicable to these layers, or rather these tensors, we can think that there will be several matrix/tensor computations required. However, the three stages of forward pass, error computation, and backward pass remain the same for most of the neural network models. We will be looking at MLP dense network and convolution network.

Dense Neural Network

Now let us understand the fundamentals of a dense network having hidden layers that are perceptron units. This is the most common neural network model that we will be using and can be visualized as shown in Figure 5-4.

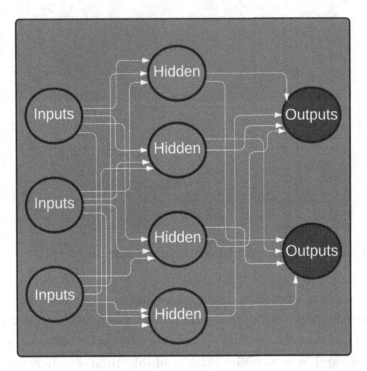

Dense Neural Network Model

Abhilash Majumder | July 24, 2020

Figure 5-4. Dense neural network with hidden layer

The interesting aspect is that the hidden layers consist of perceptron modules having different activation functions. These perceptron units of the hidden layer are then superimposed to generate a cumulative loss function. In this case, we will consider the three stages as mentioned—the forward pass, error computation, and the backward pass.

Forward pass: In this case, let us assume that the perceptrons in the hidden layer have only sigmoid activation. Also the weights and the inputs are tensors or matrices. Let us assume that l represents the hidden layer and (l-1) represents the input layer. The corresponding weights for the connection between the kth neuron in the $(l-1)^{th}$ and the jth neuron in the lth layer are denoted by w^l_{jk}. Now if we assume a bias tensor in the lth layer as b^l and the input tensor from the kth neuron in the previous $(l-1)^{th}$ layer as x^{l-1}_k, the forward pass equation or the weighted neuron function can be framed as:

$$y^l_j = \sigma \left(\sum w^l_{jk} x^{l-1}_k + b^l_j \right)$$

Generally if the activations are different for each Perceptron model, then the equation can be modified as:

$$y^l_j = f \left(\sum w^l_{jk} x^{l-1}_k + b^l_j \right),$$

where f is any activation function such as tanh, softmax, and so on. Once we have attained the loss function, we have to determine the errors, which is also known as the cost function.

Error computation: We will consider the mean squared error metric, which is also referred to as the quadratic cost or loss function. Correspondingly, this can be represented by the equation:

$$\Delta_{mse} = 0.5 \left(y' - y \right)^2$$

Now in this dense network case, we will have a sampled cost function across n training samples. Also the y should be replaced by the new loss function that we have explored. Changing these details leads to the similar equation:

$$\Delta_{mse} = (1/2n) \sum (y' - y^l_j)^2$$

For one particular training sample, this equation can be simplified as:

$$\Delta_{mse} = C = (1/2) \sum (y' - y^l_j)^2,$$

where we denote it by using the symbol C for simplicity.

Backward pass: In this case, as mentioned, the most important aspects are gradient computation and error backpropagation. In this case we will be using partial derivatives to find out gradients like before, with the exception that in this case there is a hidden layer.

- Backpropagation: This implies that instead of computing a single layer derivative with respect to the weights like in simple perceptrons, we have to compute these gradients for all the perceptrons in the hidden layer, and then we have to backpropagate these gradients to the input layer. First we will be computing the gradient flow between the outer layer and the hidden layer.

Output-Hidden Layer Gradient Flow

We will be partially differentiating with respect to the weights w^l_{jk} as well as the biases b^l_j. This can be represented as $\partial C / \partial w^l_{jk}$ and $\partial C / \partial b^l_j$, respectively. For the sake of simplicity, we will be regarding the bias as constant. However, we also have to compute the hidden layer gradients. For computing this we have to partially differentiate the cost function in the form shown here:

$$\partial C / \partial w^l_j = [\partial C / \partial y^l_j] \, [\partial y^l_j / \partial w^l],$$

where the weights w^l_j represent the weights of the jth neuron in the lth layer and is y^l_j the output tensor for that layer. This implies we have to perform differentiation of the sigmoid activation-based output for $\partial y^l_j / \partial w^l$. For simplicity, let us consider the differentiated formula for this layer as:

$$\partial y^l_j = [d(\sigma(z))/d \, w^l_j] \, \partial w^l,$$

where z is defined as $z = \sigma \left(\sum w^l_{jk} x^{l-1}_k + b^l_j \right)$ for a particular neuron in the hidden layer. If we simplify this equation, we can represent this in a reduced form:

$$\Delta^l_j = \partial C / \partial w^l_j = [\partial C / \partial y^l_j] \, [d(\sigma(z))/d \, w^l_j]$$

This can also be represented as:

$$\Delta^l_j = [\partial C / \partial y^l_j] \sigma'(z),$$

where $\sigma'(z) = [d(\sigma(z))/d\, w^l{}_j]$

The next step is the propagation of these gradients through the hidden layer to the input layer. This also implies that if we had another hidden layer in between the current input and hidden layers, then the gradients would have flowed through this layer as well. This implies that as the layers increase, we have to compute the partial derivatives repeatedly using the chain rule.

Hidden to Input Layer or Hidden to Internal Hidden Layers:

Because, in our case, we have the hidden layer directly being fed from the input layer, gradient propagation step is simple as:

$$\partial C/\partial\, w^l{}_j = \sum (w^l{}_{jk}\, x^{l-1}{}_k)\, \sigma'(z)$$

This is because we have already computed the gradients with respect to the weights through the single hidden layer. The only step now remaining is to update the weights by subtracting/ adding the gradients for a better optimality:

$$w^l{}_{jk} = w^l{}_{jk} - \alpha[\partial C/\partial\, w^l{}_j],$$

where α is the learning rate. For our dense network consisting of a single hidden layer, this pretty much concludes the backpropagation step and the gradient updates. It has to be kept in mind that these computations are performed on tensors, and generally for computation, Hadamard product is used. Hadamard product of two tensor or two matrices is a pairwise multiplication of the elements of the matrices present in the same location inside the matrices. In other words, it forms an element-wise multiplication of the two tensors (vectors). For instance:

$$[1\ 2]\ \odot$$

$$[4\ 5] = [1*4\ 2*5\ ]$$

$$= [4\ 10]$$

Now we will look into the case when the hidden layer feeds from another hidden layer, which is the most common architecture in a multi-layered dense network. In this case, if we assume that there is another hidden layer, we have to partially differentiate that layer as well. Let us consider w^{l-1}_{ki}, which represents the weights for the connection between the ith neuron in the $(l-1)^{th}$ and the kth neuron in the lth layer. Now effectively the weighted neuron function would be similar to this:

$$y^l_j = \sigma\left(\sum w^l_{jk}\left(\sigma\left(\sum w^{l-1}_{ki} x^{l-2}_i + b^l_k\right)\right) + b^l_j\right)$$

In this case, we replaced the x^{l-1}_k part of the output layer with the weighted neuron function of the previous hidden layer. In this case, we are looking into a two-hidden-layer-based model, where the input layer i directs data to the first hidden layer k which inturn directs data to the second hidden layer j. Every layer has their corresponding biases, and for simplicity we will consider them to be nonfunctional constants. That is why the second hidden layer (j^{th} layer) essentially takes as input the first weighted neuron hidden layer given by $\sigma\left(\sum w^{l-1}_{ki} x^{l-2}_i + b^l_k\right)$, and the first hidden layer is just a sigmoid activated weighted hidden layer taking input from the input layer. In this case, if we were to backpropagate the gradients, it would be a chain partial derivative rule as follows.

For the outer-last hidden layer, the gradient can be represented as:

$$\partial C/\partial w^l_j = [\partial C/\partial y^l_j]\, [\partial y^l_j/\partial w^l]$$

For this layer the weight update rule can be written as discussed earlier:

$$w^l_{jk} = w^l_{jk} - \alpha[\partial C/\partial w^l_j]$$

For the last hidden layer to the second last hidden layer (or the first hidden layer in our case):

$$\partial C/\partial w^{l-1}_k = [\partial C/\partial y^l_j]\, [\partial y^l_j/\partial w^l]\, [\partial w^l/\partial y^{l-1}_k]\, [\partial y^{l-1}_k/\partial w^{l-1}]$$

Now for the weight update in this first hidden layer we just have to compute:

$$w^{l-1}_{ki} = w^{l-1}_{kl} - \alpha[\partial C/\partial w^{l-1}_k]$$

Now let us generalize this approach for n-hidden-layer-based dense networks. The gradient flow can be generalized as:

$$\partial C / \partial \, w^{net} = [\partial C / \partial y^{net}] \, [\partial \, y^{net} / \partial \, w^{net}] \, [\partial C / \partial y^{net-1}] \, [\partial \, y^{net-1} / \partial \, w^{net-1}] \dots$$

$$\dots . [\partial C / \partial y^{net}] \, [\partial \, y^{1} / \partial \, w^{1}]$$

This is the generic form of gradient flow through dense networks where the optimization functions assist in the global convergence. This forms the backpropagation algorithm, which is the heart of deep learning and convergence. This is important, as when we design networks for our ML Agents using different RL algorithms such as deep Q-network (DQN), actor critic networks, policy gradients, and other off-policy algorithms, we will be using the dense MLP neural network library from Keras (Tensorflow). To summarize the backpropagation module, the weight update for the outer neuron (outer-hidden layer) is $\partial C / \partial \, w^{net} = [\partial C / \partial y^{net}] \, [\partial \, y^{net} / \partial \, w^{net}]$, whereas for other neurons (hidden–previous hidden or hidden-input), the update rule becomes the chain partial differentiation of the individual weighted functions (with activations) with respect to the weights.

We have understood the dense neural network architecture and also found how partial derivatives play an important role in determining the error updates and the gradient flow through the network. This is important in the supervised form of learning, which learns by minimizing the error at each step. The DQN on CartPole that we created in the first chapter is based on minimization of the error on the value Function via a multi-layer perceptron neural network (dense network). As we would progress more, we would see how value and policy functions interact and why policy gradients are very important in deep RL. But before we venture into the algorithms, we should be familiar with writing our own dense networks using Keras. Let us also explore another neural network model before going to the code segment-CNN.

Convolution Neural Network

This is another variant of neural networks, which are most commonly used for image analysis. The CNN consists of applying certain nonlinear functions for spatial analysis of pixels in an image. These are termed as features which are extracted from the image.

These features are then passed as an input through a dense neural network model. This is very important because in GridWorld, the PPO algorithm uses convolution layers (2D) for image analysis and then instructs the agent to make decisions accordingly. In most of the Atari 2D games, these CNN models are extremely important to understand the image (pixels) present in particular frame; for example, guide an agent to play the game of ping pong ("Pong" in the Gym environment) through analyzing the image of the gameplay at a particular frame and then passing it through the CNN model.

Now let us consider the architecture of a sample convolution model. It consists of a convolution layer, pooling layer, and a dense network layer. Although there are several other layers, such as the padding layer/flattening layer, that are applied, the fundamental parts remain the same. In this case, the image is passed as an input to the network, which is analyzed and passed to the dense network. Based on the depth of the input (RGB or grayscale), the channels can be either 3 or 1, respectively. To illustrate, the convolution model looks like the one shown in Figure 5-5.

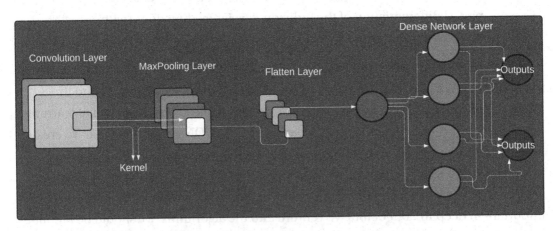

Figure 5-5. Convolution neural network model

Depending on the parameters of the input, the CNN can have different dimensions.

- **Convolution 1D:** This is applied when the input is a one-dimensional sequence of probabilistic data. Such data is generally in the form of a 1D vector such as an array. This kind of model is used in time-series forecasting where the input data is a sequence of probability values.

- **Convolution 2D:** This is the most important dimension for our use-case. The input layer consists of image data—pixels (either 3 or 1 channel[s]). In this case, the CNN model is applied on static images that do not have temporal attributes. Spatial attributes or features are extracted based on the height and width of the image. Hence the size of input for 2D convolutions can be five units (height, width, and three channels for RGB) or three units (height, width, and one channel for grayscale) for RGB or grayscale data, respectively. In our use-case, we will be studying this model, as it will analyse the images of each frame of the ML Agents environment (Gridworld) in RGB format (five channels) and pass it to dense networks.

- **Convolution 3D:** This is used for analyzing video information. Hence, along with spatial data, there is an associated temporal component to each pixel data. The temporal component defines the changes in the pixels for each frame of a video. With the addition of the temporal channel, the effective input size (channels) for the convolution 3D model becomes six units (height, width, and three channels for RGB; one temporal channel) and four units (height, width, and one channel for grayscale; one temporal channel) for RGB and grayscale pixels, respectively.

Now, let us study the convolution network in terms of its components.

- Convolution layer: This layer is associated with extracting spatial features from pixels in an image. It consists of certain filters or kernels that try to extract those features by convolving. Convolution is a mathematical operation where an image I is passed through a filter (kernel) K of dimensions k_1 x k_2, can be represented as:

$$I*K = \sum_{m}^{k1-1}\sum_{n}^{k2-1} I(i-m, j-n)K(m, n) = \sum_{m}^{k1-1}\sum_{n}^{k2-1} I(i+m, j+n)K(-m,-n)$$

This operation is similar to cross-correlation operation with a kernel that can change its signs, implying $K(m, n)=k(-m,-n)$. Now if we consider the input to be in the form of RGB, then the number of channels will be 5–width, height, and three channels for RGB. Hence the dimensions of the image I will be of order H x W x C, where H, W, and C represent the height, width, and the color channels. For D number of kernels of sizes, we can have the total kernel dimensions as k_1 x k_2 x C x D. If we assume bias for D filters as b, then we can frame the convolution weighted neuron equation as :

$$(I*K)= \sum_{m}^{k1-1}\sum_{n}^{k2-1}\sum_{c=1}^{C} K(m, n, c).I(i+m, j+n) + b$$

This is a general convolution equation to extract the features. There are certain metrics associated with convolution, which are referred to as hyperparameters.

- **Depth:** This signifies the depth of the kernel or filters, which also computed the different features to extract from the input image. In the dense network at the end layer of the CNN model, the depth also signifies the number of hidden layers in the dense model.

- **Stride:** This controls the depth columns around the spatial dimensions (height and width). If we specify a stride value of 1, then the kernel will move one pixel at a time, which may lead to overlapping of the extracted fields. If a value of 2 is assigned, then it jumps two pixels at a time. Generally as the stride increases to a value more than 3, the spatial dimension of the output decreases. We denote the stride using the symbol S.

- **Padding:** The padding layer or zero padding layer is used to pad the input image dimensions spatially (along height and width). This feature enables us to control the spatial size of the output volume.

It is important to mention the relationship between the dimensions of the input and the output of a convolution layer. Convolution between the input feature map of dimension H X W and weight kernel of dimension k_1 X k_2 produces an output feature map of dimensions:

$$\dim(O) = (H - k1 + 1) \times (W - k2 + 1).$$

There is another formulation of the output volume based on the stride S and the zero padding P, given by:

$$\dim(O) = ([(H \times W) - (k1 \times k2) + 2P]/S) + 1 = ([Z-K+2P]/S + 1,$$

where Z represents the input volume and K represents the kernel dimensions.

This value should be an integer so that the neurons fit perfectly to extract the features. For instance if we take an input image of dimensions [11,11,4] (Z = 11), and we take a kernel size of value 5 (K = 5), and we use no zero padding (P = 0) followed by a stride value of 2 (S = 2), we can get the dimension of the output layer as:

$$\dim(O) = ([11-5 + 2*0]/2)+1 = 4$$

This implies the output dimension is of size 4 X 4. For this case we get an integer output as 4, but in many cases, we see that some invalid combinations of these values may give fractional results in output dimensions. For instance, if Z = 10 with no zero padding(P = 0) and kernel dimension of 3 (K = 3), then it would not be possible to have a stride of 2 as, $([Z-K+2P]/S + 1 = ([10-3+0]/2)+1 = 4.5$, which is a fractional value. In this way, the constraints are applied on the strides, and in many cases, automatic exceptions are thrown if there are invalid combinations of these values. An illustration with input dimension Z = 3 with 1 zero-padding (P = 1), kernel size of 1(K = 1), and stride of 2, which gives an output dimension of $([Z-K+2P]/S + 1 = ([3-1+2*1]/2)+1 = 3$ is shown in Figure 5-6.

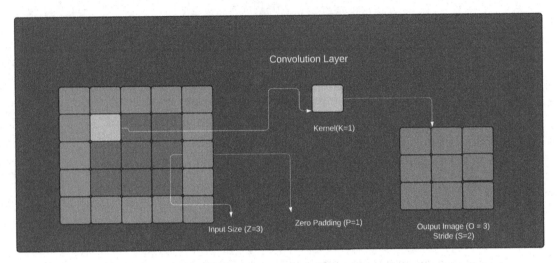

Figure 5-6. Convolution layer in CNN and convolved image dimensions

There is another interesting fact of this layer, which is called parameter sharing. This helps to reduce the dimensions of the input to reduce the computation. This is based on the assumption that if one feature is useful to compute at some spatial position (x, y), then it should be useful to compute at a different position (x_2, y_2). Let us assume that we have an output of a convolution layer with the dimensions [55*55*96] with a depth channel of 96, then we can apply the same weights and biases to constrain the neurons in each depth slice, instead of having different biases and weights for all the 96 different depth slices. This aids in the backpropagation step, because the gradients (which flow through the layers) will be added across each individual depth slice and update a single set of weight instead of 96 different weights.

- **Pooling layer:** This layer is used to reduce the spatial dimensions progressively by reducing the parameters and also the computation in the network. It is used in between convolution layers as well as at the end of the convolution layer. This layer operates on an individual depth slice or depth channel using the maximization operation, and hence this is termed MaxPooling. The most generic form of max pooling is done with filters of size 2 X 2 applied with a stride of 2, which downsamples every depth channel by 2 along both the width and the height. The output of this layer can be computed as:

$$\dim(O) = ([Z\text{-}K]/S) + 1,$$

where Z represents the height or the width of the image, K is the dimension of the kernel, and S is the stride (like earlier). In addition to max pooling, there are other metrics of pooling that are applied, one of the most important being the L2-Norm pooling. L2–Norm is a Euclidean regularization metric that uses squared error function as the regularizing equation. This is also referred to as an AveragePooling method.

- **Flattening layer:** This layer is used to compress or flatten the outputs of the pooling layer or the convolution layer to produce a sequence of values that are essentially the inputs to the dense neural network. As we already studied the dense network architecture, this compression is required to produce a sequence of inputs that can be used by the input layer of the dense network. For instance, after applying a kernel size of [3,3] on a 64 layer depth convolution 2D layer on an input image of dimensions [32,32,3], a stride of 2, and zero padding of value 1, we get the output shape as:

$$([Z\text{-}K+2P]/S + 1= ([32\text{-}3 + 1]/2)+1= 16,$$

which implies an output dimension of [16,16,64]. Now if we apply the flatten layer on this output sequence, the effective dimension would be 16*16*64 = [16384]. Thus this layer produces a one-dimensional input sequence that can be fed to the dense network. This layer does not affect the batch size.

- **Dense network:** This forms the final part of a traditional CNN model. Here the most interesting part is the backpropagation of the convolved, max-pooled, weighted neuron model. Before we enter into this layer, let us understand the backpropagation in the convolution layer that we mentioned.

Backpropagation in convolution layer: In backpropagation of the convolution layer, we also follow the chain rule of partial differentiation to update the gradients similar to the dense network. The gradient component for the individual weights can be obtained by:

$$\partial C / \partial w^l_{m,n} = \sum_i^{H-k1} \sum_j^{W-k2} [\partial C / \partial y^l_{m,n}] [\partial y^l_{m,n} / \partial w^l_{m,n}],$$

where H X W are the input dimensions, and C is the cost function or the quadratic loss function. $w^l_{m,n}$ refers to the weights of the mth neuron in the lth layer. $y^l_{m,n}$ represents the sigmoid activated weighted neuron equation of:

$$y^l_{m,n} = \sigma(\sum_m \sum_n w^l_{m,n} x^{l-1}_{i+m, j+n} + b^l)$$

Since in this case we have an image as an input instead of a 1D array, the backpropagation model for the convolution network takes as input the dimensions along the different channels of inputs along with the kernel weights and biases. The rest of the derivatives are similar to the generic chain rule, which can be reframed as:

$$\partial C / \partial w^l_{m,n} = \partial / \partial w^l_{m,n} [\sigma(\sum_m \sum_n w^l_{m,n} x^{l-1}_{i+m, j+n} + b^l)]$$

We can expand this equation further according to the depth of the convolution layer and perform the chain rule of partial differentiation as long as the depth channel is not exhausted. In this case, we used the sigmoid activation; however, in general convolution 2D networks we use "Relu" or regularized linear unit as the activation function. The Relu can be denoted as:

$$ReLu(x) = max(0, x)$$

Therefore, this activation is a straight line for x greater than 0 and is on the negative x axis for x less than 0. This implies it takes the maximum positive values.

Backpropagation in dense network: This is similar to the backpropagation and gradient flow in the dense network that we studied. After the flatten layer, we get a compressed layer composed of weights, inputs, and biases. Based on the type of problem, we can associate different activation functions. For instance, in the case of a binary classification problem, we will be using the sigmoid function as mentioned in the previous sections. For multiclass classifications, we have to use the "softmax" activation function, which was represented in Chapter 1 in the Multi-Armed Bandits section.

This completes the architecture of the convolution 2D neural network, which we will be creating using the Keras library in the next section.

Deep Learning with Keras and TensorFlow

We will now create dense and convolution neural networks using the Keras/Tensorflow framework. Keras is a high-level API that uses the Tensorflow as its back end for creating the neural networks and is very easy to use. In this section we will first create a dense MLP neural network, and then we will be creating standard convolution neural network models, which are state of the art and are used extensively in computer vision.

Dense Neural Network

We will be creating this using the Keras framework, and we require certain libraries for this. We have already installed Tensorflow and Keras in our previous chapters, and we will import these in our Notebook. Open "Intro-To-Keras-Sequential.ipynb" Jupyter Notebook, and in the first section we will see the following commands:

```
import tensorflow as tf
import numpy as np
import pandas as pd
from keras.models import Sequential
from keras.layers import Dense, Flatten
from datetime import datetime
from tensorflow import keras
```

In our case, we will be creating the dense network for a binary classification problem. A binary classification problem has only two outcomes, and in this case, the sigmoid function is used as the activation function. The Keras API has a module called as "models," which contain the different architecture of the models inside that framework. The sequential model specifies that the different layers of the deep learning model will be placed sequentially one after another, which implies the output of a layer will be the input to the next layer, as in the case of a dense MLP. The layers module in Keras specifies the different types of layers we would want to include in our model; for example, dense specifies a dense MLP network with hidden layers, flatten" specifies the flattening layer that we looked at in convolution neural networks, Convolution2D for a convolution layer, and many more. We will be exploring these layers as the chapter progresses. There are different ways of writing code for creating a deep learning network, but there are certain restrictions. In the most common cases, we will be using the Keras API and will be calling functions such as Dense() to create a dense MLP layer; however, there are alternate writing techniques that use the Keras functional API from Tensorflow. To create the same dense layer using the second form, we will be writing as keras.layers. Dense(). We will be using these notations to represent the models in our chapter.

In the next section, we have an "inp_data" method that creates synthetic data for running our deep learning model. We initialize a tensor of size [512,512] with random values called the data and also create a [512,1] dimension tensor as the labeling set that contains the binary outputs, 1 or 0s. All these are assigned randomly just for simplicity. In generic supervised learning, we have an initial labeling set associated with the data, which is our validation data set. Based on the outcomes of the deep learning model for each epoch, the errors are computed based on the difference of these outcomes with the validation data sets.

```
def inp_data():
  data=np.random.random((512,512))
  labels=np.random.randint(2, size=(512,1))
  return data, labels
```

The next part contains the model building function–"build_model" method. This method contains the sequential module from Keras.models as mentioned. Then we have the dense network represented by the method "Dense()." There are several parameters inside this dense network, including:

- **units:** This represents the dimensionality of the output space, which in our case is binary; hence, we require a 1D container (vector, array) as output.

- **input_dim:** This represents the dimensions of the input to the dense network.

- **activation:** This represents the activation function, such as sigmoid, softmax, relu, elu etc.

- **use_bias:** This specifies whether we would want to use bias in our dense network.

- **bias_initializer:** This signifies the initialized bias tensor in the network. There are several initializers, such as zeros, ones, etc.

- **kernel_initializer:** This initializes the weight tensor and can have different initializers. The most common, which we will be using, is glorot_uniform, which is a Xavier initializer. There are variants such as uniform or normal initializers as well.

- **bias_regularizer:** This signifies the regularization of the bias tensor. This is used when we would want to prevent excessive overfitting in deep learning and assists in gradient descent by modifying the steps sizes.

- **kernel_regularizer:** This is similar to bias regularizer but for the kernel weight tensor. There are variants that use the L1 and L2 regularization norm for penalizing the learning rate to assist in gradient descent.

- **bias_constraints:** The constraints applied to the bias tensor

- **kernel_constraints:** The constraints applied on the kernel weight tensor

Now we have an overview of the parameters of the Dense method, and we can write a single dense neural network model using Keras. The "model.compile" method is used for compiling the model and associating the inputs and outputs of the neural network. This part contains:

- **optimizers:** This includes different gradient descent optimizers that assist in finding the global minima, such as SGD, RMSProp, Adam, Adagrad, Adadelta, and many more.

- **loss:** This signifies the entropy loss and can be binary or categorical based on our requirements. The binary loss is a logistic (sigmoid) entropy loss while the categorical is a softmax entropy loss.

- **metrics:** These specify the metrics on which to benchmark the model such as accuracy, mean-squared-error(mse), mean-absolute-error(mae) and others.

We can now create the function as follows:

```
def build_model():
  model=Sequential()
  model.add(Dense(1, input_dim=512, activation="softmax",
  use_bias=True,
  bias_initializer='zeros',
  kernel_initializer='glorot_uniform',
  kernel_regularizer=None, bias_regularizer=None,
  kernel_constraint=None, bias_constraint=None))

  model.compile(optimizer='rmsprop',
  loss='binary_crossentropy',
  metrics=['accuracy'])

  return model
```

The next part contains the "train" method, which calls the models and fits the input data for training. The "model.fit" method is used for fitting the input data for training in different batches, each batch containing a certain portion of the input, which in our case is designated by using the batch size. The parameters used here are:

- **inputs:** the input data to train the model
- **labels:** the labels present in the data for prediction and classification
- **epochs:** the number of epochs we would want to train the model
- **batch_size:** the size of the individual batch of input to be passed to the input layer. In our case, we use a value of 64.
- **verbose:** This signifies the pattern in which the logs of the training for each epoch would be displayed.

This can be done using the following lines:

```
def train(model, data, labels):
  model.fit(data, labels, epochs=20, batch_size=64)
```

The final part of the segment contains the "main()" method, which calls the "inp_data" method to generate randomized tensors as inputs and labels, then calls the "build_model" method to create the sequential model, and finally trains the model using the "train" method. The "model.summary" method provides a view of the architecture of the sequential model.

```
if __name__=='__main__':
  data, labels=inp_data()
  model=build_model()
  model.summary()
  train(model, data, labels)
```

Now if we train this model we would see the epochs, the accuracy for each step of training, the loss, and the associated details. To summarize the model, it would appear like Figure 5-7.

```
[→  Model: "sequential_1"
    _____
    Layer (type)                Output Shape              Param #
    =============================================================
    dense_1 (Dense)             (None, 1)                 513
    =============================================================
    Total params: 513
    Trainable params: 513
    Non-trainable params: 0
    _____
    Epoch 1/200
    8/8 [==============================] - 0s 5ms/step - loss: 7.9225 - accuracy: 0.4805
    Fnoch 2/200
```

Figure 5-7. *Sequential model containing a single dense neural network*

Now let us visualize this training with the help of a Tensorboard. For this we will be using the same model with a different coding format. In this section we would see that we replace the "dense()" method with "keras.layers.Dense()" and the sequential method with the "keras.models.Sequential()" method. We also use the "keras.optimizers. RMSProp()" method, which contains the learning rate for the gradient descent. In this case, we are using the Keras API of the Tensorflow framework and the "build_model" method looks like this:

```
def build_model():
  model=keras.models.Sequential()
  model.add(keras.layers.Dense(1, input_dim=512,
```

```
activation="softmax", use_bias=True, bias_initializer='zeros',
kernel_initializer='glorot_uniform',
kernel_regularizer=None, bias_regularizer=None,
kernel_constraint=None, bias_constraint=None))

model.compile(keras.optimizers.RMSprop(learning_rate
=1e-4), loss='binary_crossentropy', metrics=['accuracy'])
return model
```

Now for integrating TensorBoard, we have to specify the logs file, which holds the logs of the training data in date–time format. During visualization it fetches these logs for representing the metrics of training: loss, accuracy, and so forth.

```
logdir= "logs/scalars/" + datetime.now().strftime("%Y%m%d-%H%M%S")
tensorboard_callback=keras.callbacks.TensorBoard
(log_dir=logdir)
```

The next step is to update the "model.fit" method in the train function. Like we saw in previous chapters, we have to add "callbacks" and specify the TensorBoard logs file as a callback resource for real-time visualization.

```
def train(model, data, labels):
  model.fit(data, labels, epochs=200, batch_size=64,
  callbacks=[tensorboard_callback])
```

If we now run the main function, we will see the training and the corresponding logs in TensorBoard. A preview is shown in Figure 5-8.

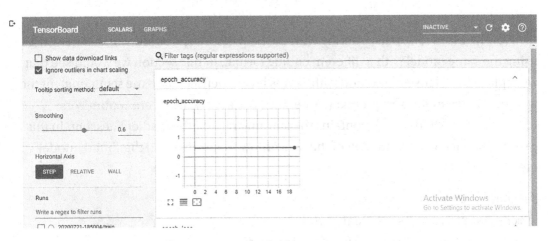

Figure 5-8. *Visualizing dense sequential model in TensorBoard*

We have created a deep learning model with Keras, and this is the first step to create more diverse and complicated models, especially deep RL. Let us try to create a simple multi-layered dense sequential model for multi-class classification. In the "build_model" method in the next segment, we initialize a sequential model using the "keras.models.Sequential" method. Then we create a dense network containing 256 units of output dimension with an input dimension of 20 units and a "Relu" activation unit. We then repeat a new dense layer that takes as input the output of the previous dense network. The dropout layer randomly sets the input units to 0 with a frequency of rate that prevents overfitting during training. Hence this layer is applicable only during training mode, as dropout does not freeze weights during training. Then we have dense layers with 64 units and "Relu" activation methods. The last layer is another dense layer, with 10 units and softmax activation for multi-class classification. The "model.compile" contains Adam optimizer from the "keras.optimizers.Adam()" method with a learning rate of 0.0001. The loss in this context is a "categorical_crossentropy" that signifies the softmax loss with the metrics as accuracy. The following method is represented as follows:

```python
def build_model():
  model= keras.models.Sequential(name="Multi-Class Dense
        MLP Network")
  model.add(keras.layers.Dense(256, input_dim=20,
          activation="relu"))
  model.add(keras.layers.Dense(256, activation="relu"))
  model.add(keras.layers.Dropout(0.2))
  model.add(keras.layers.Dense(64, activation="relu"))
  model.add(keras.layers.Dense(10, activation="softmax"))
  model.compile(keras.optimizers.Adam(lr=1e-3,
  name="AdamOptimizer"),
  loss="categorical_crossentropy", metrics=['accuracy'])
  return model
```

When we call "model.summary" method, we can see the sequential networks as shown in Figure 5-9.

```
Model: "Multi-Class Dense MLP Network"

Layer (type)                 Output Shape              Param #
=================================================================
dense_4 (Dense)              (None, 256)               5376

dense_5 (Dense)              (None, 256)               65792

dropout (Dropout)            (None, 256)               0

dense_6 (Dense)              (None, 64)                16448

dense_7 (Dense)              (None, 10)                650
=================================================================
Total params: 88,266
Trainable params: 88,266
Non-trainable params: 0
```

Figure 5-9. Sample multi-class classification model with dense networks

Now that we are familiar with dense neural networks, let us explore CNNs in Keras.

Convolution Neural Networks

The CNN is a standard network model for computer vision exclusively for image classification, image generation, motion capture, and many other tasks. Before we venture into the Keras implementation of this network, we will look into the pretrained state-of-the-art models that we mentioned in our previous chapters, such as Resnet50, VGG16, and their variants. The first model that we will be looking into is the VGG-16 model, the 16 here refers to the number of layers inside the neural network.

VGG-16 Model: This is a classic model that has sequential architecture. The following are the parts of this model:

- 2 convolution-2D layers with 64 depth channels and Kernel (Filter) size 3 x 3 with padding kept as Same. "Same" padding is given by the ceiling value of the division of image width or height with stride—that is, dim(O)=ceil(Z/S)

- 1 max pooling layer with 2 x 2 pool size and a stride value of 2

- 2 convolution-2D layers with 128 depth channels and Kernel (Filter) size 3 x 3 with padding kept as Same

- 1 max pooling layer with 2 x 2 pool size and a stride value of 2

- 3 convolution-2D layers with 256 depth channels and Kernel (Filter) size 3 x 3 with padding kept as Same

- 1 max pooling layer with 2 x 2 pool size and a stride value of 2

CHAPTER 5   DEEP REINFORCEMENT LEARNING

- 3 convolution-2D layers with 512 depth channels and Kernel (Filter) size 3 x 3 with padding kept as Same

- 1 max pooling layer with 2 x 2 pool size and a stride value of 2

- 3 convolution-2D layers with 512 depth channels and Kernel (Filter) size 3 x 3 with padding kept as Same

- 1 max pooling layer with 2 x 2 pool size and a stride value of 2

The activation functions for all the layers are kept as "Relu." This convolution network is extensively used in image classification and provides an output containing the following attribute after flattening the data:

1 dense neural layer with 4096 units

This can then be passed as input to the dense MLP network with the corresponding activation functions—sigmoid for binary classification or softmax for multi-class classification. Now let us visualize this model, which is already pretrained and built inside the Keras framework. For this, we would import the VGG-16 model already built inside the Keras framework inside the keras.applications module.

```
from keras.applications.vgg16 import VGG16
```

The "build_auto_VGG16_model()" method approaches how to build this model. We simply have to load the VGG-16 model and return it as follows:

```
def build_auto_VGG16_model():
    model=VGG16()
    return model
```

By running the "model.summary" method on this model, we can see the architecture of this model. Since the trainable parameters are large, a sample view of the model is shown in Figure 5-10.

```
Downloading data from https://github.com/fchollet/deep-learning-models/releases/download/v0.1/vgg16_weights_tf_dim_ordering_tf_kernels.h5
553467904/553467096 [==============================] - 34s 0us/step
Model: "vgg16"
_________________________________________________________________
Layer (type)                 Output Shape              Param #
=================================================================
input_1 (InputLayer)         (None, 224, 224, 3)       0
_________________________________________________________________
block1_conv1 (Conv2D)        (None, 224, 224, 64)      1792
_________________________________________________________________
block1_conv2 (Conv2D)        (None, 224, 224, 64)      36928
_________________________________________________________________
block1_pool (MaxPooling2D)   (None, 112, 112, 64)      0
_________________________________________________________________
block2_conv1 (Conv2D)        (None, 112, 112, 128)     73856
_________________________________________________________________
block2_conv2 (Conv2D)        (None, 112, 112, 128)     147584
_________________________________________________________________
block2_pool (MaxPooling2D)   (None, 56, 56, 128)       0
_________________________________________________________________
block3_conv1 (Conv2D)        (None, 56, 56, 256)       295168
_________________________________________________________________
block3_conv2 (Conv2D)        (None, 56, 56, 256)       590080
_________________________________________________________________
block3_conv3 (Conv2D)        (None, 56, 56, 256)       590080
_________________________________________________________________
block3_pool (MaxPooling2D)   (None, 28, 28, 256)       0
_________________________________________________________________
block4_conv1 (Conv2D)        (None, 28, 28, 512)       1180160
_________________________________________________________________
```


Figure 5-10. *VGG-16 prebuilt model from the Keras framework*

If we would like to build our own variant of this model, we have to import certain layers from Keras. We will be importing the convolution-2D layer, flatten layer, dense layer, MaxPooling layer, and a zero-padding layer, all of which are fundamental components in a traditional CNN. We will also be importing the Adam optimizer from the Keras.optimizers module and will be using the sequential model.

```
from tensorflow import keras
from keras.models import Sequential
from keras.layers import Dense, Convolution2D, MaxPooling2D, Dropout,
Flatten, Activation, ZeroPadding2D
from keras.optimizers import Adam
```

We first initialize the sequential model in the "build_sample_VGG_model()" and then we initially add a zero-padding 2D layer to add row and column of 0s to the input image tensor. The zero-padding layer has the following parameters.

- **padding:** An integer or a tuple of two integer values are provided. If a single integer is provided, it implies the same padding is applied to height and width, and if a tuple of two integers are provided, it signifies the symmetric height pad and symmetric weight pad.
- **data_format:** The dimensions of the input image tensor with height, width, and the number of channels.

The code for zero-padding 2D with the associated details is as follows:

```
model.add(ZeroPadding2D((1,1), input_shape=(3,224,224)))
```

Then we have the convolution-2D model in Keras, which has the following parameters.

- **filters:** the dimensionality of the output tensor, the number of output filters in the convolution

- **kernel_size:** the size of the kernel for convolution to take place; generally consists of a list of two integers specifying the height and the width of the kernels

- **padding:** refers to the padding of the input tensor; Valid implies no padding, whereas Same specifies an equal padding along the height and the width to maintain the same output dimensions as the input

- **data_format:** refers to the format of the data depending on the position of the channels. If channels_first type is chosen, then the format for this is (batch_size, channels, height, width), and if channels_last is chosen, then the format of input data is (batch_size, height, width, channels). By default it is of "image_data_format" from Keras, but if unspecified it defaults to channels_last.

- **dilation_rate:** This is used to specify the rate for dilated convolution (not required for our present scenario).

- **groups:** An integer that specifies the groups along which the input is split along the channel axis. Each group is convolved separately with the filters. The output is a concatenation of all the filters along a channel.

- **activation:** the activation function to use, which in our case will be "Relu"

- **use_bias:** specifies whether we would want to use bias.

- **bias_initializer:** This specifies the initialization for the bias, similar to the dense network.

- **kernel_initializer:** This controls the initialization of the kernel, such as glorot_uniform in our case.

- **bias_regularizer:** the regularizer for the bias

- **kernel_regularizer:** the regularizer for the kernel weight tensor

- **activity_regularizer:** This is a regularizer for the activation function that controls the output of the convolution layer.

- **kernel_constraint:** the constraints applied on the kernel

- **bias_constraint:** the constraints applied on the bias.

The convolution-2D layer with the filters, kernel_size, activation and input data_format is used in this case:

```
model.add(Convolution2D(64, 3, 3, activation='relu', input_
shape=(3,224,224)))
```

Then we have the MaxPooling-2D layer inside this code, which downsamples the data by extracting the maximum value over the pooling size. The following are its parameters.

- **pool_size:** This signifies the window size over which to compute the maximum. If a single value is specified, then the same dimensions are applied for both the height and width. If a tuple of two integers are specified, then these correspond to the height and the width of the pooling window.

- **stride:** This can be either an integer or a tuple of two integers, specifying the stride for pooling. When not specified, it defaults to pool_size.

- **padding:** This is similar to before, where Valid represents no padding and Same represents equal padding.

- **data_format:** This decides the format for the data and can be in channels_first or channels_last format.

The MaxPooling 2D layer has the following code:

```
model.add(MaxPooling2D((2,2), strides=(2,2)))
```

The rest of the model uses flatten, dropout, and dense network layers, as mentioned before. To build the model, we have to first stack two convolution 2D layers with a channel depth of 64 with the input data and then apply a MaxPooling 2D layer with stride 2 x 2, as shown here:

```
model.add(Convolution2D(64, 3, 3, activation='relu', input_
shape=(3,224,224)))
model.add(Convolution2D(64, 3, 3, activation='relu'))
model.add(MaxPooling2D((2,2), strides=(2,2)))
The same pattern is repeated with 2 Convolution 2D layers of depth channels
128 and a MaxPooling 2D layer.
model.add(Convolution2D(128, 3, 3, activation='relu'))
model.add(Convolution2D(128, 3, 3, activation='relu'))
model.add(MaxPooling2D((2,2), strides=(2,2)))
```

The next part consists of a pattern of three convolution layers of depth 256 and 512 on the data with a MaxPooling layer in between three convolution 2D layers. The convolution 2D layer of depth 512 is repeated with the MaxPooling layer as shown here:

```
model.add(Convolution2D(256, 3, 3, activation='relu'))
model.add(Convolution2D(256, 3, 3, activation='relu'))
model.add(Convolution2D(256, 3, 3, activation='relu'))
model.add(MaxPooling2D((2,2), strides=(2,2)))

model.add(Convolution2D(512, 3, 3, activation='relu'))
model.add(Convolution2D(512, 3, 3, activation='relu'))
model.add(Convolution2D(512, 3, 3, activation='relu'))
model.add(MaxPooling2D((2,2), strides=(2,2)))

model.add(Convolution2D(512, 3, 3, activation='relu'))
model.add(Convolution2D(512, 3, 3, activation='relu'))
model.add(Convolution2D(512, 3, 3, activation='relu'))
model.add(MaxPooling2D((2,2), strides=(2,2)))
```

The last part contains a flatten layer to make the outputs of the convolved input tensor suitable for input to the dense network. The dense network has 4096 units with "Relu " and "softmax" activation functions. The dropout layer in between is for setting half of the input units as 0 for the training phase. The final layer of the VGG model is:

```
model.add(Flatten())
model.add(Dense(4096, activation='relu'))
model.add(Dropout(0.5))
model.add(Dense(4096, activation='relu'))
model.add(Dropout(0.5))
model.add(Dense(1000, activation='softmax'))
```

Then we compile the model using Adam optimizer with cross_entropy loss and accuracy as the metric.

Resnet-50: This is another benchmark model for image processing and is the abbreviation of residual network. Generally in complex sequential convolution models, there is a gradual degradation in terms of the accuracy, which gets saturated. To avoid this saturated accuracy, residual blocks are incorporated. We consider a stacked layer produces an output tensor Y after passing through an input tensor X through the function F(X). This is a traditional sequential CNN model structure. However, if we were to add a residual network, instead of getting the output F(X), the input tensor is added to it making Y = F(X) + X. Now in generic CNN models, it is very hard to maintain the accuracy with the increase of depth in the network due to degradation. That is where the residual equation: Y = F(X) + X comes into the picture. Essentially this implies an identity transform of the input tensor to the output tensor. To understand this, we can draw an analogy that if F(X) = 0, then we get an identical tensor output (Y), which is the same as X, after passing through nonlinear activation units. Figure 5-11 illustrates this residual block.

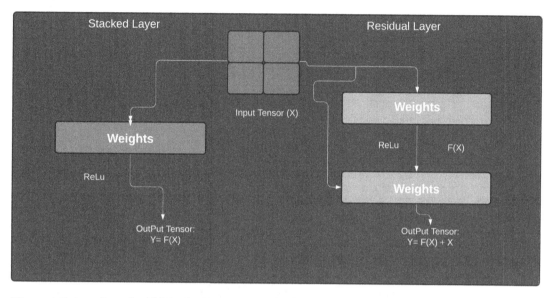

Figure 5-11. *Residual block diagram in ResNet*

Residual networks thus preserve the accuracy, even after applying thousands of convolution-2D/MaxPooling layers in the model. In the worst case, if the dimensions of the input and output tensors do not match, then a padding layer is added, given by the equation:

$$Y = F(X,\{W_i\}) + W_i X$$

The Resnet-50 model has five stages with residual and convolution blocks. The residual blocks are also called identity blocks. Each convolution block has three convolution 2D layers and each identity/residual block has three convolution 2D layers. There are more than 23 million trainable parameters in this model.

We will use the Resnet-50 model already built in the keras.applications module. Then we will load the Resnet-50 model in the build_model function as follows:

```
from keras.applications.resnet50 import ResNet50
def build_model():
  model=ResNet50()
  return model

resnet_model= build_model()
resnet_model.summary()
```

When we summarize the model we will see that the model is being downloaded, and then the trainable parameters are presented along with the layers, as shown in Figure 5-12.

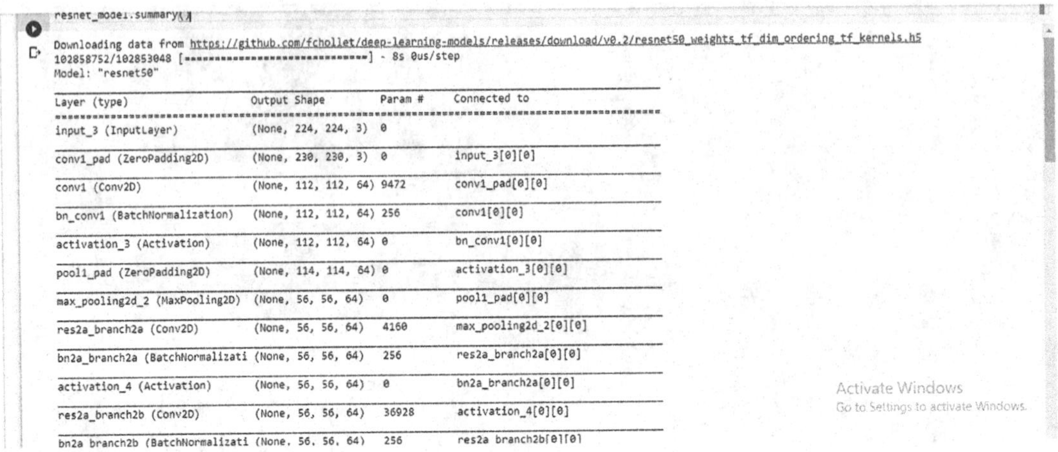

```
resnet_model.summary()

Downloading data from https://github.com/fchollet/deep-learning-models/releases/download/v0.2/resnet50_weights_tf_dim_ordering_tf_kernels.h5
102858752/102853048 [==============================] - 8s 0us/step
Model: "resnet50"
```

Layer (type)	Output Shape	Param #	Connected to
input_3 (InputLayer)	(None, 224, 224, 3)	0	
conv1_pad (ZeroPadding2D)	(None, 230, 230, 3)	0	input_3[0][0]
conv1 (Conv2D)	(None, 112, 112, 64)	9472	conv1_pad[0][0]
bn_conv1 (BatchNormalization)	(None, 112, 112, 64)	256	conv1[0][0]
activation_3 (Activation)	(None, 112, 112, 64)	0	bn_conv1[0][0]
pool1_pad (ZeroPadding2D)	(None, 114, 114, 64)	0	activation_3[0][0]
max_pooling2d_2 (MaxPooling2D)	(None, 56, 56, 64)	0	pool1_pad[0][0]
res2a_branch2a (Conv2D)	(None, 56, 56, 64)	4160	max_pooling2d_2[0][0]
bn2a_branch2a (BatchNormalizati	(None, 56, 56, 64)	256	res2a_branch2a[0][0]
activation_4 (Activation)	(None, 56, 56, 64)	0	bn2a_branch2a[0][0]
res2a_branch2b (Conv2D)	(None, 56, 56, 64)	36928	activation_4[0][0]
bn2a_branch2b (BatchNormalizati	(None, 56, 56, 64)	256	res2a_branch2b[0][0]

Figure 5-12. *Resnet-50 model from Keras*

There are several variants of VGG and Resnet models with different numbers of hidden and convolution layers, and there are other state-of-the-art models such as AlexNet and GoogleNet.

Building an Image Classifier Model with Resnet-50

Now that we have understood the fundamentals of neural networks and building models in Keras, let us build a image classifier model in a few lines of code using the Keras framework and the ResNet-50 Model. Open the Resnet50 Convolution Networks.ipynb notebook, and in this case we will be using this model to let the machine decide whether the given image is that of a cat or dog. To build this binary classification model first, we have to import the libraries from Keras—namely, the Resnet-50 model from keras.applications and img, img_to_array module from the keras.preprocessing module. These layers help us to decode and preprocess the input image to make it usable for the Resnet model. We also require numpy for reshaping the image tensor and "matplotlib" for presenting the image on the screen.

```
from keras.applications.resnet50 import ResNet50, decode_predictions,
preprocess_input
from keras.preprocessing.image import image, img_to_array
```

```
import numpy as np
import matplotlib.pyplot as plt
```

In the next stage, we import the data set and unzip it. This contains a large database of images of cats and dogs correctly labeled where we can use our supervised Resnet model.

```
!wget -qq http://sds-datacrunch.aau.dk/public/dataset.zip
!unzip -qq dataset.zip
```

Now let us see the first image of the data set by plotting it using matplotlib in dimensions of [244,244].

```
img = image.load_img
("dataset/single_prediction/cat_or_dog_1.jpg", target_size = (224, 224))
plt.imshow(img)
```

On running this, we will see an image of a Labrador dog on the screen like that in Figure 5-13.

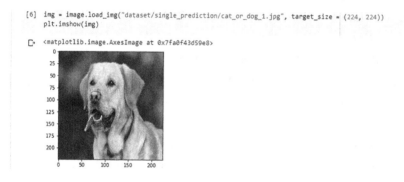

Figure 5-13. *Image of a dog from data set*

We will be using this image to verify whether the model can classify it correctly as a dog. In the next stage, we have to convert this image into a tensor. This is done by converting the image in a numpy array and then expanding it along an axis to make it a input tensor:

```
img=image.img_to_array(img)
img=np.expand_dims(img, axis=0)
img=preprocess_input(img)
```

In the next step we train that image using the Resnet-50 model, and we will get the predictions from the model. Now we would want to predict the most probable classification of the given image, which in our case is the dog. This is done by using the "decode_predictions" method, which states the predicted value of the model predictions, whether it is a dog or cat.

```
model=ResNet50(weights='imagenet')
model.summary()
#predict image
predictions= model.predict(img)
print("Accuracy of predictions")
print(decode_predictions(predictions, top=1)[0])
```

Now if we run this model, we would instantly see that the Resnet model predicts the image to be that of a Labrador_retriever with 56.7% accuracy. We have built a binary classification model with Resnet-50 and we can create a multi-class classification model as well. The Convolution Network-Classification.ipynb Notebook contains a multi-class classification model using a custom convolution-2D neural network (implementing a variant of VGG-16) to classify a CIFAR data set. CIFAR is a benchmark image classification data set, which is present in the keras.datasets module and is extensively used for image analysis and classification. However, the model specifications and the implementations are kept for an interested reader, who would like to venture into depths of image analysis, processing, classification models, and other computer vision models.

These neural network models, both MLP (dense) and convolution, will be extensively used in our deep RL algorithms, and now that we have a fair idea of these networks we will study them.

Deep Reinforcement Learning Algorithms

In Chapter 1 we learned about the contrast as well as the relation between value and policy functions in RL. We used Bellman functions to update the values and also changed the policies to lead to a better value estimate. All of these were based on discrete data. Before we dive into the main algorithms, we should have an idea of the different types of algorithmic paradigms in deep RL.

On Policy Algorithms

These algorithms depend on policy performance and optimization. This family of algorithms try to optimize a policy and provide a good performance. In this section, we will analyze the traditional RL space by comparing Q-learning (off-policy) and SARSA (state, action, reward, state, action; on-policy) algorithms.

Traditional RL: Q-Learning and SARSA

In this case, the policy function is updated to get an optimal Q-value. In the discrete RL scenario where we read about the Bellman equation and the Q-learning algorithm, we also mentioned policy functions. Another variant of discrete RL that updates the policy function rather than the values is the SARSA algorithm. In generic Q-learning, we have the following equation of Q–value update:

$$Q(S, A) = Q(S, A) + \alpha \left[R + y \max_a Q(S`, a) - Q(S, A) \right]$$

$$S = S`$$

where α is the learning rate and y is the discount factor and S, A, and R represent the states, actions, and reward space, respectively. Q(S, A) represents the value retrieved by taking an action A from state S. In this form of learning, the agent chooses an action A from S using the Q-value policy (greedy policy). It then receives the R (rewards) and observes the next state S`. Thus there is a dependency on the older states that is useful for off-policy algorithms. In contrast to Q-learning, we have the SARSA algorithm. The update equation for SARSA is given by the equation:

$$Q(S, A) = Q(S, A) + \alpha \left[R + y Q(S`, A`) - Q(S, A) \right]$$

$$A = A`$$

$$S = S`$$

Although both these equations come from Bellman equation, the fundamental difference is that SARSA chooses an action A from a state S based on a Q policy, then it observes the R (rewards) and new state (S`) and then chooses another action A` from state S` by using the policy derived from Q. update of policy makes SARSA an on-policy algorithm in discrete RL space. In SARSA, the agent learns optimal policy and behaves using the same policy, such as the Epsilon-Greedy policy. In case of SARSA, the update policy is the same as behavioral policy.

To see this comparison, we can open the Q-Learning|SARSA-FrozenLake.ipynb
Notebook to see the contrast in on-off policy techniques in traditional learning
algorithms in discrete space. Most of the code segment is the same except for the Q and
SARSA functions. In the "Q_learning" method, we see that the Q-policy tries to apply a
greedy maximization policy and goes to the next steps based on the computed Q-values
as mentioned earlier. This is accomplished by the following lines of code:

```
best_value, info = best_action_value(table, obs1)
Q_target = reward + GAMMA * best_value
Q_error = Q_target - table[(obs0, action)]
table[(obs0, action)] += LEARNING_RATE * Q_error
```

The accuracy (reward) steps graph for Q-learning can be observed as shown in
Figure 5-14.

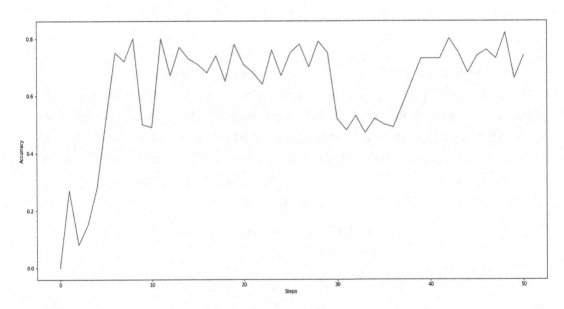

Figure 5-14. *Accuracy steps graph for Q-learning*

Now in the case of the SARSA algorithm, the "SARSA" method implements the on–
policy update method that updates the policies:

```
target=reward + GAMMA*table[(state1, action)]
predict=table[(state0, action)]
table[(state0, action)]+= LEARNING_RATE*(target- predict)
```

346

On running this segment, we can visualize the reward-steps graph and can compare the difference between on- and off-policies in discrete space, as shown in Figure 5-15.

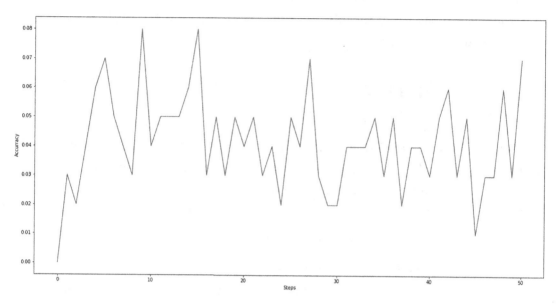

Figure 5-15. *Accuracy steps graph for SARSA*

Deep RL: Continuous Spaces Deep On-Policy Algorithms

Now in many complex environments, there can be a continuous distribution of values related to a particular policy. Although this set of algorithms can be extended to discrete spaces, we will consider continuous distributions. For continuous spaces, we have to use deep RL algorithms. In the case of on-policy algorithms for optimizing the policy, the most important class of algorithms are called policy gradients. The policy gradient method models and optimizes the policy directly. Generally we associate a parameterized function $\pi_\theta(a|s)$, which signifies the policy and policy gradients try to optimize θ to get a better reward. The reward function generally in policy gradients are denoted as:

$$J(\theta) = \sum_s d^\pi(s)V^\pi(s) = \sum_s d^\pi(s)\sum_A \pi_\theta(a|s)Q^\pi(s, a),$$

where $d^\pi(s)$ represents the stationary distribution of Markov chain for π_θ policy, which is an on-policy distribution. This can be generalized as if the agent travels along the Markov chain indefinitely the probability of the agent ending up at a state becomes unchanged, which is referred to as the stationary probability. In this context, we will explore most of the on-policy algorithms such as vanilla policy gradient (VPG), advantage actor critic (A2C), PPO, along with variants of asynchronous actor critic (A3C) and its variants, which include ACER (off policy A3C) and ACKTR. However, most importantly we will be understanding the PPO policy since ML Agents use it extensively.

Policy Gradient – REINFORCE

It can be expected that policy-based deep RL is more useful than value-based learning, in continuous spaces. This is due to the infinite number of actions that can estimate the values; hence, value-based approaches are too computationally intensive. In policy gradient method of on policy training, there is a concept of gradient ascent. This implies the policy improvement takes place according to the equation:

$$Q^\pi(s' \,|a'\,) = \text{argmax}_A \, Q^\pi(s\,|a\,)$$

To maximize the policy update, we generally require computation of the gradient of the policy $J(\theta)$, so that we can move θ toward the direction of highest return on that policy π_θ. This is done by using the policy gradient theorem and is the backbone of most of the deep RL algorithms present in continuous space.

Policy Gradient Theorem

Computing the gradient is a difficult problem, as it depends on the action selection space as well as the stationary distribution of states, particularly policy behavior π_θ. The latter part is difficult to compute, as it is not possible to know the stationary distribution of states in a dynamic environment. We denote the gradient of the policy as $\Delta_\theta J(\theta)$, where Δ_θ represents the grad operator on the parameter space θ. The policy gradient theorem provides a reformation of the partial derivative of the objective function without involving the derivative of the state distribution. The policy gradient can be simplified as follows:

$$\Delta\theta \, J(\theta) = \Delta\theta \sum S \, d\pi(s)V\pi(s) = \Delta\theta \sum S \, d\pi(s) \sum A \, \pi\theta(a|s)Q\pi(s, a)$$

$$\alpha \sum_s d^\pi(s) \sum_A \Delta_\theta \, \pi_\theta(a|s)Q^\pi(s, a),$$

where α represents proportionality. Therefore, instead of computing the derivatives on the state space, we are effectively calculating the derivative of the policy function. The derivation of this theorem can be done by starting with the state value function $\Delta_\theta V^\pi(s)$ and then expanding it to include the policy function and the $Q^\pi(s, a)$ state as follows:

$$\Delta_\theta V^\pi(s) = \Delta_\theta \left(\sum_A \pi_\theta(a|s)Q^\pi(s, a) \right)$$

$$= \sum_A \left(\Delta_\theta \pi_\theta(a|s)Q^\pi(s, a) + \pi_\theta(a|s) \, \Delta_\theta \, Q^\pi(s, a) \right) \text{By Chain Rule of Derivatives}$$

Extending Q with future state values

$$= \sum_A \left(\Delta_\theta \pi_\theta(a|s)Q^\pi(s, a) + \pi_\theta(a|s) \, \Delta_\theta \sum_{S, R} P(s`, r|s, a) \, (r+V^\pi(s`)) \right)$$

Reward r not function of θ

$$= \sum_A \left(\Delta_\theta \pi_\theta(a|s)Q^\pi(s, a) + \pi_\theta(a|s) \sum_{S, R} P(s`, r|s, a) \, \Delta_\theta V^\pi(s`) \right)$$

As $P(s`, r|s, a) = P(s`|s, a)$

$$= \sum_A \left(\Delta_\theta \pi_\theta(a|s)Q^\pi(s, a) + \pi_\theta(a|s) \sum_{S, R} P(s`|s, a) \, \Delta_\theta V^\pi(s`) \right)$$

Thus we have a recursive formulation of the gradient update policy, as mentioned in the following equation:

$$\Delta_\theta V^\pi(s) = \sum_A \left(\Delta_\theta \pi_\theta(a|s)Q^\pi(s, a) + \pi_\theta(a|s) \sum_{S, R} P(s`|s, a) \, \Delta_\theta V^\pi(s`) \right)$$

If we observe closely, we will see that if we extend $\Delta_\theta V^\pi()$ indefinitely, it is easy to find out that we can transition to any state from a starting state s through the recursive unrolling process and by adding all the visitation probabilities, we will get $\Delta_\theta V^\pi(s)$. This can be proved simply by using the $\pi_\theta(a|s) \sum_{S, R} P(s`|s, a) \, \Delta_\theta V^\pi(s`)$ repeatedly to transition into new states s``, s```, and others. This form can be represented as:

$$\Delta_\theta V^\pi(s) = \sum_S \sum_K p^\pi(s \rightarrow x, k)\Phi(s),$$

where $p^\pi(s \rightarrow x, k)$ represents the transition probability from state s to x after k steps, and $\Phi(s)$ signifies $\Delta_\theta \pi_\theta(a|s)Q^\pi(s, a)$.

Now passing this into the policy gradient function for gradient ascent, we get:

$$\Delta_\theta J(\theta) = \Delta_\theta V^\pi(s)$$

$$= \sum_S \sum_K p^\pi(s_0 \rightarrow s, k)\Phi(s) \text{ Starting from state } S_0 \text{ through Markov distribution and}$$
$$\text{recurrence}$$

$$= \sum_S \eta(s) \, \Phi(s) \text{ Let } \eta(s) = \sum_K p^\pi(s_0 \rightarrow s, k)$$

$$= \left(\sum_S \eta(s) \right) \left[\sum_S \eta(s) / \left(\sum_S \eta(s) \right) \right] \Phi(s) \text{ Normalize } \eta(s)$$

$$\alpha \left[\sum_S \eta(s) / \left(\sum_S \eta(s) \right) \right] \Phi(s) \sum_S \eta(s) \text{ is constant}$$

$$= \sum_S d^\pi(s) \sum_A \Delta_\theta \pi_\theta(a|s)Q^\pi(s, a) \; d^\pi(s) = \sum_S \eta(s) / \left(\sum_S \eta(s) \right) \text{ stationary distribution}$$

That completes the proof of the policy gradient theorem, and we can simplify the equation as follows:

$$\Delta_\theta J(\theta) \propto \sum_s d^\pi(s) \sum_A \Delta_\theta \pi_\theta(a|s) Q^\pi(s, a)$$

$$= \sum_s d^\pi(s) \sum_A \pi_\theta(a|s) Q^\pi(s, a) [(\Delta_\theta \pi_\theta(a|s))/ \pi_\theta(a|s)]$$

This modification is added to produce a new form of generic policy gradient algorithms in the form of expectations using the fact that the derivative of $\ln(x)$ $(\log_e x)$ is $1/x$:

$$\Delta_\theta J(\theta) = E[Q^\pi(s, a) \Delta_\theta \ln(\pi_\theta(a|s))]$$

Generally, this equation is represented as:

$$\Delta_\theta J(\theta) = E[\sum_t \Psi_t \Delta_\theta \ln(\pi_\theta(a|s))],$$

where may be the following functions:

- **Reward trajectory:** $\sum_t r_t$

- **State-action value:** $\sum_t Q^\pi(s_t, a_t)$

- **Advantage function:** $\sum_t A^\pi(s_t, a_t)$

- **Temporal difference residual:** $r_{t+} V^\pi(s_{t+1}) - V^\pi(s_t)$

Advantage function is defined as:

$$A^\pi(s_t, a_t) = Q^\pi(s_t, a_t) - V^\pi(s_t)$$

In VPG, which we will be reviewing closely, we have the advantage function in the policy gradient equation, represented as:

$$\Delta_\theta J(\theta) = E[\sum_t \Delta_\theta \ln(\pi_\theta(a|s)) A^\pi(s_t, a_t)]$$

Now, we have seen that an optimal policy tries to maximize the rewards, and the gradients are used to compute the maxima in high-dimensional space. In deep RL using policy methods, this is the gradient ascent step, which is stochastic in nature and tries to maximize the parameter θ as follows:

$$\Theta_{k+1} = \Theta_k + \alpha \Delta_\theta J(\theta),$$

where α is the learning rate. Policy gradients compute the advantage function estimates based on rewards and then try to minimize the errors in the value function by normal gradient descent (SGD/Adam) using the quadratic loss function that we discussed in neural networks:

$$\Phi_{k+1} \, \alpha \, \sum_s \sum_t (V^{\pi}(s_t) - R_t)^2,$$

where α signifies proportionality and Φ_{k+1} is the error gradient on mean squared loss.

To understand this deep reinforcement on–policy algorithm, we will look into the simple implementation of the VPG algorithm. Open the Policy Gradients.ipynb Notebook. We will be using the CartPole environment from OpenAI, as in most of our previous examples, and will develop the algorithm. Then we will use this on other trainable deep RL environments in Gym, such as Atari Games (Pong) and MountainCar.

We define the class PGAgent and declare the initial variables that control the exploration-exploitation rate (gamma), learning rate, state size, action size, and initialize arrays to contain the list of rewards, actions, states, and probabilities. This is signified by the following lines:

```
class PGAgent:
  def __init__(self, state_size, action_size):
    self.state_size=state_size
    self.action_size=action_size
    self.gamma=0.99
    self.learning_rate=0.001
    self.states=[]
    self.rewards=[]
    self.labels=[]
    self.prob=[]
    self.model=self.build_model()
    self.model.summary()
```

Now let us see the model part of this algorithm, which is responsible for the gradient ascent of the advantage as well as the gradient descent to minimize the error in value estimates. We will be using dense MLP network in our case. We can also use convolution networks in this case. The initial two dense use 64 units with "Relu" activation and glorot_uniform as the kernel initializing functions. Then we have a dense layer with softmax activation and self.action_size as the output dimension. Since in CartPole the action space consists of either moving toward the left or right, we can use sigmoid

activation as well. Then we have a "model.compile" method with Adam optimizer and
a categorical cross entropy loss. Since this code is made to provide a policy gradient
approach to most of OpenAI Gym's environments; hence, we have used softmax
activation for multi-class classification and cross-entropy loss. For CartPole, we can
make changes to the loss by making it binary_crossentropy and using sigmoid activation
in the last dense layer.

```
model=Sequential()
    model.add(Dense(64, input_dim=self.state_size, activation='relu',
    kernel_initializer='glorot_uniform'))
model.add(Dense(64, activation='relu', kernel_initializer='glorot_
uniform'))
model.add(Dense(self.action_size, activation='softmax'))
    model.compile(optimizer=Adam(learning_rate=self.learning_rate),
    loss='categorical_crossentropy')
 return model
```

The next method is memory, which fills the array of actions, rewards, and states. In
this method, whenever an action is chosen, it is marked in the array as 1. This can be
thought of as a one-hot encoding mechanism.

```
y=np.zeros([self.action_size])
y[action]=1
self.labels.append(np.array(y).astype('float32'))
self.states.append(state)
self.rewards.append(reward)
```

In the "act" method, we use the model to predict an action that an agent should take
based on the advantage estimate (GAE) function. The "model.predict" method is used to
predict the probabilities. The action having the highest probability is chosen as the next
action based on the GAE policy.

```
  def act(self, state):
    state=state.reshape([1, state.shape[0]])
    probs=self.model.predict(state, batch_size=1).flatten()
    self.prob.append(probs)
    action=np.random.choice(self.action_size,1, p=probs)[0]
    return action, probs
```

The "discount_rewards" method provides a discounted reward by using the exploration-exploitation factor gamma. This is a generic discount rewards policy and will be used across algorithms.

```
def discount_rewards(self, rewards):
    discounted_rewards = np.zeros_like(rewards)
    running_sum = 0
    for t in reversed(range(len(rewards))):
        if rewards[t] != 0:
            running_add = 0
        running_add = running_add * self.gamma + rewards[t]
        discounted_rewards[t] = running_add
    return discounted_rewards
```

In the next method, the "train" method, we will be training the neural network. For this, we normalize the rewards array. Then we use the "model.train_on_batch" method to train the neural network and pass inputs as the states ("self.states") and outputs as the actions ("self.labels").

```
def train(self):
    labels=np.vstack(self.labels)
    rewards=np.vstack(self.rewards)
    rewards=self.discount_rewards(rewards)
    rewards=(rewards-np.mean(rewards))/np.std(rewards)
    labels*=-rewards
    x=np.squeeze(np.vstack([self.states]))
    y=np.squeeze(np.vstack([self.labels]))
    self.model.train_on_batch(x, y)
    self.states, self.probs, self.labels, self.rewards
    =[],[],[],[]
```

In the load_model and save_model functions, we load and save the weights of the model as follows:

```
def load_model(self, name):
    self.model.load_weights(name)

  def save_model(self, name):
    self.model.save_weights(name)
```

In the "main()" method, we create the environment from Gym using the "gym. make" method. This method also has the action space and observation space along with the rewards. We create an object of the PGAgent class and pass in the action size and state size as arguments from the Gym environment. We train our model for 200 epochs, and for each episode of training, we observe the rewards, states, and actions and correspondingly add the rewards to cumulative rewards. For each episode of training represented by the "agent.train" method, we record the corresponding action and the rewards. If the reward is negative, it is reset to 0 and the training starts again.

```
if __name__=="__main__":
  env=gym.make('CartPole-v0')

  state=env.reset()

  score=0
  episode=0
  state_size=env.observation_space.shape[0]
  action_size=env.action_space.n
  agent=PGAgent(state_size, action_size)
  j=0
  while j is not 2000:
    screen = env.render(mode='rgb_array')
    action, prob=agent.act(state)
    state_1, reward, done,_=env.step(action)
    score+=reward
    agent.memory(state, action, prob, reward)
    state=state_1
    plt.imshow(screen)
    ipythondisplay.clear_output(wait=True)
    ipythondisplay.display(plt.gcf())

    if done:
      j+=1
      agent.rewards[-1]=score
      agent.train()
```

```
print("Episode: %d - Score: %f."%(j, score))
score=0.0
state=env.reset()

env.close()
```

Finally after training is completed, we close the environment. We can also see the CartPole in action as we used the "ipythondisplay" methods, which we saw in the first chapter. Figure 5-16 illustrates this.

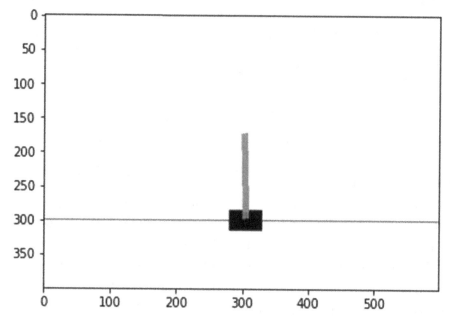

Figure 5-16. *CartPole environment training using policy gradient algorithm*

This code segment can be used for solving the MountainCar problem in the Gym environment where a car is stuck between two slopes of a mountain and has to climb up to reach the destination. By changing the env.make (MountainCar-v0), we can simulate this GAE policy gradient algorithm for this use-case, as shown in Figure 5-17.

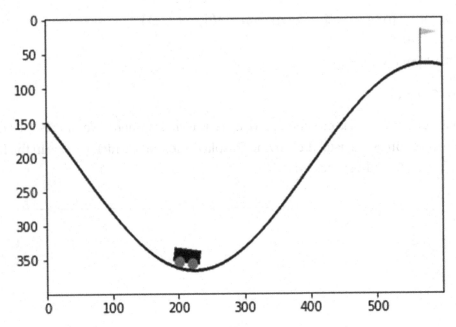

Figure 5-17. *MountainCar problem training in policy gradients*

Actor Critic Algorithm

Let us now venture into the actor critic set of algorithms, which is an on-policy technique. As we saw in policy gradients, there is a gradient ascent of the gradient function for choosing better returns and there is a standard gradient descent or minimization function for reducing the error in the value estimates. In actor critic, a modification is made by introducing two competitive neural network models and storing previous value estimates pertaining to a particular policy. Hence actor critic consists of two neural network models or agents:

- **Critic:** updates the value function parameters w and modifies the policy gradient by updating the state-action value $\sum_t Q^\pi(s_t, a_t)$ or state value $\sum_t V^\pi(s_t)$

- **Actor:** relies on the critic to update the policy parameters θ for $\pi_\theta(a|s)$

For the critic update step, we can consider the policy gradient theorem and function with state action value instead of advantage function as follows:

$$\Delta_\theta J(\theta) = E[\sum Q^\pi(s, a) \, \Delta_\theta \ln(\pi_\theta(a|s)) \,],$$

with the gradient ascent step denoted by

$$\Theta_{k+1} = \Theta_k + \alpha \, \Delta_\theta J(\theta)$$

The actor can upgrade its policies to have a better reward. There is also a value estimate that governs the critic in deciding the value of the next state. Depending on the current policy $\pi_\theta(a|s)$, the critic estimates whether the action to be taken by the actor is most rewarding or not. Hence, the general architecture of actor critic can be visualized as shown in Figure 5-18.

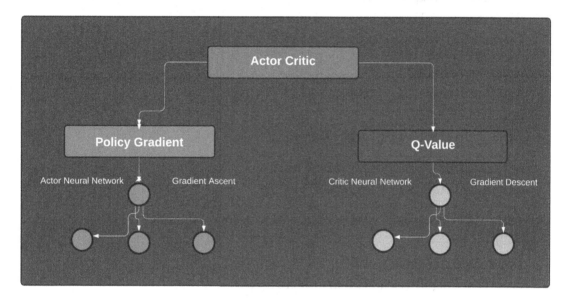

Figure 5-18. *Actor critic network architecture*

With respect to this, we will be understanding some of the variants of actor critic algorithm.

A2C algorithm: This uses the actor critic concept mentioned before with the modification that instead of a value update, it updates the advantage estimate (GAE), which is given by the following equation:

$$A^\pi(s_t, a_t) = Q^\pi(s_t, a_t) - V^\pi(s_t)$$

The A2C algorithm can be found in the A2C.ipynb Notebook. This algorithm has been built using the same code base of the policy gradient algorithm that we observed, and all the functions are the same. The only changes in the A2C algorithm is that we train two different neural network models–the actor and critic. This can be observed in the "build_actor_model" and "build_critic_model" methods inside the A2Cagent class. The actor model contains two dense MLP layers with 64 units with activation "Relu" (this can be changed to convolution-2D layers as per requirement) and kernel initializers. Then it has a softmax distributed outer dense layer with the action spaces as the output. We finally compile the actor model with categorical cross-entropy loss and Adam optimizer.

```
def build_actor_model(self):
    logdir= "logs/scalars/" + datetime.now().
    strftime("%Y%m%d-%H%M%S")
    tensorboard_callback=keras.callbacks.
    TensorBoard(log_dir=logdir)

    Actor=Sequential()
    Actor.add(Dense(64, input_dim=self.state_size,
    activation='relu',
    kernel_initializer='glorot_uniform'))

    Actor.add(Dense(64, activation='relu',
    kernel_initializer='glorot_uniform'))

    Actor.add(Dense(self.action_size, activation='softmax'))

    Actor.compile(optimizer=
    Adam(learning_rate=self.learning_rate),
    loss='categorical_crossentropy')
    return Actor
```

In the next stage, we have the build_critic_model function, which has a similar architecture with respect to the actor model. However, we can make changes to this architecture by introducing different dense/convolution layers and/or changing the activation functions.

```
def build_critic_model(self):
    logdir= "logs/scalars/" + datetime.now().
    strftime("%Y%m%d-%H%M%S")

    tensorboard_callback=keras.callbacks.
    TensorBoard(log_dir=logdir)
```

```
Critic=Sequential()
Critic.add(Dense(64, input_dim=self.state_size,
activation='relu',
kernel_initializer='glorot_uniform'))

Critic.add(Dense(64, activation='relu',
kernel_initializer='glorot_uniform'))
Critic.add(Dense(self.action_size, activation='softmax'))

Critic.compile(optimizer=
Adam(learning_rate=self.learning_rate),
loss='categorical_crossentropy')
return Critic
```

The "memory" method has the similar implementation as that in the policy gradient. However, in the "act" method, we will use the critic model to predict the actions as follows:

```
def act(self, state):
    state=state.reshape([1, state.shape[0]])
    probs=self.Critic.predict(state, batch_size=1).flatten()
    self.prob.append(probs)
    action=np.random.choice(self.action_size,1, p=probs)[0]
    return action, probs
```

Then we have the "discount_rewards" method, which is similar to policy gradient. The "train" method has changes, as in this case, we have to train both the actor and critic models. We take the inputs of the actions ("labels") and the discounted rewards and then specify the states and actions, (self.states, self.labels) to the actor and critic models. The "train_on_batch" method is used for training specifically on user-defined batches, and in this case, we can use the "model.fit" method to train as well. The difference is that in the latter case, the "fit" method automatically converts the sampled data into batches for training and may also include a generator function.

```
def train(self):
    labels=np.vstack(self.labels)
    rewards=np.vstack(self.rewards)
    rewards=self.discount_rewards(rewards)
```

```
rewards=(rewards-np.mean(rewards))/np.std(rewards)
labels*=-rewards
x=np.squeeze(np.vstack([self.states]))
y=np.squeeze(np.vstack([self.labels]))
self.Actor.train_on_batch(x, y)
self.Critic.train_on_batch(x, y)
self.states, self.probs, self.labels, self.rewards=[],[],[],[]
```

The rest of the code segment is the same as the policy gradient, and hence methods like "load_weight" and "save_weight" are similar. On running this in the CartPole environment, we can visualize the training as well as the rewards/loss. Thus we built an A2C agent that uses two neural networks using policy gradient and advantage value-estimate to predict the output actions. This can also be used for training the Acrobot environment in OpenAI Gym. The Acrobot consists of two joints and two links, where the joint between the two links is underactuated. The goal is to swing the end of the lower link to a given height, as shown in Figure 5-19.

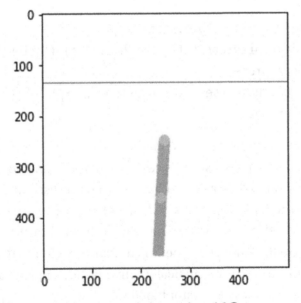

Figure 5-19. *Acrobot environment training using A2C*

A3C: This is an asynchronous version of the A2C algorithm, which mainly relies on threading. This implies that there are several worker threads that work in parallel to update the parameters θ. The importance of this on-policy algorithm is that the

A3C agent learns the value function when multiple actors are trained in parallel, and these are synced with the global parameters periodically. While this algorithm runs especially well in GPUs, we will implement a very simple version for the CPU, using the same code base that we have. The effect of different parallel actor implies that the training is faster due to faster updates on the parameters which assist in upgrading the policy.

Open the A3C.ipynb Notebook in Colab or Jupyter Notebook. This code segment can be made to run on Cloud GPUs, which are provided with the Colab, with some code changes. In our case, we have to import the threading library and its associated modules such as Lock and Thread. The concept of lock and release is important for process scheduling (thread scheduling) and prevents deadlock in the operating system. While a subthread updates the global parameters, the other subthreads should not be reading or using those parameters; this is done by a classic mutex lock (mutual exclusion). This is analogous to the "Readers-Writers" problem in Operating System Theory, where readers are unable to read unless the writers complete writing to the same disk or file.

```
import threading
from threading import Lock, Thread
```

We have most of the functions that implement the A3CAgent class, similarly to the A2CAgent class. The difference lies in the fact that here we will use threading to make multiple copies of the Actor model. The "train_thread" method creates "daemon" threads, depending on the number of threads specified in the "n_threads" attribute. Now each of these daemon threads calls the "thread_train" method, which has an associated lock for reading an updating the global parameters set.

```
def train_thread(self, n_thread):
    self.env.close()
    envs=[gym.make('CartPole-v0') for i in range(n_thread)]
    threads=(threading.Thread(target=self.thread_train(),
    daemon=True, args=(self, envs[i], i)) for i
    in    range(n_thread))
    for t in threads:
      time.sleep(1)
      t.start()
```

The "thread_train" method calls the "agent.train()" method inside every lock stage, trains a particular worker actor thread, and updates the global parameter set (states, actions, rewards).

```
def thread_train(self):
    lock=Lock()
    lock.acquire()
    agent.train()
    lock.release()
```

This completes the A3C modification of the A2C algorithm. As mentioned, there are other variants that are faster and have a greater performance on GPUs, but in this case we are simply using a smaller CPU version. We can train MountainCar with this algorithm as well and compare the results with A2C. To illustrate, the A3C architecture is shown in Figure 5-20.

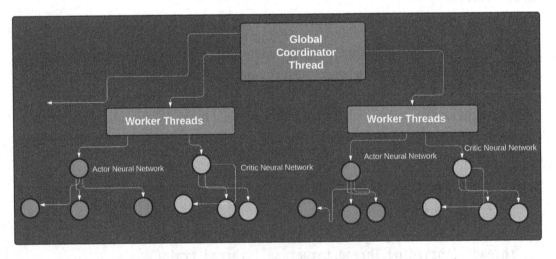

Figure 5-20. *A3C architecture*

Actor critic using Kronecker factored trust region (ACKTR): This is a variant of the actor critic class of algorithms where natural gradient is used in place of Adam/SGD/ RMSProp optimizers. It is faster than gradient descent, as it acquires the loss landscape by using the Fisher Information Matrix (FIM) as a curvature of the loss function. A generic FIM of a probabilistic model that outputs a conditional probability of y given the value of x is denoted by:

$$F_\theta = E_{(x,\,y)} \left[\Delta \log p(y|x;\theta) \, \Delta \log p(y|x;\theta)^T \right]$$

In generic classification tasks, we normally use mean value of log likelihood (mse error) as the loss function. We can derive the relationship between the FIM and the Hessian (2nd order partial derivative matrix of scalar fields) of a negative log likelihood loss $E(\theta)$:

$$H(E)\,(\theta) = \Delta^2 E_{(x,\,y)} \left[- \log p(y|x;\theta) \right]$$

$$= - E_{(x,\,y)} \left[\Delta^2 \log p(y|x;\theta) \right]$$

$$= - E_{(x,\,y)} \left[- (\Delta \log p(y|x;\theta) \, \Delta \log p(y|x;\theta)^T)/ p(y|x;\theta)^2 + \Delta^2 p(y|x;\theta)/ p(y|x;\theta) \right]$$
$$\text{(Chain Rule)}$$

$$= F_\theta - E_{(x,\,y)} \left[\Delta^2 p(y|x;\theta)/ p(y|x;\theta) \right]$$

The gradient update rule is given by:

$$\Theta_{k+1} = \Theta_k - \alpha \, (F_\theta)^{-1}{}_k \, \Delta \, E(\theta_k),$$

where α is the learning rate and Δ denotes the grad operator (for derivative).

We will use the ACKTR model from Baselines (stable-baselines) to train four instances of the CartPole environment in parallel. Open the ACKTR.ipynb Notebook In the first step, we have to make the necessary imports, including the stable baselines, the policies (MLP/MLPLSTM), the ACKTR model, and ipythondisplay for visualization.

```
import gym

from stable_baselines.common.policies import MlpPolicy, MlpLstmPolicy,
MlpLnLstmPolicy
from stable_baselines.common import make_vec_env
from stable_baselines import ACKTR
import matplotlib.pyplot as plt
from IPython import display as ipythondisplay
from pyvirtualdisplay import Display
display = Display(visible=0, size=(400, 300))
display.start()
```

Then we load the CartPole-v1 environment and load the ACKTR model with MLP (dense neural network) policy with 25000 time-steps.

```
env = make_vec_env('CartPole-v1', n_envs=4)
```

```
model = ACKTR(MlpPolicy, env, verbose=1)
model.learn(total_timesteps=25000)
model.save("acktr_cartpole")
model = ACKTR.load("acktr_cartpole")
```

```
obs = env.reset()
```

Then we have a loop for execution of the algorithm and observe the state, rewards, and actions per step of training.

```
while True:
    action, _states = model.predict(obs)
    obs, rewards, dones, info = env.step(action)
    screen = env.render(mode='rgb_array')
    plt.imshow(screen)
    ipythondisplay.clear_output(wait=True)
    ipythondisplay.display(plt.gcf())
```

On running this module, we can visualize the training happening on four instances with ACKTR policy, as shown in Figure 5-21.

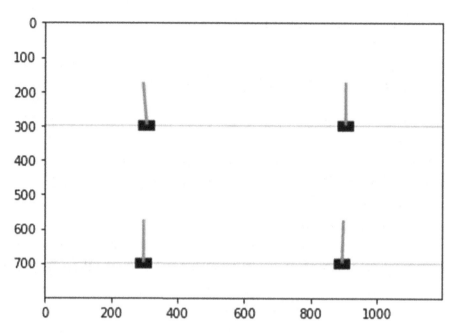

Figure 5-21. *ACKTR algorithm in CartPole*

We can also modify our existing code base that we used in the previous cases. We will see the A2C_ACKTR class, and in place of the Adam optimizer present in the "build_actor_model" class, we will be using the "kfac" (Kronecker Factor) as the optimizer for natural gradient descent. This uses the "kfac" module from Tensorflow, and there have not been any upgrades of the module to be compatible with Tensorflow 2.0. Hence, there may be error mismatches. However, the code remains the same, with the only modification in the inclusion of the "kfac" module instead of the Adam optimizer.

Stochastic actor critic for continuous spaces: This is another variant of actor critic algorithms that uses a Gaussian distribution instead of a softmax distribution. This parameterized distribution assists in continuous spaces. For this the Gaussian equation (distribution) for the policy $\pi_\theta(a|s)$ can be written as:

$$\pi_\theta(a|s)) = 1/(\sqrt{2\pi}\sigma_\theta\,(s)) \exp\left(-\,(a-\mu_\theta\,(s)^2)/2\,\sigma_\theta\,(s)^2\right)$$

This is implemented in the Stochastic Continuous Normal AC.ipynb Notebook, with the simple replacement in the "build_actor_model" method with the kernel initializing as "normal," which represents a Normal (Gaussian kernel) and a sigmoid activation unit.

```
Actor.add(Dense(64, input_dim=self.state_size, activation='relu',
kernel_initializer='normal'))
Actor.add(Dense(64, activation='relu', kernel_initializer='normal'))
Actor.add(Dense(self.action_size, activation='sigmoid'))
```

This can also be implemented by writing a custom Gaussian activation unit and making it consistent with Tensorflow.

The variants of actor critic algorithms that we read in this section are entirely on-policy actor critic versions. There are off-policy actor critic algorithms (ACER) as well that we will look briefly in the next few sections.

Proximal Policy Optimization

Now we have explored the actor critic algorithms, we can learn about the PPO algorithm. This is based on A3C; however, there are fundamental differences. In this policy gradient on-policy algorithm, comparison is made between two policies based on their returns. Before we get into the details of PPO, let us understand the trust region policy optimization (TRPO) algorithm, which is the starting point of PPO.

Trust region policy optimization: To improve the stability of the actor critic variants, TRPO was designed, which avoids frequent policy updates by avoiding certain constraints based on Kullback-Leiblar (KL) divergence. The KL divergence provides the divergence relation between two probabilistic distributions, p and q, on variable x given by the equation:

$$D_{KL} = - \sum p(x) \log (p(x)/q(x))$$

Generally TRPO is a minorization-majorization (MM) algorithm that provides an upper and lower bound on the expected returns of the policies for comparison and thresholds them using the KL divergence. TRPO tries to find an optimal policy upgrade rule by comparing against the running gradient defined by $\Delta_\theta J(\theta)$, which is called the surrogate gradient, and the corresponding policy gradient equation as the surrogate objective function. The TRPO algorithm can be analyzed as an optimization problem with the following conditions:

- Adding KL divergence constraint on the distribution of the old and the new policies with the problem of maximizing the $\Delta_\theta J(\theta)$:

$$\text{Max}_\theta \, \Delta_\theta J(\theta)$$

$$\text{Subject to } D_{KL}(\pi_{\theta old}(a|s)/ \, \pi_\theta(a|s)) < \partial$$

- Regularization of the gradient objective function with KL divergence:

$$\text{Max}_\theta\ L\theta)= J(\pi_\theta) - C\ D_{KL}(\pi_{\theta old}(a|s)/\ \pi_\theta(a|s))$$

The equations depend on the parameters of C and ∂. Now we apply sampling in this context, which implies finding the advantage taken at each step. Now if we refer to the Policy Gradient Theorem and the gradient function, given by the equation:

$$\Delta_\theta\ J(\theta) = E[\textstyle\sum_t \Psi_t \Delta_\theta \ln(\pi_\theta(a|s))\ ]$$

we will reframe the policy $\pi_\theta(a|s)$ part to contain a ratio of old and present policies, and in place of Ψ_t, we will be using the advantage function, $A^\pi(s_t, a_t)$. The new gradient objective function for policy update becomes:

$$\Delta_\theta\ J(\theta) = E[\textstyle\sum_t A^\pi(s_t,\ a_t), \Delta_\theta \ln(\pi_\theta(a|s)/\ \pi_{\theta old}(a|s)))\ ],$$

which can be simplified to:

$$\Delta_\theta\ J(\theta) = E[\ A^\pi(s_t,\ a_t)\ (\pi_\theta(a|s)/\ \pi_{\theta old}(a|s))\ ]$$

Now the maximization problem can be simplified as:

$$\text{Max}_\theta\ E[\textstyle\sum_t A^\pi(s_t,\ a_t), \Delta_\theta \ln(\pi_\theta\ (a|s)/\ \pi_{\theta old}\ (a|s)))\ ]$$

$$\text{Subject to } D_{KL}(\pi_{\theta old}(a|s)/\ \pi_\theta(a|s)) < \partial$$

This is the main concept behind the TRPO algorithm. There are methods like natural gradient that are applied using the FIM for faster convergence. The ratio of policies is used to compute the importance sampling on a set of parameters θ. Now we will try to use this concept to build a TRPO agent. As we saw, the TRPO is an optimization over the actor critic method. Hence we will understand two variants of TRPO—one by OpenAI Baselines and the other by updating the same code base of actor critic.

Open the TRPO.ipynb Notebook. First we will use the Baselines TRPO module from OpenAI. For this we will import the library modules required for us.

```
import gym
from stable_baselines.common.policies import MlpPolicy
from stable_baselines import TRPO
import matplotlib.pyplot as plt
from IPython import display as ipythondisplay
from pyvirtualdisplay import Display
display = Display(visible=0, size=(400, 300))
display.start()
```

This is the same as in the previous case, with the exception that in this case we will be using the TRPO algorithm. In this case, we will be using the Pendulum-v0 as our environment. The Pendulum is a classic RL environment, similar to CartPole, where there is an inverted pendulum that starts in a random position. The goal is to swing this pendulum up so that it stays upright—a classic control problem. First we load the environment using the Gym, and then we load the TRPO model using MLP (dense) as our neural network architecture.

```
env = gym.make('Pendulum-v0')
model = TRPO(MlpPolicy, env, verbose=1)
model.learn(total_timesteps=25000)
model.save("trpo_pendulum")
del model
model = TRPO.load("trpo_pendulum")
```

Inside the while loop, we run the algorithm for 25000 iterations and observe the states, rewards, and action spaces.

```
while True:
    action, _states = model.predict(obs)
    obs, rewards, dones, info = env.step(action)
    screen = env.render(mode='rgb_array')
    plt.imshow(screen)
    ipythondisplay.clear_output(wait=True)
    ipythondisplay.display(plt.gcf())
```

On running the code segment, we can visualize the Pendulum trying to be upright, as shown in Figure 5-22.

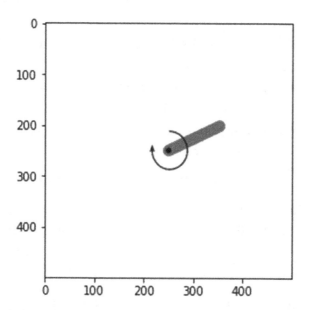

Figure 5-22. *Pendulum environment using the TRPO algorithm*

Now we are going to modify our previous code base, which is the A2C variant of actor critic. Most of the code segment will remain the same, with the exception that in the "build_actor_model" method in the TRPOAgent class, we will add a new loss function-trpo_loss. This loss function computes the KL divergence of the predicted outcomes with the previous outcomes and has an entropy factor to govern the constraints. The loss is measured by taking the negative log likelihood of the KL divergence distribution and is used with the Adam optimizer for the actor neural network.

```
def trpo_loss(y_true, y_pred):
    entropy=2e-5
    old_log= k.sum(y_true)
    print(old_log)
    pred_log=k.sum(y_pred)
    print(pred_log)
    kl_divergence= k.sum(old_log* k.log(old_log/pred_log))
    prob=1e-2
    loss=-k.mean(kl_divergence +
    entropy*(-(prob*k.log(prob+1e-10))))
    return loss
Actor.compile(optimizer=Adam(learning_rate=self.learning_rate),
loss=trpo_loss)
```

Thus we can now use TRPO on the A2C variant. We can also add this loss function in the A3C variant to make the TRPO-A3C agent variant. We can also play with the hyperparameters to estimate our values on particular policies.

Proximal Policy Optimization (PPO): Using the TRPO concept, PPO is developed to increase simplicity and ease of use. The PPO algorithm relies on clipping of the surrogate gradient objective function while retaining the performance on the value estimates. Let us look at the previous objective equation of TRPO, which was:

$$\Delta_\theta J(\theta) = E[\ A^\pi(s_t, a_t)\ (\pi_\theta(a|s)/\ \pi_{\theta old}(a|s))\ ]$$

TRPO does not limit the distance between the policies $\pi_\theta(a|s)$, $\pi_{\theta old}(a|s)$). And in many cases, this may lead to instability in training. PPO uses a clipped threshold value given by $[(1+\varepsilon), (1-\varepsilon)]$, where ε is a hyperparameter. Hence, the effective formulation of the gradient function based on PPO is defined as:

$$\Delta_\theta J(\theta) = E[\min(r(\theta)A^\pi(s_t, a_t), clip(r(\theta), 1+\varepsilon, 1-\varepsilon)\ A^\pi(s_t, a_t)],$$

where $r(\theta) = \pi_\theta(a|s)/\ \pi_{\theta old}(a|s)$ and $clip(r(\theta), 1+\varepsilon, 1-\varepsilon)$ clips the ratio $r(\theta)$ to be no more than $(1+\varepsilon)$ and no less than $(1-\varepsilon)$.

This is the concept behind the PPO algorithm. There are other variants of the PPO algorithm such as PPO-Penalty, which penalizes the KL divergence similar to TRPO with the exception that in TRPO there is a hard constraint. This clipping controls the divergence between the old and new policies in the following way, which is governed by the advantage as follows.

- If the advantage $A^\pi(s_t, a_t)$ is positive, the objective function will increase if the action becomes more likely—that is, $\pi_\theta(a|s)$ increases. However, due to the minimization term, there is a limit how much the objective can increase. Once the ratio $\pi_\theta(a|s) > (1+\varepsilon)\ \pi_{\theta old}(a|s))$, the minimization operation takes control and hence avoids the new policy to go far away from the older policy.

- If the advantage $A^\pi(s_t, a_t)$ is negative, the objective function will decrease if the action becomes less likely—that is, $\pi_\theta(a|s)$ will decrease. However, due to the maximization term, there is a limit how much the objective can decrease. Once the ratio $\pi_\theta(a|s) < (1-\varepsilon)$ $\pi_{\theta old}(a|s))$, the maximization will kick in and avoid the new policy to go far away from the old one.

Now let us implement a PPO agent using the Baselines from Open AI, and then we will explore how to modify the TRPO source (the loss function) to make it PPO.

Open the PPO-Baselines.ipynb Notebook. We will be using the stable Baselines like before and will import all the libraries and neural networks associated with PPO. Since we will be using the clipped PPO version, we have to import PPO2 from the Baselines as well as the "MlpPolicy," which signifies we will be using dense networks for our training.

```
import gym
from stable_baselines.common.policies import MlpPolicy
from stable_baselines.common import make_vec_env
from stable_baselines import PPO2
```

In the next step, we will set up the environment, and in this case, we will be using the CartPole environment. We will load the model as well. This is done using the following lines of code.

```
env = make_vec_env('CartPole-v1', n_envs=4)
model = PPO2(MlpPolicy, env, verbose=1)
model.learn(total_timesteps=2000)
model.save("ppo2_cartpole")
model = PPO2.load("ppo2_cartpole")
```

In the next step, we train our PPO agent for 2000 iterations over four instances of the CartPole environment similar to the previous ones.

```
obs = env.reset()
while True:
    action, _states = model.predict(obs)
    obs, rewards, dones, info = env.step(action)
```

Once completed, we will again visualize the four CartPole environments, as shown in Figure 5-23.

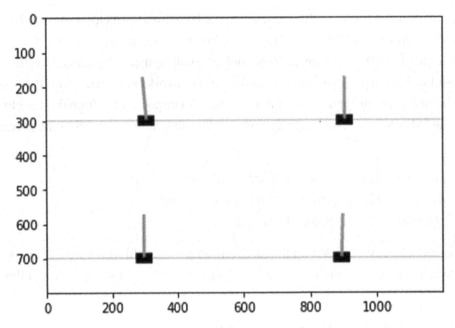

Figure 5-23. *CartPole environment training with PPO policy*

Now we will implement both the PPO-penalty version and the PPO-clipped version. Open the PPO-A2C.ipynb Notebook, since we will be running PPO on A2C baseline, similarly to TRPO.

- **PPO-penalty:** This requires penalizing the KL divergence of the distributions of TRPO and removing a hard constraint. The only change required is in the loss function inside the "build_actor_ model" method inside the PPOAgent class. The "trpo_ppo_penalty_ loss" method uses the predictions policy and the old policy. Then it finds the KL divergence similarly to the case of TRPO. After that, it computes the advantage estimate and provides a minimization bound on the ratio of the new and old policies given by the ratio r(θ). This is a penalized clipped variant of PPO algorithm.

```
def trpo_ppo_penalty_loss(y_true, y_pred):
    entropy=2e-5
    clip_loss=0.2
    old_log= k.sum(y_true)
    print(old_log)
    pred_log=k.sum(y_pred)
```

```
print(pred_log)
r=pred_log/(old_log + 1e-9)
kl_divergence= k.sum(old_log* k.log(old_log/pred_log))
advantage=kl_divergence
p1=r*advantage
p2=k.clip(r, min_value=
1-clip_loss, max_value=1+clip_loss)*advantage
prob=1e-2
loss=-k.mean(k.minimum(p1, p2) +
entropy*(-(prob*k.log(prob+1e-10))))
return loss

Actor.compile(optimizer=Adam(learning_rate=self.learning_rate),
loss=trpo_ppo_penalty_loss)
```

- **PPO-clipped:** This is the standard PPO clipping policy. This is
  implemented by the "trpo_ppo_clip_loss" method and is passed with
  the Adam optimizer. Here the advantage is computed by subtracting
  the Q-value from the value estimate of the previous policy. Then we
  have the clip method to clip the ratio $r(\theta)$ bounded by the "epsilon"
  threshold.

```
def trpo_ppo_clip_loss(y_true, y_pred):
    entropy=2e-5
    clip_loss=0.2
    old_log= k.sum(y_true)
    print(old_log)
    pred_log=k.sum(y_pred)
    print(pred_log)
    r=pred_log/(old_log + 1e-9)
    advantage=pred_log-old_log
    p1=r*advantage
    p2=k.clip(r, min_value=
    1-clip_loss, max_value=1+clip_loss)*advantage
    prob=1e-2
    loss=-k.mean(k.minimum(p1, p2) +
```

```
        entropy*(-(prob*k.log(prob+1e-10)))))
        return loss

    Actor.compile(optimizer=Adam(learning_rate=self.learning_rate),
    loss=trpo_ppo_clip_loss)
```

Thus we have seen the PPO algorithm and understood the fundamental concept behind this algorithm, which is the default training algorithm for ML Agents. In the next sections, when we will be building newer agents with ML Agents, we can create our own PPO model like the one mentioned earlier or use the Baseline model as well. In this context, it is important to mention that we can use convolution-2D neural network as well in place of dense networks, and some implementations have been provided with the Pong Atari game (2D) from the Gym environment. This is controlled with the help of image processing where pixels are passed into convolution-2D neural network, and then policy gradient algorithms are applied, as shown in Figure 5-24.

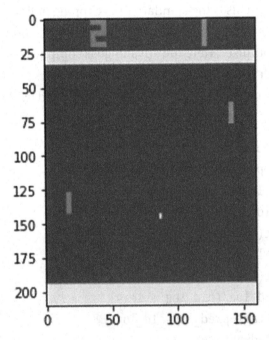

Figure 5-24. *Pong Atari game with policy gradient using convolution-2D neural network*

Unity ML Agents has their own built PPO model, which we were using till now to train our agents. In the next section, we will explore the off-policy algorithms in deep RL, which includes DQN, DDQN, D3QN, SAC, ACER, and other algorithms.

Off-Policy Algorithms

This class of algorithms relies on a buffer containing past estimates and take decisions accordingly. In this case, sampling of past data is done with the help of the Bellman equation with which a Q-function can be trained to satisfy the interaction between the agent and the environment. There is a concept of experience replay that involves extensive sampling of past states and the value estimates to optimize the Bellman function. As we have mentioned, Q-learning is an off-policy technique. In the deep learning context, we have DQN, DDQN, D3QN, DDPG, TD3, ACER, and SAC as off-policy algorithms. In this section we will be looking into the variants of DQN extensively.

Deep Q-network: This is a deep RL variant of Q-learning. This makes Q-learning more stable over continuous and discrete spaces, as in this case the Q-function is approximated by a nonlinear activation. Off-policy DQN algorithm computes the values of all possible states before updating the policy, while the on-policy methods upgrade the policy by comparing with the gradient of the objective function. The two fundamental concepts involved in DQN are:

- **Experience replay:** This implies sampling of the past states, values, actions.

- **Training updated target network:** This involves applying a deep learning layer to update the policy by calculating the value estimates.

The loss or the objective function in this case is defined as:

$$Y(s, a, r, s`) = r + y \max_a Q_\theta(s`, a`)$$

$$L(\theta) = E_\theta [(Y(s, a, r, s`) - Q_\theta(s, a))^2],$$

where y (gamma) is the exploration-exploitation factor. Depending on the type of the network, different neural networks can be used. For image-specific DQN, convolution neural networks can be used.

In the next case, we will study the DQN implementation, which we had a glimpse of in Chapter 1. Open the CartPole-Rendering.ipynb Notebook. As usual we have to import all the necessary libraries and modules from keras for building the dense model. We will also import the ipythondisplay for visualization algon with Tensorboard for visualization of the training phase. We will also have a deque data structure to store our states, actions, rand ewards for each training phase.

```
import gym
from gym import logger as gymlogger
from gym.wrappers import Monitor
gymlogger.set_level(40)
from keras.callbacks import TensorBoard
from keras.models import Sequential
from keras.layers import Dense
from keras.optimizers import Adam
import numpy as np
import random
import pandas as pd
import math
import matplotlib.pyplot as plt
from collections import deque
import glob
import io
import base64
from IPython.display import HTML

from IPython import display as ipythondisplay
%load_ext tensorboard
%tensorboard --logdir logs
```

In the "__init__" method inside the DeepQLearning class, we will include all the hyperparameters required for building the Q-network. This includes the exploration-exploitation factor, learning factor, epsilon, alpha decay, batch_size, the replay memory (deque), and other parameters.

```
self.replay_memory= deque(maxlen=1000)
self.env=gym.make('CartPole-v0')
self.gamma=gamma
self.epsilon=epsilon
self.epsilon_min=epsilon_min
```

```
self.log_epsilon=log_epsilon
self.alpha=alpha
self.alpha_decay=alpha_decay
self.no_episodes=no_episodes
self.no_complete=no_complete
self.batch_size=batch_size
self.quiet=quiet
if env_steps is not None:
  self.env._max_episode_steps=env_steps
```

In the next step we build the sequential model with dense layers with Keras. The dense layers have 48 units each with "tanh" activation. The last layer of the dense network has 2 units that signify that the CartPole can move either in the left or right direction with "sigmoid" activation.

```
self.model=Sequential()
    self.model.add(Dense(48, input_dim=4, activation="tanh"))
    self.model.add(Dense(48, activation="tanh"))
    self.model.add(Dense(2, activation="sigmoid"))
     self.model.compile(loss='mse', optimizer=Adam
    (lr=self.alpha,
    decay=self.alpha_decay))
```

In the next step, we have the "remember" method, which contains the states, rewards, and actions in a container for storage and sampling.

```
def remember(self, state, action, reward, next_state, done):
    self.replay_memory.append((state, action, reward,
    next_state, done))
```

The "choose_step" method is used to select a particular action is the value estimate of the action is greater than a certain threshold value denoted by the epsilon.

```
def choose_step(self, state, epsilon):
    return self.env.action_space.sample() if(np.random.random()<=epsilon)
  else np.argmax(self.model.predict(state))
```

The "preprocess" method is used to transform (flatten) the states so that it can be fed into the dense network.

```
def preprocess_state(self, state):
    return np.reshape(state, [1, 4])
```

The "get_epsilon" and "decay_epsilon" are methods to modify the epsilon decay in which will be used in the training step for experience replay.

```
def get_epsilon(self, t):
    return max(self.epsilon_min, min(self.epsilon,
    1.0-math.log((t+1)*self.log_epsilon)))

  def decay_epsilon(self):
    if self.epsilon>self.epsilon_min:
      self.epsilon*=self.log_epsilon
```

The "replay" method is used to collect the states, actions, and rewards in the form of a sampled distribution from the memory buffer. It then uses the trained model to predict the next probable action and updates the value of the action (reward), by using the epsilon and gamma factors. This is where the off-policy logic plays. The experience replay allows the algorithm to sample information from the deque (memory) and then lets the model predict an action corresponding to the highest return in the value estimates or rewards.

```
def replay(self, batch_size):
    x_batch, y_batch=[],[]
    minibatch=random.sample(
     self.replay_memory, min(len(self.replay_memory), batch_size))
    for state, action, reward, next_state, done in minibatch:
      y_target=self.model.predict(state)
      y_target[0][action]=reward if done
     else reward+self.gamma*(np.max(self.model.predict(next_state)[0]))
      x_batch.append(state[0])
      y_batch.append(y_target[0])
```

In the next phase, we have the "run" method, where we control the logic of the algorithm. In this case, we load the CartPole environment, then record the states, actions, and rewards in the memory, and preprocess the states to make the input suitable for the dense network. The deque has a memory limit of 100, and we train the model until the mean score of the algorithm exceeds a certain threshold. Each epoch of training has 100 episodes internally to collect the rewards and compute the mean score.

```python
def run(self):
    print(self.env.action_space)
    total_scores=deque(maxlen=100)
    for i in range(self.no_episodes):
        state= self.preprocess_state(self.env.reset())
        done=False
        j=0
        while not done:
            action= self.choose_step(state, self.get_epsilon(i))
            next_state, reward, done,_=self.env.step(action)
            next_state=self.preprocess_state(next_state)
            self.remember(state, action, reward, next_state, done)
            state=next_state
            j+=1
        total_scores.append(j)
        mean_score=np.mean(total_scores)
        if mean_score >=self.no_complete and i>=100:
            if not self.quiet:
                print("Ran {} episodes.Solving after
                {} trainings".format(i, i-100))
                return i-100
        if i%100==0 and not self.quiet:
            print("Episode Completed {}.
            Mean score {}".format(i, mean_score))

        self.replay(self.batch_size)
    if not self.quiet:
        print("Not solved after {} episodes", format(i))
    return i
```

On running this model, we will visualize the DQN algorithm performing a value estimated off-policy control for the CartPole environment. We can now understand and relate with the outputs that we achieved in the introductory section of Chapter 1. The TensorBoard visualization is shown in Figure 5-25.

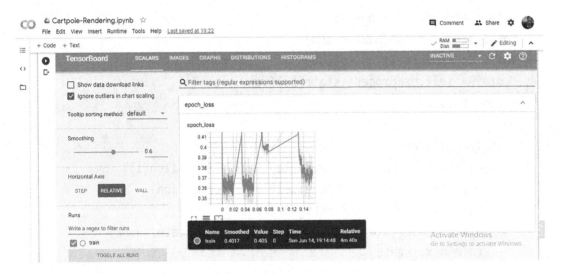

Figure 5-25. *CartPole environment training using DQN*

Double deep Q-networks: In many cases, DQN leads to overestimation of the return of values because we use the same policy $Q_\theta(s, a)$ to predict the best probable action and also estimate the rewards/values with the same policy $Q_\theta(s`, a`)$. DDQN employs two neural networks to decouple the action selection and the value estimation stages. The effective loss or objective function involves two Q-networks, $Q_{\theta 1}(s, a)$ and $Q_{\theta 2}(s, a)$, as follows:

$$Y_1(s, a, r, s`) = r + y \max_a Q_{\theta 1}(s`, \text{argmax}_a Q_{\theta 2}(s`, a`))$$

$$Y_2(s, a, r, s`) = r + y \max_a Q_{\theta 2}(s`, \text{argmax}_a Q_{\theta 1}(s`, a`))$$

This helps increase the stability of training, as two policies are involved in the sampling strategy. The first Q-network (original Q-network) uses the maximum value estimate from the second Q network (target Q-network) and the second Q network (target Q Network) updates its policies from the returns of the first network.

We will be exploring this network, and for this we have to open the Double Deep Q Network.ipynb Notebook. We will be building on top of the previous DQN with the changes being made inside the "__init__" and the "replay" methods in the

DoubleDeepQLearning class. In the "__init__" method, we have two neural networks—namely, the "model" and "target_model," which are similar to each other (like in DQN) with the same parameters. However, this can be changed according to requirements.

```
self.model=Sequential()
    self.model.add(Dense(48, input_dim=4, activation="tanh"))
    self.model.add(Dense(48, activation="tanh"))
    self.model.add(Dense(2, activation="sigmoid"))
    self.model.compile(loss='mse', optimizer=
    Adam(lr=self.alpha,
    decay=self.alpha_decay))
    self.target_model=Sequential()
    self.target_model.add(Dense(48, input_dim=4,
    activation="tanh"))
    self.target_model.add(Dense(48, activation="tanh"))
    self.target_model.add(Dense(2, activation="sigmoid"))
    self.target_model.compile(loss='mse', optimizer=
    Adam(lr=self.alpha,
    decay=self.alpha_decay))
```

The next change is in the "replay" method, where we have to assign the inputs (states, actions, rewards) from the deque to the two networks. We assign the predictions of the target network in place of the original network and pass it to the model. The contrast between the DQN and DDQN is mentioned in the comments in the program.

```
    x_batch, y_batch=[],[]
    minibatch=random.sample(
    self.replay_memory, min(len(self.replay_memory), batch_size))
    for state, action, reward, next_state, done in minibatch:
      y_target=self.model.predict(state)
      y_next_target=self.model.predict(next_state)
      y_next_val=self.target_model.predict(next_state)
      #DQN Update
      #y_target[0][action]=reward if done
      else reward +self.gamma*(np.max
    (self.model.predict(next_state)[0]))
      #DDQN Update
```

```
y_next_target[0][action]=reward if done
else reward+self.gamma*(np.max(y_next_val[0]))
x_batch.append(state[0])
#DQN
#y_batch.append(y_target[0])
#DDQN
y_batch.append(y_next_target[0])
```

These are the only changes required to make the network DDQN. On running the code segment, we can see the CartPole being trained, as shown in Figure 5-26.

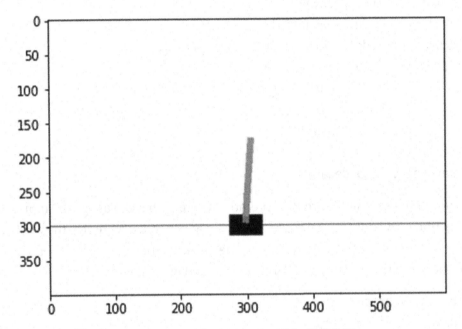

Figure 5-26. *CartPole environment being trained in DDQN*

Dueling double Q-network: The dueling network in an enhancement on the D2QN network architecture as the output layer is partitioned into two major components—the value estimate $V^\pi(s_t)$ and the advantage estimate $A^\pi(s_t, a_t)$. The relation between them with the Q-policy is given by the relation (which we studied in policy gradients):

$$A^\pi(s_t, a_t) = Q^\pi(s_t, a_t) - V^\pi(s_t)$$

Effectively the estimated advantage sums to 0 ($\sum A^\pi(s_t, a_t)\pi(a|s) = 0$) in this context, and we have to subtract the mean value of the Advantage

$[1/|A^\pi(s_t, a_t)|]\sum A^\pi(s_t, a_t)$) from the value estimates $V^\pi(s_t)$ to get the Q-value $Q^\pi(s_t, a_t)$. This is represented by the following equation, which is the driving force of dueling DQN.

$$Q^\pi(s_t, a_t) = V^\pi(s_t) + (A^\pi(s_t, a_t) - [1/|A^\pi(s_t, a_t)|]\sum A^\pi(s_t, a_t))$$

To see this in action, let us open the Dueling Double DQN.ipynb Notebook. We maintain the similar code base of the DDQN with the inclusion of an advantage loss (named as "advantage_loss") in the "model" part of the "__init__" method. In the "advantage_loss" method, we compute the advantage of Q–value with respect to the value estimate. Then we compute the mean of the advantage and fit it accordingly in the loss estimate. All of this is done in Keras using the back-end module. We then pass it into the "model.compile" method with Adam as our optimizer.

```
def advantage_loss(y_true, y_pred):
    q_val=y_pred
    v_val=y_true
    advantage=(q_val-v_val)
    adv_mean=k.mean(advantage)
    adv_factor=1/adv_mean*(k.sum(advantage))
    loss=- adv_factor*self.epsilon
    return loss
self.model.compile(loss=advantage_loss, optimizer=Adam(lr=self.alpha,
decay=self.alpha_decay))
```

The rest of the code segment being the same, we now train this on our CartPole environment to get an understanding of its performance, as shown in Figure 5-27.

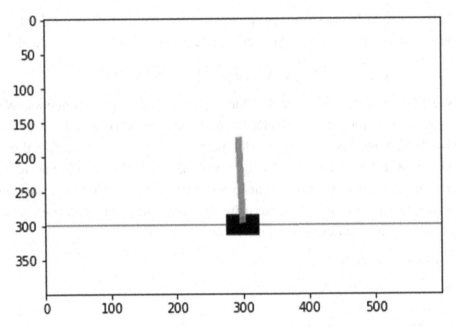

Figure 5-27. *CartPole environment being trained in D3QN*

Actor critic experience replay: This is an off-policy variation of the A3C algorithm that we saw previously. It includes sampling of the previous states along with retracing the Q-value estimate. The three major conditions that are applied in this context include:

- retrace Q-value estimate

- truncate weights with bias correction

- applying a KL divergence bound TRPO

The retracing part is an off-policy sampling technique that uses an error term to move toward a proper value estimated policy. This is denoted by the formulation:

$$Q^\pi(s_t, a_t) = Q^\pi(s_t, a_t) + \Delta\, Q^\pi(s_t, a_t),$$

where,

$$\Delta\, Q^\pi(s_t, a_t) = \alpha\, \partial_t,$$

where $\Delta\, Q^\pi(s_t, a_t)$ is the incremental error update that is referred to as temporal difference (TD) error. The incremental update is then formulated as the ratio of two policies $((\pi_\theta(a|s)/\,\pi_{\theta old}(a|s)))$ with an error term ∂_t from previous value estimates. The simplified version looks like this:

$$\Delta Q\pi ret(st,\ at) = yt\ \Pi((\pi\theta(a|s)/\,\pi\theta old(a|s))\partial t)$$

384

This is where the off-policy sampling is used with the policy gradient update of a generic actor critic/TRPO method. ACER is considered as an off-policy mainly due to the incremental update of the error estimate from previous values.

ACER also has a weight truncation rule to reduce the variance of the policy gradient. Generally in AC algorithms, the advantage estimate (GAE) is signified with the equation:

$$A^\pi(s_t, a_t) = Q^\pi(s_t, a_t) - V^\pi(s_t)$$

Now with retracing in ACER, the advantage estimate for policy gradient becomes:

$$A^\pi(s_t, a_t) = Q^\pi_{ret}(s_t, a_t) - V^\pi(s_t)$$

Thus, the policy gradient estimate becomes:

$$\Delta_\theta J(\theta) = E[\sum(Q^\pi_{ret}(s, a) - V^\pi(s_t)) \, \Delta_\theta \ln(\pi_\theta(a|s))\,]$$

Now we will be building the Baseline version of the ACER algorithm. Open the ACER-Baselines.ipynb Notebook. We will import the libraries and the modules from stable Baselines like before.

```
import gym
from stable_baselines.common.policies import MlpPolicy, MlpLstmPolicy,
MlpLnLstmPolicy
from stable_baselines.common import make_vec_env
from stable_baselines import ACER
import matplotlib.pyplot as plt
from IPython import display as ipythondisplay
from pyvirtualdisplay import Display
display = Display(visible=0, size=(400, 300))
display.start()
```

In this case, we will instantiate four instances of the CartPole environment, where the ACER agent will be using MLP (dense) network.

```
env = make_vec_env('CartPole-v1', n_envs=4)
model = ACER(MlpPolicy, env, verbose=1)
model.learn(total_timesteps=25000)
model.save("acer_cartpole")
del model
model = ACER.load("acer_cartpole")
```

Then we have the while loop, which controls the ACER algorithm and runs for 25000 iterations. It collects the rewards, states, and actions for each epoch of training and presents the motion of the four CartPoles on the screen.

```
while True:
    action, _states = model.predict(obs)
    obs, rewards, dones, info = env.step(action)
    screen = env.render(mode='rgb_array')
    plt.imshow(screen)
    ipythondisplay.clear_output(wait=True)
    ipythondisplay.display(plt.gcf())
```

On running this model, we get to visualize the CartPoles. We can compare this result with the other variants of actor critic models that we read earlier, as shown in Figure 5-28.

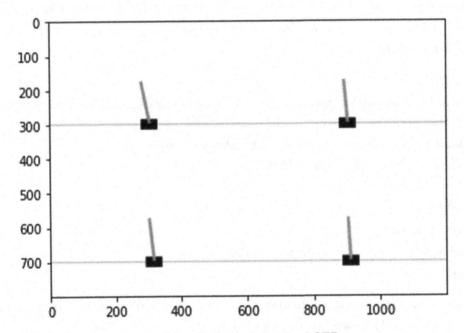

Figure 5-28. *Four instances of CartPole training in ACER*

Soft actor critic: This is another off-policy algorithm, which relies on entropy-based modeling. It is a stochastic actor critic policy, which uses entropy regularization to maximize the trade-off between expected return and entropy. The entropy of a probabilistic variable with a density function, can be defined as:

$$H(P) = E\left[-\log(P(x))\right]$$

In entropy regularized form, the agent gets a bonus reward at each time-step proportional to the entropy of the policy at the particular time-step. This is denoted by:

$$\pi_\theta(a|s) = \arg\max_\pi E[\sum_t y^t (R(s_t, a_t, s_{t+1}) + \alpha H(\pi_\theta(.|s_t)))],$$

where R is the reward and is the trade-off coefficient. With entropy regularization, the value estimate and the Q-policy is related as:

$$V^{\pi\theta}(s_t)) = E[Q^{\pi\theta}(s_t, a_t)] + \alpha H(\pi_\theta(.|s_t))$$

In ML Agents, SAC is present as an off-policy algorithm and we will look into its implementation from the Baselines as well as by modifying the TRPO-A2C/PPO-A2C program.

Open the SAC- Baselines.ipynb Notebook. This is an implementation of the SAC algorithm without parallelization. First we will import the necessary libraries, modules, and networks from Baselines.

```
import gym
import numpy as np

from stable_baselines.sac.policies import MlpPolicy
from stable_baselines import SAC
import matplotlib.pyplot as plt
from IPython import display as ipythondisplay
from pyvirtualdisplay import Display
display = Display(visible=0, size=(400, 300))
display.start()
```

Then we load the model and declare it to use the MLP or dense networks, although we can specify other types of policies which include LSTM. We create the Pendulum environment for our algorithm and load it in.

```
env = gym.make('Pendulum-v0')
model = SAC(MlpPolicy, env, verbose=1)
model.learn(total_timesteps=50000, log_interval=10)
model.save("sac_pendulum")
del model
model = SAC.load("sac_pendulum")
```

Then we run the Pendulum environment for 50000 iterations using MLP policy with the SAC algorithm. At each step we record the parameters of training, which includes the states, actions, and rewards.

```
while True:
    action, _states = model.predict(obs)
    obs, rewards, dones, info = env.step(action)
    screen = env.render(mode='rgb_array')
    plt.imshow(screen)
    ipythondisplay.clear_output(wait=True)
    ipythondisplay.display(plt.gcf())
```

After a considerable amount of training, we can see the Pendulum balancing itself in an upright manner, as shown in Figure 5-29.

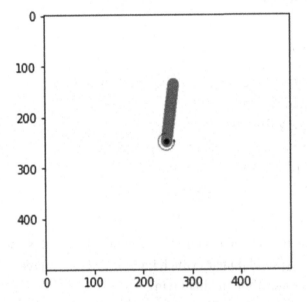

Figure 5-29. *Pendulum environment training with SAC*

Now we can also modify our source code of A2C variants to make it a soft actor critic module, by introducing the entropy factor. For this we change the loss function in the "build_actor_model" method. In this case, we will train the "MountainCar" environment using our implementation of SAC. In the "sac_loss" method, we compute the rewards for the previous step as well as the entropy of the current step using the entropy equation. After applying the policy update formula, which involves addition of the rewards and the entropy regularized form, we can calculate a negative log likelihood loss. We then return this loss function to be used with the Adam optimizer.

```
def sac_loss(y_true, y_pred):
    entropy=2e-5
    pred_reward= k.sum(y_true)
    entropy_val=k.sum(- (k.log(y_pred)))
    expectation = pred_reward + entropy_val
    prob=1e-2
    loss=-k.mean(expectation +
     entropy*(-(prob*k.log(prob+1e-10))))
    return loss
Actor.compile(optimizer=Adam(learning_rate=self.learning_rate), loss=sac_
loss)
```

On training this algorithm, we can see that the MountainCar tries to go to the top of the mountain on the right side of the screen. In this way, it moves back and forth several times to gain necessary momentum, as shown in Figure 5-30.

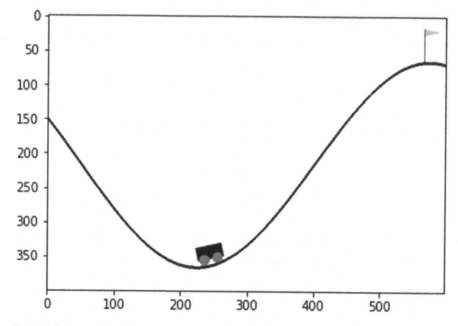

Figure 5-30. *MountainCar training with custom SAC*

There are several other off-policy algorithms, such as deep deterministic policy gradients (DDPG) and its variants, along with model-free deep RL algorithms, which we will be focusing on in the next chapter.

Model-Free RL: Imitation Learning–Behavioral Cloning

In the context of ML Agents, there is also a module on imitation learning, which falls under behavioral cloning algorithms. Specifically we will be exploring generative adversarial imitation learning (GAIL), which uses general adversarial networks (GAN), a different form of neural networks from Dense or convolution networks. Let us discuss GAIL briefly. GAIL falls under the model-free RL paradigm, which also uses entropy, and it learns a cost/objective function from expert demonstrations. Imitation learning algorithms such as GAIL are used in inverse RL. But before, let us understand GANs.

General adversarial networks: This kind of neural network has two components: a generator and a discriminator. The task of the generator is to prepare a false replica of original data to fool the discriminator into thinking that it is real. While the task of the discriminator is to correctly identify the false data from the generator. This is done with the help of entropy regularization. Mathematically, if $p(x)$ defines the distribution of the data on sample x, and $p(z)$ is the distribution of data from the generator G with samples as z, then the GAN is a maximization-minimization function with respect to generator G and discriminator D:

$$\min_G \max_D V(D, G)$$

$$V(D, G) = E_{x \sim p(x)}[\log(D(x))] + E_{z \sim p(z)}[\log(1 - D(G(z)))]$$

The first term of the equation is the entropy distribution of samples x, that is the original data. The discriminator tries to maximize this to 1. The second term is the generated data from the samples z, and the task of the discriminator is to reduce this part to 0 as it contains synthetic data. The task of the generator is to maximize this second part of the equation. This is how GANs work, as a competitive neural network model between the generator and the discriminator.

The architecture of a GAN can be visualized as shown in Figure 5-31.

General Adversarial Network -GAN Model

Ashilash Majumder | August 1, 2020

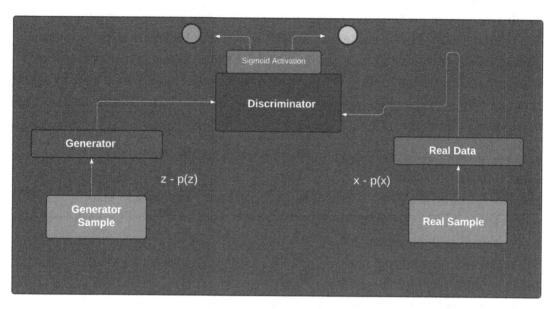

Figure 5-31. *GAN model architecture for classification*

General adversarial imitation learning: GAIL is a variant of behavioral cloning that uses GAN to learn a cost function. The discriminator tries to separate expert trajectories from the generated trajectories. The trajectories involve the direction of the gradient toward a proper return on the value estimates. Initially, we train a SAC model as the expert model and then use it as the real sampled data. The GAIL then builds its own generator and discriminator network to generate synthetic trajectories and compares them against the expert trajectories that are produced by the SAC algorithm. We will be using the GAIL algorithm from Baselines. Open the GAIL-Baselines.ipynb Notebook. In the first case, we initially run the Pendulum environment and train it with the SAC algorithm as mentioned. The SAC trains it on a MLP policy and generates the expert trajectories, signified by the "generate_expert_traj" method.

```
from stable_baselines import SAC
from stable_baselines.gail import generate_expert_traj
# Generate expert trajectories (train expert)
model = SAC('MlpPolicy', 'Pendulum-v0', verbose=1)
generate_expert_traj(model, 'expert_pendulum', n_timesteps=6000, n_
episodes=10)
```

Then we have the GAIL code segment. After we have saved the trajectories produced by the SAC policy in a data set (provided by the "ExpertDataSet" method), we then use this data set for the GAIL to generate the generator data and the discriminator. The GAIL algorithm is then trained on an MLP network for 1000 time-steps, where the discriminator tries to optimize the policy so that the value estimates are consistent with that produced by the SAC policy. The generator, on the other hand, tries to modify and generate synthetically similar trajectories that are difficult to segregate from the real SAC trajectories.

```
dataset = ExpertDataset(expert_path='expert_pendulum.npz', traj_
limitation=10, verbose=1)
model = GAIL('MlpPolicy', 'Pendulum-v0', dataset, verbose=1)
model.learn(total_timesteps=1000)
model.save("gail_pendulum")
del model
model = GAIL.load("gail_pendulum")
env = gym.make('Pendulum-v0')
obs = env.reset()
while True:
  action, _states = model.predict(obs)
  obs, rewards, dones, info = env.step(action)
  env.render()
```

On training with GAIL, we can see the different parameters and the scores of training, as shown in Figure 5-32.

```
   3    0.000348     0.0566
   4    0.00075      0.0861
   5    8.18e-05     0.242
   6    0.00113      0.283
   7    0.000344     0.295
   8    8.09e-05     0.409
   9    1.8e-05      0.458
  10    1.34e-05     0.507
done in 0.022 seconds
Expected: 0.014 Actual: 0.007
Stepsize OK!
vf
done in 0.043 seconds
Optimizing Discriminator...
generator_loss |   expert_loss |      entropy | entropy_loss | generator_acc |   expert_acc
     0.69405 |       0.69093 |      0.68563 |     -0.00069 |      0.50195 |      0.56543
------------------------------------------------------
| EpLenMean                   | 200          |
| EpRewMean                   | 141.34862    |
| EpThisIter                  | 5            |
| EpTrueRewMean               | -1.31e+03    |
| EpisodesSoFar               | 5            |
| TimeElapsed                 | 4.79         |
| TimestepsSoFar              | 1024         |
| entloss                     | 0.0          |
| entropy                     | 1.4192339    |
| explained_variance_t...     | 0.00718      |
| meankl                      | 0.0057204687 |
| optimgain                   | 0.0070504355 |
| surrgain                    | 0.0070504355 |
```

Figure 5-32. *Training GAIL using generated trajectories from SAC*

We have covered most of the major algorithms in deep RL in terms of on- and off-policy models, including model-free RL (GAIL). In the next context, we will create a deep learning model for Puppo, which would include joint motion and will be trained using the PPO algorithm.

Building a Proximal Policy Optimization Agent for Puppo

We now have a fair understanding why the PPO algorithm is the most widely used form of deep RL policies due to its robustness and clipping to prevent instability of the TRPO policy gradient. We will build a PPO agent for Puppo whose task is to find the stick in the environment. However, in this case, it will move using its joint vectors that are constrained with PPO policy. For this we will be using the Puppo Unity scene. The joint system is used in this case to train Puppo to reach the target by actuating and applying force on it. The reward function that is applied on the joints can be formulated as:

$$r(\theta) = v.d \, X \, (-\theta) + 1,$$

where the reward is parameterized by the angular force θ, which is applied along the y axis. v signifies the normalized velocity vector of Puppo, and d signifies the normalized direction of Puppo toward the target. In Unity this is controlled using the joint drive

393

controller script. An additional reward of 1 is provided if Puppo successfully reaches the target and 0 if it does not. This is the control logic of the agent, and we will be training it with PPO.

We can open the Puppo agent Unity file and observe the components present in the scene. We can see that the component scripts like BehavorialParameters.cs, Decision Requester, and Model Overrider are added to it. This is similar to the previous chapters, where we attached these components to the agents. However, in this case, we will be using the joint drive controller script in addition to all these components. Then we have an associated PuppoAgent.cs script, which is what we will be exploring in this section. This script controls the joint motion of the agent and records observations from the environments with the help of the joint locomotion. Figure 5-33 shows a preview of the environment.

Figure 5-33. *Puppo agent in Unity Editor*

Now let us open the PuppoAgent.cs script. Like before, we include the Unity ML Agents module and also the sensors module to record the observations.

```
using System.Collections;
using System.Collections.Generic;
using UnityEngine;
using Unity.MLAgents;
```

```
using System;
using System.Linq;
using Unity.MLAgents.Sensors;
using Random = UnityEngine.Random;
using Unity.MLAgentsExamples;
```

Inside the PuppoAgent class, which inherits from the agent class, we declare the variables that would be present in the environment. We have the transforms, such as the target and dog (Puppo), and we have variables for the joints. These include 11 joints forming the lower legs, upper legs, mouth, and the torso (body). All these joints are associated with a turning force (torque) and a corresponding turning speed (angular velocity). These are denoted in the following lines.

```
public Transform target;
 public Transform dog;
 // These items should be set in the inspector
 [Header("Body Parts")]
 public Transform mouthPosition;
 public Transform body;
 public Transform leg0_upper;
 public Transform leg1_upper;
 public Transform leg2_upper;
 public Transform leg3_upper;
 public Transform leg0_lower;
 public Transform leg1_lower;
 public Transform leg2_lower;
 public Transform leg3_lower;
 public bool vectorObs;
 [Header("Body Rotation")]
 public float maxTurnSpeed;
 public ForceMode turningForceMode;
 EnvironmentParameters m_params;
```

We also have variables that control the joint driver controller script and vectors that control the direction to the target. In the "Initialize" method, we assign the dog and the target variables. We instantiate an instance of the joint driver controller script and associate the joint variables with that instance.

```
dog=GetComponent<Transform>();
target=GetComponent<Transform>();
jdController = GetComponent<JointDriveController>();
jdController.SetupBodyPart(body);
jdController.SetupBodyPart(leg0_upper);
jdController.SetupBodyPart(leg0_lower);
jdController.SetupBodyPart(leg1_upper);
jdController.SetupBodyPart(leg1_lower);
jdController.SetupBodyPart(leg2_upper);
jdController.SetupBodyPart(leg2_lower);
jdController.SetupBodyPart(leg3_upper);
jdController.SetupBodyPart(leg3_lower);

m_params = Academy.Instance.EnvironmentParameters;
```

Then we have the "Collect Observations" method, which uses Vector Sensors. For this we first get the associated joint forces with the help of the "GetCurrentJointForces()" method. Then we assign sensors that collect information such as the distance between the target and Puppo. The sensors also collect information related to the body's angular velocity, normal velocity, direction of normal as well as the direction of upward vector to control the force acting on the body of Puppo. Then we have a loop that runs for all the joints that are touching the ground and compute the normalized angular rotation with the help of "currentXNormalizedRot" along the respective axes. Then we add a sensor that records the current strength applied on a joint normalized with the maximum shear force limit on that particular joint. To summarize this method controls the sensor information related to the joints, angular velocity, rotation, and force as well as the body's orientation and distance and direction with respect to the target.

```
public override void CollectObservations(VectorSensor sensor)
{if(vectorObs==true)
    {
        jdController.GetCurrentJointForces();
        sensor.AddObservation(dirToTarget.normalized);
        sensor.AddObservation(body.localPosition);
        sensor.AddObservation(jdController.
        bodyPartsDict[body].rb.velocity);
        sensor.AddObservation(jdController.
```

```
        bodyPartsDict[body].rb.angularVelocity);
        sensor.AddObservation(body.forward);
         sensor.AddObservation(body.up);
foreach (var bp in jdController.bodyPartsDict.Values)
        {

                                var rb = bp.rb;
        sensor.AddObservation(bp.groundContact.
         touchingGround ? 1 : 0);
        if(bp.rb.transform != body)
        {
            sensor.AddObservation(bp.currentXNormalizedRot);
            sensor.AddObservation(bp.currentYNormalizedRot);
            sensor.AddObservation(bp.currentZNormalizedRot);
            sensor.AddObservation(bp.currentStrength/
            jdController.maxJointForceLimit);
        }
        }}

    }
```

The "RotateBody" method is used to apply a torque or angular force on Puppo. It takes as input the corresponding action at a particular step of decision-making process. It lerps the speed between 0 and the "maxturnspeed." It then applies a force in the normalized direction of rotation and in the direction of the forward vector and multiplies it with the speed. This is done with the help of the "AddForceAtPosition" method, which is applied on the body.

```
void RotateBody(float act)
    {
        float speed = Mathf.Lerp(0, maxTurnSpeed
        , Mathf.Clamp(act, 0, 1));
        Vector3 rotDir = dirToTarget;
        rotDir.y = 0;
        // Adds a force on the front of the body
        jdController.bodyPartsDict[body].
        rb.AddForceAtPosition(
```

```
        rotDir.normalized * speed * Time.deltaTime
      , body.forward, turningForceMode);
      // Adds a force on the back of the body
      jdController.bodyPartsDict[body].
        rb.AddForceAtPosition(
            -rotDir.normalized * speed * Time.deltaTime
          , -body.forward, turningForceMode);
}
```

In the next step, we have the "OnActionsReceived" overridden method, which assigns the vector observations from the environment to the corresponding joints. As we see there are 20 vectorized observations from the sensors, which are received during the training stage. Now we are using dense neural networks for this model, and we are using only ray sensor information.

```
public override void OnActionReceived(float[] vectorAction)
    {

        var bpDict = jdController.bodyPartsDict;
      Debug.Log(vectorAction.Length);

        // Update joint drive target rotation
        bpDict[leg0_upper].SetJointTargetRotation(vectorAction[0],
        vectorAction[1], 0);
        bpDict[leg1_upper].SetJointTargetRotation(vectorAction[2],
        vectorAction[3], 0);
        bpDict[leg2_upper].SetJointTargetRotation(vectorAction[4],
        vectorAction[5], 0);
        bpDict[leg3_upper].SetJointTargetRotation(vectorAction[6],
        vectorAction[7], 0);
        bpDict[leg0_lower].SetJointTargetRotation(vectorAction[8], 0, 0);
        bpDict[leg1_lower].SetJointTargetRotation(vectorAction[9], 0, 0);
        bpDict[leg2_lower].SetJointTargetRotation(vectorAction[10], 0, 0);
        bpDict[leg3_lower].SetJointTargetRotation(vectorAction[11], 0, 0);

        // Update joint drive strength
        bpDict[leg0_upper].SetJointStrength(vectorAction[12]);
        bpDict[leg1_upper].SetJointStrength(vectorAction[13]);
```

```
bpDict[leg2_upper].SetJointStrength(vectorAction[14]);
bpDict[leg3_upper].SetJointStrength(vectorAction[15]);
bpDict[leg0_lower].SetJointStrength(vectorAction[16]);
bpDict[leg1_lower].SetJointStrength(vectorAction[17]);
bpDict[leg2_lower].SetJointStrength(vectorAction[18]);
bpDict[leg3_lower].SetJointStrength(vectorAction[19]);

    rotateBodyActionValue = vectorAction[19];
}
```

Next we have the "FixedUpdate" method, where we control the simulation loop and keep track of the decision counter; if the counter has a value of 3, a new request is sent through the academy to the external training environment to sample a new set of decisions. This is done with the help of the communicator module, which we saw in the last chapter. In this method there is the "UpdateDirToTarget" method, which takes the distance from the body of the joint to the corresponding target agent. There is also an energy conservation step that controls the turn frequency of Puppo. This adds a negative reward whenever Puppo turns very fast multiple times. Also we have a penalty for time during which Puppo is not able to reach the target.

```
void FixedUpdate()
    {
        UpdateDirToTarget();

        if (decisionCounter == 0)
        {
            decisionCounter = 3;
            RequestDecision();
        }
        else
        {
            decisionCounter--;
        }

        RotateBody(rotateBodyActionValue);

        var bodyRotationPenalty =
        -0.001f * rotateBodyActionValue;
        AddReward(bodyRotationPenalty);
```

```
    // Reward for moving towards the target
    RewardFunctionMovingTowards();
    // Penalty for time
    RewardFunctionTimePenalty();
}
```

The "OnEpisodeBegin" overridden method is used to reset the environment whenever one episode of training is complete. This method resets the joints and the forces on them and calculates the direction toward the target from the current episode.

```
public override void OnEpisodeBegin(){

    if (dirToTarget != Vector3.zero)
        {
            transform.rotation
            = Quaternion.LookRotation(dirToTarget);
        }

        foreach (var bodyPart
        in jdController.bodyPartsDict.Values)
        {
            bodyPart.Reset(bodyPart);
        }
        //SetResetParameters();

}
```

The "RewardFunctionMovingTowards" method is used to reward Puppo whenever it moves toward the goals, and this is where the reward function that we mathematically mentioned at the start of the section is written. Also on reaching the target, we can conclude the episode of training by assigning rewards.

```
void RewardFunctionMovingTowards()
{
    float movingTowardsDot = Vector3.Dot(
    jdController.bodyPartsDict[body].rb.velocity
      ,   dirToTarget.normalized);
    AddReward(0.01f * movingTowardsDot);
```

```
  var dist=Vector3.Distance(dog.position, target.position);
  if(dist<0.02f)
 {
    SetReward(3.0f);
    EndEpisode();
 }
}
```

That completes the entire script for the agent. Now we will train this agent using the external brain through the communicator in Tensorflow. We will be using the generic "trainer_config.yaml" file, which contains the hyperparameters for PPO training algorithm. We will be using the default hyperparameter set, which we used in our previous training scope.

```
default:
  trainer: ppo
  batch_size: 1024
  beta: 5.0e-3
  buffer_size: 10240
  epsilon: 0.2
  hidden_units: 128
  lambd: 0.95
  learning_rate: 3.0e-4
  learning_rate_schedule: linear
  max_steps: 5.0e5
  memory_size: 128
  normalize: false
  num_epoch: 3
  num_layers: 2
  time_horizon: 64
  sequence_length: 64
  summary_freq: 100
  use_recurrent: false
  vis_encode_type: simple
  reward_signals:
```

```
extrinsic:
  strength: 1.0
  gamma: 0.99
```

We now open Anaconda prompt and navigate to the "config" folder to run the "mlagents-learn" command. After writing the command

```
mlagents-learn <path to trainer_config.yaml> --run-id=Puppoagent -train,
```

we can visualize the training starting in the Anaconda prompt. We will also be prompted to run the current Unity scene for training on PPO policy with the help of Tensorflow, as shown in Figure 5-34.

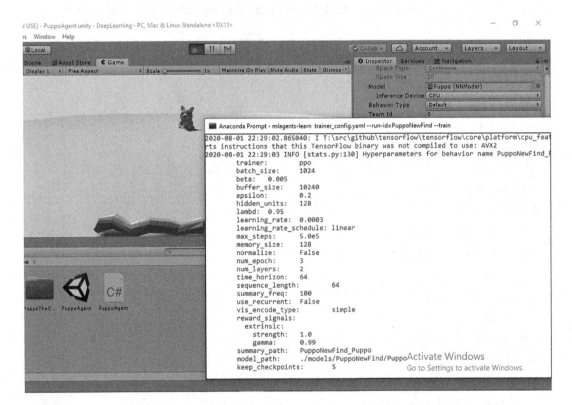

Figure 5-34. *Puppo agent being trained in PPO using Tensorflow*

Now let us visualize this learning in TensorBoard, and we know the steps to start it. We navigate to the "config" folder and then we type the command:

```
tensorboard -logdir=summaries
```

This records the observations, actions, and rewards in the summaries folder inside the config folder.

On running the command, we can see the losses, estimated rewards, cumulative rewards, entropy, and other details on TensorBoard. Once the training is completed, we can close the training and the connection with the external brain. Then we assign the trained PPO neural network to the Puppo agent. We now have an agent that we are ready to build. In the final step, we built the agent and saved it to the environments folder. Inside that folder we have a Puppo Unity simulation with the trained PPO neural network agent. Figure 5-35 shows the Tensorboard visualization of training.

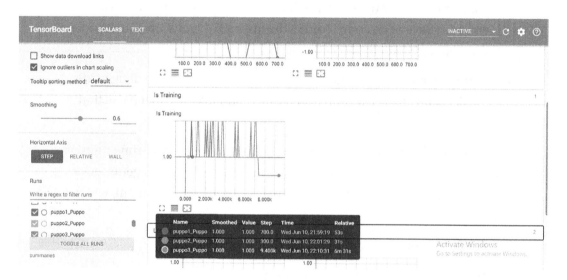

Figure 5-35. *Tensorboard visualization of PPO*

Now let us try to interact with the Python API. The Python API controls the observations, decisions, and actions through the Communicator port 5004.

Interfacing with Python API

For this let us open the Python-API-MLagents.ipynb Notebook. In this context, we will learn how the Python API controls the interaction between the Unity environment and controls the decision steps, terminal steps, and the agent ID and the behavior names.

- **Unity environment:** This controls the interface between the Unity application and the training code. This is done through the communicator for external training.

- **Agent ID:** Unique identifier ID for the agents undergoing training in the scene

- **Behavior name:** The behavior on which the agent is trained (PPO, SAC, GAIL)

- **Decision steps:** Contains the observation, rewards data for the agent being trained on a particular behavior. Only agents that requested a decision in the last call of the "env.step()" method are included here.

- **Terminal steps:** This also controls the observation and reward data for the currently trained agent. In this case, the agents whose episodes have been completed in the last call of "env.step()" method are included here.

- **Behavior spec:** Determines the shapes of the observation data inside the decision and the terminal steps and contains the expected action steps.

Now let us load the Unity environment, in the Notebook for real-time training and interaction. For this we import the Unityenvironment from "mlagents_envs. environment" module. In the next stage we create the Unityenvironment, which takes the following arguments:

- **File location:** The location of the Unity executable

- **Seed:** This controls the random number generation algorithm, which is used in RL for hyperparameters. For deterministic learning, similar seed values are provided for the agents.

- **Worker ID:** This controls the port for interaction with the agent. If we are using parallelization algorithms such as on-policy A3C, then we have to specify this part.

- **Side_channels:** This controls the interface of transfer of information between the Unity environment and the Python environment, which is not related to the RL training loop. This may include some configurations.

The following segment is used for interacting with the Puppo environment:

```
from mlagents_envs.environment import UnityEnvironment
import matplotlib.pyplot as plt
import numpy as np
import sys
import tensorflow as tf
env=UnityEnvironment(file_name="G:/DeepLearning/environments/DeepLearning",
seed=1, side_channels=[])
```

Now let us interact with the training environment. The "BaseEnv" interface in Unity has the following attributes:

- **Reset:** This is "env.reset" method, which resets the environment.

- **Close:** This is the "env.close()" method (similar to OpenAI Gym), which sends a signal to close the communication channel.

- **Step:** This is equivalent to the Gym implementation of "env.step()," which we used in the training loop to record the observations, actions, and rewards.

- **Get Behavior Names:** This is denoted by "env.get_behavior_names()" method. This controls the behavior names in the environment.

- **Get Behavior Spec:** This is denoted by the "env.get_behavior_spec()" method. This controls the shapes of the observation and the action spaces whether they are continuous/multi-discrete.

- **Get States:** This is denoted by "env.get_steps()" method, which controls the decision and the terminal steps of the agent.

- **Set Actions:** This is denoted by the "env.set_actions()" method. This sets the actions for all the agents in the scene. For discrete cases, we have 2D numpy arrays with int32 data type, and for continuous distributions, we have numpy arrays with float32 data types. The first dimension controls the number of agents whose actions are being set, and the second dimension controls the number of discrete actions in multi-discrete space or number of actions in continuous type.

- **Set Action For agent:** This is denoted by the "env.set_action_for_ agent()" method. This is a 1D numpy array similar to the previous method that controls the attributes for a particular agent.

In our case, we will see the observation space of the Puppo agent through this API:

```
def_behaviours= env.get_behavior_names()
print(def_behaviours)
env.step()
BehaviorSpec(observation_shapes=[(59,)], action_type=<ActionType.
CONTINUOUS: 1>, action_shape=20)
steps=env.get_steps('Puppo?team=0')
print(steps)
print(steps[0])
print(behaviour_specs.action_shape)
print(behaviour_specs.observation_shapes[0])
print(behaviour_specs.count)
print(behaviour_specs)
steps=env.get_steps('Puppo?team=0')
print(steps.count)
```

In this case, we provide a continuous action control for the PPO agent. The decision step has the following four attributes:

- **Obs:** This signifies the observation space.

- **Rewards:** This signifies the rewards for the corresponding steps.

- **agent ID:** The unique ID for the agent.

- **Action Mask:** This is a 2D array for the agent that controls the batch size and branching in discrete/multi-discrete action spaces.

For the terminal step we have four attributes:

- **Obs:** This signifies the observation space.

- **Rewards:** This signifies the rewards for the corresponding steps.

- **Agent ID:** The unique ID for the agent.

- **Max Step:** The batch size during the last simulation step.

We can visualize the different attributes in the environment such as the states, observations, and actions through this API in real-time. Figure 5-36 shows the simulation.

Figure 5-36. *Real-time Python interfacing with Puppo agent Unity.exe*

Interfacing with Side Channels

There is also a scope of passing information not related to the training step. This may include engine configurations and are generally task-agnostic with respect to the learning step. There are two variants of side channels for interfacing:

- **Engine configuration channel:** This controls the time-scale, resolution, and graphics of the environment and can be useful for fine-tuning performance during training. It has two parameters.

  - **Set configuration parameters:** This controls the height, width, quality, time-scale, target frame rate, and capture frame rates during the simulation/training phase.

  - **Set configuration:** This has an argument "Config," which contains a tuple of the associated parameters.

This is denoted by the following lines from the documentation:

```
from mlagents_envs.environment import UnityEnvironment
from mlagents_envs.side_channel.engine_configuration_channel
import EngineConfigurationChannel

channel = EngineConfigurationChannel()

env = UnityEnvironment(side_channels=[channel])

channel.set_configuration_parameters(time_scale = 2.0)

i = env.reset()
```

- **Environment parameters:** This controls the numerical properties in the environment or some numerical properties related to the agent. It has only one method:

  - **Set float parameter:** This sets the float values in the Unity environment against a particular key.

This is denoted by the following lines of code segment from the documentation:

```
from mlagents_envs.environment import UnityEnvironment
from mlagents_envs.side_channel.environment_parameters_channel
import EnvironmentParametersChannel

channel = EnvironmentParametersChannel()

env = UnityEnvironment(side_channels=[channel])

channel.set_float_parameter("parameter_1", 2.0)

i = env.reset()
```

Once a property has been modified in Python, we can access it in C# as follows:

```
var envParameters = Academy.Instance.EnvironmentParameters;
float property1 = envParameters.GetWithDefault("parameter_1",
0.0f);
```

Thus we have now realized how Unity ML Agents interface with the Python API. This is very important as in the next section we will be training our environments using PPO/SAC algorithms from the Baselines or our own implementations as well.

Training ML Agents with Baselines

Now that we can interact with the Python API, we can use the Gym wrapper to train the ML Agents using the Baselines from OpenAI. The gym wrapper provides an interface on top of the "UnityEnvironment" class. Open the Interfacing with MLAgents.ipynb Notebook. First we will install the "gym_unity" wrapper as follows:

```
!pip install gym_unity
```

We will be using the "UnityToGymWrapper" for interfacing with the Gym environment. It has the following parameters:

- **Unity environment:** The Unity environment to be wrapped

- **Use visual:** This signifies if visual observations would be used for the environment in place of vector observations during the decision steps and terminal steps.

- **Uint8_visual:** This controls the output format of visual observations as uint8 values (0-255), and most Atari games use this (e.g., Pong). Defaults to float values in range (0.0-1.0), which refers to grayscale image.

- **Flatten_branched:** This is used to flatten a branched discrete action space into Gym discrete to make it compatible for interfacing with the Gym environment.

- **Allow_multiple_visual_obs:** This allows multiple visual observations instead of one observation.

Now let us use the GridWorld environment in Unity ML Agents and train it using custom off-policy dueling DQN from the Baselines. We will be using the implementation provided in the documentation for simplicity. For this, we have to create a file with a

name–for example, "baseline-dqn-gridworld-train.py"—and we have to save it in the /
env folder of our repository. Then we have to include the libraries, wrappers, and the
algorithms, which we will be using:

```
from mlagents_envs.environment import UnityEnvironment
from gym_unity.envs import UnityToGymWrapper
```

Then inside the "main" method, we load the Unity environment and convert it into a
Gym environment by using the "UnityToGymWrapper" method. Because in GridWorld
image analysis is done using convolution neural networks and we will be using CNN
policy for our dueling DQN while training GridWorld. We will set the unint8_visuals to
"True," as we will require the output format to be of type (0-255) as it is converted to a 2D
Atari-like environment. We will also set "use_visual" to true, as we will be taking visual
observations as input.

```
unity_env = UnityEnvironment("./envs/GridWorld")
env = UnityToGymWrapper(unity_env, 0, use_visual=True, uint8_visual=True)
logger.configure('./logs') # Change to log in a different directory
```

In the next step, we will call on the "deepq.learn" method from Baselines, as it
provides the implementation of DQN. The following parameters are to be used in this
context.

- Env: This sets the Gym converted environment.

- cnn: This is the neural network policy that will be used—in this case,
  convolution 2D neural networks.

- learning rate: This is the learning rate for the algorithm.

- total_timesteps: The total episodes for which the training will happen

- buffer_size: Controls the depth of the buffer for experience replay

- exploration_fraction: Controls the exploration factor

- exploration_final_episode: Tracks the exploration for the final
  episode

- print_freq: Printing logs on screen

- train_freq: Training on samples with the assigned frequency

- learnin_starts: After how many steps the weight updates take place for learning

- target_network_update_freq: The frequency of update of the neural network

- gamma: Exploration-exploitation factor

- prioritized_replay: This is used if we use DDQN with priority replay buffer, implying certain observations are used ahead of others.

- checkpoint_freq: For controlling the frequency of logs

- checkpoint_path: The path for storing the frequency of logs

- duelling: This controls the nature of the policy; in this case we will use dueling DQN.

The following program segment represents this:

```
act = deepq.learn(
        env,
        "cnn", # conv_only is also a good choice for GridWorld
        lr=2.5e-4,
        total_timesteps=1000000,
        buffer_size=50000,
        exploration_fraction=0.05,
        exploration_final_eps=0.1,
        print_freq=20,
        train_freq=5,
        learning_starts=20000,
        target_network_update_freq=50,
        gamma=0.99,
        prioritized_replay=False,
        checkpoint_freq=1000,
        checkpoint_path='./logs',
      # Change to save model in a different directory
        dueling=True
    )
```

Then we save the model and use the "main" method to train it.

```
print("Saving model to unity_model.pkl")
    act.save("unity_model.pkl")

if __name__ == '__main__':
    main()
```

Then we have to navigate to the folder location where this file is located. Then we have to run the following command in Anaconda prompt.

```
python -m baseline-dqn-gridworld-train.py
```

After we run this command, we can see the training happening in the console and the GridWorld environment being trained on a dueling DQN policy. We can see the training while the Unity executable is running, as shown in Figure 5-37.

Figure 5-37. *GridWorld training using dueling DQN from Baselines*

We can also use ML Agents PPO method for training this by using the command:

```
mlagents-learn <pah to trainer_config.yaml> --run-id=GridWorldNew -train
```

The training phase appears as shown in Figure 5-38.

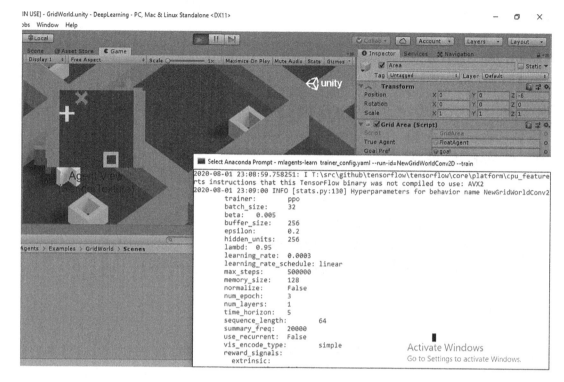

Figure 5-38. *Training on PPO policy of ML Agents*

Now let's use the Baseline PPO2 (clipped) version from Gym to train this environment. We load the Unity GridWorld environment, as mentioned before, and we will be creating a monitored environment in this context. This is an example of multi-instance training using the PPO2 algorithm from the Baselines as mentioned in the documentation. We use the "UnityToGymWrapper" to convert the environment and also apply "use_visuals" for visual observation. Then we use the "SubprocVecEnv" method to create subprocesses for instantiating multiple instances of the GridWorld environment.

```
from mlagents_envs.environment import UnityEnvironment
from gym_unity.envs import UnityToGymWrapper
from baselines.common.vec_env.subproc_vec_env import SubprocVecEnv
from baselines.common.vec_env.dummy_vec_env import DummyVecEnv
from baselines.bench import Monitor
from baselines import logger
import baselines.ppo2.ppo2 as ppo2

import os
```

413

```python
try:
    from mpi4py import MPI
except ImportError:
    MPI = None

def make_unity_env(env_directory, num_env, visual, start_index=0):
    def make_env(rank, use_visual=True):
        def _thunk():
            unity_env = UnityEnvironment(env_directory)
            env = UnityToGymWrapper(unity_env,
            rank, use_visual=use_visual, uint8_visual=True)
            env = Monitor(env, logger.get_dir()
            and os.path.join(logger.get_dir(), str(rank)))
            return env
        return _thunk
    if visual:
        return SubprocVecEnv([make_env(i + start_index)
         for i in range(num_env)])
    else:
        rank = MPI.COMM_WORLD.Get_rank() if MPI else 0
        return DummyVecEnv([make_env(rank, use_visual=False)])
```

Then we have the PPO2 algorithm from the Baselines, which uses the MLP policy or dense networks, and this can be modified to use convolution neural networks as well. In this context we create four environments of GridWorld for multi-threaded training. We train for 100000 episodes:

```python
def main():
    env = make_unity_env('./envs/GridWorld', 4, True)
    ppo2.learn(
        network="mlp",
        env=env,
        total_timesteps=100000,
        lr=1e-3,
    )

if __name__ == '__main__':
    main()
```

414

On running this using the Python –m command, we can visualize simultaneous training of four GridWorld environment instances. We can visualize the training in Tensorboard as well by using the log files.

Now we can use our own implementations of the on-/off-policy algorithms that we discussed in the previous section as well to train our ML Agents without custom models. This is left for interested readers to try using the previous implementations of on-/off-policy algorithms with Unity ML Agents through the Gym interface. In the next section we will look into a certain aspects of "mlagents," which are inside the ML Agents repository; this would include a brief overview of the different policies implemented in the ML Agents in Unity for the PPO algorithm as well as understanding memory-based neural networks—namely, LSTM networks.

Understanding Deep RL policies in Unity ML Agents and Memory-Based Networks

In this context, we will be going through certain scripts inside the ML Agents repository that we mentioned in the last chapter—namely, the ModelOverrider script in Examples/SharedAssets/Scripts directory of the repository. This is used alongside the BehaviorParameters and the DecisionRequester scripts for our agents in Unity.

Model Overrider Script

This script is a utility class that overrides the neural network model during inference mode and is used to validate the training internally after the episodes are completed. This works with a 1:1 ratio between the agents and the environments. First we have the type of the neural network model file that is used by Barracuda for inference, either in ".nn" or ".onnx" format. Then we specify arguments that refer to the neural network model path and location as well as the training steps, extension, episodes, and directory of the neural network model and other details.

```
HashSet<string> k_SupportedExtensions = new HashSet<string>{"nn", "onnx"};
      const string k_CommandLineModelOverrideFlag = "--mlagents-override-
         model";
      const string k_CommandLineModelOverrideDirectoryFlag = "--mlagents-
         override-model-directory";
```

```
    const string k_CommandLineModelOverrideExtensionFlag = "--mlagents-
    override-model-extension";
    const string k_CommandLineQuitAfterEpisodesFlag = "--mlagents-quit-
    after-episodes";
    const string k_CommandLineQuitOnLoadFailure = "--mlagents-quit-on-
    load-failure";
```

Then it has variables that control the agent, a dictionary containing asset paths and the behavior names as key-value pairs, another dictionary that stores the behavior name and the neural network model as a key-value pair. It also contains variables for number of steps, previous number of steps, number of completed episodes, and Boolean value to check whether to load on failure and also contains static variables for the same.

```
Agent m_Agent;
Dictionary<string, string> m_BehaviorNameOverrides = new Dictionary<string,
string>();
string m_BehaviorNameOverrideDirectory;
string m_OverrideExtension = "nn";
Dictionary<string, NNModel> m_CachedModels = new Dictionary<string,
NNModel>();
int m_MaxEpisodes;
int m_NumSteps;
int m_PreviousNumSteps;
int m_PreviousAgentCompletedEpisodes;
bool m_QuitOnLoadFailure;
[Tooltip("Debug values to be used in place of the command line for
overriding models.")]
public string debugCommandLineOverride;
static int s_PreviousAgentCompletedEpisodes;
static int s_PreviousNumSteps;
```

Then there are methods such as "TotalCompletedEpisodes," "TotalNumSteps," "HasOverrides," and "GetOverridenBehaviorName," which control the total steps completed during training, the total steps of training, a Boolean function that asserts whether a particular behavior overriding is possible, and the name of the overridden behavior, respectively.

```
int TotalCompletedEpisodes
{
    get { return m_PreviousAgentCompletedEpisodes + (m_Agent == null ? 0 :
    m_Agent.CompletedEpisodes);  }
}

int TotalNumSteps
{
    get { return m_PreviousNumSteps + m_NumSteps; }
}

public bool HasOverrides
{
    get { return m_BehaviorNameOverrides.Count > 0
    || !string.IsNullOrEmpty(m_BehaviorNameOverrideDirectory);  }
}

public static string GetOverrideBehaviorName(string originalBehaviorName)
{
    return $"Override_{originalBehaviorName}";
}
```

The "GetAssetPathFromCommand" line method is used to load the assets from the command line arguments. It does this by splitting the arguments. Since the assets are stored (.nn/.onnx) in a key–value pair format, the splitting enables to extract the behavior names and the type of the asset. This is done by the following lines of code:

```
m_BehaviorNameOverrides.Clear();
    var maxEpisodes = 0;
    string[] commandLineArgsOverride = null;
    if (!string.IsNullOrEmpty
      (debugCommandLineOverride)
        && Application.isEditor)
    {
        commandLineArgsOverride
        =   debugCommandLineOverride.Split(' ');
    }
```

```
var args
 = commandLineArgsOverride
 ??    Environment.GetCommandLineArgs();
for (var i = 0; i < args.Length; i++)
{
    if (args[i] == k_CommandLineModelOverrideFlag &&
    i < args.Length-2)
    {
        var key = args[i + 1].Trim();
        var value = args[i + 2].Trim();
        m_BehaviorNameOverrides[key] = value;
    }
```

It also contains the conditions for controlling the extensions during splitting the arguments (at the time of writing this book .onnx files are not supported in this context), and also controls "on load failure" property if the model loading fails. There is a condition that specifies the number of episodes of training used before quitting.

```
else if (args[i] == k_CommandLineModelOverrideExtension
  Flag && i < args.Length-1)
    {
        m_OverrideExtension = args
        [i + 1].Trim().ToLower();
        var isKnownExtension
      = k_SupportedExtensions.Contains
      (m_OverrideExtension);
        var isOnnx = m_OverrideExtension.Equals("onnx");
        if (!isKnownExtension || isOnnx)
        {
            Debug.LogError($"loading unsupported format
             : {m_OverrideExtension}");
            Application.Quit(1);
#if UNITY_EDITOR
                        EditorApplication.isPlaying = false;
#endif
        }
    }
```

```
    else if (args[i] == k_CommandLineQuit
    AfterEpisodesFlag && i < args.Length-1)
    {
        Int32.TryParse(args[i + 1], out maxEpisodes);
    }
    else if (args[i] == k_CommandLineQuitOnLoadFailure)
    {
        m_QuitOnLoadFailure = true;
    }
}
```

The "OnEnable" method is used for setting and resetting the parameters, such as episodes completed, agent behavior, and whether the behavior has overrides and is used in case we are resetting the Unity scene.

```
void OnEnable()
{
    m_PreviousNumSteps = s_PreviousNumSteps;
    m_PreviousAgentCompletedEpisodes
    = s_PreviousAgentCompletedEpisodes;
    m_Agent = GetComponent<Agent>();
    GetAssetPathFromCommandLine();
    if (HasOverrides)
    {
        OverrideModel();
    }
}
```

The "OnDisable" method is used for updating the static variables that control the episodes and the steps counts.

```
void OnDisable()
{
    s_PreviousAgentCompletedEpisodes
    = Mathf.Max(s_PreviousAgentCompletedEpisodes,
      TotalCompletedEpisodes);
```

```
    s_PreviousNumSteps = Mathf.Max
    (s_PreviousNumSteps, TotalNumSteps);
}
```

We then have the "Fixed Update" method, which has the maxSteps attribute which controls the maximum steps required for training and lets the agent train for at least the maximum steps specified before terminating. It also checks for any errors during the training stage by extending the training for a few more time-steps.

```
void FixedUpdate()
{
    if (m_MaxEpisodes > 0)
    {
        if (TotalCompletedEpisodes >= m_MaxEpisodes
        && TotalNumSteps > m_MaxEpisodes * m_Agent.MaxStep)
        {
            Debug.Log($"ModelOverride
              reached {TotalCompletedEpisodes} episodes
             and {TotalNumSteps} steps. Exiting.");
            Application.Quit(0);
#if UNITY_EDITOR
            EditorApplication.isPlaying = false;
#endif
        }
    }
    m_NumSteps++;
}
```

The "GetModelFromBehaviorName" method is used to retrieve the neural network model through the arguments specified in the behavior names. It takes the path to the neural network model asset and then uses a key-value pair to generate the behavior name and the neural network model. Then it reads the bytecodes of the model for inference mode. It also caches the files (assets) for future reference during inference training.

```
public NNModel GetModelForBehaviorName(string behaviorName)
{
    if (m_CachedModels.ContainsKey(behaviorName))
    {
        return m_CachedModels[behaviorName];
    }
    string assetPath = null;
    if (m_BehaviorNameOverrides.ContainsKey(behaviorName))
    {
        assetPath = m_BehaviorNameOverrides[behaviorName];
    }
    else if(!string.IsNullOrEmpty(m_BehaviorNameOverrideDirectory))
    {
        assetPath = Path.Combine(m_BehaviorNameOverrideDirectory,
        $"{behaviorName}.{m_OverrideExtension}");
    }

    if (string.IsNullOrEmpty(assetPath))
    {
        Debug.Log($"No override for
        BehaviorName {behaviorName}, and no directory set.");
        return null;
    }

    byte[] model = null;
    try
    {
        model = File.ReadAllBytes(assetPath);
    }
    catch(IOException)
    {
        Debug.Log($"Couldn't load file {assetPath}
        at full path {Path.GetFullPath(assetPath)}", this);
        m_CachedModels[behaviorName] = null;
        return null;
    }
```

```
    var asset = ScriptableObject.CreateInstance<NNModel>();
    asset.modelData
    = ScriptableObject.CreateInstance<NNModelData>();
    asset.modelData.Value = model;
    asset.name = "Override - " + Path.GetFileName(assetPath);
    m_CachedModels[behaviorName] = asset;
    return asset;
}
```

The "OverrideModel" method contains the actual overriding logic for the
neural network models. It extracts the parameters that assign the brain from the
BehaviorParameters script attached to the agent, and then assigns the neural network
model in the form of bytecodes. It gets the corresponding behavior name and checks
whether the name is valid and present in the assets inside Unity. It then assigns the
trained neural network model for inference after the agent has been loaded. This is done
by the following lines:

```
void OverrideModel()
{
    bool overrideOk = false;
    string overrideError = null;

    m_Agent.LazyInitialize();
    var bp = m_Agent.GetComponent<BehaviorParameters>();
    var behaviorName = bp.BehaviorName;

    var nnModel = GetModelForBehaviorName(behaviorName);
    if (nnModel == null)
    {
        overrideError =
            $"Didn't find a model for
            behaviorName {behaviorName}. Make " +
            $"sure the behaviorName is set correctly
            in the commandline " +
            $"and that the model file exists";
    }
    else
```

```
    {
        var modelName = nnModel != null ?
        nnModel.name : "<null>";
        Debug.Log($"Overriding behavior {behaviorName}
        for agent with model {modelName}");
        try
        {
            m_Agent.SetModel(GetOverrideBehaviorName
            (behaviorName), nnModel);
             overrideOk = true;
        }
        catch (Exception e)
        {
            overrideError = $"Exception
            calling Agent.SetModel: {e}";
        }
    }
    if (!overrideOk && m_QuitOnLoadFailure)
    {
        if(!string.IsNullOrEmpty(overrideError))
        {
            Debug.LogWarning(overrideError);
        }
        Application.Quit(1);
#if UNITY_EDITOR
        EditorApplication.isPlaying = false;
#endif
    }

}
```

Thus we have had an overview of the Model Overrider script in Unity, which is an important script used for overriding inference models in Unity. Next we will be looking briefly into the actual neural networks built inside Unity. We will also explore the LSTM module inside the model scripts in ML Agents.

In this context, let us navigate toward the mlagents/trainers/tf folder, which contains the Tensorflow implementation of the actual neural network models in Unity. We will look into the Models.py script.

Models Script: Python

This is the fundamental script used by PPO/SAC/GAIL/Ghost and other training algorithms inside ML Agents. It controls the entire Tensorflow specifications of the neural network as well as the hyperparameters. We will be looking at certain parts of this script. We have the epsilon mentioned at the start of the script, which can be changed as well. Then we have the different classes that contain the parameters for encoding. This also contains the encoding parameters for the Tensors (height, width, and channels for convolution networks). There is also an associated minimum resolution for the different neural networks used, and we can see "RESNET:15" being mentioned in this context, which specifies that for CNN-based models, we can use ResNet as our neural network.

```python
EPSILON = 1e-7

class Tensor3DShape(NamedTuple):
    height: int
    width: int
    num_channels: int

class NormalizerTensors(NamedTuple):
    update_op: tf.Operation
    steps: tf.Tensor
    running_mean: tf.Tensor
    running_variance: tf.Tensor

class ModelUtils:

    MIN_RESOLUTION_FOR_ENCODER = {
        EncoderType.SIMPLE: 20,
        EncoderType.NATURE_CNN: 36,
        EncoderType.RESNET: 15,
    }
}
```

Then we specify the global training steps in Tensorflow, and we also freeze certain weights in the network that is specified by the "trainable=False" command. Then we have the method "create_schedule," which controls the learning rate tensor and controls the base learning rate, global steps, and maximum steps. There are two types of trainers: linear and constant.

```
if schedule == ScheduleType.CONSTANT:
          parameter_rate = tf.Variable(parameter
           , trainable=False)
elif schedule == ScheduleType.LINEAR:
          parameter_rate = tf.train.polynomial_decay(
          parameter, global_step, max_step,
          min_value, power=1.0
          )
else:
          raise UnityTrainerException(f"The
          schedule {schedule} is invalid.")
return parameter_rate
```

Then we have variance scaling initializers and Swish activation methods for creating initializers for our trainable weights in the neural networks. Now we have methods that take the visual observations from the Unity scene through the camera and transform them to a 3D Tensor containing the height, width, and channels("create_visual_input").

```
visual_in = tf.placeholder(
        shape=[None, o_size_h, o_size_w, c_channels], dtype=tf.float32,
        name=name
```

In case we are not using visual observations, we have to convert the vector observations (ray sensor data) in the form of a 1D Tensor ("create_vector_input").

```
vector_in = tf.placeholder(
        shape=[None, vec_obs_size], dtype=tf.float32, name=name
        )
```

There are methods ("normalize_vector_obs") that normalize the input vectors and the visual observations (Tensors), which is done by dividing with the square root of the variance.

425

```
normalized_state = tf.clip_by_value(
        (vector_obs - running_mean)
        / tf.sqrt(
            running_variance / (tf.cast(normalization_steps,
            tf.float32) + 1)
        ),
        -5,
        5,
        name="normalized_state",
    )
```

The "create_normalizer" method is used to create a Tensor that contains the next value to normalize based on the current running mean and variance (used in batch normalization). It also contains the normalization steps for the nontrainable weights.

```
vec_obs_size = vector_obs.shape[1]
 steps = tf.get_variable(
     "normalization_steps",
     [],
     trainable=False,
     dtype=tf.int32,
     initializer=tf.zeros_initializer(),
 )
 running_mean = tf.get_variable(
     "running_mean",
     [vec_obs_size],
     trainable=False,
     dtype=tf.float32,
     initializer=tf.zeros_initializer(),
 )
 running_variance = tf.get_variable(
     "running_variance",
     [vec_obs_size],
     trainable=False,
     dtype=tf.float32,
     initializer=tf.ones_initializer(),
 )
```

```
update_normalization
= ModelUtils.create_normalizer_update(
    vector_obs, steps, running_mean, running_variance
)
return NormalizerTensors(
    update_normalization, steps,
     running_mean, running_variance
)
```

The next method "create_vector_observation_encoder" is an important method as it contains the actual implementation of the Dense neural network (MLP) for the vector observations. As we have studied the dense network in Keras, here the dense network from Tensorflow is used. We have the parameters, such as hidden layers, units, and kernel initializers, which in this case is variance_scaling, the activation function, and other details.

```
with tf.variable_scope(scope):
        hidden = observation_input
        for i in range(num_layers):
            hidden = tf.layers.dense(
                hidden,
                h_size,
                activation=activation,
                reuse=reuse,
                name=f"hidden_{i}",
                kernel_initializer=tf.initializers.variance_
                scaling(1.0),
            )
return hidden
```

Then we have the "create_visual_observation_encoder" method which contains the convolution-2D neural network architecture used in ML Agents. This is the one used in GridWorld environment when training with PPO policy and cnn as the neural network type. As we have studied, we have the convolution layer, flattening/pooling layer and then a dense network in a traditional CNN.

- **Convolution layers in ML Agents:** We can understand here the ML
  Agents uses convolution-2D neural network with kernel size of [8,8]
  and stride of [4,4] with an activation of "Relu" for the first convolution
  network. For the second CNN, we have a kernel size of [4,4] and
  stride of [2,2] with "elu" (exponential linear unit) as the activation
  function and 32 being the channel depth.

- **Dense layers:** The output of the 2nd convolution layer is passed into
  the dense network, which is created using the (dense neural network)
  "create_vector_observation_encoder" method in the previous case.

The following lines represent this, and we can change this code according to our
requirements and add pooling/dropout or other layers that we have studied previously.

```
with tf.variable_scope(scope):
        conv1 = tf.layers.conv2d(
            image_input,
            16,
            kernel_size=[8, 8],
            strides=[4, 4],
            activation=tf.nn.elu,
            reuse=reuse,
            name="conv_1",
        )
        conv2 = tf.layers.conv2d(
            conv1,
            32,
            kernel_size=[4, 4],
            strides=[2, 2],
            activation=tf.nn.elu,
            reuse=reuse,
            name="conv_2",
        )
        hidden = tf.layers.flatten(conv2)
```

```
with tf.variable_scope(scope + "/" + "flat_encoding"):
        hidden_flat = ModelUtils.create_vector_observation_encoder(
            hidden, h_size, activation, num_layers, scope, reuse
        )
return hidden_flat
```

In the next method, "create_nature_cnn_visual_observation_encoder," there is a residual network or ResNet type of network built for ML Agents. Now we have studied the importance of residual blocks in ResNet architecture to increase accuracy in training as the depth of the neural network model increases. This is done in Tensorflow by using the reuse=reuse parameter, which is mentioned in this context. Here we have three convolution-2D neural network models with "elu" as the common activation function and different kernel sizes (8, 4, and 3, respectively) and different strides (4, 2, and 1, respectively). The depth of the channels changes from 32 to 64 units in second and third layers. Then we have the usual dense MLP network included from the vector observations method.

```
with tf.variable_scope(scope):
        conv1 = tf.layers.conv2d(
            image_input,
            32,
            kernel_size=[8, 8],
            strides=[4, 4],
            activation=tf.nn.elu,
            reuse=reuse,
            name="conv_1",
        )
        conv2 = tf.layers.conv2d(
            conv1,
            64,
            kernel_size=[4, 4],
            strides=[2, 2],
            activation=tf.nn.elu,
            reuse=reuse,
            name="conv_2",
        )
```

```
            conv3 = tf.layers.conv2d(
                conv2,
                64,
                kernel_size=[3, 3],
                strides=[1, 1],
                activation=tf.nn.elu,
                reuse=reuse,
                name="conv_3",
            )
            hidden = tf.layers.flatten(conv3)
with tf.variable_scope(scope + "/" + "flat_encoding"):
            hidden_flat
            = ModelUtils.create_vector_observation_encoder(
             hidden, h_size, activation, num_layers,
             scope, reuse
            )
return hidden_flat
```

The "create_resnet_visual_observation_encoder" is another variant of the ResNet model, and in this case, we have additional hidden layers with "Relu" activation in between the usual convolution blocks. Also in this case, a MaxPooling layer is present with pool size of [3,3] and stride size of [2,2]. Additionally the convolution layers now have "same" padding applied to them.

```
n_channels = [16, 32, 32] # channel for each stack
n_blocks = 2 # number of residual blocks
with tf.variable_scope(scope):
            hidden = image_input
            for i, ch in enumerate(n_channels):
                hidden = tf.layers.conv2d(
                    hidden,
                    ch,
                    kernel_size=[3, 3],
                    strides=[1, 1],
                    reuse=reuse,
                    name="layer%dconv_1" % i,
```

```
            )
            hidden = tf.layers.max_pooling2d(
                hidden, pool_size=[3, 3], strides=[2, 2],
                padding="same"
            )
            # create residual blocks
            for j in range(n_blocks):
                block_input = hidden
                hidden = tf.nn.relu(hidden)
                hidden = tf.layers.conv2d(
                    hidden,
                    ch,
                    kernel_size=[3, 3],
                    strides=[1, 1],
                    padding="same",
                    reuse=reuse,
                    name="layer%d_%d_conv1" % (i, j),
                )
                hidden = tf.nn.relu(hidden)
                hidden = tf.layers.conv2d(
                    hidden,
                    ch,
                    kernel_size=[3, 3],
                    strides=[1, 1],
                    padding="same",
                    reuse=reuse,
                    name="layer%d_%d_conv2" % (i, j),
                )
                hidden = tf.add(block_input, hidden)
        hidden = tf.nn.relu(hidden)
        hidden = tf.layers.flatten(hidden)

with tf.variable_scope(scope + "/" + "flat_encoding"):
        hidden_flat
        = ModelUtils.create_vector_observation_encoder(
          hidden, h_size, activation, num_layers,
```

```
                scope, reuse
            )
return hidden_flat
```

Then we have the "break_into_branches" method, which takes a concatenated set of logits that represent multiple discrete branches and breaks it into a single Tensor per branch, and the "create_discrete_action_masking_layer" method, which applies a masking layer on the discrete actions. It uses a softmax activation to mask over the logits and uses a multinomial distribution for the output.

```
branch_masks = ModelUtils.break_into_branches(action_masks, action_size)
raw_probs = [
            tf.multiply(tf.nn.softmax(branches_logits[k])
          + EPSILON, branch_masks[k])
            for k in range(len(action_size))
        ]
normalized_probs = [
            tf.divide(raw_probs[k]
          , tf.reduce_sum(raw_probs[k],
            axis=1, keepdims=True))
            for k in range(len(action_size))
        ]
output = tf.concat(
            [
                tf.multinomial(tf.log(normalized_probs[k]
              + EPSILON), 1)
                for k in range(len(action_size))
            ],
            axis=1,
        )
return (
            output,
            tf.concat([normalized_probs[k]
            for k in range(len(action_size))], axis=1),
            tf.concat(
                [
```

```
            tf.log(normalized_probs[k] + EPSILON)
            for k in range(len(action_size))
        ],
        axis=1,
    ),
)
```

The "create_observation_streams" uses the previous methods, which contain the neural network architecture for building the observation streams, used in training. The next method, "create_recurrent_encoder," is another important method that uses recurrent neural network or LSTM networks for memory-based processing. We will be studying about LSTMs shortly; however, in this case, this method creates a neural network that stores a part of the actions/states/rewards in the memory and uses it for future reference. The "BasicLSTMCellMethod" from Tensorflow (or Keras) is used for this purpose.

```
s_size = input_state.get_shape().as_list()[1]
m_size = memory_in.get_shape().as_list()[1]
lstm_input_state = tf.reshape(input_state, shape=[-1, sequence_length, s_
size])
memory_in = tf.reshape(memory_in[:, :], [-1, m_size])
half_point = int(m_size / 2)
with tf.variable_scope(name):
        rnn_cell
      = tf.nn.rnn_cell.BasicLSTMCell(half_point)
        lstm_vector_in = tf.nn.rnn_cell.LSTMStateTuple(
         memory_in[:, :half_point],
         memory_in[:, half_point:]
        )
        recurrent_output, lstm_state_out
         = tf.nn.dynamic_rnn(
            rnn_cell, lstm_input_state
            , initial_state=lstm_vector_in
        )
```

```
recurrent_output = tf.reshape(recurrent_output, shape=[-1, half_point])
return recurrent_output, tf.concat([lstm_state_out.c, lstm_state_out.h],
axis=1)
```

This script is the most important script, as it governs the network architecture for the different on-/off-policy algorithms present in Unity ML Agents, and we can modify these hyperparameters (such as kernel size/stride in convolution-2D neural network or activations) and try to understand the outcome of the training. In the next section we will see the PPO script very briefly and then venture into LSTM-based networks.

PPO in Unity ML Agents

In Unity ML Agents, we have to navigate to the mlagents/trainers/ppo folder, and inside we can see that there are two python scripts: optimizers and trainer.

- **Trainer Python script:** This controls the actual implementation of the PPO algorithm in ML Agents. It takes the hyperparameters, such as batch size, episodes, policies, learning rate, gamma, and epsilon from the config files ("trainer_config.yaml"), and checks the validity. One of the important methods in this context is the "_process_ trajectory" method. This controls the initial trajectory built using the PPO policy and gets the value estimates (observation, rewards, states) following that particular policy. It computes and stores the rewards in a buffer. After that it computes the GAE, which we mentioned in the PPO section in deep RL. It calculates the advantages based on the value estimates and the returns for the particular policy.

```
tmp_advantages = []
tmp_returns = []
for name in self.optimizer.reward_signals:
    bootstrap_value = value_next[name]

    local_rewards = agent_buffer_trajectory[
        "{}_rewards".format(name)

    ].get_batch()
    local_value_estimates = agent_buffer_trajectory[
        "{}_value_estimates".format(name)
```

```
].get_batch()
local_advantage = get_gae(
    rewards=local_rewards,
    value_estimates=local_value_estimates,
    value_next=bootstrap_value,
    gamma=self.optimizer.reward_signals[name].
    gamma,
    lambd=self.trainer_parameters["lambd"],
)
local_return = local_advantage
+ local_value_estimates
agent_buffer_trajectory["{}_returns".
format(name)].set(local_return)
agent_buffer_trajectory["{}_advantage".
format(name)].set(local_advantage)
tmp_advantages.append(local_advantage)
tmp_returns.append(local_return)
```

This is computed both locally and globally. The "_update_policy"
method is used to update the current policy by comparing the
returns with the GAE of the older policy. It updates the policy in
mini-batches of training. The "create_policy" method is used for
creating the PPO policy and has several parameters, such as brain
parameters, seed, and "is training" (Boolean)—all of which are
derived from the NNPolicy class. The "add_policy" method adds
the current training policy to the trainer. The "discount_rewards"
method is the same as we had written in previous sections
to provide a discounted return on the rewards. The method
"get_gae" returns the GAE advantage estimate, which is used for
updating the policy, represented by the equation:

$$A^\pi(s_t, a_t) = Q^\pi(s_t, a_t) - V^\pi(s_t)$$

The following lines of code signify this formulation.

value_estimates = np.append(value_estimates, value_next)

delta_t = rewards + gamma * value_estimates[1:] - value_estimates[:-1]

advantage = discount_rewards(r=delta_t, gamma=gamma * lambd)

return advantage

- **Optimizer Python script:** This script contains a complex variant of the PPO optimizer that we created in our deep RL section. This controls the loss and the learning rate and fine-tunes the optimization by updating the policy gradient. It contains certain hyperparameters that control the epsilon, beta, maximum steps, number of layers, and other attributes. It also contains the type of the neural network architecture to be used—whether recurrent networks, convolution networks, or dense networks are to be used. The "create_cc_critic" method signifies the creation of a continuous controlled critic value network, and in the case of recurrent networks, it uses the "create_recurrent_encoder" method from the Model.py script that we mentioned.

```
if self.policy.use_recurrent:
        hidden_value, memory_value_out
        = ModelUtils.create_recurrent_encoder(
            hidden_stream,
            self.memory_in,
            self.policy.sequence_length_ph,
            name="lstm_value",
        )
        self.memory_out = memory_value_out
```

The "create_dc_critic" represents a discrete controlled critic network, and if the policy is CNN, then it uses the "create_visual_observation_encoder" method from the Model.py script. It can also use other variations of visual encoders such as Resnet. In the discrete case, we take the topmost index of the buffer for analysis.

```
hidden_stream = ModelUtils.create_observation_streams(
        self.policy.visual_in,
        self.policy.processed_vector_in,
        1,
        h_size,
        num_layers,
        vis_encode_type,
    )[0]
```

The "_create_losses" method contains the actual clipping of policies that we saw in the PPO section of deep RL. The clipping is done based on the GAE returns on the old policy and is represented by the following lines of code:

```
r_theta = tf.exp(probs - old_probs)
p_opt_a = r_theta * advantage
p_opt_b = (
    tf.clip_by_value(r_theta, 1.0 - decay_epsilon, 1.0
    + decay_epsilon)
    * advantage
)
```

where epsilon is the hyperparameter used in this context.

That concludes the section on PPO, and we have an idea as to how the PPO algorithm is created internally by Unity for use in ML Agents. We also understood that the hyperparameters mentioned in the "trainer_config.yaml" are used in these scripts to control the training and policy gradient optimization. Now let us briefly understand LSTM and try to understand the hyperparameters with which it is associated.

Long Short-Term Memory Networks in ML Agents

Recurrent Neural Network

LSTMs are modified versions of recurrent neural networks (RNNs). RNNs are networks that pass the processed information through the hidden layers toward its own input and hence are used for retaining memory inside the network. RNNs learn information from the previous step and store this information. Internally the hidden layers have some activations that try to retain the data. In the gradient descent part of training a RNN, due to successive gradient flow through the RNN, the network is useful for storing certain error gradients from previous time-steps and helps in the learning process, which is not possible in the case of traditional neural networks. However, in traditional RNN, there are two problems that occur due to the recursive looping of the gradient updates.

- **Vanishing gradient problem:** This implies as the training length increases, the successive gradients decrease, as very little error gets propagated to the previous layers. This leads to a nonconverging learning curve, and the algorithm oscillates in the regions of the global minima without converging.

- **Exploding gradient problem:** Due to frequent recursive updates in training, the model weights may get updated by a large quantity. This causes instability in the training phase, as in many cases, the algorithm oversteps from the global minima.

LSTM Network

To counteract this issue of gradients, LSTMs were devised to stabilize the weight updates and the gradient flow during training, along with retaining memory. The typical architecture of a LSTM module looks like that shown in Figure 5-39.

LSTM Network

Abhilash Majumder | August 2, 2020

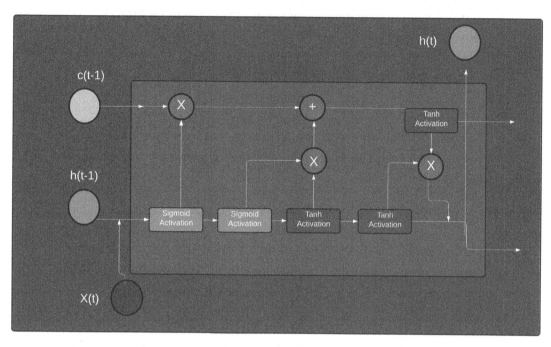

Figure 5-39. *LSTM architecture*

Now we have a separate activation unit here, which is denoted by "tanh." This is used because the second derivative of "tanh" does not dissipate as the learning progresses. The first derivative is given by the formulation:

$$\partial tanh(z) = [(1-z^2)]\partial z$$

In LSTM, there are four major gates that control the flow of information and memory. The h(t-1) controls the outputs of the previous LSTM cell, and c(t-1) controls the memory of the previous LSTM cell. X(t) is the input to the current cell. We will understand the gates going from left to right starting with the sigmoid activation unit.

- **Forward gate:** This controls the sigmoid activated output of the previous LSTM cell [h(t-1) with weights(W)] and the current input X(t) with some bias.

$$f_t = \sigma \left(W_f \left[h_{t\text{-}} X_t \right] + b_f \right)$$

439

- **Input Gate:** This also controls the sigmoid activated output of previous h(t-1) with the weights W. Additionally there is a "tanh" activation applied on the previous output with the input X(t) with corresponding bias.

$$i_t = \sigma\left(Wi[h_{t\text{-}}X_t] + b_i\right)$$

$$C_t^{'} = \tanh(Wc[h_{t\text{-}}X_t] + b_c)$$

- **Forget gate:** This controls the information that we want the LSTM network to forget. This is computed by the following formula using c(t-1):

$$C_t = f_t {}^*C_{t\text{-}1} + i_t {}^* C_t^{'}$$

- **Output gate:** This contains a sigmoid activated unit that decides what we would want to output. This is follows by a "tanh" activation, which clamps between (-1,1) to get the current LSTM contents h(t):

$$o_t = \sigma\left(Wo[h_{t\text{-}}X_t] + b_o\right)$$

$$h(t) = o_t {}^* \tanh(C_t)$$

Through these gates, the LSTM network tries to alleviate the drawbacks of a traditional RNN. We have observed the case in the Model.py script where we mentioned the RNNs use-case.

LSTM in ML Agents Models

In ML Agents, we have seen the importance of RNNs for training the models in the Model.py script. Here again is a representation of the same.

```
s_size = input_state.get_shape().as_list()[1]
m_size = memory_in.get_shape().as_list()[1]
lstm_input_state = tf.reshape(input_state, shape=[-1, sequence_length, s_
size])
memory_in = tf.reshape(memory_in[:, :], [-1, m_size])
half_point = int(m_size / 2)
with tf.variable_scope(name):
        rnn_cell
        = tf.nn.rnn_cell.BasicLSTMCell(half_point)
        lstm_vector_in = tf.nn.rnn_cell.LSTMStateTuple(
```

```
      memory_in[:, :half_point],
      memory_in[:, half_point:]
    )
    recurrent_output, lstm_state_out
     = tf.nn.dynamic_rnn(
        rnn_cell, lstm_input_state
        , initial_state=lstm_vector_in
    )
```

```
recurrent_output = tf.reshape(recurrent_output, shape=[-1, half_point])
return recurrent_output, tf.concat([lstm_state_out.c, lstm_state_out.h],
axis=1)
```

Here the important part is the "BasicLSTMCell," which has units denoted by "m_size/2." These signify the number of units in the LSTM block. The "LSTMStateTuple" method is used for including the extents of memory for use in processing the observations. Internally these are passed through the series of sigmoid and tanh activated cells to get the current output. Now this model file is used across SAC/GAIL and other algorithms in ML Agents. We can definitely view the source of SAC, especially to get an idea of the use of LSTM networks in that algorithm. Also the different attributes of LSTMs are also present in the trainer_config.yaml file, which is used for training the PPO agent. We will explore LSTM networks in more depth in the next chapter when we study adversarial memory-based networks.

Simplified Hyperparameter Tuning For Optimization

Optimization is an important aspect when it comes to deep RL. In all the sections we have focused in this chapter, we see that there are a lot of hyperparameters that govern the on/off policy as well as model-free algorithms, including neural network architectures. We will be considering the PPO configurations inside ML Agents that is present in the trainer_config.yaml file. For SAC-based configurations, most of the parameters remain the same, with certain exceptions. Some of the common hyperparameters include the following.

- **Trainer:** SAC- or PPO-based on the policies required

- **Summary Freq:** This controls the frequency of the summary of training. This can also be viewed using TensorBoard.

- **Batch size:** This controls the batch size for training. This should be multiple times smaller than the buffer size. Typically for PPO (continuous), it should be between 512 and 5120, whereas for SAC (continuous), it should be between 128 and 1024. For discrete variants, it should be 32 to 512.

- **Buffer size:** This controls the number of observations/actions/states for each policy. It should be typically larger than the batch size. In PPO this is around 2048 to 409600, and for SAC it should be around 5000 to 1000000.

- **Hidden units:** The number of hidden units in a fully connected neural network architecture. Typically, it should be around 32 to 512.

- **Learning rate:** The learning rate for gradient descent algorithm. This typically should be within 1e-5 to 1e-3 (0.00001 to 0.001).

- **Learning rate schedule:** This controls the variation of the learning rate that we looked at in the Models.py script. It can be linear or constant. For PPO, a linear decaying policy is applied on the learning rate, while for SAC it is kept constant.

- **Max steps:** The maximum steps required for the algorithm; this should be within 5e5 and 1e7.

- **Normalize:** This controls normalization on the vector observations using the running mean and variance.

- **Num layer:** Controls how many hidden layers are present after the observation layer. Typically should be between 1 and 3 (CNN).

- **Time horizon:** The number of experiences of observations, states, and actions collected before it was saved in the replay buffer.

- **Vis encoder type:** This controls the type of encoders for visual observations. As we saw in the previous sections, it can be either "cnn_natural," "resnet," and its variants.

- **Init_path:** This controls the path to a trainer used previously for training. A past behavioral neural network model that was previously used is signified with this parameter.

- **Threaded:** This controls whether the model can update its weights when the environment is being stepped. It is recommended to keep it to False when policy training algorithms like PPO are used.

Hyperparameters for PPO

These are certain hyperparameters that are important in the context of PPO in addition to the standard training parameters.

- **Beta:** This controls the strength of the entropy regularization so that the agent can explore spaces during training. This typically has a value between 1e-4 and 1e-2.

- **Epsilon:** This controls how swiftly the policy can diverge from an older policy. A smaller value has stable updates on the policy. This typically has a value between 0.1 and 0.3.

- **Lambd:** The regularization factor that is used in calculating GAE. Typically a low value resembles using the current advantage value and a high value signifies using the actual advantages received from the environment (high variance). This typically has a value between 0.9 and 0.95.

- **Num_epoch:** The number of passes to be made through the buffer before gradient descent step is applied. Decreasing this will lead to slower and stable updates. This typically has a value between 3 and 10.

Analyzing Hyperparameters through TensorBoard Training

We will look into a Unity environment called Tiny Agent, which is a cart racing environment. While we will explore this in the next chapter, it is important to show the tradeoff made in training when different sets of hyperparameters are applied. For training this particular environment, we have used the default set of hyperparameters that is present for PPO.

```
default:
  trainer: ppo
  batch_size: 1024
  beta: 5.0e-3
```

```
buffer_size: 10240
epsilon: 0.2
hidden_units: 128
lambd: 0.95
learning_rate: 3.0e-4
learning_rate_schedule: linear
max_steps: 5.0e5
memory_size: 128
normalize: false
num_epoch: 3
num_layers: 2
time_horizon: 64
sequence_length: 64
summary_freq: 100
use_recurrent: false
vis_encode_type: simple
reward_signals:
  extrinsic:
    strength: 1.0
    gamma: 0.99
```

And for the sake of training and understanding, we modify the values of certain hyperparameters such as gamma, batch_size, learning rate, and hidden units. While it is generally recommended to follow the guidelines as mentioned in this section for the hyperparameters, it has been observed that a compatible value range of 256 to 512 as the hidden units with a batch size of 1024 provides a suitable learning curve with stable updates and proper convergence. In this case, we will analyze the plot in TensorBoard made using different training instances of the Tiny Agent, as shown in Figure 5-40.

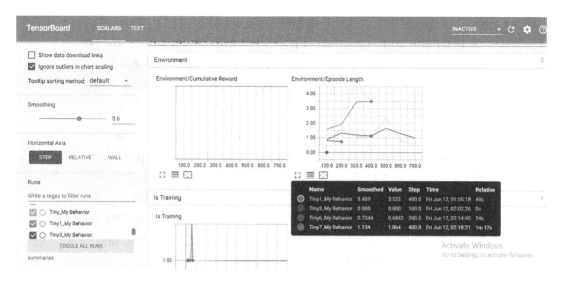

Figure 5-40. Hyperparameter tuning in Tiny Agent

While we can play with the hyperparameters accordingly and visualize the training in Tensorboard, it is important to mention that change in policies from "mlp" to "cnn" to other networks ("mlplstm") also plays a significant role in the training process. We can visualize this effect when we train the GridWorld environment using both CNN and dense neural networks. In the default hyperparameters for PPO, we can change the "use_recurrent" value to True, and then it will become a LSTM form of PPO policy training.

Summary

We have reached the end of this chapter that revolved around complex and fundamental concepts. To summarize:

- We understood the fundamentals of neural network architectures from dense to convolution networks. We also learned how to write custom neural network models using Keras and Tensorflow.

- We explored the different variations of the convolution-2D neural networks and its associated components such as activations, relation between kernels, strides, padding, and different associated layers such as MaxPooling. We also learned about Resnet and VGG-16 as the traditional state-of-the-art model.

- We then studied in depth about deep RL algorithms. We understood the two paradigms–on- and off-policy learning. In on-policy, we saw the contrast between Q-learning and SARSA in the traditional RL space. Then we ventured in depth into the different on policy deep RL algorithms.

- We studied policy gradients and built corresponding agents using OpenAI Gym environments. Then we studied actor critic paradigms of learning, which includes advantage actor critic (A2C) and asynchronous advantage actor critic (A3C) and built agents using those policies using Baselines as well as using custom code. Then we studied actor critic Kronecker factor trust region (ACKTR) and stochastic actor critic algorithms.

- We learned about the PPO algorithm and its derivation from trust region policy optimization (TRPO) including writing custom neural network models and using the Baselines. We learned the importance of clipping in PPO to stabilize the training.

- After that, we learned about off-policy algorithms, which exclusively covers deep Q-networks (DQN) and its variants such as dueling DQN and double DQN. We also analyzed the importance of these algorithms using sampling of past states from the buffer. Then we explored off-policy actor critic such as ACER.

- Then we studied soft actor critic (SAC), where we introduced entropy regularization as a means to stabilize off-policy algorithms.

- We briefly learned about one model-free RL algorithm that relies on behavioral cloning and general adversarial networks called GAIL and saw how it imitates a different policy (such as SAC) by using a generator and a discriminator.

- We then created a PPO agent for Puppo that used joint articulation and vectorized direction of motion and angular force to move the agent. We then trained it using the default parameters for PPO learning and visualized them using TensorBoard.

- We then learned about the Python API and its interaction with the Unity environment. We also converted the Unity environment to an equivalent Gym environment and trained it using Baselines algorithms–DQN and PPO.

- Then we learned about some of the most important scripts present in ML Agents (the Model Overrider script and Models.py script) and the trainers and optimizers Python file inside the PPO policy and understood how Unity internally implements the neural networks as well as the PPO policy.

- Then we understood LSTM networks in memory-based training and briefly saw the importance of this version of RNNs in training ML Agents on certain policies.

- In the last section of the chapter, we studied extensively about hyperparameters optimization in Unity ML Agents. We learned the default and standard values with respect to certain hyperparameters that are generic for SAC and PPO. Then we exclusively saw some characteristic hyperparameters for PPO. Lastly we trained a Unity environment named Tiny Agent (which we will discuss in the next chapter) with different sets of hyperparameters and observed it using TensorBoard.

That conclusively summarizes this entire chapter, which had a lot of core concepts. In the next chapter we will be looking into a few complex algorithms, curriculum learning, and adversarial agents and will be building a cart game.

CHAPTER 6

Competitive Networks for AI Agents

In the last chapter, we studied the different parts of deep reinforcement learning (RL) and also studied the interactivity of the Python API to build custom models. Since there are various paradigms inside RL, we will be exploring adversarial and cooperative learning in addition to curriculum learning. Since we have an idea of the actor critic class of algorithms, including proximal policy operation (PPO), we will also look into an off-policy counterpart that we mentioned in the last chapter: deep deterministic policy gradient (DDPG). The important aspects in this chapter include understanding the significant improvement in training when curriculum learning is applied along with a policy gradient variant. This allows the agent to learn in incremental steps when placed in a new dynamic environment. In this section, we will be exploring more samples of machine learning (ML) agents to get an overview of adversarial self-play, where an agent has to compete with an adversary to gain rewards. After covering the fundamental topics, we will also be looking at certain simulations using ML Agents, including the Kart game (which we mentioned in the previous chapter). Let us begin with curriculum learning, and then we will explore competitive networks.

Curriculum Learning

Curriculum learning is an approach that involves increasing the complexity of the learning environment gradually. In practical cases, the agent gets scalar rewards after achieving its goal, and in complex environments it may be difficult for the agent to accomplish that task. This method provides incremental rewards at each step to stabilize the learning of the agent. This can be thought of as an agent that is getting trained with an increasing level of difficulty at each step. The two major policies that are considered in curriculum learning include:

449

A. Majumder, *Deep Reinforcement Learning in Unity*, https://doi.org/10.1007/978-1-4842-6503-1_6

- Designing a metric to quantify the difficulty of a task for sorting tasks accordingly

- Providing a sequence of tasks with increasing levels of difficulty to the agent during training and increased stabilization

There are several variants of curriculum learning that are dependent on different policies. Some of the variants of include:

- **Task-specific curriculum learning:** This involves gradually increasing the complexity of the tasks to be performed by the agent. Some of the generalizations arising out of this form of learning include:

  - cleaner examples that lead to better generalization

  - introducing more difficult examples gradually to speed up training

If we are using an incremental increase of level complexity as our main metric, there is a requirement to quantify the difficulty (complexity) of the level. This can be resolved by using a minimal loss deep network with respect to another network while the former is getting trained. This allows the agent to learn sequentially using an improving network as the complexity of the level increases. In this section, we will be exploring this category of curriculum learning with PPO policy using ML Agents. Task-specific curriculum learning uses procedural content generation, which is used to randomize a particular level or environment in a game. We can get an idea of this when we study about PCG in the Obstacle Tower Challenge in the next chapter, as we will understand how the levels use curriculum learning to increase the complexity of the environment. We can also modify some features from the previous lessons on different deep RL algorithms to make it task-specific or reward-specific curriculum learning. Since we were using the OpenAI Gym environments such as CartPole and MountainCar for our implementations, we are unable to modify the inherent environments. However, we can increase or decrease the rewards after each step of training. This has an indirect effect of modifying the gradient convergence of the deep networks. In case of decreasing the rewards successively at each step of training, we apply the agent to a harsh condition where the rewards effectively decrease; as a result, the gradient ascent step in policy gradient algorithms such as A2C will decrease. The opposite will be the case when the rewards are increased at each step, which signifies an incremental curriculum learning approach. In the PPO-A2C

Curriculum Reward Specific.ipynb Notebook, we can see the contrast in the rewards for each iteration of training for the two cases; in the first case, we have the original implementation of the algorithm, whereas in the second case, we have an incremental reward strategy where the reward gets doubled after each successive iteration. The change is in the "agent.run" method, where in place of directly assigning the rewards to the next step, we multiply the rewards by two and then pass it on.

```
action, prob=agent.act(state)
state_1, reward, done,_=env.step(action)
reward*=2
score+=reward
agent.memory(state, action, prob, reward)
state=state_1
```

Alternatively the "discount_reward" method can also be changed to define the rewards for the next steps by providing an incremental discount. The outcome can be visualized with the help of Tensorboard training as well. The contrast in the rewards can be observed as shown in Figure 6-1.

```
1/1 [==============================] - 0s 2ms/step - loss: -9.2103e-07
Episode: 997 - Score: 10.000000.
1/1 [==============================] - 0s 2ms/step - loss: -9.2103e-07
Episode: 998 - Score: 10.000000.
1/1 [==============================] - 0s 2ms/step - loss: -9.2103e-07
Episode: 999 - Score: 10.000000.
1/1 [==============================] - 0s 2ms/step - loss: -9.2103e-07
Episode: 1000 - Score: 9.000000.
1/1 [==============================] - 0s 2ms/step - loss: -9.2103e-07
Episode: 1001 - Score: 8.000000.
1/1 [==============================] - 0s 2ms/step - loss: -9.2103e-07
Episode: 1002 - Score: 10.000000.
1/1 [==============================] - 0s 2ms/step - loss: -9.2103e-07
```

Figure 6-1. *Rewards with original PPO-A2C on CartPole environment*

The second case shows the increase in rewards, which also implies an increase in the gradient ascent of the policy functions, as shown in Figure 6-2.

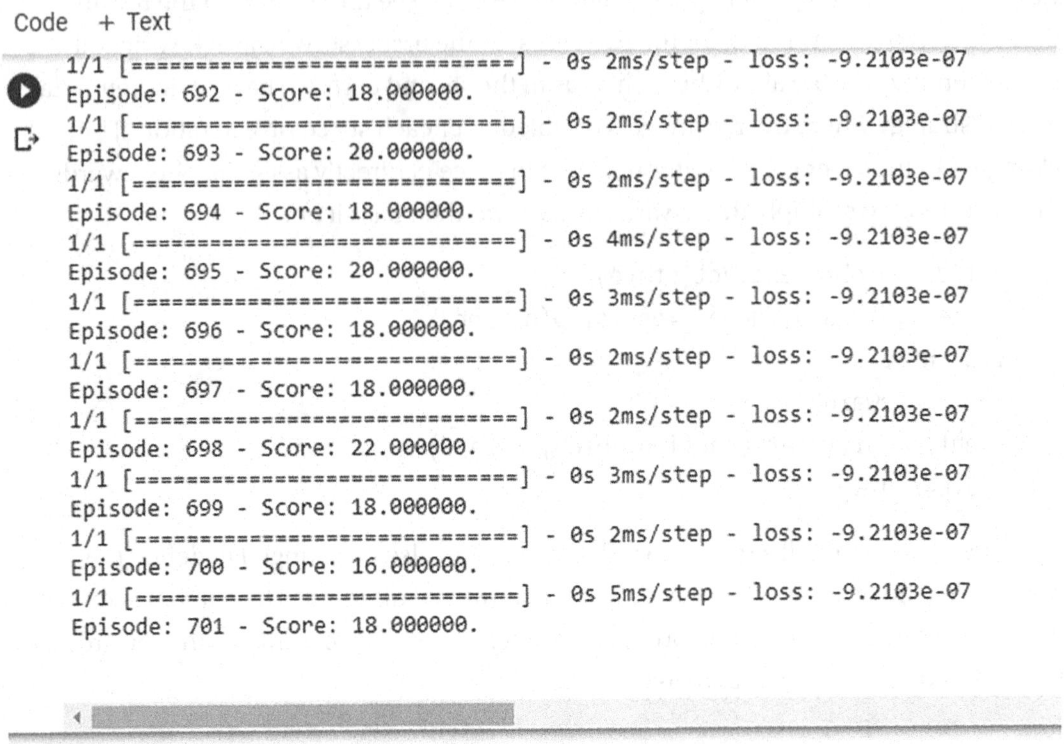

Code   + Text

```
1/1 [==============================] - 0s 2ms/step - loss: -9.2103e-07
Episode: 692 - Score: 18.000000.
1/1 [==============================] - 0s 2ms/step - loss: -9.2103e-07
Episode: 693 - Score: 20.000000.
1/1 [==============================] - 0s 2ms/step - loss: -9.2103e-07
Episode: 694 - Score: 18.000000.
1/1 [==============================] - 0s 4ms/step - loss: -9.2103e-07
Episode: 695 - Score: 20.000000.
1/1 [==============================] - 0s 3ms/step - loss: -9.2103e-07
Episode: 696 - Score: 18.000000.
1/1 [==============================] - 0s 2ms/step - loss: -9.2103e-07
Episode: 697 - Score: 18.000000.
1/1 [==============================] - 0s 2ms/step - loss: -9.2103e-07
Episode: 698 - Score: 22.000000.
1/1 [==============================] - 0s 3ms/step - loss: -9.2103e-07
Episode: 699 - Score: 18.000000.
1/1 [==============================] - 0s 2ms/step - loss: -9.2103e-07
Episode: 700 - Score: 16.000000.
1/1 [==============================] - 0s 5ms/step - loss: -9.2103e-07
Episode: 701 - Score: 18.000000.
```

Figure 6-2. *Rewards with reward-based curriculum on PPO-A2C on CartPole*

Now for a better effect the hyperparameters inside the loss function ("trpo_ppo_penalty_loss") can also be changed. A gradual increment or decrement in the hyperparameters can affect the learning of the agent, which is analogous to increasing or decreasing the difficulty of the tasks. By changing the hyperparameter "prob" in the "trpo_ppo_penalty_loss," we can visualize the change in the epoch loss through Tensorboard, as shown in Figure 6-3.

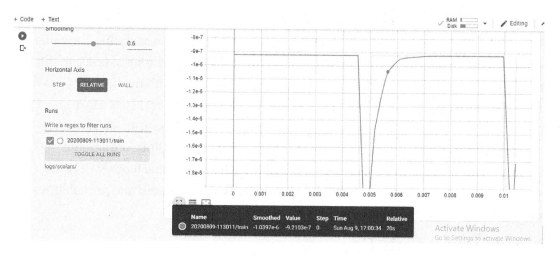

Figure 6-3. *Changing the epoch loss by gradually changing the hyperparameters*

- **Teacher student curriculum learning:**

  - In this context, the agent learns through an N-task curriculum and an adaptive policy. The concept of this form of curriculum learning involves two strategies:

  - The loss function changes before and after every iteration of learning, and this helps the agent to optimize the rewards for each level. In this case, the change in loss functions triggers a change in the reward signals, which also changes the gradient ascent for a particular policy.

  - In case of policy gradient algorithms such as PPO, the KL divergence between two networks—the teacher and the student networks—helps the agent to learn in the direction of increasing difficulty. The model complexity increases when it modestly generalizes the training samples and stabilizes the networks to allow the agent to learn.

In this form of curriculum learning, the teacher network provides a policy for the student network to learn. The student can then learn complex tasks by following the policy of the teacher. Generally this leads to a faster learning, but owing to consistent changes in the loss function, the student may forget the previous training. To simplify, both the teacher and student are deep learning networks where the task of the teacher network is to propose a set of complex activities that the student network can perform.

There are discrete and continuous space variants of this form of curriculum learning. The teacher network can also use Epsilon-Greedy and Thompson sampling and other exploration-exploitation algorithms to increase the difficulty of the set of tasks. In this case, we will study about teacher student curriculum learning with the help of "PPO-A2C Teacher Student Curriculum Learning.ipynb" Notebook. We will use the original A2C algorithm, which will be our student network, and we will have an alternate A2C algorithm with changing loss functions as the teacher network. Since the student network is the same as in the previous chapter, we will focus on the teacher network. For this, we have separate arrays for retaining the rewards, labels, states, and probabilities for the teacher network, as mentioned here.

```
self.teacher_labels=[]
self.teacher_states=[]
self.teacher_rewards=[]
self.teacher_prob=[]
self.Teacher_Actor=self.build_teacher_actor_model(True)
self.Teacher_Critic=self.build_teacher_critic_model()
```

In the next section we will look into the "build_teacher_actor_model" method, which is similar to the "build_actor_model" (student network). The difference in this case is that we pass a Boolean value in the arguments for alternating between two different loss functions: the clipped PPO loss and the KL divergence PPO loss. We also changed some of the hyperparameter values in this method—namely, the epsilon, prob, and clip_loss values. The rest of the code segment is similar to the previously written PPO algorithm. The requirement for changing the loss function is to optimize the reward signals, and this is mentioned as follows:

```
def build_teacher_actor_model(self, loss_fn):
    logdir= "logs/scalars/" + datetime.now().
    strftime("%Y%m%d-%H%M%S")
    tensorboard_callback=keras.callbacks.
    TensorBoard(log_dir=logdir)

    Actor=Sequential()
    Actor.add(Dense(64, input_dim=self.state_size,
    activation='relu', kernel_initializer='glorot_uniform'))
    Actor.add(Dense(64, activation='relu', kernel_initializer
```

```
='glorot_uniform'))
Actor.add(Dense(self.action_size, activation='softmax'))
def trpo_ppo_clip_loss(y_true, y_pred):
  entropy=2e-4
  clip_loss=0.3
  old_log= k.sum(y_true)
  print(old_log)
  pred_log=k.sum(y_pred)
  print(pred_log)
  r=pred_log/(old_log + 1e-8)
  advantage=pred_log-old_log
  p1=r*advantage
  p2=k.clip(r, min_value=
  1-clip_loss, max_value=1+clip_loss)*advantage
  prob=1e-3
  loss=-k.mean(k.minimum(p1, p2) +
  entropy*(-(prob*k.log(prob+1e-9))))
  return loss

def trpo_ppo_penalty_loss(y_true, y_pred):
  entropy=2e-4
  clip_loss=0.3
  old_log= k.sum(y_true)
  print(old_log)
  pred_log=k.sum(y_pred)
  print(pred_log)
  r=pred_log/(old_log + 1e-8)
  kl_divergence= k.sum(old_log* k.log(old_log/pred_log))
  advantage=kl_divergence
  p1=r*advantage
  p2=k.clip(r, min_value=
  1-clip_loss, max_value=1+clip_loss)*advantage
  prob=1e-3
  loss=-k.mean(k.minimum(p1, p2) +
  entropy*(-(prob*k.log(prob+1e-9))))
  return loss
```

```
if loss_fn==True:
  Actor.compile(optimizer=Adam
  (learning_rate=self.learning_rate),
  loss=trpo_ppo_penalty_loss)
  loss_fn=False
else:
  Actor.compile(optimizer=Adam
  (learning_rate=self.learning_rate),
  loss=trpo_ppo_clip_loss)
  loss_fn=True
return Actor
```

The "teacher_memory" method is used for one hot-encoding the actions as well as storing the rewards, labels, and probabilities, similarly to the "memory" method in A2C. The "teacher_act" method is for selecting the actions with the highest probabilities, similarly to the "act" method in original A2C. We have similar methods as the A2C code (student network) in the teacher network, as we see the methods are prefixed with "teacher_<method name>." In the main method, after we initialize the states, actions, and rewards for the student and the teacher networks, we train them separately. In case the rewards from the teacher network exceed the student network, it assigns the rewards and trains it in the new policy. The alternating policy at each stage of training also optimizes the rewards signal. In the normal A2C algorithm without teacher network supervision, the Tensorboard plot shows the epoch loss (error reduction in the value estimates denoted by the red segment) and the rewards (blue segment), as shown in Figure 6-4.

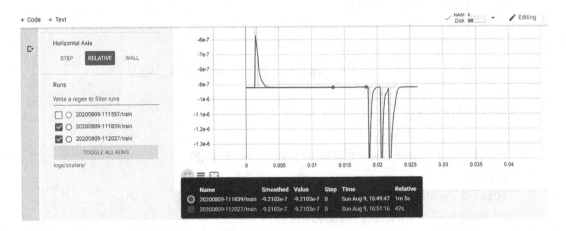

Figure 6-4. *Original PPO-A2C without teacher student curriculum learning*

With the teacher network in place, we can see the rewards getting spiked due to change in the gradient ascent as well as in the policy. The rewards for this case can be represented by the orange segment, as shown in Figure 6-5.

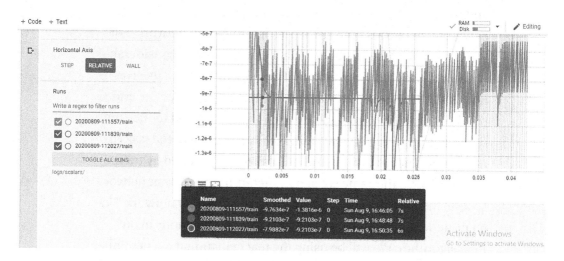

Figure 6-5. *PPO-A2C with teacher student curriculum learning*

- **Curriculum learning through self-play:** In this case, agents learn through self-play, which uses a similar teacher student type to curriculum learning, with certain changes. The difference from the teacher student framework is that here an adversarial approach is used for training the agent. We have two different networks. The task of the first network is to retrieve rewards from the environment by attaining a state S_1 from S_0 and set the initial benchmarks for attaining that reward. The second network has to reach the state S_1 in a shorter time span and retrieve the same rewards. Hence the two networks are in an adversarial positioning with respect to each other; the first network has to cover the maximum rewards and set a proper benchmark, while the second network has to attain that in a smaller time span as compared to the first one. In this case, we have two different methods that take place for the second network.

  - In self-play mode, the first network alters state from S_0 to S_1 and then the second network has the task to reset the environment back to initial state S_0

- In target task mode, the second network receives a reward signal if it reaches the particular new state in a shorter time span.

Let us represent the first network as the teacher in this case and the second network as the student. The task of the teacher network is to increase the efficiency of the student network. For this the teacher tries to choose a task that will take a considerable time for the student to complete. The student network receives rewards when it completes the task faster than the teacher, and as the difficulty of the task increases, the teacher should reduce the difference between the timestamps of completion of the tasks to enable the student to learn. In self-play this is attained by training a network with the same set of parameters as the current network so as to increase the efficiency of training of the first network. Now let us understand this concept with a few modifications in our PPO algorithm. We will be using the teacher student curriculum learning code segment as our base and will only modify the "main" method. Open the "PPO-A2C Self Play Curriculum Learning.ipynb" Notebook. In the "main" method, we have a list of rewards that will be provided for three time-steps denoted by the "reward_level" array.

```
reward_level=[800.0,900.0,1000.0]
```

We then run through this array and grant the teacher network its rewards on completing a new task. The student network then has a task to complete the activity in a shorter timespan, which is controlled by the "min_time" variable. Once the student completes the tasks the teacher rewards, the student network for that particular level and the process continues. We can see a sharp contrast in the values of the student and the teacher rewards. If the difference is too high, this implies the student network is unable to get sufficient rewards or perform faster than the teacher network. Although the cumulative rewards of this system increase, there is a sufficient margin between the two networks. This can be addressed by changing the hyperparameters as well as defining

alternate loss functions that would penalize the teacher network
in case the difference between the rewards goes above a certain
threshold. This is implemented by the following lines:

```
if teacher_score>reward_level[1]:
        teacher_score=reward_level[1]
    #Train the Student to get that score in minimum time
        counter+=1
        if(counter<min_time):
        min_time=counter
    if(teacher_score<score):
        agent.rewards[-1]=teacher_score
```

The Tensorboard visualization of the epoch loss for this form of curriculum
learning is provided in Figure 6-6.

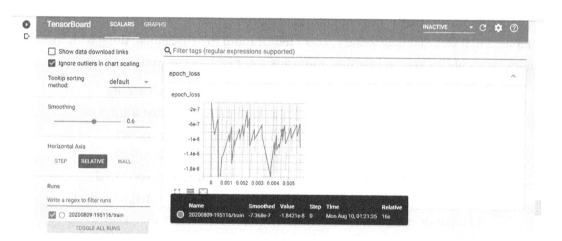

Figure 6-6. *PPO-A2C with self-play curriculum learning*

Now if we compare this (orange segment) with the epoch loss for
teacher student curriculum learning (blue segment), we will see that
the latter has a lower loss gradient as compared to self-play, whereas the
rewards are more for self-play. This is due to the adversarial nature of the
teacher and student networks in self-play, which leads to more rewards
in this case. This also implies a faster convergence than ordinary teacher
student curriculum learning. In the initial stages, the self-play has a
more deep loss gradient owing to the student network not being able to
compete with the teacher, but that decreases as the levels increase.
This is demonstrated by the Tensorboard plot, as shown in Figure 6-7.

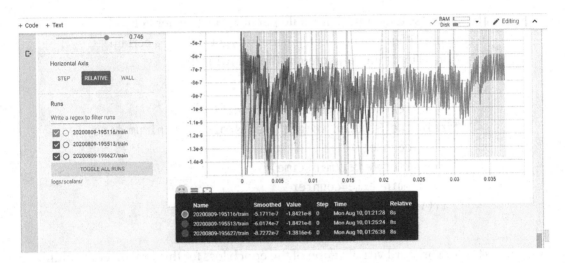

Figure 6-7. *Epoch loss comparison between teacher student and self-play (CL)*

Adversarial self-play is the major form of learning that we will see in detail in this chapter when we will analyze the soccer environment in ML Agents. Along with these major forms of curriculum learning, there are other variants as well.

- **Automatic Goal Generation:** This form of curriculum learning relies on generated goals and chooses a feasible goal that the agent can solve with the current policy. This is an interesting aspect of curriculum learning, as the goals are generated randomly for the agent to achieve. This is achieved with the help of adversarial networks or GAN, which we studied in the last chapter in the context of the model-free GAIL algorithm. Since we are aware that a GAN has a generator and a discriminator that are in competition against each other, we can use this concept to train the agent. The objective of the generator is to produce intermediate goals that the agent has to achieve. These are referred to as "GOID," which implies goals of intermediate difficulty. The generator network then has to be trained to produce such intermediate goals and has associated minimum and maximum values, denoted by R_{min} and R_{max}, respectively, which controls the maximum and minimum probability of attaining the goal by the agent during T time-steps. The role of the discriminator is to determine whether the goal can be achieved by the agent during the time slot provided and also to verify whether the goal is from the GOID set. The policy gradient function can be used in this case as :

$$\pi^* (a_t|s_t, g) = \arg \max_\pi E[R^g(\pi)],$$

where $R^g(\pi)$ is the success probability of reaching the goal g and a and s are actions and states, respectively. This principle of learning using GANs is called goal GAN. The generator and the discriminator functions for goal GAN curriculum learning can be defined as follows:

$$L_{GoalGAN}(G) = (\tfrac{1}{2}) E_z[(D(G(Z)) - c)^2]$$

$$L_{GoalGAN}(D) = (\tfrac{1}{2}) E_g[(D(g) - b)^2 + (1 - y_g) (D(g) - a)^2] + (\tfrac{1}{2}) E_z[(D(G(Z)) - a)^2],$$

where a is the label for fake data, b is the label for real data, and c is the value that generator G wants discriminator D to believe for fake data. y_g is a Boolean variable that signifies whether the goal is real (1) or not (0). There are three main components in this form of curriculum learning, which include:

- policy solver: The policy solver gets a goal g and receives a reward signal $R^g(\pi)$ when the goal is attained.

- discriminator D: This predicts whether the goal is attainable by the agent and generally uses a classification model.

- generator G: The generator is responsible for generating goals g within a feasible score limit.

This form of curriculum learning that uses GANs as the internal architecture is used for systematic training of the agent with increasing difficulty level. This is illustrated in Figure 6-8.

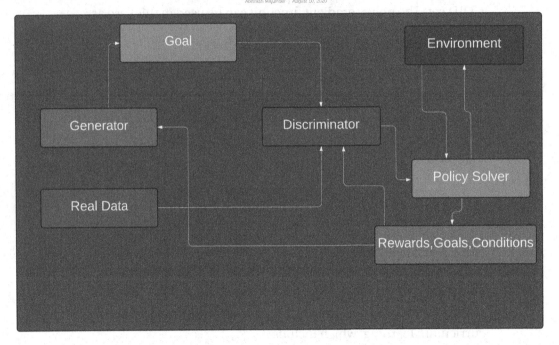

Figure 6-8. *Goal GAN for automatic goal generation curriculum learning*

We will be using the "AGG.ipynb" to determine the effects of goal GAN in curriculum learning with the help of a custom generator and discriminator model. The "build_generator_model" method is responsible for creating the generator network, and the "build_discriminator_model" is responsible for creating the discriminator network. We will look into the generator model, which is almost similar to the critic model with the change in the kernel size and kernel initializer.

```
def build_generator_model(self):

    logdir= "logs/scalars/" + datetime.now()
    .strftime("%Y%m%d-%H%M%S")
    tensorboard_callback=keras.callbacks.
    TensorBoard(log_dir=logdir)

    generator=Sequential()
    generator.add(Dense(128, input_dim=self.state_size,
    activation='relu', kernel_initializer='he_uniform'))
    generator.add(Dense(64, activation='relu',
```

```
    kernel_initializer='he_uniform'))
generator.add(Dense(self.action_size,
    activation='softmax'))
generator.compile(optimizer=Adam(learning_rate=
self.learning_rate), loss='categorical_crossentropy')
return generator
```

The discriminator network has an additional "LeakyReLU" with the normal dense neural network model architecture. This assists the network to segregate between original goals (rewards) and fake goals (rewards). This is denoted by the following lines:

```
def build_discriminator_model(self):

    logdir= "logs/scalars/" + datetime.now()
    .strftime("%Y%m%d-%H%M%S")
    tensorboard_callback=keras.callbacks.
    TensorBoard(log_dir=logdir)

    discriminator=Sequential()
    discriminator.add(Dense(128, input_dim=self.state_size,
    activation='relu', kernel_initializer='he_uniform'))
    discriminator.add(Dense(64, activation='relu',
    kernel_initializer='he_uniform'))
    discriminator.add(keras.layers.LeakyReLU(alpha=0.1))
    discriminator.add(Dense(self.action_size,
    activation='softmax'))
    discriminator.compile(optimizer=Adam(learning_rate=
    self.learning_rate), loss='categorical_crossentropy')
    return discriminator
```

The next segment is the "train" method, where we use five samples from the original states and labels for the generator network to generate fake samples. Then we train the generator with these samples. Similarly we train the entire states and labels with the discriminator model. The actor critic model is also present, which is the policy solver in our case. This is done by the following lines:

```
labels=np.vstack(self.labels)
rewards=np.vstack(self.rewards)
rewards=self.discount_rewards(rewards)
```

```
rewards=(rewards-np.mean(rewards))/np.std(rewards)
labels*=-rewards
x=np.squeeze(np.vstack([self.states]))
y=np.squeeze(np.vstack([self.labels]))
#tensorboard.set_model(self.Actor)
#Assign a small part of the input to the generator
print("Generator Sampling")
x_g, y_g=np.squeeze(np.vstack([self.states[:5]]))
,np.squeeze(np.vstack
([self.labels[:5]]))
self.generator.fit(x_g, y_g, callbacks=
[tensorboard_callback])
#Train Discriminator network
print("Discriminator Sampling")
self.discriminator.fit(x, y, callbacks
=[tensorboard_callback])
#Solver Network training
print("A2C-PPO policy solver")
self.Actor.fit(x, y, callbacks=[tensorboard_callback])

self.Critic.train_on_batch(x, y)
self.states, self.probs, self.labels, self.rewards=[],
[],[],[]
```

If we train this GAN on the PPO-A2C policy, then we clearly visualize the rewards that are generated by the generator and the discriminator along with the epoch loss of the policy solver (agent). This is shown in Figure 6-9.

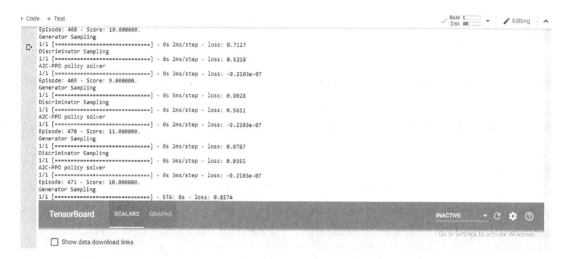

Figure 6-9. *Scores and epoch loss of goal GAN curriculum learning*

Now we have covered the details of the different aspects of curriculum learning, there are some other methods such as skilled-based curriculum learning and curriculum learning through distillation.

- **Skilled-based curriculum learning:** This relies on analyzing different tasks simultaneously to determine which tasks provide a better reward signal. This is done with the help of expectation maximization or variation EM method and helps the agent to learn in an unsupervised manner. This is also related to meta RL, where the agent tries to figure a proper policy to get the best rewards.

- **Curriculum learning through distillation:** This involves using transfer learning to generate different skills and to prevent catastrophic forgetting. Progressive neural networks and long short-term memory (LSTM)-based memory networks play an important role in training the agent to learn with the help of transfer learning methods.

Curriculum Learning in ML Agents

We will consider curriculum learning in ML agents with the help of the Wall Jump Unity Scene in Unity. The target of the blue agent in this case, is to reach the green target area by crossing a wall. This wall can be scaled with the help of the yellow block, which acts as a platform on which the agent can jump to reach the target on the other side of the wall. Based on the height of the wall, the agent has to move the yellow block so as to scale the wall. If originally the agent was trained in an environment having a big wall, it would have taken a larger time for the agent to figure out by using PPO or SAC algorithm. Hence, the concept of curriculum learning plays an important role here. The height of the wall is initially 0 and then it gradually increases, and this gives the agent an idea where the original green target is placed. Thus for successive iterations of training, as the height of the wall increases, the agent has to use the yellow platform to cross it. In the initial stages there is no wall present, and in this case the agent has to jump over the yellow platform to reach the target; as the level increases, the height of the wall increases systematically. This increases the cumulative reward for each successive level. The comparison between two levels of training is shown in Figure 6-10(a, b).

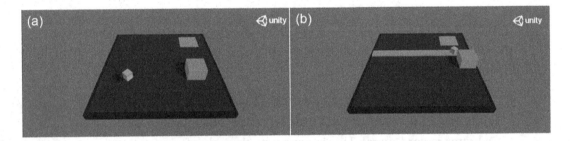

Figure 6-10. *(a & b). Changing the wall height to simulate curriculum learning*

Let us first understand the Wall Jump environment through the scripts, and then we will be training this environment through curriculum learning. For this we will look into the WallJumpAgent C# script that controls the agent's movements. Along with this script, there are also Behavior Parameters, Model Overrider, and Decision Requester scripts attached to the agent as in our previous cases. The blue agent also uses RayPerceptionSensorComponent3D for collecting observations. In the first section, there are three different types of neural network brains that are used for inference: noWallBrain, smallWallBrain, and bigWallBrain. Each of these is separately used depending on the height of the wall for curriculum learning. Then there are variables that control the agent, the ground material, and the properties of jumping—height, time, start position, and end position. The variables also control the spawn area, the bounds of spawn area, colliders, target area, and the yellow platform.

```
int m_Configuration;
public NNModel noWallBrain;
public NNModel smallWallBrain;
public NNModel bigWallBrain;

public GameObject ground;
public GameObject spawnArea;
Bounds m_SpawnAreaBounds;

public GameObject goal;
public GameObject shortBlock;
public GameObject wall;
Rigidbody m_ShortBlockRb;
Rigidbody m_AgentRb;
Material m_GroundMaterial;
Renderer m_GroundRenderer;
WallJumpSettings m_WallJumpSettings;

public float jumpingTime;
public float jumpTime;

 public float fallingForce;
public Collider[] hitGroundColliders = new Collider[3];
Vector3 m_JumpTargetPos;
Vector3 m_JumpStartingPos;

EnvironmentParameters m_ResetParams;
```

The "Initialize" method is used for initializing the variables that were declared in the previous step. This method is the overridden method that was used in our previous samples as well.

```
m_WallJumpSettings
= FindObjectOfType<WallJumpSettings>();
m_Configuration = Random.Range(0, 5);

m_AgentRb = GetComponent<Rigidbody>();
m_ShortBlockRb = shortBlock.GetComponent<Rigidbody>();
m_SpawnAreaBounds
```

```
    = spawnArea.GetComponent<Collider>().bounds;
    m_GroundRenderer = ground.GetComponent<Renderer>();
    m_GroundMaterial = m_GroundRenderer.material;

    spawnArea.SetActive(false);

    m_ResetParams
    = Academy.Instance.EnvironmentParameters;
```

Then we have the "Jump" method, which is used to trigger jumps with a frequency value denoted by the jumpingTime float variable. This also allows the blue agent to jump from its current position.

```
public void Jump()
{
    jumpingTime = 0.2f;
    m_JumpStartingPos = m_AgentRb.position;
}
```

The "DoGroundCheck" method is used for evaluating the current position of the agent depending on whether it is grounded or not. It does this with the help of colliders. The "Physics.OverlapBoxNonAlloc" method is used for storing the colliders within a given box. This method is controlled by the Boolean variable smallCheck, and depending on this value, it determines whether the agent's colliders are colliding with the platform, wall, and the ground. This provides the agent information related to the current environment by checking against different tags for collision.

```
if (!smallCheck)
    {
        hitGroundColliders = new Collider[3];
        var o = gameObject;
        Physics.OverlapBoxNonAlloc(
            o.transform.position +
            new Vector3(0, -0.05f, 0),
            new Vector3(0.95f / 2f, 0.5f, 0.95f / 2f),
            hitGroundColliders,
            o.transform.rotation);
        var grounded = false;
```

```
        foreach (var col in hitGroundColliders)
        {
            if (col != null && col.transform !=
                transform &&
                  (col.CompareTag("walkableSurface") ||
                   col.CompareTag("block") ||
                   col.CompareTag("wall")))
            {
                grounded = true; //then we're grounded
                break;
            }
        }
        return grounded;
    }
    else
    {
        RaycastHit hit;
        Physics.Raycast(transform.position
        + new Vector3(0, -0.05f, 0), -Vector3.up, out hit,
            1f);

        if (hit.collider != null &&
            (hit.collider.CompareTag("walkableSurface") ||
             hit.collider.CompareTag("block") ||
             hit.collider.CompareTag("wall"))
            && hit.normal.y > 0.95f)
        {
            return true;
        }

        return false;
    }
```

The "MoveTowards" method is used for moving the agent in the direction of the target. This is done with the help of the "Vector3.MoveTowards" method, which controls the motion based on the agent's velocity and position.

```
void MoveTowards(
        Vector3 targetPos, Rigidbody rb,
        float targetVel, float maxVel)
    {
        var moveToPos = targetPos - rb.worldCenterOfMass;
        var velocityTarget = Time.fixedDeltaTime *
        targetVel * moveToPos;
        if (float.IsNaN(velocityTarget.x) == false)
        {
            rb.velocity = Vector3.MoveTowards(
                rb.velocity, velocityTarget, maxVel);
        }
    }
```

Then we have the overridden method "CollectObservations," similarly to our previous projects, which collects observations with the help of ray sensors. The sensors check for the distance between the agent and the target, as well as the distance from the ground, and use the DoGroundCheck to check for colliders in the environment.

```
public override void CollectObservations(VectorSensor sensor)
    {
        var agentPos = m_AgentRb.position
            - ground.transform.position;

        sensor.AddObservation(agentPos / 20f);
        sensor.AddObservation(DoGroundCheck(true) ? 1 : 0);
    }
```

The "GetRandomSpawnPos" is a method that is used by the agent and the yellow platform to spawn randomly anywhere within the bounds of the ground platform. This is done with the help of "Random.Range" method.

```
public Vector3 GetRandomSpawnPos()
    {
        var randomPosX = Random.
          Range(-m_SpawnAreaBounds.extents.x,
            m_SpawnAreaBounds.extents.x);
        var randomPosZ = Random.
```

```
        Range(-m_SpawnAreaBounds.extents.z,
          m_SpawnAreaBounds.extents.z);

    var randomSpawnPos = spawnArea.transform.position +
        new Vector3(randomPosX, 0.45f, randomPosZ);
    return randomSpawnPos;

}
```

The "Moveagent" method is used to control the motion of the agent by analyzing the vector observation space from the ray sensors. It uses the "DoGroundCheck" to validate the current location and colliders, and based on the observation array, the agent can move forward, upward, or right. The agent uses the "AddForce" method to trigger the jump in a particular direction.

```
public void MoveAgent(float[] act)
    {
        AddReward(-0.0005f);
        var smallGrounded = DoGroundCheck(true);
        var largeGrounded = DoGroundCheck(false);

        var dirToGo = Vector3.zero;
        var rotateDir = Vector3.zero;
        var dirToGoForwardAction = (int)act[0];
        var rotateDirAction = (int)act[1];
        var dirToGoSideAction = (int)act[2];
        var jumpAction = (int)act[3];

        if (dirToGoForwardAction == 1)
            dirToGo = (largeGrounded ? 1f : 0.5f)
            * 1f * transform.forward;
        else if (dirToGoForwardAction == 2)
            dirToGo = (largeGrounded ? 1f : 0.5f)
           * -1f * transform.forward;
        if (rotateDirAction == 1)
            rotateDir = transform.up * -1f;
        else if (rotateDirAction == 2)
            rotateDir = transform.up * 1f;
```

471

```
        if (dirToGoSideAction == 1)
            dirToGo = (largeGrounded ? 1f : 0.5f)
                  * -0.6f * transform.right;
        else if (dirToGoSideAction == 2)
            dirToGo = (largeGrounded ? 1f : 0.5f)
                  * 0.6f * transform.right;
        if (jumpAction == 1)
            if ((jumpingTime <= 0f) && smallGrounded)
            {
                Jump();
            }

    transform.Rotate(rotateDir,
     Time.fixedDeltaTime * 300f);
    m_AgentRb.AddForce(dirToGo
       * m_WallJumpSettings.agentRunSpeed,
         ForceMode.VelocityChange);

    if (jumpingTime > 0f)
    {
        m_JumpTargetPos =
            new Vector3(m_AgentRb.position.x,
                m_JumpStartingPos.
              y + m_WallJumpSettings.agentJumpHeight,
                m_AgentRb.position.z) + dirToGo;
        MoveTowards(m_JumpTargetPos,
          m_AgentRb, m_WallJumpSettings.agentJumpVelocity,
            m_WallJumpSettings.agentJumpVelocityMaxChange);
    }
    if (!(jumpingTime > 0f) && !largeGrounded)
    {
        m_AgentRb.AddForce(
            Vector3.down *
            fallingForce, ForceMode.Acceleration);
    }
    jumpingTime -= Time.fixedDeltaTime;
}
```

The "OnActionReceived" method is an overridden method that uses raycasts (ray sensors) to provide the observation space. It then uses the "SetReward" method to provide a negative reward every time the agent is not able to reach the target and also terminates that episode of training. It also signals the reward phase by triggering a change in the ground material.

```
public override void OnActionReceived(float[] vectorAction)
    {
        MoveAgent(vectorAction);
        if ((!Physics.Raycast
            (m_AgentRb.position, Vector3.down, 20))
            || (!Physics.Raycast(m_ShortBlockRb.
             position, Vector3.down, 20)))
        {
            SetReward(-1f);
            EndEpisode();
            ResetBlock(m_ShortBlockRb);
            StartCoroutine(
                GoalScoredSwapGroundMaterial
                (m_WallJumpSettings.failMaterial, .5f));
        }
    }
```

The "Heuristic" method is used for heuristic control of the agent. This relies on the heuristic brain and is used when no trained inference models or external brains are used.

```
public override void OnActionReceived(float[] vectorAction)
    {
        MoveAgent(vectorAction);
        if ((!Physics.Raycast
            (m_AgentRb.position, Vector3.down, 20))
            || (!Physics.Raycast(m_ShortBlockRb
                .position, Vector3.down, 20)))
        {
            SetReward(-1f);
            EndEpisode();
```

```
            ResetBlock(m_ShortBlockRb);
            StartCoroutine(
                GoalScoredSwapGroundMaterial
                (m_WallJumpSettings.failMaterial, .5f));
        }
    }
```

The "OnTriggerStay" method checks if the agent has reached the goal, and then it uses the "SetReward" method to provide a positive reward if the agent is successful. The agent does this by checking whether the collider has "goal" tag as mentioned in the code segment here:

```
void OnTriggerStay(Collider col)
    {
        if (col.gameObject.CompareTag("goal")
          && DoGroundCheck(true))
        {
            SetReward(1f);
            EndEpisode();
            StartCoroutine(
                GoalScoredSwapGroundMaterial
                (m_WallJumpSettings.goalScoredMaterial, 2));
        }
    }
```

The "ResetBlock" method is used for resetting the position of the yellow block in the scene at the start of every episode of training.

```
void ResetBlock(Rigidbody blockRb)
    {
        blockRb.transform.position = GetRandomSpawnPos();
        blockRb.velocity = Vector3.zero;
        blockRb.angularVelocity = Vector3.zero;
    }
```

The "OnEpisodeBegin" method is an overridden method that resets the agent's position, velocity, and direction using the "ResetBlock" method. The "FixedUpdate" method controls the actual game logic and calls the "ConfigureAgent" method as follows:

```
public override void OnEpisodeBegin()
    {
        ResetBlock(m_ShortBlockRb);
        transform.localPosition = new Vector3(
            18 * (Random.value - 0.5f), 1, -12);
        m_Configuration = Random.Range(0, 5);
        m_AgentRb.velocity = default(Vector3);
    }

    void FixedUpdate()
    {
        if (m_Configuration != -1)
        {
            ConfigureAgent(m_Configuration);
            m_Configuration = -1;
        }
    }
```

The "ConfigureAgent" method controls the inference neural networks to be used based on the height of the wall and is associated with the curriculum learning part. If the value of "config" is 0, it implies that there is no wall (wall with 0 height), and the agent uses noWallBrain brain for inference. This is by using the "SetModel" method. If the height of the wall is 1 unit, then the agent uses "smallWallBrain" as the inference brain. For wall height values greater than 1 unit, the agent uses bigWallBrain for inference. The agent computes the height of the wall with the help of localScale variable after receiving inputs from the ray sensors. This is shown by the following lines of code:

```
void ConfigureAgent(int config)
    {
        var localScale = wall.transform.localScale;
        if (config == 0)
        {
```

```
        localScale = new Vector3(
            localScale.x,
            m_ResetParams.GetWithDefault("no_wall_height", 0),
            localScale.z);
        wall.transform.localScale = localScale;
        SetModel("SmallWallJump", noWallBrain);
    }
    else if (config == 1)
    {
        localScale = new Vector3(
            localScale.x,
            m_ResetParams.GetWithDefault("small_wall_height", 4),
            localScale.z);
        wall.transform.localScale = localScale;
        SetModel("SmallWallJump", smallWallBrain);
    }
    else
    {
        var min = m_ResetParams.GetWithDefault("big_wall_min_height", 8);
        var max = m_ResetParams.GetWithDefault("big_wall_max_height", 8);
        var height = min + Random.value * (max - min);
        localScale = new Vector3(
            localScale.x,
            height,
            localScale.z);
        wall.transform.localScale = localScale;
        SetModel("BigWallJump", bigWallBrain);
    }
}
```

That is the script that controls the blue agent, and in this case, we can see that depending on the height of the wall, the agent pushes the yellow platform accordingly to scale it. Also the agent uses a different inference brain, depending on the height of the wall. There is also an associated script, WallJumpSettings, which controls the different properties of the environment such as ground material color, the speed, jump height, and the jump velocity of the agent.

```
using UnityEngine;

public class WallJumpSettings : MonoBehaviour
{
    [Header("Specific to WallJump")]
    public float agentRunSpeed;
    public float agentJumpHeight;

    public Material goalScoredMaterial;

    public Material failMaterial;

    [HideInInspector]
    public float agentJumpVelocity = 777;
    [HideInInspector]
    public float agentJumpVelocityMaxChange = 10;

}
```

Now that we have read about the script that controls the agent in the environment, let us understand another unique script before we use the "mlagents-train" method to train the agent.

Since we will be using curriculum learning to train our agents, we have to use a different "yaml" script that controls the hyperparameters to systematically increase the level of rewards and height of the wall. This can be found in the Curricula folder inside the Config folder. Inside the Curricula folder, we have the Wall_Jump.yaml script. Here we see, we have BigWallJump and SmallWallJump as the curriculum learning parameters for the two modes of inference. The measure, min_lesson_length, and signal_smoothing are the same for both of them. In the BigWallJump set of curriculum learning, we observe that the rewards threshold increases from 0.1 to 0.3 and then to 0.5. This is again task (reward)-specific curriculum learning, which we studied. Also we have the big_wall_min_height, which gradually increases from 0.0 to 8.0 in steps of 2 units. We have the big_wall_max_height, which determines the maximum height that the wall should be limited to for a particular episode. In this case, for the first episode, the maximum wall height is 4 units, while the minimum is 0 units, and this pattern follows successively as the height increases with an increase in the reward.

```
BigWallJump:
  measure: progress
```

```
thresholds: [0.1, 0.3, 0.5]
min_lesson_length: 100
signal_smoothing: true
parameters:
  big_wall_min_height: [0.0, 4.0, 6.0, 8.0]
  big_wall_max_height: [4.0, 7.0, 8.0, 8.0]
```

In the SmallWallJump case, we have the threshold of rewards for each level. This increases from 1.0 to 5.0 in steps of 2 units. The "small_wall_height" also increases from 1.5 to 4.0 units with a step size of 0.5 units.

```
SmallWallJump:
  measure: progress
  thresholds: [0.1, 0.3, 0.5]
  min_lesson_length: 100
  signal_smoothing: true
  parameters:
    small_wall_height: [1.5, 2.0, 2.5, 4.0]
```

This is the script that has to be added with our original trainer_config.yaml file (PPO-policy) to train the agent in curriculum learning. The hyperparameters and properties for the PPO network are the same as in the previous cases. Now for training the agent we have to write the following command from the config folder:

```
mlagents-learn trainer_config.yaml --curriculum=curricula/wall_jump.yaml
--run-id=NewWallJump --train
```

To generalize this syntax:

```
mlagents-learn <path to trainer_config.yaml> --curriculum=<path to
curricula/wall_jump.yaml> --run-id=<new id> --train
```

On running this, we can visualize the training, and in this case we will be using the BigWallJump parameters for curriculum learning, as shown in Figure 6-11a.

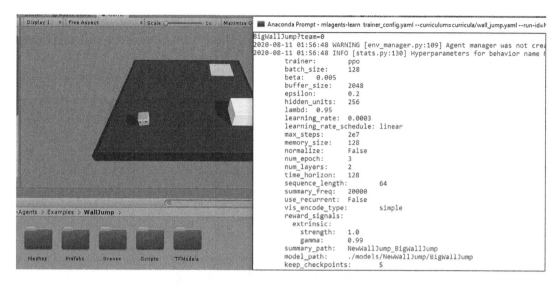

Figure 6-11a. *Curriculum training on wall jump with no wall*

In this case, we can see the training as the height of the wall increases, as shown in Figure 6-11b.

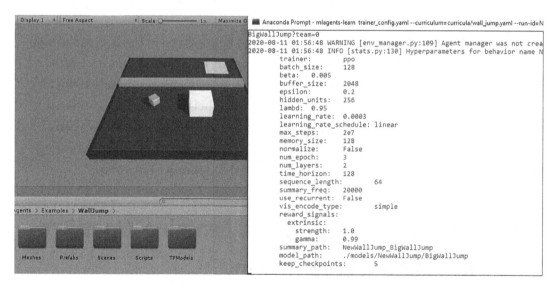

Figure 6-11b. *Curriculum training on wall jump with wall height*

Now that we know how to visualize this training with the help of Tensorboard, let us write the command again for starting tensorboard as follows:

```
tensorboard --logdir=summaries
```

479

This is run from the config folder and starts on the port 6006. We can then evaluate the rewards (cumulative), episode length, and epoch loss. A preview of the training using curriculum learning is provided in Figure 6-12.

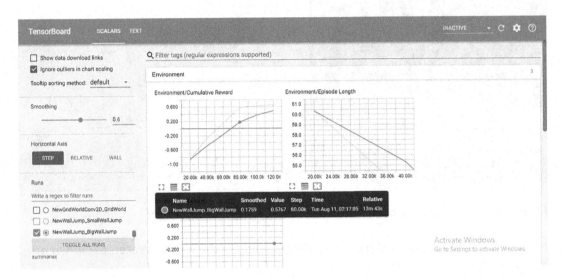

Figure 6-12. *Tensorboard visualization of curriculum learning in wall jump*

We have observed how curriculum learning can be triggered in Unity with the help of an additional yaml file in the Curricula folder. For any new simulations or games that we create using ML Agents, we can add our own set of yaml parameters script for curriculum learning using the same pattern mentioned before. There are additional curriculum learning scripts as well for soccer and test, which can be read for a better understanding. In the next section we will be focusing on another deep RL algorithm, DDPG, before moving on to adversarial self-play and cooperative networks.

Extended Deep Reinforcement Learning Algorithms
Deep Deterministic Policy Gradient

In this context, we will be studying the DDPG algorithm, which is an off-policy actor critic variant. This algorithm combines the deep Q-network (DQN) for continuous action spaces with a traditional actor critic policy. It is closely related to the original Q-learning algorithm, which uses the Bellman update with the exception that this occurs only in continuous spaces. The need for continuity in the algorithm comes from the fact that for discrete spaces, computing the maximum Q-value (rewards) is feasible. However, in the case of continuous action spaces, there are uncountable computations that are required before arriving at the maximum value. We can recall from the previous section that in the original DQN algorithm, there is a replay buffer that stores the past action/observation spaces as well as a frozen target network whose weights cannot be changed. The same approach is applied here as well, but the action space is continuous, and that is where gradient comes into the picture. There are two distinct attributes in the DDPG framework:

- **Deep Q Learning:** This part of DDPG relies on a traditional DQN that uses the Bellman equation for computing the error in the Q-values. This error, which is termed mean squared Bellman error (MSBE), is the quadratic loss function, which the algorithm has to minimize through gradient descent. The equations can be written as follows:

$$Y(s,a,r,s`) = r + y \max_a Q_\theta(s`,a`)$$

$$L(\theta) = E_\theta [(Y(s,a,r,s`) - Q_\theta(s,a))^2],$$

where y(gamma) is the exploration-exploitation factor. This forms the initial part of the DDPG algorithm, and since the algorithm relies on continuous action spaces, the gradient is computed by partial differentiation of the quadratic loss function. The modified loss function can be represented as :

$$L(\theta) = E_\theta [(Q_\theta(s,a) - (r + Y(1-d) \max_{a`} (Q_\theta(s`,a`)))^2],$$

where the (1-d) value determines whether the agent is in the terminal or nonterminal step of the training process. The gradient computation with respect to the Q-value can be computed by using partial derivatives:

$$\partial L(\theta)/\partial Q_\theta(s,a) = \partial E_\theta [(Q_\theta(s,a) - (r + Y(1-d) \max_{a`} (Q_\theta(s`,a`)))^2] / \partial Q_\theta(s,a).$$

Now from our previous concept of DQN, we know that replay buffers and target network training are the two most important characteristics for an off-policy network. The replay buffer allows the DDPG algorithm to choose between most recently used to older samples to prevent overfitting. Because in DDPG, we have to determine the maximum Q-value in continuous spaces, this is done with the help of the target network. The target network is trained to maximize the value of $Q_\theta(s`, a`)$, and this is represented using $\mu_\theta(s`)$. In many cases additional noise is added to improve efficiency. Also the trained target network works on the quadratic MSBE loss function to update the Q-value:

$$Q_\theta(s`,a`) = Q_\theta(s,a) - \alpha\, \partial L(\theta)/\partial Q_\theta(s,a),$$

where α is the learning rate of the algorithm.

- **Policy network:** The policy for DDPG involves using the policy gradient algorithm to maximize the value estimates from a policy. This is the simplest form of gradient ascent-based policy optimization technique, which we studied in the previous chapter and can be formulated as:

$$\Delta_\theta J(\theta) = \max E[Q_\theta(s`,\mu_\theta(s`))]$$

This completes the mathematical aspects of this off-policy algorithm. Now we will look into the details of its implementation with the help of stable baselines on the MountainCarContinuous environment. Open the DDPG_Baselines.ipynb Python Notebook in Google Colab. Since most of the libraries and frameworks are similar to the previous use-cases, we will concentrate on the core implementation. We get the action spaces from the Gym environment, and then we apply a noise to the action (mentioned before). This noise is to increase stability in training the DQN and is called the OrnsteinUhlenbeckActionNoise. Then we call the DDPG policy from Baselines and pass on the required parameters using the action and parameter noises. This is done by the following lines:

```
env = gym.make('MountainCarContinuous-v0')
# the noise objects for DDPG
n_actions = env.action_space.shape[-1]
param_noise = None
action_noise = OrnsteinUhlenbeckActionNoise(mean=np.zeros(n_actions),
sigma=float(0.5) * np.ones(n_actions))

model = DDPG(MlpPolicy, env, verbose=1, param_noise=param_noise, action_
noise=action_noise)
```

```
model.learn(total_timesteps=4000)
model.save("ddpg_mountain")

del model
model = DDPG.load("ddpg_mountain")
```

Then we run a loop to train the agent on DDPG policy for 4000 iterations, and the model predicts the rewards for each stage of training. The visualization of the training is also updated on the screen with the help of "ipythondisplay" library.

```
obs = env.reset()
while True:
    action, _states = model.predict(obs)
    obs, rewards, dones, info = env.step(action)
    screen = env.render(mode='rgb_array')
    plt.imshow(screen)
    ipythondisplay.clear_output(wait=True)
    ipythondisplay.display(plt.gcf())
```

On running this, we will get to see the different attributes such as reference Q mean values, rollout Q mean values, as well as the training episode length, duration, epochs, steps, the critic, and actor loss, as shown in Figure 6-13.

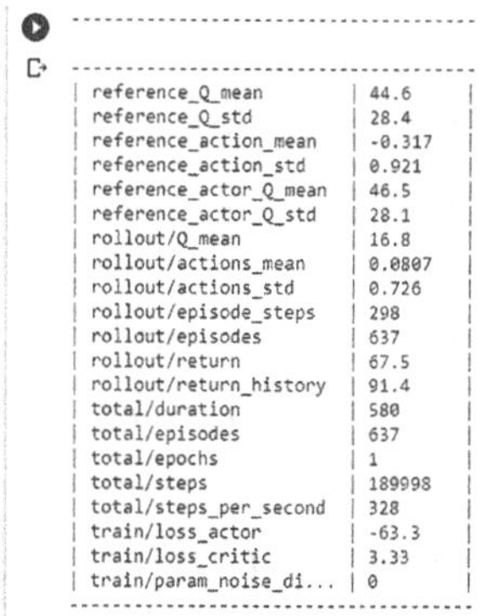

reference_Q_mean	44.6
reference_Q_std	28.4
reference_action_mean	-0.317
reference_action_std	0.921
reference_actor_Q_mean	46.5
reference_actor_Q_std	28.1
rollout/Q_mean	16.8
rollout/actions_mean	0.0807
rollout/actions_std	0.726
rollout/episode_steps	298
rollout/episodes	637
rollout/return	67.5
rollout/return_history	91.4
total/duration	580
total/episodes	637
total/epochs	1
total/steps	189998
total/steps_per_second	328
train/loss_actor	-63.3
train/loss_critic	3.33
train/param_noise_di...	0

***Figure 6-13.** Output of training DDPG on the MountainCarContinuous environment*

We can also see the car trying to get up the cliff to reach the flag, as shown in Figure 6-14.

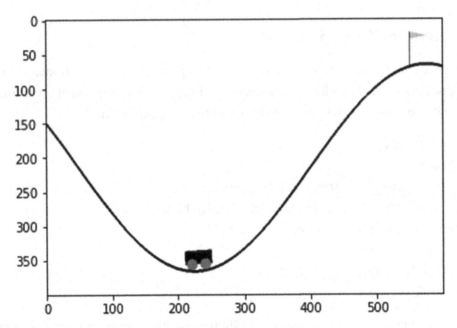

Figure 6-14. *Mountain car training visualization*

This algorithm is a classic off-policy algorithm and can also be used in case of training the Reacher environment in Unity ML Agents. In this case, we can use the Baseline implementation of the algorithm. As we read in Chapter 3 regarding the different environments, the Reacher is a complex robotic arm simulation environment where the robot is credited with rewards if it keeps the arms within the green spherical balls. Some of the best implementations of solving this problem require PPO with DDPG for continuous spaces. As DDPG uses actor critic mechanism as the policy network, PPO provides a good stability in training. As mentioned in the last chapter, we can use the Python API for interfacing and running our Baseline Gym models on Unity ML Agents to train them. This is left for an enthusiastic reader to try training the Reacher agent with DDPG. Figure 6-15 shows a preview of training the environment with DDPG.

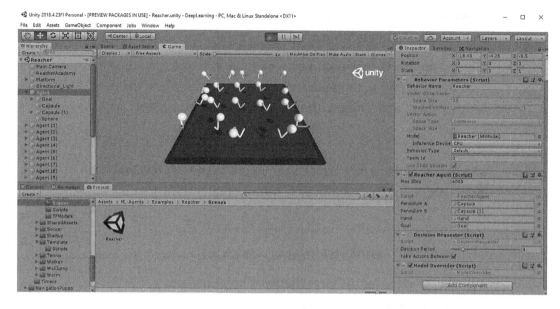

Figure 6-15. *Reacher environment with PPO-DDPG off-policy training*

Now we will be looking briefly into some variants of the DDPG algorithm.

Twin Delayed DDPG

This is a variant of the DDPG algorithm that improves over DDPG by using clipping of the policy updates, similarly to clipped PPO, and uses delayed policy updates to prevent it from overestimating the Q-value. Twine-delayed DDPG (TD3) is almost similar to DDPG with certain modifications:

- **Target policy smoothing:** As mentioned in the case of DDPG, we have a target network that uses MSBE loss as the metric. This is modified in TD3 algorithm by clipping the noise added to the target network. This is bounded within the range $a_{low} \leq a \leq a_{high}$. The target actions are computed in this case as:

$$a`(s`) = clip(\mu_\theta(s`) + clip(\varepsilon, -c, c), a_{low}, a_{high}),$$

where (-c, c) are the hyperparameters. The clipping factor plays an important role in regularization of the algorithm and removes the drawbacks of DDPG. DDPG exploits sharp points on the curve and this gives brittle and unstable rewards in many cases. Smoothing the curve using TD3 plays an important role in stabilizing it.

- **Clipped double Q-learning:** This technique acts as a minimization objective that tries to minimize the Q-values coming from the two networks in double DQN. We have the formulation as follows:

$$R(y,s`,d) = r + y(1-d) \min (Q_{\theta 1}(s`,a`), Q_{\theta 2}(s`,a`)),$$

where symbols have their usual meaning. Based on this rewards value, the two DQNs are trained with their corresponding MSBE loss as follows:

$$L_1(\theta) = E_{\theta 1} [(Q_{\theta 1}(s,a) - R(y,s`,d))^2]$$

$$L_2(\theta) = E_{\theta 2} [(Q_{\theta 2}(s,a) - R(y,s`,d))^2]$$

A smaller Q-value for the target network helps prevent overestimation and stabilizes the training.

- **Delayed policy control:** TD3 updates the policies in a delayed manner and also uses the basic maximization of the policy gradient as the core function:

$$\Delta_\theta J(\theta) = \max E[Q_\theta(s`,\mu_\theta(s`))]$$

It is recommended to update the policy after every two Q-function (value) updates.

This completes the twin delayed DDPG algorithm. This can be visualized in the TD3-Baselines.ipynb Notebook, which contains the OpenAI implementation of the algorithm. Most of the code segment is the same as in DDPG, with the only change in the policy of the algorithm.

```
n_actions = env.action_space.shape[-1]
action_noise = NormalActionNoise(mean=np.zeros(n_actions), sigma=0.1 *
np.ones(n_actions))
model = TD3(MlpPolicy, env, action_noise=action_noise, verbose=1)
model.learn(total_timesteps=50000, log_interval=10)
model.save("td3_pendulum")
```

In this case, we are using the Pendulum environment for training this algorithm, as shown in Figure 6-16.

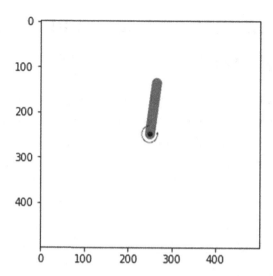

Figure 6-16. *TD3 training in the pendulum environment*

Some of the other variants include:

- **Distributed deep deterministic policy gradient (D4PG):** This uses a distributional critic as the core functionality. This allows a distributed training of the DDPG network using prioritized experience replay. D4PG uses multiple distributed actors working in parallel and feeding data into the same replay buffer.

- **Multi-agent deep deterministic policy gradient (MADDPG):** This is a multi-agent version of the DDPG algorithm where the environment changes in response to all the agents working in the scene. This can be compared to a multi-agent Markov Decision Process (MDP). The critic in this case learns from a centralized action value function for a particular agent. This may give rise to conflicting reward functions and also a competitive environment. In this case there are multiple actors that are present for each agent that update the policy gradient.

We have completed learning about most of the algorithms related to on- and off-policy deep RL. DDPG is an important off-policy algorithm for continuous vector spaces and can be used in ML Agents where the mode in the Behavior Parameters script is of type Continuous. In the next section we will be focusing on adversarial self-play and cooperative networks.

Adversarial Self-Play and Cooperative Learning

Adversarial Self-Play

This is an important aspect of training agents to play in a dynamic environment. In addition to the obstacles present in the environment, there is also another agent whose reward signals are antagonistic with respect to the player agent. This adversarial agent controls the player. Adversarial self-play is used when the agents also perceive another agent to be an obstacle along with the environment. Self-play involves the player agent trying to win over a past state of itself, which is the scenario in adversarial play. The adversarial agent forces the player agent to change its policies and attain better Q-value estimates than what it achieved in its previous states. However, in most of the cases, the level of difficulty should be properly controlled so as to prevent the player agent from getting penalized. This can be observed in the case of the tennis environment, where the player agent has to compete against an adversarial agent to get points. Depending on the level of gameplay of the adversary, the player agent has to adjust its policies accordingly. At the start of the gameplay, if a strong adversary is provided, then the player agent may not be able to learn significantly. In contrast, if the opponent becomes weaker as the training progresses, this may lead to an instability in learning of the player agent. Using the same policy for the above two cases can be problematic for the player, as it may not learn significantly. This makes adversarial play very difficult to estimate. In self-play, as mentioned, an agent tries to compete against its past self, by changing its policy and gets rewarded if the current self is better than the past self. This improvement of the agent can only come from the increasing level of difficulty of the gameplay, including the strength of the adversary. Curriculum learning plays a significant role here to moderate and control the level of difficulty as the gameplay progresses. With the help for curriculum learning (task-specific), the player utilizes adversarial self-play to methodically update its policies to reach a specific goal, as shown in Figure 6-17.

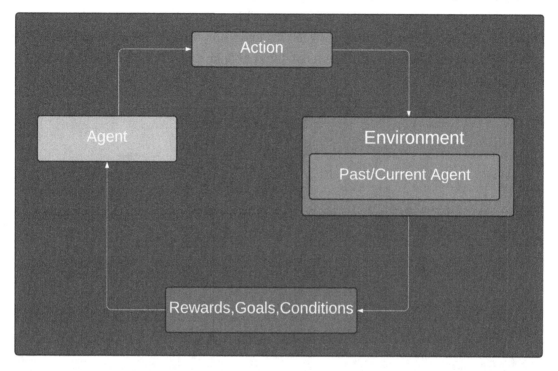

Figure 6-17. *Agent in an adversarial self-play environment*

Cooperative Learning

Cooperative networks are used in multi-agent environments, where we have multiple agents in a particular group compete against adversarial agents in a different group. The groups can be greater than two, and in this case, we have a cluster of agents with the same policies and reward estimates trained to reach the same goal. In adversarial gameplay, we have two or more deep RL neural networks that compete against each other for value maximization. In cooperative gameplay, we have two or more deep RL neural networks that are similar in architecture, policies, and loss functions trained with the same motive. However, modifications can be made between the cooperating agents to learn to change their policies by observing each other. This is another important metric where one of the agents uses a policy gradient technique as A2C and the other cooperating agent can imitate it using GAIL. This kind of cooperative network-based agents are generally found in group-based games such as soccer. In the soccer environment(two players), we have two different teams, each having two players. Among the players in a particular team, one of them is a goalie while the other is a striker. Both these players (agents) must work in cooperation with each other to defeat the opponent team, which also contains a goalie and a striker. This environment is beautifully crafted to show both cooperative learning between the agents on the same team as well as adversarial self-play between the agents of different teams. Figure 6-18 shows a preview of the environment.

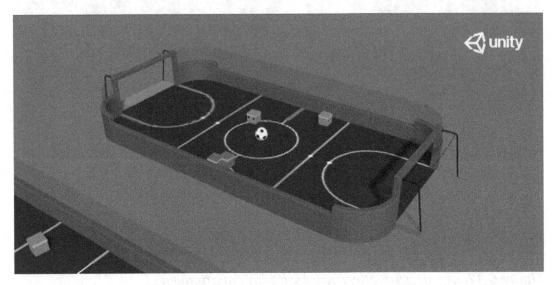

Figure 6-18. *Adversarial and cooperative learning in the soccer environment*

Let us understand the soccer environment in detail in this section.

Soccer Environment for Adversarial and Cooperative Learning

We may have played AI-based football or soccer games like FIFA, where we have seen intelligent AI agents (players) playing along with us as well as against us. This is a classic example where both adversarial and cooperative networks play an important role. In the Unity scene, we have two different teams: blue and purple. Each team consists of two players that are effectively agents. Each of these agents contain the Behavior Parameters and Model Overrider as well as the Decision Requester scripts attached to it. Additionally we have the RayPerceptionSensorComponent3D script, which control the discrete observation space for the agents. In this case, we will first study the

"AgentSoccer script. At the start of the script, we have the types of the team— 0 and 1, which represent the blue and the purple Teams, respectively. It also contains types of the players based on their locations on the platform; if the agent is placed closer to the goal, it becomes a goalie, whereas for other locations it becomes a striker.

```
public enum Team
    {
        Blue = 0,
        Purple = 1
    }

    public enum Position
    {
        Striker,
        Goalie,
        Generic
    }
```

Then we have the different variables that control the position, ID of the agent, the kick power, the speed of the agent (lateral, existential, forward), and the parameters that control the team, rigidbodies of the agents.

```
[HideInInspector]
    public Team team;
    float m_KickPower;
    int m_PlayerIndex;
    public SoccerFieldArea area;
    // The coefficient for the reward for colliding with a ball. Set using
        curriculum.
    float m_BallTouch;
    public Position position;

    const float k_Power = 2000f;
    float m_Existential;
    float m_LateralSpeed;
    float m_ForwardSpeed;

    [HideInInspector]
```

```
public float timePenalty;

[HideInInspector]
public Rigidbody agentRb;
SoccerSettings m_SoccerSettings;
BehaviorParameters m_BehaviorParameters;
Vector3 m_Transform;

EnvironmentParameters m_ResetParams;
```

The overridden "Initialize" method is used for assigning the different agents to their respective teams and also assigns their IDs respectively. Depending on the position of the agent, it is assigned a lateral and forward velocity, and we can see different values for goalie and striker. It also assigns the rigidbodies and the maximum angular velocities of the agents.

```
m_Existential = 1f / MaxStep;
m_BehaviorParameters = gameObject.GetComponent
<BehaviorParameters>();
        if (m_BehaviorParameters.TeamId == (int)Team.Blue)
        {
            team = Team.Blue;
            m_Transform = new Vector3(transform.
            position.x - 4f, .5f, transform.position.z);
        }
        else
        {
            team = Team.Purple;
            m_Transform = new Vector3(transform.position.x
            + 4f, .5f, transform.position.z);
        }
        if (position == Position.Goalie)
        {
            m_LateralSpeed = 1.0f;
            m_ForwardSpeed = 1.0f;
        }
```

```
else if (position == Position.Striker)
{
    m_LateralSpeed = 0.3f;
    m_ForwardSpeed = 1.3f;
}
else
{
    m_LateralSpeed = 0.3f;
    m_ForwardSpeed = 1.0f;
}
m_SoccerSettings = FindObjectOfType<SoccerSettings>();
agentRb = GetComponent<Rigidbody>();
agentRb.maxAngularVelocity = 500;

var playerState = new PlayerState
{
    agentRb = agentRb,
    startingPos = transform.position,
    agentScript = this,
};
area.playerStates.Add(playerState);
m_PlayerIndex
  = area.playerStates.IndexOf(playerState);
playerState.playerIndex = m_PlayerIndex;

m_ResetParams
= Academy.Instance.EnvironmentParameters;
```

The "MoveAgent" method moves the agents after receiving the ray observations. Depending on the actions received, the switch code block moves the agents along a particular axis (forward and lateral motion) and also allows it to rotate. Then it uses the "AddForce" method to trigger the motion of the agent along a particular direction.

```
 var dirToGo = Vector3.zero;
var rotateDir = Vector3.zero;

m_KickPower = 0f;
```

```
var forwardAxis = (int)act[0];
var rightAxis = (int)act[1];
var rotateAxis = (int)act[2];

switch (forwardAxis)
{
    case 1:
        dirToGo = transform.forward * m_ForwardSpeed;
        m_KickPower = 1f;
        break;
    case 2:
        dirToGo = transform.forward * -m_ForwardSpeed;
        break;
}

switch (rightAxis)
{
    case 1:
        dirToGo = transform.right * m_LateralSpeed;
        break;
    case 2:
        dirToGo = transform.right * -m_LateralSpeed;
        break;
}

switch (rotateAxis)
{
    case 1:
        rotateDir = transform.up * -1f;
        break;
    case 2:
        rotateDir = transform.up * 1f;
        break;
}
```

```
transform.Rotate(rotateDir, Time.deltaTime * 100f);
agentRb.AddForce(dirToGo
* m_SoccerSettings.agentRunSpeed,
    ForceMode.VelocityChange);
```

The "OnActionReceived" overridden method controls the rewards received by the agent based on its position. If the position is that of a goalie, a positive reward is provided. If the position is that of a striker, a negative existential reward is provided. For all other generic cases, a small negative reward is provided to the agent.

```
if (position == Position.Goalie)
    {
        // Existential bonus for Goalies.
        AddReward(m_Existential);
    }
    else if (position == Position.Striker)
    {
        // Existential penalty for Strikers
        AddReward(-m_Existential);
    }
    else
    {
        // Existential penalty cumulant for Generic
        timePenalty -= m_Existential;
    }
    MoveAgent(vectorAction);
```

We have the "Heuristic" method, which is common for all the ML Agents scripts, and uses different keys (W, A [forward], S, D [rotate], E, Q [right]) to control the agent. Used mainly as a player brain and also in imitation learning.

```
if (Input.GetKey(KeyCode.W))
    {
        actionsOut[0] = 1f;
    }
```

```
if (Input.GetKey(KeyCode.S))
{
    actionsOut[0] = 2f;
}
//rotate
if (Input.GetKey(KeyCode.A))
{
    actionsOut[2] = 1f;
}
if (Input.GetKey(KeyCode.D))
{
    actionsOut[2] = 2f;
}
//right
if (Input.GetKey(KeyCode.E))
{
    actionsOut[1] = 1f;
}
if (Input.GetKey(KeyCode.Q))
{
    actionsOut[1] = 2f;
}
```

The "OnCollisionEnter" method is important for rewarding the agent and the team when the ball enters the opponent's goal. The force of kicking the ball by the agent also increases if it is at the goalie position. Normally for each goals scored, the agent gets a reward of +1.0 and for each goal conceded, a negative score of -1.0 is received. In all other cases, a negative score of -0.0003 units is received.

```
var force = k_Power * m_KickPower;
        if (position == Position.Goalie)
        {
            force = k_Power;
        }
        if (c.gameObject.CompareTag("ball"))
        {
```

```
        AddReward(.2f * m_BallTouch);
        var dir = c.contacts[0].point
                  - transform.position;
        dir = dir.normalized;
        c.gameObject.GetComponent<Rigidbody>
        ().AddForce(dir * force);
    }
```

The "OnEpisodeBegin" method is used for resetting the agent, and the positions of the different agents in the scene. It also resets the velocity, force and the penalty time of the environment.

```
    timePenalty = 0;
    m_BallTouch = m_ResetParams.GetWithDefault
                  ("ball_touch", 0);
    if (team == Team.Purple)
    {
        transform.rotation = Quaternion.Euler
        (0f, -90f, 0f);
    }
    else
    {
        transform.rotation = Quaternion.Euler
        (0f, 90f, 0f);
    }
    transform.position = m_Transform;
    agentRb.velocity = Vector3.zero;
    agentRb.angularVelocity = Vector3.zero;
    SetResetParameters();
```

This completes the agent script. This script is added to both the players on both the teams. For a particular team, the respective properties are triggered (based on enums). There are other additional scripts that assist this script, such as the SoccerBallController script. This controls the collisions with the different game objects, particularly what game object the ball has touched (blue team player, purple team player, goal)

```
void OnCollisionEnter(Collision col)
    {
        if (col.gameObject.CompareTag(purpleGoalTag))
          //ball touched purple goal
        {
            area.GoalTouched(AgentSoccer.Team.Blue);
        }
        if (col.gameObject.CompareTag(blueGoalTag))
          //ball touched blue goal
        {
            area.GoalTouched(AgentSoccer.Team.Purple);
        }
    }
```

The SoccerField area controls the platform or the ground on which the game is being played. This includes lighting the platform when a goal is scored as well as adding rewards of +1.0 units for the goal scoring agent, and a negative reward is attributed to the conceded agent.

```
foreach (var ps in playerStates)
        {
            if (ps.agentScript.team == scoredTeam)
            {
                ps.agentScript.AddReward(1
                + ps.agentScript.timePenalty);
            }
            else
            {
                ps.agentScript.AddReward(-1);
            }
            ps.agentScript.EndEpisode();
            //all agents need to be reset
            if (goalTextUI)
            {
                StartCoroutine(ShowGoalUI());
            }
        }
```

There is also a "ResetBall" method that is called in the Socceragent script during the start of each episode. This resets the ball to the middle of the platform and resets its rotation, scale, and direction.

```
ball.transform.position = ballStartingPos;
ballRb.velocity = Vector3.zero;
ballRb.angularVelocity = Vector3.zero;

var ballScale
= m_ResetParams.GetWithDefault("ball_scale", 0.015f);
ballRb.transform.localScale = new Vector3
  (ballScale, ballScale, ballScale);
```

The last script in this context is the SoccerSettings script, which has variables controlling the materials of the blue and purple teams, the speed of the agents, as well as a Boolean variable for randomizing the agents during training.

```
public Material purpleMaterial;
public Material blueMaterial;
public bool randomizePlayersTeamForTraining = true;
public float agentRunSpeed;
```

Now we will be training this scene with the help of PPO-based curriculum learning to see the adversarial self-play and cooperative learning in action.

Training Soccer Environment

We will be using curriculum learning since for any team (player agents) the level of difficulty of training should increment gradually. This allows the agents of both the teams to learn using a stable policy for optimal rewards. Similar to training the Wall Jump environment in the previous section, we will use the following code to start the training process from the Anaconda prompt (Command prompt) terminal:

```
mlagents-learn trainer_config.yaml --curriculum=curricula/soccer.yaml –run-id=NewSoccer --train
```

On running this command, we can see that the PPO algorithm uses the hyperparameters as we saw in the previous chapters. Additionally we are also using the parameters present in the Soccer.yaml curriculum learning script. We can observe that the rewards threshold increases by 0.05 units starting from 0.05, and also the ball_touch parameter decreases gradually from 1.0 to 0.0. This implies as the difficulty increases, it becomes harder for the agent in a particular team to retain the ball for a longer time. For the initial levels, the agents can have the ball for a longer time span, and as the levels increase, this time decreases. In a practical football or soccer match, it can be observed that if two teams are very competitive, the ball possession ratio decreases for both the teams.

```
SoccerTwos:
  measure: progress
  thresholds: [0.05, 0.1]
  min_lesson_length: 100
  signal_smoothing: true
  parameters:
    ball_touch: [1.0, 0.5, 0.0]
```

The training scene appears as shown in Figure 6-19.

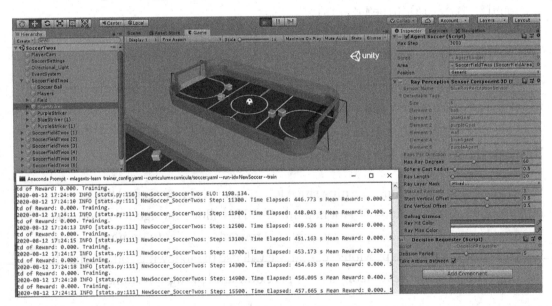

Figure 6-19. *Training soccer environment using adversarial–cooperative learning*

Tensorboard Visualization

Let us visualize this training process in Tensorboard as well. We will be using the command:

```
tensorboard --logdir=summaries
```

This command needs to be called from the config folder inside the ML Agents repository. We can visualize the cumulative rewards, the loss and other parameters of the training. Figure 6-20 shows a preview of the Tensorboard visualization.

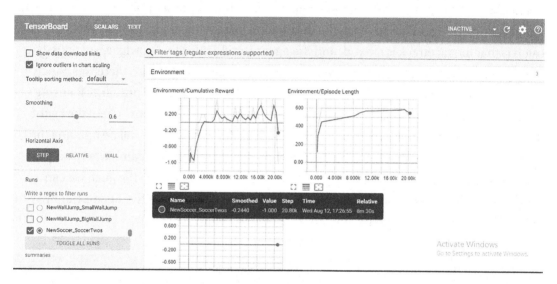

Figure 6-20. *Tensorboard visualization of the training*

We can change the hyperparameters to visualize how it affects the training, the loss, and the rewards. After a considerable amount of training period, we can see that the agents are playing really well. We have seen how the effect of adversarial (different teams) and cooperative (same teams) learning mode affects the agents' ability to tackle the environment. We can use different algorithms apart from PPO, such as SAC (or other soft Q-learning technique) to see the difference in the training process. While the tennis environment is a pure competitive (adversarial) learning-based environment, in the soccer environment, we have the flavors of both adversarial as well as cooperative learning. It has to be kept in mind that we can also change the hyperparameter properties, including the neural network parameters present in the Model.py script that

501

we mentioned in the last chapter and see the changes in the outputs. Significantly it can be observed how changing the recurrent network properties (LSTM network properties) can change the learning of the agent.

Building an Autonomous AI Agent for a Mini Kart Game

We will now build an autonomous driving agent for a miniature Kart game using ML Agents. We will be training this on PPO policy as well, but any other policies can be used. In this scenario, the agent has to reach the destination by moving along a small racetrack. The catch is that the racetrack is curved, and the agent should be able to navigate seamlessly through it. As the path length increases, the training episode length also increases. Since we will not be using visual observation sensors (no CNNs), we will be primarily focusing on using ray perception sensors to get information from the current position of the agent, the distance from the goal as well as the current direction. For this we will be opening the Tinyagent Unity scene. This is a miniature version of a racetrack Kart game where only one agent is present. If we can make the agent learn the trajectory to reach the goal, we can even extend it to create a full-fledged game using more such competitive agents (along with curriculum learning). The scene appears as shown in Figure 6-21.

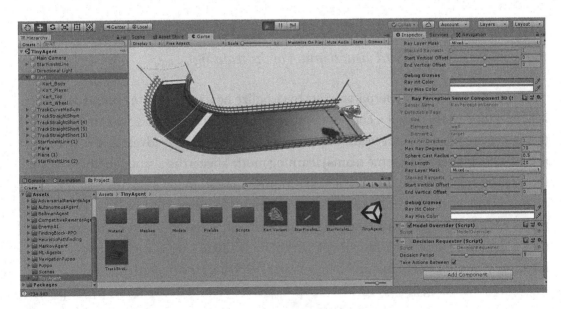

Figure 6-21. *Autonomous AI agent in tiny agent Unity scene*

We have an agent (blue-colored) that is inside a Kart. The agent has a RayPerceptionSensorComponent3D script for collecting the observations. It also has the Behavior Parameters, Model Overrider, and Decision Requester scripts attached with it. For this case, we are using a discrete distribution and let us explore the Tinyagent script. The main idea behind designing is that the agent computes the distance between the target and its current position. For any movement along the direction of the target, the agent is incrementally rewarded. If the agent crashes against the boundary of the poles, then it gets a negative reward. The time for reaching the goal is also a factor in deciding the rewards—the more the time it takes, the more penalty the agent receives. As we progress, we will see that we compute the direction as well as the relative distance between the agent (Kart) and the destination. If the agent moves in the opposite direction as the target, then it also gets a negative reward. With this concept, let us understand the script. The script contains the variables such as the game objects, the target, and the current position of the agent with respect to the target. It also controls materials for coloring the ground when it collides with the track boundaries (red) or on reaching the destination (green). For computing the relative distance, we will be using three variables: prev_spawn_dist, prev_target_dist, and prev_dist. These are used for adjusting the positions of the agent at the start of each episode of training and also to compute the distance from the target.

```
float rewards = 0f;
public GameObject main_agent;
public GameObject target;
Transform target_pos;
Transform agent_pos;
Rigidbody agent_body;
float prev_dist = 0f;
float prev_spawn_dist = 0f;
float prev_target_dist = 0f;
public GameObject ground;
public bool vectorObs;
public Material green_material;
public Material default_material;
public Renderer ground_renderer;
Vector3 previous_position = new Vector3
                    (28.88f, 1.9f, -34.5f);
```

We then have the "Initialize" overridden method, which initializes the target position, and the Kart agent position assigns its rigidbody component.

```
agent_pos = GetComponent<Transform>();
target_pos = GetComponent<Transform>();
agent_body = GetComponent<Rigidbody>();
```

We then have the "CollectObservations" method, which is used for collecting discrete vector observations. It computes the relative distance between the Kart and the destination and uses it as an observation. The velocity of the agent (Kart) is also taken as an observation.

```
if (vectorObs == true)
        {
            var relative_position
            = target_pos.position - agent_pos.position;

            sensor.AddObservation(transform.
              InverseTransformDirection(agent_body.velocity));

            sensor.AddObservation(relative_position);
        }
```

Then we have the MoveAgent script, which controls the motion of the Kart depending on the observation received from the sensors. Since the agent can move in the forward and up direction and can also rotate along a particular axis, we have a total of 6 vectors in the action spaces, -2 for each x and z axes for rectilinear motion (positive and negative), and 2 along the rotational axis. Then we use the AddForce component to add a force to the Kart agent.

```
var direction = Vector3.zero;
var rotation = Vector3.zero;
// var velocity = Vector3.zero;

var action = Mathf.FloorToInt(acts[0]);
switch (action)
{
    case 1:
        direction = transform.forward * 1.0f;
        break;
```

```
    case 2:
        direction = transform.forward * (-1.0f);
        break;
    case 3:
        rotation = transform.up * 1.0f;
        break;
    case 4:
        rotation = transform.up * (-1.0f);
        break;

}
transform.Rotate(rotation, Time.deltaTime * 100f);

agent_body.AddForce(direction * 0.1f, ForceMode.VelocityChange);
```

Then we have the "OnActionReceived" overridden method, which controls the distance of the Kart from the starting position, as well as from the destination. This is required because the agent gets credited if its distance increases from the starting position. For every forward motion toward the target, the agent gets a reward of 0.009 units, and on reaching the target, it gets a reward of 5 units. For every time-step the agent does not reach the vicinity of the target, it gets a negative credit of -0.005 units. To prevent the agent from moving along the y axis, a negative reward of -2 units is added each time the Kart topples. We can create more such conditions according to our will to change the environment reward signals.

```
float dist_target = Vector3.Distance
(agent_pos.position, target_pos.position);
float dist_spawn = Vector3.Distance
(new Vector3(2.88f, 2.35f, -43.5f), agent_pos.position);
float dist_prev = Vector3.Distance
  (previous_position, agent_pos.position);

// if (dist_target < 0.00005f)
// {Debug.Log("Near Target");
//      AddReward(5f);
//      rewards += 5f;

// }
```

```
if (dist_prev > prev_dist)
{

    Debug.Log("Going forward");
    AddReward(0.009f);
    rewards += 0.009f;

}

if (agent_pos.position.y < -0.5f
  || agent_pos.position.y > 5f)
{

    Debug.Log("Going Down");
    AddReward(-2.0f);
    rewards -= 2.0f;
    reset();

}

// if (agent_pos.rotation.x != 0f
//      || agent_pos.rotation.z != 0f)
// {
//      //agent_pos.rotation.x=0f;
//      //agent_pos.rotation.z=0f;
//      Debug.Log("Rotating");
//      AddReward(-1.0f);
//      rewards -= 1.0f;
//      reset();

// }

AddReward(-0.005f);
rewards += -0.005f;
Debug.Log(rewards);
//prev_dist_target = dist_target;
//prev_dist_spawn = dist_spawn;
//prev_dist = dist_prev;
prev_spawn_dist = dist_spawn;
```

```
prev_target_dist = dist_target;
previous_position = agent_pos.position;

moveAgent(vect);
```

The "OnCollisionEnter" method is used for checking whether the Kart has collided with the boundary of the track or has reached the destination. For the former case, a negative reward of -0.5 units is credited and the episode is terminated, very similar to the case when in a racing game we collide with the boundary and are eliminated. For the latter case, we again receive a positive reward of 3 units and the ground color changes (green), signaling that the agent has reached the goal.

```
if (collision.gameObject.CompareTag("wall"))
    {
        Debug.Log("Collided with Wall");
        SetReward(-0.5f);
        rewards += -0.5f;
        Debug.Log(rewards);
        EndEpisode();
    }
    else if (collision.gameObject.CompareTag("target"))
    {
        Debug.Log("Reached Target");
        SetReward(3f);
        rewards += 3f;
        StartCoroutine(Lightupground());
        Debug.Log(rewards);
        //gameObject.SetActive(false);
        EndEpisode();
    }
```

Then we have the "OnEpisodeBegin" method, which calls the "Reset" method to reset the scene at the start of every episode. It places the Kart at the starting position again and resets its velocity, angular velocity, and also its rotation.

```
// var rotate_sample = Random.Range(0, 4);
// var rotate_angle = 90f * rotate_sample;
agent_pos.transform.Rotate(new Vector3(0f, 0f, 0f));
```

```
//agent.Rotate(new Vector3(0f, -90f, 0f));
agent_pos.position = new Vector3
  (28.88f, 1.9f, -33.5f);
agent_body.velocity = Vector3.zero;
agent_body.angularVelocity = Vector3.zero;
```

That conclusively completes the agent script. We have created an autonomous agent that will be using ray sensors to collect observations to reach the target. Now we have to train this agent.

Training Tiny Agent with PPO Policy

We will be using the default hyperparameters of PPO to train this agent, but it has to be mentioned that in this case we are not using curriculum learning. It is left for the reader to create a yaml script for training this agent with curriculum learning (task-specific) by following the previous sections. Since this is a practically challenging environment, this requires several hours (days even) for training on a CPU. Thus it is recommended to train this with curriculum learning approach by creating a yaml script that controls the start position of the Kart agent. In the initial stages, we can position the agent closer to the target so that it comes in direct line of sight, and the agent can get credited with rewards. For successive levels of training, the position can be changed by moving the agent far from the target position. We use the command:

```
mlagents-learn --trainer_config.yaml --run-id=NewTinyAgent --train
```

Tuning the hyperparameters can also be done to find the different characteristic parameters that affect the agent. Training the Kart agent appears as shown in Figure 6-22.

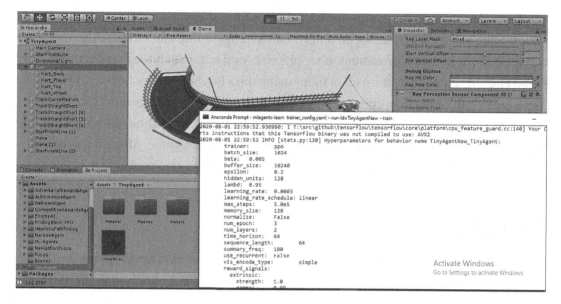

Figure 6-22. *Training tiny agent with PPO policy in ML Agents*

Visualization and Future Work

Let us visualize this training in Tensorboard. This can be done by using the command:

```
tensorboard -logdir=summaries
```

The visualization provides an estimate of the cumulative rewards and epoch loss for the Kart agent. A typical visualization is shown in Figure 6-23.

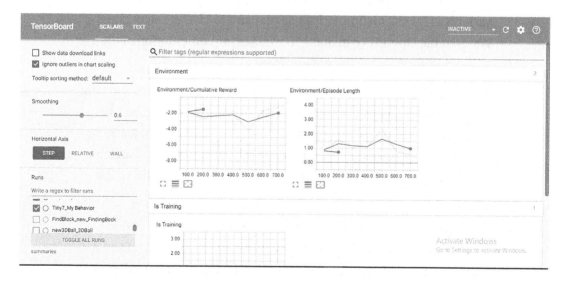

Figure 6-23. *Tensorboard visualization of tiny agent*

This project is a starting point for further development by the readers. The template provides the sample for building an autonomous AI agent that can navigate through certain terrains in the environment. If we place several other such Kart agents in the scene and simultaneously train all of them using the PPO/SAC policy, we can build an AI-based racing game. However, training these agents requires a huge amount of time (probably days for multiple agents). We can also create the curriculum learning script to include adversarial components in case of a multi-agent Kart game. After all the agents are trained, we can play against those trained agents and see who comes first.

Summary

This completes the chapter that has been a descriptive projection of the different aspects of curriculum learning and adversarial Learning as well as creating simulations and games. To summarize:

- We studied curriculum learning and its different branches, including task-specific learning, teacher student curriculum learning, as well as automatic goal generation using goal GAN algorithms.

- We then visualized the steps to train the Wall Jump environment in ML Agents with the help of PPO-based curriculum learning.

- The next section was based on extended deep RL algorithms, including the off-policy DDPG algorithm. We also covered the variants of DDPG including TD3, D4P,G and MADDPG algorithms. We used the OpenAI Gym Stable Baselines implementation of the algorithms for training the environments.

- Next we learned about adversarial self-play and cooperative learning, which is important in the context of multi-agent-based games and simulations. We saw the contrast between the two forms of learning and also understood the importance of self-play. We then visualized this process using the Soccer environment and trained it using the PPO policy.

- The last section was based on building an autonomous AI agent for a miniature Kart game. The agent had to reach the target from a given starting position without colliding with the track boundary. We trained this agent with the PPO policy of ML Agents and visualized the training process with Tensorboard. There are further scopes in terms of building more autonomous agent-based racing games with this template.

In the next and the last chapter, we will be focusing on additional algorithms, certain case studies from Unity Technologies, as well as different platforms for deep RL.

CHAPTER 7

Case Studies in ML Agents

At this stage, we have gained considerable knowledge as to the flexibility of the ML Agents Toolkit. We have also learned different complex algorithms that are related to deep RL. If we analyze, we can visualize that the main idea of any RL algorithm is to provide a set of decisions that the agent can follow to achieve a particular goal. Although we covered most of the deep learning algorithms, there is a set of algorithms that do not follow the traditional approach of backpropagation and gradient ascent/descent. In this chapter, we will explore evolutionary algorithms, which have been in practice for quite some time. These algorithms follow the principle of Darwinism—only the fittest offspring survive to produce the next generation. We will also look into the most famous case study of Unity ML Agents: Obstacle Tower Challenge. This challenge was created by Unity Technologies to help foster research in the AI community by providing a "challenging new benchmark for Agent performance." The Obstacle Tower is a procedurally generated environment that the agent has to solve with the help of computer vision, locomotion, and generalization. The agent has a goal to reach successive floors by arriving at a step of stairs for each level. Each floor has its unique challenges in terms of puzzles, layouts, and visual appearance and forms a proper environment where traditional RL algorithms often fail to make the agent progress further. We will also be looking into the Unity ML Agents Challenge, which was organized by Unity. Since these are case studies, we will be briefly exploring the suggestions and steps followed by participants whose algorithms were benchmarked for performance. We will also be exploring certain other platforms for deep RL—namely, the Google Dopamine platform. Also in this chapter, we will be focusing more on the applicability of the algorithms that we have learned in these challenges.

© Abhilash Majumder 2021
A. Majumder, *Deep Reinforcement Learning in Unity*, https://doi.org/10.1007/978-1-4842-6503-1_7

Evolutionary Algorithms

Throughout this book, we have learned about different complex algorithms that enable the agent to take decisions. We have looked at algorithms that extensively require deep learning and neural networks. In this section, we will look into a different set of algorithms that use the biological concept of natural evolution. Throughout the history of human evolution, we have seen genes play an important role. From Neanderthals to Homo sapiens, the transformation was due to continuous change in our DNA, which contains the alleles (genes). DNA is a molecule containing two polynucleotide chains in a double helical orientation (Watson and Crick Model), containing Adenine, Cytosine, Thymine, and Guanine bases. Human reproduction is the process of transforming, splitting, and recombining these DNA strands in our system that inherently change or mutate the genes for the next generation of offspring. In sexual reproductive organisms, cell division through the process of meiosis takes place. In this eight-step procedure, chromosomes (fundamental part of genes) undergo splitting and combination several times to produce new permutations of chromosomes that are transferred to the next generation. The two most important stages in this process are crossover of the chromosomes and mutation of the chromosomes. The survivability of the new combination of chromosomes (mutated chromosome) depends on the theory of natural selection proposed by Darwin. According to Darwin's theory, the fittest offspring survives to produce more offspring for the next generation. Combining this theory of Darwin (Principle of Natural Selection) with the chromosome transformation steps, the evolutionary algorithms come into picture. The evolutionary algorithms set is a collection of algorithms that are proposed to generate stronger samples for each new generation to complete a given task. The fitness of a particular offspring depends on its score to optimize a task—that is, to what extent the new offspring performs better as compared to the older ones. These tasks can be optimizing a mathematical function, or matching a pattern, or even making an agent to make a decision that would maximize the value returned. The combination of evolutionary algorithms with RL has given rise to a vast set of algorithms that are commonly referred to as evolutionary strategies (ES). Mostly, these algorithms are randomized and do not rely on neural networks or backpropagation for weight updates, as in the case of traditional deep RL algorithms. However, these can be extended to contain neural networks for training the crossover and mutation steps through a loss function with the help of gradient descent optimizers. Let us first formalize the steps of evolutionary algorithms, and then we will look at two simplest forms of these algorithms for better understandability.

The following are the steps of evolutionary algorithms.

- **Initialization:** This is the first step of the algorithm where an initial population (samples) is initialized along with the chromosome set (possible variables), which can include characters for pattern matching, floats or integers for optimizing a function, and so forth. This also contains the target genome, which is the target value of the optimization process that is required to be reached.

- **Selection:** This process involves selecting the fittest offspring from the new generation based on certain logic. Depending on the fitness, the selection process can either mate the new offspring or mutate it.

- **Crossover:** This process is derived from splitting different parts of the chromosome and recombining them at different locations, effectively interchanging the gene sequences at different positions. Crossover causes mutation, as new combinations of the sequences are produced. Similarly, in our context, crossover is implemented using a random function to create new combinations of the offspring solution.

- **Mutation:** The new offspring population is then made to mutate, which is again controlled by a random function. The random function mutates parts of the solution based on the crossed over solution to optimize the target value. This introduces a variation in the population.

- **Termination:** Once the target function or value is achieved, the process terminates, as in this case we have produced the fittest generation.

This process can be visualized in Figure 7-1.

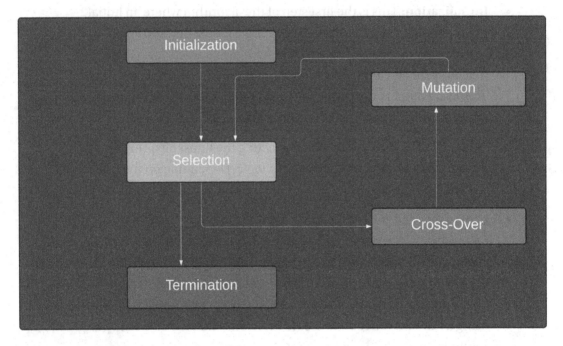

Figure 7-1. *Evolutionary algorithm steps*

We will be focusing on two different algorithms in this section: the genetic algorithm and the evolution strategy.

Genetic Algorithm

The most primitive form of evolutionary algorithms is the genetic algorithm. As the name suggests, it follows the traditional pipeline of evolutionary algorithm mentioned in the previous section including mutation and selection. The aim of the algorithm is to optimize a function by adjusting the randomly generated results for each episode of training. The episodes of training are referred to as the generation, and the results of such episodes are termed as the offspring. We will be building a genetic algorithm that would try to match a phrase by performing mutation and selection. Open the Genetic Algorithm.ipynb Notebook. In our case, we have a target string as the phrase that the algorithm has to match. The initial population is produced randomly by selecting characters from the "gene_pool" (character set).

Initially we start with declaring the class "GA" and including the "parameters" method. This controls the variables such as population, which signifies the length of the generated offspring string at each generation; the chromosome, which is the gene pool or all the characters present for building the population (alphabets, numbers, punctuations, space, and special characters); and the target_genome, which specifies the target string to match.

```
def parameters(self,population_size,chromosomes,
target_genome):
    self.population=population_size
    self.chromosomes=chromosomes
    self.target_genome=target_genome
```

The "mutation" method is used to randomly select a particular character from the set of characters referred to as the gene pool. In reality mutation is the process of randomly changing a particular gene in a genome sequence, and in this case, the method randomly selects a particular character from the set.

```
def mutation(self,chromosomes):
    gene_chromosome= random.choice(self.chromosomes)
    return gene_chromosome
```

The "create_sequence" method uses the "mutation" method to create the genome sequence for each new offspring in a generation. It returns a list of the character sequence.

```
def create_sequence(self,target_genome,chromosomes):
    sequence=[]
    for _ in range(len(self.target_genome)):
        sequence.append(self.mutation(self.chromosomes))
    return sequence
```

We then have the "offspring" method, which is a simplified version of crossing over of genes during mating. We take two different parent strings or character sequences as the parent genomes, and based on the output of the random function, we either clamp the parent's genome to the child or mutate it using the "mutation" method. The "random" method provides an output probability, and if this value lies between 0 and 0.35, the child genome takes the first parent's genome; if it is between 0.35 and 0.70, the child genome takes the second parent's genome. For probabilities between 0.70 to 1.0, we produce a new genome sequence for the child with the mutation algorithm.

```
def offspring(self,seq1,seq2):
    child_sequence=[]
    for s1,s2 in zip(seq1,seq2):
      if(random.random()<0.35):
        child_sequence.append(s1)
      elif(random.random()<0.7):
        child_sequence.append(s2)
      else:
        child_sequence.append(self.mutation(self.chromosomes))
    return child_sequence
```

The "fitness" method computes the decreasing fitness value for each offspring. Since we have to match a phrase or string, the fitness of a child genome sequence is calculated as the number of characters that are mismatched with respect to the target genome sequence. As the training would progress, we would see that the fitness would decrease, implying that the offspring sequences (strings) almost or completely match the target sequence (string).

```
def fitness(self,child_seq,target):
    fitness=0
    for i,j in zip(child_seq,target):
      if i!=j:
        fitness+=1
    return fitness
```

We have the "main" method where we initialize the class. We assign an initial population size of 100 randomly created genomes. The target genome sequence is the phrase "Genetic algorithm," which the algorithm has to match. We then have a "while" loop, which runs as long as the target genome is not attained. Internally, we sort the new generation of offspring sequences based on their fitness value and use 10% of them (fittest offspring) for the next generation. The remaining 90% of the population is then mated (50-50 ratio) using the "offspring" method. This procedure is completed with the help of the following lines:

```
if __name__=='__main__':
  ga=GA()
  gene_pool='''abcdefghijklmnopqrstuvwxyzABCDEFGHIJKLMNOPQRS
  TUVWXYZ 1234567890, .-;:_!"#%&/()=?@${[]}'''
  target_gene='Genetic Algorithm'
  ga.parameters(100,gene_pool,target_gene)
  generation=0
  gene_match=False
  fitness_array=[]
  gen_array=[]
  pop=[]
  for i in range(ga.population):
    ind_gene=ga.create_sequence(ga.chromosomes,
    ga.target_genome)
    pop.append(ind_gene)

  while not gene_match:
    pop = sorted(pop, key = lambda x:ga.fitness(x,
    ga.target_genome))
    z=pop[0]
    if ga.fitness(z,ga.target_genome) <= 0 :
        gene_match = True
        break
    new_generation=[]
    sample=int((10*ga.population)/100)
    new_generation.extend(pop[:sample])
    mate_sample=int((90*ga.population)/100)

    for j in range(mate_sample):
      parent1=random.choice(pop[:50])
      parent2=random.choice(pop[:50])
      child=ga.offspring(parent1,parent2)
      new_generation.append(child)
    pop=new_generation
    w=ga.fitness(pop[0],ga.target_genome)
    fitness_array.append(w)
```

```
gen_array.append(generation)
print("Generation: {}\tString: {}\tFitness:
{}". format(generation, "".join(pop[0]),w))
generation += 1
```

We then use the "matplotlib" library to visualize the downward trend of fitness score with the new generations. It has to be mentioned that in this case, we consider the most fit to be the ones with the least fitness score—that is, almost completely matches the target genome or phrase. However, this logic can be reversed as well, and we can either maximize or minimize according to our needs.

```
plt.plot(gen_array,fitness_array)
plt.title('Genetic Fitness Curve')
plt.xlabel('Generations')
plt.ylabel('Fitness')
plt.show()
```

On running this, we can visualize the generations being produced by the algorithm and the corresponding fitness score,as shown in Figure 7-2.

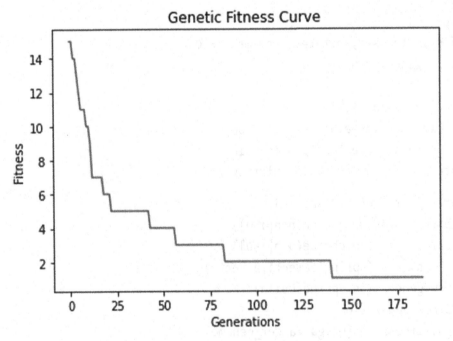

Figure 7-2. *Fitness vs. generations curve in genetic algorithm*

The parameters inside the algorithm, such as the target_genome, population size, and the percentages for producing new generations, can be changed as well to analyze the effect of each parameter on training.

Evolution Strategies

This is another set of algorithms that rely on crossover and mutation steps extensively for generation of new progenies. In the case of genetic algorithm we tried to match a phrase with values from a gene pool, which in our case was a subset of the ASCII character set. If we had to optimize a given mathematical function with a genetic algorithm, we would have used the binary set {0,1} to generate fit offspring. In the case of ES, for the same problem, we will be using real numbers to generate new generations. ES is a set of deterministic algorithms based on certain probabilistic distribution of the samples of a particular generation. Due to the deterministic nature of these algorithms, the dependency on gradient computation to maximize or minimize a function can be avoided. The simplest form of this includes simple Gaussian evolution strategies, and before we move into the implementation details of this, let us summarize the steps of ES.

We have to optimize a given function f(x) to an optimized variant $p_\theta(x)$ using the parameter set θ. The following steps are required:

- Generate an initial population D = {$(x_i, f(x_i))$} where $x_i \sim p_\theta(x)$

- Evaluate the fitness of D

- Use Darwin's best fit strategy to select a subset of offspring to update θ and produce the next generation of offspring.

There are various algorithms inside this set, and we will be implementing the Gaussian Evolution Strategy.

Gaussian Evolution Strategy

We mentioned the randomness in ES is due to the distributions. When we apply a Gaussian kernel on the mutation and offspring generation process, we create this strategy. We create a normal distribution with mean μ and standard deviation σ, which is tracked by θ as follows:

$$\theta = (\mu, \sigma), \text{ and } p_\theta(x) \sim N(\mu, \sigma^2 I) = \mu + \sigma N(0, I),$$

where $N(\mu,\sigma^2 I)$ is the normal distribution. The steps for this process can be mathematically simplified as follows:

- **Initialization:** Initialize $\theta = \theta_0$ and counter t=0

- **OffSpring generation:** By using crossover and mutation, we create the next set of population using the form:

$$D^{(t+1)} = \{\, x^{(t+1)} \mid x^{(t+1)} = \mu^{(t)} + \sigma^{(t)} y^{(t+1)} \text{ where } y^{(t+1)} \sim N(x|0,I) \,\}$$

- **Survival of fittest:** The most elite offspring are sampled from the new population based on their fitness scores. Let λ be the sample of the fittest generation of offspring:

$$D^{(t+1)}{}_{elite} = \{\, x_i{}^{(t+1)} \mid x_i{}^{(t+1)} \,\varepsilon\, D^{(t+1)} \text{ and } i=1,....,\lambda \,\}$$

- **Update μ and θ:** The mean and the standard deviation is updated using the fittest offspring set:

$$\mu^{(t+1)} = avg(D^{(t+1)}{}_{elite}) = (1/\lambda) \left(\sum_{i=1..\lambda} x_i{}^{(t+1)} \right)$$

$$\sigma^{(t+1)2} = var(D^{(t+1)}{}_{elite}) = (1/\lambda) \left(\sum_{i=1..\lambda} x_i{}^{(t+1)} - \mu^{(t)} \right)^2$$

Now we will create a simplified version of this algorithm that will be used to find the maximum value in a curve. In our case, we will use a general superposed harmonic oscillator as our function, although we can change the function according to our needs. Open the Evolutionary Algorithm.ipynb Notebook. We create the class "EA" and declare the "parameters" method, which controls the "chrom_size" (since we want to find the maximum float value of the equation, it is 1); the "chrom_bound," which specifies the range in which to find the maxima; the "generations," which signifies the number of generations to produce; the "population," which controls the population size per generation; "n_offspring," which controls the number of offsprings produced; and a Boolean variable "mutation," which controls whether mutation will take place.

```
def parameters(self,chrom_size,chrom_bound,n_generations,
population_size,
n_offspring,mutation):
    self.chrom_size=chrom_size
    self.chrom_bound=chrom_bound
    self.generations=n_generations
```

```
self.population=population_size
self.n_offspring=n_offspring
self.mutation=mutation
```

Then we have the methods "harmonic," "sigmoid," and "function," which are different functions that we would like to optimize (maximize) in a given range. These are normal algebraic functions in the real plane bounded by the "chrom_bound" variable. In our case we will be using the "harmonic" method:

```
def sigmoid(self,x):
    return 1/(1+np.exp(-x))
  def function(self,x):
    return 2*x*x - np.cos(2*x)
  def harmonic(self,x):
    return np.cos(2*x) + np.sin(2*x)
```

The "fitness" method is used to flatten the input into a list so that it can be used by the "survival_of_fittest" method later. A small bias of 1e-3 is added to it to avoid 0:

```
def fitness(self,z):
    return z.flatten() + 1e-3
```

The "offspring" method is used to mate two parents to produce a child and perform crossover and mutation (if "mutation" is set to True). We create a dictionary that contains the offspring number with its corresponding chromosome (float value). Each organism in the population consists of a value and produces similar offspring containing another float value, and as the training progresses, the offspring tries to produce the maximum float value for the function. The dictionary keeps a track of the float values or the chromosomes for each offspring. In the crossover method, two random parents (each containing a float value) are taken, and a new child offspring is generated. Since we are using mutation, we also create an array that contains the mutated float values (randomized) for each of the offspring. Then while updating the mutated gene, we use a normal distribution with mean of 0.2. Finally we return the newly generated offspring containing its own chromosome (float).

```
def offspring(self,population,n_offspring):

    children=dict({"chromosome":np.zeros((n_offspring,
    self.chrom_size))})
```

```
if self.mutation==True:
  children['mutate']=np.zeros_like(children['chromosome'])

  for i,j in zip(children['chromosome'],
  children['mutate']):
    sample1,sample2=np.random.choice
   (np.arange(self.population),size=2)
    crossover=np.random.randint
   (0,2,self.chrom_size,dtype=np.bool)
    i[crossover]=population['chromosome']
                 [sample1,crossover]
    i[~crossover]=population['chromosome']
                 [sample2,~crossover]
    j[crossover]=population['mutate']
                 [sample1,crossover]
    j[~crossover]=population['mutate']
                 [sample2,~crossover]
    j[:]=np.maximum((j + np.random.rand(*j.shape)-0.2),0)
    i+=j*np.random.rand(*i.shape)
    i[:]=np.clip(i,*self.chrom_bound)
  return children
```

We then have the "survival_of_fittest" method, and in this case we are using the mutation array as well. We stack the dictionary containing the float value (chromosome) and the mutated output value (float). Then we flatten this container and pass it to the "harmonic" function to generate float values. The resultant output is then sorted, and the highest values are passed to the next generation of offspring. This can be illustrated using the following lines:

```
def survival_of_fittest(self,pop, kids):
    if self.mutation==False:
      pass
    for key in ['chromosome', 'mutate']:
        pop[key] = np.vstack((pop[key], kids[key]))

    fit = self.fitness(self.harmonic(pop['chromosome']))
```

```
# calculate global fitness
idx = np.arange(pop['chromosome'].shape[0])
good_idx = idx[fit.argsort()][-self.population:]
for key in ['chromosome', 'mutate']:
    pop[key] = pop[key][good_idx]
#print(pop)
return pop
```

In the "main" method, we initialize the values of the parameters. We are providing a bound –[0,5] for determining the maxima of the function("chrom_size"), with a population size of 100 ("population"), for 200 generations ("generations") and 50 offspring for each generation ("n_offspring") with "mutation" set to "True." We initialize the population with a normal distribution. For each loop of training, we create a new offspring using the "offspring" method and generate a new population based on the output of the "survival_of_fittest" method. A scatter plot, created using "matplotlib," is used to visualize the final position of the maximum value of the function.

```
if __name__=='__main__':
  ea=EA()
  ea.parameters(1,[0,5],200,100,50,True)
  population=dict(chromosome=5*np.random.rand
 (1,ea.chrom_size).repeat(ea.population,axis=0),
  mutate=np.random.rand(ea.population,ea.chrom_size))
  ea.plot()
  for m in range(ea.generations):

    child = ea.offspring(population, ea.n_offspring)
    #print(child)
    population = ea.survival_of_fittest(population, child)
    print("Generation",m)
    #print("Population",population)
  scatter_pl = plt.scatter(population['chromosome']
  , ea.harmonic(population['chromosome']), s=200,
  lw=0, c='orange', alpha=0.5); plt.pause(0.05)

  plt.show()
```

On running this, we can visualize the maxima being pointed out by a yellowish-orange glow, as shown in Figure 7-3. Since we are using a superposed sinusoidal curve, the maximum value can be at either of the two peaks in the range [0,5]. The algorithm shows the result to be the one on the right.

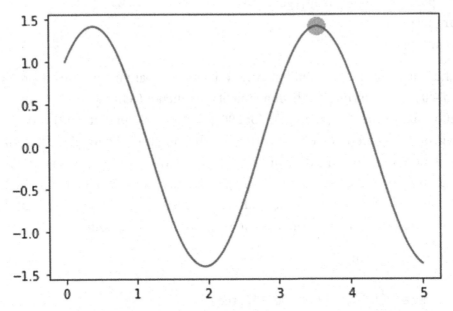

Figure 7-3. *Maximizing a harmonic function with Gaussian Evolutionary Strategy*

We can change the function to check the maxima for them as well. There are other algorithms in this section such as Covariance Matrix Adaptation (CMA)-ES and Natural Evolution Strategy (NES), which we will briefly discuss.

Covariance Matrix Adaptation Evolution Strategy

This is a stochastic evolutionary strategy that uses covariance matrix for updating the mean and standard deviation for each cycle of offspring. We use the Gaussian distribution, which we used in the previous part, with a covariance matrix instead of plain floats and integers. This is represented by the form:

$$\theta = (\mu, \sigma), \text{ and } p_\theta(x) \sim N(\mu, \sigma^2 C) = \mu + \sigma N(0, C),$$

where C is the covariance matrix. The covariance matrix on Gaussian distribution has non-negative Eigen values, and the corresponding vectors form an orthonormal basis. Most of the process is the same as before, with the exception of mean and standard deviation update. The mean is updated using the form:

$$\mu^{(t+1)} = \text{avg}(D^{(t+1)}_{elite}) = \alpha(1/\lambda)\left(\sum_{i=1..\lambda} x_i^{(t+1)}\right),$$

where α is the learning rate. The most important aspect is the step size for producing new samples. Without the covariance matrix, the samples for the next generations are controlled by the standard deviation, σ, as mentioned in the previous section (Offspring Generation). A larger value updates the parameters using a large step size, and to control this we use the evolution strategy with the covariance matrix. Thus, at each step the parameters are updated by moving the new generation along the evolution path. This is done by updating y according to the relation:

$$(1/\lambda)\left(\sum_{i=1..\lambda} y_i^{(t+1)}\right) \sim (1/\sqrt{\lambda})C^{(t)0.5} N(0,I)$$

The $C^{(t)0.5}$ can be calculated easily since the matrix forms an orthonormal basis. We can assign higher weights to the recent offspring with the help of polyak averaging. The adaptation of the covariance matrix is done with the help of rank minimization. The CMA-ES algorithm is more stable than the vanilla ES algorithm (simple Gaussian), as it controls the exploration rate along with adapting the covariance matrix with the help of rank minimum updates. It combines the effect of Gaussian distribution on a covariance matrix for step-size modulation as well as updates the standard deviation using an adaptive strategy.

Natural Evolution Strategy

NES is related to the policy gradient update method to optimize a function. It uses the log likelihood method used in the vanilla policy gradients and reinforce algorithms, denoted by:

$$\Delta_\theta J_\theta = E_{x\text{-}p\theta}\left[f(x)\,\Delta_\theta \log p_\theta(x)\right]$$

The fundamental parts of this algorithm are listed here.

- NES uses rank-based fitness. This implies that NES uses ranks to determine monotonically increasing fitness.

- NES uses adaptation sampling for the hyperparameters. In this case, natural gradient descent is applied to update the weights, which are denoted as the ratio between the previous generation offspring fitness with respect to the current fitness.

$$w`_i = p_\theta(x) / p_{\theta'}(x)$$

- It also uses Kullback-Leiblar (KL) divergence as a measure to find the divergence between the probabilistic distributions during the sampling stage, and as in natural gradient descent, the algorithm tries to determine the steepest direction along a small step.

These are some of the important algorithms under ES. There are several other algorithms that control and update the variance and the mean of the population using different metrics. The OpenAI ES is a gradient-free black box optimizer variant of NES that uses Gaussian noise and then uses the log likelihood (similar to policy gradient). These types of gradient algorithms are called evolved policy gradient ES algorithms. Thus, there is much scope of development using this category of algorithms in addition to the traditional deep RL. We will see that these algorithms have been used in the Obstacle Tower Challenge by the topmost performers in the next section.

Case Study: Obstacle Tower Challenge

The Obstacle Tower Challenge (February - August 2019) was designed to provide improvised benchmarks in the context of deep RL. The challenge was created to foster research among developers as well as scientists to outperform contemporary state-of-the-art (SOTA) algorithms. We will be looking at the challenge from an objective view-point and will also be looking at some of the most successful submissions of the challenge by the winners. The Obstacle Tower Challenge was created to be difficult to solve for the SOTA algorithms during that time. While AI generalization was the main aim of the challenge, the challenge is renowned for the feature of procedural level generation. The Obstacle Tower Challenge contains an AI agent whose task is to move from level 0 to level 100, and in each level, the agent has to complete a set of tasks in a given room. The challenge had 100 different procedurally generated environments, each containing a starting point and an ending point. Each particular room (level) consisted of puzzles, enemies, obstacles, and keys to unlock the next room (level). The research behind this project is attributed to the ML Agents team from Unity Technologies. The paper related to this is "Obstacle Tower: A Generalization Challenge in Vision, Control and Planning" by Juliani et al. The paper is published at the following link: `https://arxiv.org/abs/1902.01378`.

Figure 7-4 shows a view of the Obstacle Tower Challenge taken from the Unity Technologies Blog (`https://blogs.unity3d.com/2019/01/28/obstacle-tower-challenge-test-the-limits-of-intelligence-systems/`).

Figure 7-4. *Obstacle Tower Challenge in Unity ML Agents*

The Details of Obstacle Tower

The Obstacle Tower Challenge was created using Unity Engine and ML Agents and can be made to run in Windows, Linux, and Mac OS. It also uses the OpenAI Gym wrapper for easy integration with existing deep RL algorithms. It consists of the features mentioned here.

Episode Dynamics

According to the details of the paper, the most interesting aspect is the procedural content generation for each room or level. Each level has a set of tasks to be completed, which can include evading obstacles, defeating enemies, collecting keys for unlocking the door to the next level, as well as evading falling into pits and traps. Each level contains "orbs" that increase the time for the agent to reach upper levels. This is a variation of the exploration-exploitation strategy that compels the agent to decide whether to collect orbs and increase time or quickly complete the level. This procedural generation of the levels allows the agent to be trained in a task-specific curriculum learning pattern. We will be looking at it in the successive sections.

Observation Space

This consists of visual as well as nonvisual auxiliary information that is required by the agent to take a decision. The visual observation space consists of a 168 X 168 RGB pixel image, which can be downscaled to 84 X 84 dimensions. The nonvisual space consists of a vector containing auxiliary attributes, such as the number of keys the agent is in possession and the time left in the episode.

Action Space

The action space is multi-discrete, implying that it consists of smaller discrete action spaces. The agent can move using the following subspaces: forward, backward, no-op, left, right no-op, clockwise, counterclockwise rotation of the camera, no-op, and jump no-op. The action space can also be flattened to a list consisting of 54 possible choices.

Reward Space

This contains both sparse and dense rewards. Sparse rewards are credited when the agent completes a particular level. In this case, a value of +1 unit is credited as the reward. In dense configuration, the agent gets credited with +0.1 unit of reward for opening doors, solving puzzles, and collecting keys. One of the aims of this challenge is to create internal reward signals that can be used by different deep RL algorithms to instigate curiosity and empowerment within the agent.

Procedural Level Generation: Graph Grammar

Procedural generation is an important aspect of designing the levels of this challenge. It includes lighting, texture, room layout, and floor layouts, which enables the agent to learn using a curriculum-based approach. This generation also allows the agent to perform well in new rooms by generalization.

- **Visual appearance:** This includes the five different themes of Obstacle Tower, which are generated procedurally using different sets of lighting, textures, intensity, and direction of real-time global illumination. The variants are ancient, moorish, industrial, modern, and future.

- **Floor layout:** The floor layout is generated using graph grammar. This layout generation consists of a mission graph and the layout grid. The mission graph suggests the actions that are required to be performed by the agent to reach the next room, such as unlocking a door with a key or solving a puzzle. The paper provides an in-depth overview of how the graph grammar technique is used to generate successive levels. The paper also uses letters and notations to provide an idea how each node in the grammar is related to the next node. Grammar recipes are involved to concatenate a sequence of grammar rules to procedurally generate a new mission graph. This is done by including randomness in the generation process. The generated mission graph is then converted to a 2D grid of rooms, which is the layout grid. This is done with the help of shape grammar and is used to generate the virtual scene.

- **Room layout:** Once the floor layout is completed, the room layout is generated with the help of templates. The paper uses the descriptions of the two templates: puzzle and key. In the former template, the agent has to push a block from start to end and avoid intermediate obstacles to unlock a different level. In the key template, the agent has to find and collect keys and avoid obstacles. Using a probabilistic approach, new samples of these templates are created that control the position of different GameObjects in a particular room. Each room can have dimensions of order 3 X 3, 4 X 4, and 5 X 5.

This is how the Obstacle Tower environment was created, mainly by using graph recipes, shape grammar, and sampling of templates to procedurally generate new levels. The difficulty of each level also increases systematically to allow the agent to learn using curriculum learning. Since a number of such levels (100) are generated using a finite number of initial levels, there is a significant requirement for generalization by the agent. Figure 7-5 illustrates the different themes and their visual appearance, which is collected from the paper.

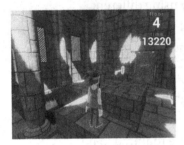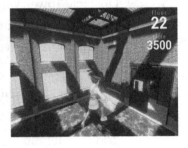

Figure 7-5. *Ancient, Moorish, and industrial themes in Obstacle Tower*

Generalization

According to the details of the paper, the Obstacle Tower contains three different generalization environments. These test the agent's capability to generalize the new levels and also for improving or changing algorithms to produce benchmark performances.

- **No generalization:** This involves training the agent on a fixed version of the Obstacle Tower environment. In this case, five random seeds of dynamics of the agent were to be used as a measure of performance.

- **Weak generalization:** This is also referred to as within-distribution generalization, which requires the agent to be trained on a fixed set of 100 seeds for the environment configurations. Then generalization is to be tested on five randomly selected tower configuration seeds for five times each, with a different set of seeds that control the agent's dynamics. This was the main focus of the challenge, as mentioned in Unity blog (`https://blogs.unity3d.com/2019/08/07/announcing-the-obstacle-tower-challenge-winners-and-open-source-release/`).

- **Strong generalization:** In addition to the weak generalization testing strategy, the agent would have to be tested on a diverse set of external visual conditions such as varying lighting, textures, and geometry. Since the testing environment was created with a different set of grammar rules from the training counterpart, it was difficult to train the agent with contemporary SOTA deep learning algorithms. The challenge also emphasized that stronger generalization forms a better strategy for agents to learn any complex environment.

The Unity Team initially benchmarked the challenge and compared the results with humans playing the game. The team used proximal policy operation (PPO) and rainbow as the algorithms and discovered that the agent could reach less than 10 levels for no generalization strategy. Rainbow outperformed PPO as a more generalized algorithm. For weak and strong generalizations, the maximum levels reached were 3.4 and 0.8, respectively, with a varied rainbow algorithm. Rainbow is a variant of N-step dueling double deep Q-network (DQN) with prioritized experience replay and distributed RL. In contrast, humans were able to solve 15 levels on average, reaching up to 22 levels. The sharp contrast of the catastrophic learning of the agent with human counterparts is illustrated by Unity in their blog, as shown in Figure 7-6.

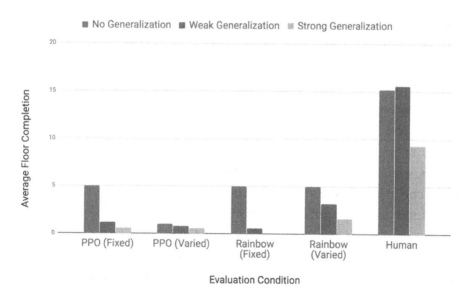

Figure 7-6. Performance of PPO, rainbow vs. human control on the Obstacle Tower Challenge

Now that we have covered the fundamentals of the Obstacle Tower Challenge, we will be looking at some of the solutions that made a breakthrough by providing extraordinary benchmarks. We will also walk through the steps to install the Obstacle Tower environment, as it was open sourced after the challenge under Apache 2.0 license.

Challenge Winners and Proposed Algorithms

The challenge was won by Alex Nichol, whose algorithm was able to solve an average of 19.4 levels. The fundamental part of the winning strategy was including behavioral cloning algorithms initially to train the agent in a supervised manner. Nichol used GAIL with a fine-tuned custom PPO implementation. The PPO policy (preirarchy) with KL divergence was used. However, behavioral cloning began overfitting the solution, and Alex designed an IMPALA convolution neural network (CNN) visual classifier to detect different objects (doors, keys, obstacles) in the room. To avoid catastrophic forgetting of the agent by using recurrent neural networks (RNNs) as the memory, he built a stack of observations from 50 time-steps as part of the input. He also tried a variety of CMA-ES evolution algorithms for exploration; however, the visual classifier (distributed IMPALA) along with fine-tuned PPO, behavioral cloning, and stacked observations provided a much better output. The agent was able to attain an average reward of 35.86 units. The detailed description of the approach is provided at Alex Nichol's blog (`https://blog.aqnichol.com/2019/07/24/competing-in-the-obstacle-tower-challenge/`), and the repository for the challenge is at (`https://github.com/unixpickle/obs-tower2`).

The second prize was won by the computational science laboratory Compscience.org (`https://www.compscience.org`) at Universitat Pompeu Fabra. The team consisted of Gianni and Miha. They reached an average of 16 levels and initially tried PPO with KL divergence term but later resorted to extensive sampling methods. Later the team used world models, which comprises creating compressed representation of the observation with an auto encoder (encoder-decoder variants using long short-term memory [LSTM]-based RNNs) and building a policy using ES.

The third prize was won by Songbin Choi from Seoul, whose agent reached an average of 13.2 floors. He used the PPO policy from the ML Agents with gated recurrent unit (GRU), which is an improvised version of LSTM and RNNs, for better performance. To reduce overfitting dropout layers were added along with adding left-right flipping in images for classification (data augmentation). The data augmentation is a standard procedure to produce samples of images with different orientations from the input image. He then used an experience buffer to collect the most relevant observations and used the entire 100 seeds as the training set.

Apart from the winners, there were honorable mentions of Joe Booth, Doug Meng, and the UEFDL team. Booth used PPO with demonstrations for training the agent and used a compressed network with RNN architecture for memory. More details as to the approach can be found at the link: `https://towardsdatascience.com/i-placed-4th-in-my-first-ai-competition-takeaways-from-the-unity-obstacle-tower-competition-794d3e6d3310` along with the repository at: `https://github.com/Sohojoe/ppo-dash`.

Booth was able to reach 10.8 levels with his policy. Meng used a variant of deepmind IMPALA with batched inference and customized replay. Having tried PPO and rainbow, he resorted to IMPALA due to the fact that it is less off-policy compared to the former ones. The UEFDL team used advantage actor critic (A2C) with LSTM from the stable baselines to train the agent, later using A2C with curiosity and PPO for better performance. Both Meng and the UEFDL team attained an average of 10 levels. More information on the approaches can be found at the Unity blog (`https://blogs.unity3d.com/2019/08/07/announcing-the-obstacle-tower-challenge-winners-and-open-source-release/`).

Installation and Resources

The Obstacle Tower source has been open sourced since the completion of the challenge at github: `https://github.com/Unity-Technologies/obstacle-tower-source`.

In order to use the repository, it is required to install Unity version 2019.4 (from Unity Hub) along with ML Agents Release 4 (the latest release as per documentation). This Release can be found at the link: `https://github.com/Unity-Technologies/ml-agents/tree/release_4`.

The repository can be downloaded in zip format or by using the command line

```
git clone https://github.com/Unity-Technologies/obstacle-tower-source
```

Once the installation is complete, we can open this in the Unity Editor. We have to load the Procedural scene from the Assets/ObstacleTower/Scenes folder. We can then click Play in the Editor to interact using human controls. There are certain important aspects in the repository that controls the procedural generation of the levels.

- When the environment is launched or reset, the definitions for the floor and room layouts are generated in advance using the FloorBuilder script located inside the Assets/ObstacleTower/Scripts/FloorLogic folder. Internally a list of FloorLayout objects, each filled with a 2D grid of RoomDefinition objects and other meta-data, are generated. The FloorGenerator and RoomGenerator scripts are responsible for generating the FloorLayout and RoomDefinition, respectively, with help of graph recipes and shape grammar.

- When the agent starts at a given floor, the FloorLayout is used to generate the specific floor (scene) on run-time. FloorBuilder and RoomBuilder scripts are used for instantiating the GameObjects inside the scene, with the help of definitions provided.

For modifying and playing with the five different visual themes, we have to navigate to the Assets/ObstacleTower/Resources/Prefabs, where the prefabs of each theme are located. The animations, meshes, and textures are located in the Assets/WorldBuilding folder. The five themes are illustrated in the Figure 7-7.

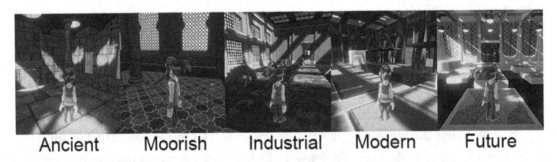

Ancient   Moorish   Industrial   Modern   Future

Figure 7-7. *The five visual themes of the Obstacle Tower Challenge*

Resources For Procedural Level Generation

As we learned from the paper, the floor for each room is generated using a set of rules using graph grammar. The FloorGeneration is used for producing FloorLayout, which returns a 2D array of RoomDefinitions. The nine different types of rooms are:

- **Normal:** normal room without any special properties

- **Lock:** a room with "KeyLock" door that requires a key to open

- **Key:** a room containing a "Key" item

- **Lever:** a room with a "LeverLock" trap door

- **Puzzle:** a room with at least one "PuzzleLock" door requiring a puzzle to be solved to open

- **Start:** a room containing a "Start" door

- **End:** a room containing "End" door

- **Basement:** a room containing both a "Start" and "End" door (only for floor 0)

- **Connection:** a room containing one-way doors

The steps for creating a new room type based on "input.txt" and "output.txt" files with graph grammar is explained at the documentation link `https://github.com/Unity-Technologies/obstacle-tower-source/blob/master/Assets/ObstacleTower/Resources/FloorGeneration/AddRoomType.md`.

According to this documentation, for creating a new type of room, we first modify the NodeType.cs script to include a new node. Then we have to modify the EnvironmentParameters.cs script to add the new room type. The documentation uses a new room type named "Hazard," and the EnvironmentParameters.cs script is updated as follows:

```
public enum AllowedRoomTypes
 {
    Normal,
    PlusKey,
    PlusPuzzle
    PlusPuzzle,
    Hazard
 }
```

The TemplateRoomGenerator script is used for modifying the templates for generation of the room. The following changes are to be made as pointed out by the documentation.

```
public class TemplateRoomGenerator : RoomGenerator
    private List<RoomDefinition> endTemplates;
    private List<RoomDefinition> keyTemplates;
    private List<RoomDefinition> basementTemplates;
    private List<RoomDefinition> hazardTemplates;
```

```
      public TemplateRoomGenerator()
      {
public class TemplateRoomGenerator : RoomGenerator
            case NodeType.Connection:
                normalTemplates = LoadTemplates($"Templates/
                 {roomSize - 2}/{targetDifficulty}/normals");
                return normalTemplates[Random.Range
                (0, normalTemplates.Count)];
            case NodeType.Hazard:
                hazardTemplates = LoadTemplates($"Templates/
                {roomSize - 2}/{targetDifficulty}/hazards");
                return hazardTemplates[Random.Range
                (0, hazardTemplates.Count)];
            default:
                normalTemplates = LoadTemplates($"Templates/
                {roomSize - 2}/{targetDifficulty}/normals");
                return normalTemplates[Random.Range
                (0, normalTemplates.Count)];
```

Then we have to create our own recipe to modify FloorGenerator.cs script

```
public class FloorGenerator
                return "graphRecipeNormal";
            case AllowedRoomTypes.PlusKey:
                return "graphRecipeKey";
            case AllowedRoomTypes.Hazard:
                return "graphRecipeHazard";
            case AllowedRoomTypes.PlusPuzzle:
                switch (environmentParameters.allowedFloorLayouts)
                {
```

After this we have to open the Procedural scene in Unity and select the
ObstacleTower-v3.0 GameObject in the hierarchy. We then navigate to the
ObstacleTower Academy component and change the row in the Reset Parameters
named "allowed-rooms" to the ordinal value of the enum. In this case, we set the value of
3 for "Hazard" room type. This is represented in Figure 7-8 from the Github page.

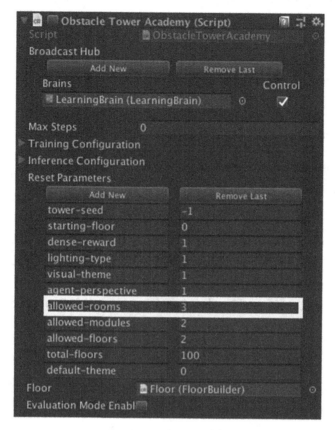

Figure 7-8. *Adding a room type to the Obstacle Tower environment*

Along with different rooms, there are different doors that are present in the scene, which includes:

- **Open:** tagent can move freely

- **KeyLock:** requires a Key to be opened

- **LeverLock:** the doors that trap the agent from behind them once the agent passes through

- **PuzzleLock:** the doors that are unlocked after the agent solves a puzzle

- **Start:** the doors where the agent is spawned at the start of the game

- **Exit:** the doors that take the agent to the next floor

- **OneWay:** these doors freely open from only one direction

The Github documentation at `https://github.com/Unity-Technologies/` `obstacle-tower-source/blob/master/extending.md` provides an overview how to programmatically add a new room. The example provided here shows how to add a Basement type of room:

```
// Create a 1x1 empty floor grid
Cell[,] cellGrid = new Cell[1, 1];

// Create a Basement room node
Node node = new Node(0, 0, NodeType.Basement);

// Pick walls for the entry and exit doors
List<int> possibleDoors = new List<int> {0, 1, 2, 3};
int doorStart = possibleDoors[Random.Range(0, possibleDoors.Count)];
possibleDoors.Remove(doorStart);
int doorEnd = possibleDoors[Random.Range(0, possibleDoors.Count)];

// Add the basement room to the floor grid
cellGrid[0, 0] = new Cell(0, 0, CellType.Normal, node);

// Set the entry and exit doors on the walls of the cellGrid
cellGrid[0, 0].doorTypes[doorStart] = DoorType.Start;
cellGrid[0, 0].doorTypes[doorEnd] = DoorType.Exit;

// Create a floor layout with the grid.
var layout = new FloorLayout
{
    floorRoomSize = 5,
    floorLayout = new RoomDefinition[1, 1],
    cellLayout = cellGrid
};
```

So we have observed how to add a new room configuration using textual node declarations and updating the EnvironmentParameters script as well as programmatically.

Resource for Generating Room Layout

For generating a new layout for the room, we have to specify a template as mentioned in the previous sections. We also understood that templates are created by using the text-based input and output files. Each RoomDefinition contains two 2D arrays—one that defines the module placement in the room and another that defines the item position in the room. The templates are located in the Assets/ObstacleTower/Resources/Templates folder. In order to access a three-level difficulty in a 5 X 5 puzzle room, we have to navigate to Assets/ObstacleTower/Resources/Templates/5/3/puzzles. Each template file (textual) contains a grid of characters that control the position of different items in the room. The first item specifies the modules, and the second specifies the items. The uppercase letters refer to specific values, while the lowercase letters signify probabilistic values. The templates are interpreted in the TemplateRoomGenerator script that contains a set of rules how each character is to be interpreted for generating the room layout. A simple example of a 3 X 3 room with a key is as follows.

Go GK Go
GX GX GX
GX Go Go

G refers to PlatformLarge prefab module, o refers to a 50% chance of placing an orb, and X refers to no item. A typical illustration of interpreting this template in the Moorish theme is provided (from Github documentation) in Figure 7-9.

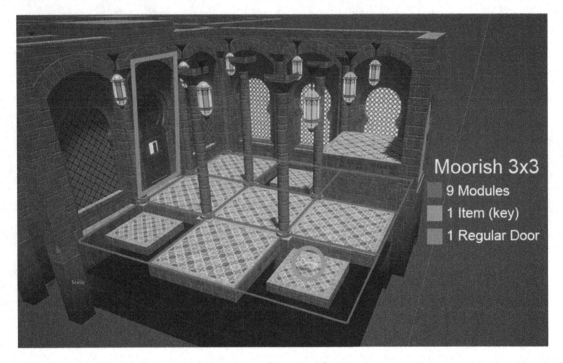

Figure 7-9. *Room layout generation after template interpretation*

The Github documentation also contains the different types of prefab modules and items available in the repository. Now that we have an idea of the procedural content generation in Obstacle Tower, we can create a simple Python script to run pre-existing algorithms (PPO, soft actor critic [SAC]) on it.

Interacting with Gym Wrapper

We will now use the obstacle-tower-env repository from https://github.com/Unity-Technologies/obstacle-tower-env to create an interaction with the OpenAI Gym wrapper. With the pre-existing settings of the Obstacle Tower Challenge, we will create an interface between the Gym and the environment through the Python API, which we studied in Chapter 5. We have to first install the Gym interface in our local machine or virtual machine through Command or Anaconda prompt by cloning the repository and running the installation with the help of the "pip install –e." command. We followed the same method for installing ML Agents in Chapter 3.

```
git clone
git@github.com:Unity-Technologies/obstacle-tower-env.git
 cd obstacle-tower-env
 pip install -e.
```

Once we have installed the required components, we can start interacting with the Gym environment for the Obstacle Tower environment. An introductory notebook for this interaction is provided by Unity at `https://github.com/Unity-Technologies/obstacle-tower-env/blob/master/examples/basic_usage.ipynb`, and this is also present in the Getting Started-Obstacle Tower Challenge.ipynb Notebook for reference. We first import the obstacle-tower-env in our Notebook along with matplotlib for plotting.

```
from obstacle_tower_env import ObstacleTowerEnv
%matplotlib inline
from matplotlib import pyplot as plt
```

We then start to analyze the environment in non-retro mode. We will be looking at the observation space and action space of the environment, which we discussed in detail in the previous sections. Since the Obstacle Tower environment can be used with the Gym wrapper, we will be using the methods "env.action_space," "env.reset," "env.close," and other Gym methods that we have used throughout this book.

```
#Launching the Environment
env = ObstacleTowerEnv(retro=False, realtime_mode=False)
print(env.action_space)
print(env.observation_space)
```

The next step is to interact with the environment and also observe the rewards associated. The "env.step" method is used in this case to provide an overview of the observations and rewards for each episode.

```
#Interacting with the Environment
obs = env.reset()
plt.imshow(obs[0])
obs, reward, done, info = env.step(env.action_space.sample())
plt.imshow(obs[0])
```

In the next step, we set the environment parameters. We set the seed value for controlling the rooms and floor, and according to the paper, in weak generalization strategy we can choose any valid seed in 0 to 100 range. We also select a floor for analysis. The config controls the agent's perspective, and in this case we set it to first-person mode. We then have the "env.reset" method from Gym, which resets the current parameters.

```
env.seed(5)
env.floor(15)
config = {'agent-perspective': 0}
obs = env.reset(config=config)
plt.imshow(obs[0])
```

We can also use the retro mode for this. For launching the retro mode, we have to set the Boolean variable "retro" to True.

```
env = ObstacleTowerEnv(retro=True)
print(env.action_space)
print(env.observation_space)
We can  interact with this retro Environment as follows:
#Interacting with the Environment in Retro mode
obs = env.reset()
print(obs.shape)
obs, reward, done, info = env.step(env.action_space.sample())
plt.imshow(obs)
For closing the Environment, we have to use the "env.close" method from Gym
#Close Environment retro mode
env.close()
```

Now, if we would like to extend the Gym Baseline algorithms for initial training of the Obstacle Tower agent, then we have to follow the steps provided in Chapter 5, where we mentioned the steps to use Gym wrapper and the Python API for training an agent using the Baselines. Among the submissions that we went through, we observed that PPO remains the default go-to algorithm for training the agent. The winners have used modified versions of PPO (with variant -1 using KL divergence), along with a set of other algorithms related to behavioral cloning, CNNs for image classification, and LSTM/GRU/RNNs for memory. The simplicity and robustness of PPO makes it very easy to use, and along with memory-based networks like GRU and LSTM, the performance greatly increases. There are certain reset parameters that can be used in the "env.reset" method and are provided by the Github documentation at the link `https://github.com/Unity-Technologies/obstacle-tower-env/blob/master/reset-parameters.md`. Additionally, Unity has provided an example implementation of the Obstacle Tower environment with predefined seeds and evaluated on a random policy. This is provided at the link `https://github.com/Unity-Technologies/obstacle-tower-env/blob/master/examples/evaluation.py` and is also present in the Obstacle_Tower_Predefined_Seeds-Unity.ipynb Notebook.

That completes this case study, and as we have learned, there is a huge scope of research and development. The Obstacle Tower provides a challenging environment for traditional deep RL algorithms to solve. With more research and advancements in the fields of RL, especially in the area of meta learning, improvised algorithms may allow the agent to complete more levels.

Case Study: Unity ML Agents Challenge I

This was a challenge organized by the ML Agents team of Unity before the Obstacle Tower Challenge around December 2017. The scope was to redefine the possibilities of Unity ML Agents to train agents to perform different tasks. The details of the challenge can be found at the Unity Connect website (`https://connect.unity.com/discover/challenges/ml-agents-1`).

We will be looking briefly at the top three submissions, while interested readers can go through the entire blog for more details. The first position was attained by Christine Barron, with the submission of "Pancake Bot." The aim of the project was to train a robotic arm to make pancakes—that is, to make the arm toss the pancake on the plate. The creator used curriculum learning for training and included three rigidbody limbs with configurable joints. All components were under the influence of gravity and torque. The initial reward signal was created to help the agent (Bot) to keep the pancake on its arm for a longer time period. The revised reward signal included the distance of the pancake from the center of the pan (robotic arm), and if the pancake hit the ground, the episode was terminated. To reduce the noise, kinematics and rotational motion were applied at the joints. On reaching a score of more than 60, the episode is terminated and the target is again placed at a random location. Curriculum learning helped to generalize the learning of the arm. Based on curriculum learning, the arm (agent) can move from 0.4 units to 0.8 and 1.2 units successively (along x and z axes). "Pass The Butter" is another bot that was designed with ray sensors to move the "butter" to a target destination. It uses nine raycasts originating from the "camera" on its head and returns 1 if it hits an obstacle. The reward signals included a +2 units of reward for successful completion of the task and -2 units if the bot hit the floor. The bot is credited with a small reward of +0.075 unit depending on its nearness to the destination, and for every frame a penalty of -0.05 is provided. If the bot hits an obstacle, it gets credited with -0.15 unit of reward. Figure 7-10 shows a preview from the blog. More details of these robots can be found at the link https://connect.unity.com/p/pancake-bot?_ga=2.240054851.151262200.1598121566-630897211.1596987781.

Figure 7-10. *Pancake bot by Christine Barron in ML Agents Challenge*

The second position was attained by Chau Chi Thien with the project "Metal Warfare." This is a real-time strategy (RTS) game where the creator wanted to leverage Unity ML Agents to create AI agents for firing and shooting missiles, as shown in Figure 7-11. Certain details that are mentioned is that ML Agents was used to credit the agent that fired the missile. Based on whether the missile hit the target or not, a positive or negative reward was credited. The creator assigned several reward signals based on whether the missile hit the enemy building or target, crediting a +1 unit of reward for each successful operation. The states array consists of five parts: action ID, rewards for previous actions (delayed rewards), is idle or not, available actions, and the learning states. More details on this RTS game, created with ML Agents, can be found at the link https://connect.unity.com/p/metal-warfare-real-time-strategy-game-special-edition-for-ai-ml-challenging?_ga=2.96402396.151262200.1598121566-630897211.1596987781.

Figure 7-11. *Metal Warfare by Chau Chi Thien in ML Agents Challenge*

The third position was attained by David Busch in his submission of Hide/
Escape: Avoidance of Pursuing Enemies. The aim behind this project was to create
an intelligent AI to hide from a patrolling agent. After creating the reward signals, the
creator tuned the hyperparameters to analyze the effect of different parameters on
the agent's training. To avoid the gameplay from continuing indefinitely, the creator
assigned a "win-zone" that the escaping agent has to reach in order to win. This,
combined with extensive hyperparameter optimization and curriculum learning, gave
rise to an intelligent AI agent that was capable of hiding and escaping from a patrolling
agent, as shown in Figure 7-12. The details of this project can be found at the link
`https://connect.unity.com/p/hide-escape-avoidance-of-pursuing-enemies?_`
`ga=2.61152876.151262200.1598121566-630897211.1596987781`.

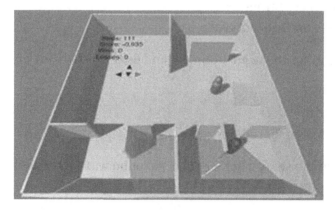

Figure 7-12. *Hide escape by David Busch in ML Agents challenge*

Along with these, there are several other submissions that are mentioned in the blog. All these were designed using an earlier version of the ML Agents, and it paved the way for the Obstacle Tower Challenge that we learned about.

At this stage, we have covered almost all of the topics relevant in the context of ML Agents that would enable the reader a clear view of the capabilities of this toolkit. We will look briefly into another deep RL platform—namely, the Google Dopamine, as it can be integrated with the ML Agents as well.

Google Dopamine and ML Agents

We have learned and used the Gym environment extensively throughout the course of the book. Now we will look into the integration of Google Dopamine with ML Agents. Dopamine is an open source framework for research in deep RL by Google and can be acccssed at the Github link (`https://github.com/google/dopamine`). Dopamine has its own implementations of DQN, rainbow, C51 variations of Rainbow, along with others. Using the Gym wrapper, we can run the ML Agents using Dopamine, and for this we have to first clone the Dopamine repository.

```
git clone https://github.com/google/dopamine
```

Dopamine recommends using a virtual environment for training agents. The following commands are required to activate a virtual environment:

```
python3 -m venv ./dopamine-venv
source dopamine-venv/bin/activate
```

Then we have to set up the environment and finally install the dependencies of Dopamine.

```
pip install -U pip
pip install -r dopamine/requirements.txt
```

Then we can test to verify whether the installation was successful by using the following command:

```
cd dopamine
export PYTHONPATH=$PYTHONPATH:$PWD
python -m tests.dopamine.atari_init_test
```

We have to copy the contents of atari folder to a new folder (e.g., unity).In the next step, we have to open the dopamine/Atari/run_experiment.py and add the following lines to import ML Agents dependencies as mentioned here:

```
from mlagents_envs.environment import UnityEnvironment
from gym_unity.envs import UnityToGymWrapper
```

Then we navigate to the "create_atari_environment" method in the same file, and then we have to instantiate a Unity environment by using the following code:

```
game_version = 'v0' if sticky_actions else 'v4'
full_game_name = '{}NoFrameskip-{}'.format(game_name, game_version)
unity_env = UnityEnvironment('./envs/GridWorld')
env = UnityToGymWrapper(unity_env, use_visual=True, uint8_visual=True)
return env
```

We use the GridWorld environment for this. Dopamine has only Atari-specific calls, and that is why we have to modify it to use our Unity ML Agents. Since Dopamine provides algorithmic variations of DQN using experienced replay it is compatible with discrete action spaces (Gym). For branched discrete action spaces, we have to enable the "flatten_branched" parameter in the "UnityToGymWrapper," which treats each combination of branched actions as separate actions. For visual observations, Dopamine does not automatically adapt to multiple channels, and that is why it is recommended to provide grayscale images as input with dimensions of 84 X 84. Since Dopamine caters to Atari environments, we have to modify the hyperparameters as well. The dopamine/agents/rainbow/config/rainbow.gin file is known to work well with GridWorld. The following hyperparameters are taken from the official Github documentation:

```
import dopamine.agents.rainbow.rainbow_agent
import dopamine.unity.run_experiment
import dopamine.replay_memory.prioritized_replay_buffer
import gin.tf.external_configurables

RainbowAgent.num_atoms = 51
RainbowAgent.stack_size = 1
RainbowAgent.vmax = 10.
RainbowAgent.gamma = 0.99
RainbowAgent.update_horizon = 3
```

```
RainbowAgent.min_replay_history = 20000  # agent steps
RainbowAgent.update_period = 5
RainbowAgent.target_update_period = 50  # agent steps
RainbowAgent.epsilon_train = 0.1
RainbowAgent.epsilon_eval = 0.01
RainbowAgent.epsilon_decay_period = 50000  # agent steps
RainbowAgent.replay_scheme = 'prioritized'
RainbowAgent.tf_device = '/cpu:0'  # use '/cpu:*' for non-GPU version
RainbowAgent.optimizer = @tf.train.AdamOptimizer()

tf.train.AdamOptimizer.learning_rate = 0.00025
tf.train.AdamOptimizer.epsilon = 0.0003125

Runner.game_name = "Unity" # any name can be used here
Runner.sticky_actions = False
Runner.num_iterations = 200
Runner.training_steps = 10000  # agent steps
Runner.evaluation_steps = 500  # agent steps
Runner.max_steps_per_episode = 27000  # agent steps

WrappedPrioritizedReplayBuffer.replay_capacity = 1000000
WrappedPrioritizedReplayBuffer.batch_size = 32
```

We can run the Dopamine variant of the GridWorld agent by running the following command:

```
python -um dopamine.unity.train \
  --agent_name=rainbow \
  --base_dir=/tmp/dopamine \
  --gin_files='dopamine/agents/rainbow/configs/rainbow.gin'
```

In this context it is recommended to copy the contents of the atari to a new folder with any name (e.g., unity).Then we have to replace "unity" in the "import dopamine. unity.run_experiment" code with the folder where we have copied the run_experiment. py and trainer.py files.

This completes the introduction to Google Dopamine integration with ML Agents using Gym wrapper. This also concludes the major topics in the book.

Summary

We come to the last section of this chapter and also the book. We will summarize the topics that we learned in this chapter.

- We learned about evolutionary algorithms and learned its relation with genetic theory of organisms as well as with Darwin's theory of evolution.

- We analyzed two variants of evolutionary algorithms—namely, the genetic algorithm and the broad class of ES. In the genetic algorithm, we created an evolution network to match a phrase by genetic process of crossing over and mutation.

- In the scope of ES, we learned about the difference between the genetic algorithm and ES, where the latter uses real numbers in place of binary values to optimize a function. We then created a simple Gaussian ES to find the maximum value of a harmonic oscillator within a specified range.

- We extended our learning of ES algorithms to CMA –ES and NES algorithms. In CMA-ES we saw the importance of Gaussian distribution on covariance matrices for updating the mean and standard deviation of the offspring population. In NES, we saw the relation between natural gradient descent and evolution sampling strategy to come up with an evolved policy gradient form for training the agent.

- In the next section, we had a descriptive overview of the Obstacle Tower Challenge. In this case study, we had a thorough understanding of the provided challenge, the requirements as well as the complex environment.The challenge was created to build a generalization (weak/strong) characteristics in agents and also to improve the benchmarks of model performance. We also looked into how procedural content generation with graph grammar was extensively used to design the floor layout and room layout.

- We then discussed the strategies and algorithms that were adopted by the winners of the competition. We saw that PPO remained as the go-to algorithm in the context of traditional deep RL and also saw hybrid combinations of behavioral cloning/GAIL along with ES and world models emerge as the major strategies adopted by the winners. LSTM/GRU with PPO remained as the core form of approach in most submissions.

- The aim of the Obstacle Tower was to foster research and to improve benchmarks. In the next section, we saw the steps to download the open source repository, which contained the codes for making new room layouts and floors. We also saw the generalization of graph grammars as the main strategy to generate complex levels.

- We saw the steps to create a script that would make the Obstacle Tower environment interact with the Gym wrapper and also observe the different Gym parameters associated with it.

- We then analyzed another case study—ML Agents Challenge I, which was created with an older version of ML Agents. We went through the top three submissions and their projects, which involved robotic arms, RTS games, and escaping AI agents.

- In the last section, we covered the steps to integrate ML Agents with Google Dopamine. Google Dopamine is a research framework for deep RL using variants of DQN algorithms (rainbow). At this stage, we can integrate with the most popular deep RL platforms, which includes Gym (OpenAI) and Dopamine (Google).

We come to the end of the book. The importance of deep RL in creating autonomous AI agents is immense. As we have seen from robotic simulation, to enemy AI, path finding to autonomous driverless agents—the possibilities are endless. We have covered most of the traditional deep RL algorithms along with some evolutionary algorithms and saw them in action using ML Agents. The ML Agents repository is under constant research and development, and it is a fantastic tool. Irrespective of profession, this tool can not only be used for automating games but also to create intelligent AI agents and complex environments as well as for extensive research. The ease of compatibility with OpenAI Gym wrapper makes it even more robust and simple to train AI agents with any algorithms. Through this book, we hope to create an enthusiasm among readers as to the endless possibilities attainable with this toolkit.

Index

A

A* algorithm
    B* algorithm, 104
    D* (D-star) algorithm, 102–104
    dynamic weighted, 94–96
    grid attributes, 86
    heuristic/cost function, 88
    heuristic term, 87
    implementation in Python, 89–93
    iterative deepening, 96–98
    lifelong planning, 98–102
    path searching algorithm, 86
    runtime, 93
    simple memory-bound, 105, 107
    simulation in Unity, 118–127
A3C, 360–362
A2C algorithm, 357–360
Academy
    AutomaticSteppingEnabled, 276
    class, 273, 274
    code segments, 278
    communicator, 277
    controlling, 279
    controls, 175, 273
    DisableAutomaticStepping
        method, 275
    Fixed Update method, 274
    InitializeEnvironment method, 276
    layer linked brain, 279

    online training, 275, 279
    parameters values, 276
    script, 273
    StatsRecorder method, 276
    variables, 274
    workflow, 279
AcademyFixedUpdateStepper
    component, 274
Academy.Instance.EnvironmentStep()
    method, 272
Actor critic algorithm, 10, 356, 357, 366
Actor critic experience replay, 384–386
Actor critic network architecture, 357
Actor critic using Kronecker factored trust
    region (ACKTR), 362–365
Adam optimizer, 333, 336, 352, 389
AddDemonstratorWriterToAgent
    method, 268
AddForceAtPosition method, 397
AddForce component, 504
AddForce method, 493
AddReward method, 293
Advantage actor critic (A2C), 348
Adversarial self-play, 480, 487–489
Agent, 1, 2, 165
    brain academy architecture linked, 287
    DecisionRequester, 285–287
    external policy, 280
    GetAction/ScaleAction, 284

A. Majumder, *Deep Reinforcement Learning in Unity*, https://doi.org/10.1007/978-1-4842-6503-1

Printed in the United States
By Bookmasters